BEST LITTLE IRONIES, ODDITIES & MYSTERIES
of the
CIVIL WAR

BEST LITTLE IRONIES, ODDITIES & MYSTERIES
of the
CIVIL WAR

C. Brian Kelly

with "Mary Todd Lincoln: Troubled First Lady" by Ingrid Smyer

CUMBERLAND HOUSE
NASHVILLE, TENNESSEE

Published by
CUMBERLAND HOUSE PUBLISHING, INC.
431 Harding Industrial Drive
Nashville, Tennessee 37211
www.CumberlandHouse.com

Cover design by Bateman Design, Nashville, Tennessee

Library of Congress Cataloging-in-Publication Data

Kelly, C. Brian.
    Best little ironies, oddities, and mysteries of the Civil War / C. Brian Kelly. With Mary Todd Lincoln : troubled First Lady / by Ingrid Smyer.
        p.   cm.
    Includes index.
    ISBN 1-58182-116-6 (pbk. : alk. paper)
    1. United States—History—Civil War, 1861–1865—Anecdotes. 2. Curiosities and wonders—United States—Anecdotes. 3. United States—History—Civil War, 1861–1865—Biography—Anecdotes. 4. Lincoln, Mary Todd, 1818–1882. 5. Presidents' spouses—United States—Biography. I. Smyer-Kelly, Ingrid, 1927– —Mary Todd Lincoln. II. Title.
    E655.K24 2000
    973.7—dc21   00-055472

Printed in the United States of America

1 2 3 4 5 6 7 8—04 03 02 01 00

*Your more verbose of the two authors writing herein
would like to dedicate this tome to his dear wife,
helpmate, and collaborator . . . in so many other things
as well. Thus, to my dear wife, Ingrid.*

Contents

Part 3: Generally Speaking I

Part 4: 1862–63: High-Water Mark Reached

Part 5: Generally Speaking II

Part 6: 1864–65: Winding Down

Dateline: Williamsburg, Virginia, May 1862

The battle of Williamsburg, a Confederate defeat, was over. Federal troops were filtering into town as presage to a long period of occupation.

On Main Street, the restored Duke of Gloucester Street of today's Colonial Williamsburg, stood a house belonging to Mrs. Elizabeth Ware. It was the scene of a minor commotion as a Confederate soldier was carried in, wounded. No Federals seen here as yet.

In a short while, the grievously wounded young man died.

Mrs. Ware and a daughter decided he should lie in the parlor for the moment.

Soon the Federals were in the area. They were seeking out the ailing, the wounded.

Told that the Ware home held a deceased Confederate soldier, a young man in Union uniform entered to investigate. While the two women stood by, he advanced on the body and drew aside the cloth covering the dead man's face.

As the women continued to watch, stunned now, the soldier fell to his knees and kissed the dead man, his enemy. And, it also seems, his own brother.

(Based upon Civil War Williamsburg *by Carson O. Hudson Jr. [Colonial Williamsburg Foundation, Williamsburg, Virginia, in association with Stackpole Books, 1997])*

Introduction

WE MAY BE IN DEEP trouble here. With sixty thousand or even more books already written about the Civil War, who needs yet another? As I heard Pulitzer prize–winning historian Mark Neely estimate out loud recently, the sixty thousand total breaks down to forty-one books for every day of the Civil War, or close to two books written for every hour of the conflict. "This," he said, "is a serious problem."

No doubt he has a point. Such an outpouring may be a wee bit superfluous. Perhaps, too, we really do need to get a handle on it "to avoid being buried in detail."

As he noted also, the river of type sometimes changes course—in recent years a shift from repeated studies of all possible causes of the Civil War to a tidal wave of books about the actions of the great conflict. Lots of details there, all right!

The fact is, though, that people—historians, writers, readers of all kinds—remain fascinated by the rift that almost split this country into two parts nearly 150 years ago. And, true, whether a reader or writer delving into its myriad facets, it becomes like the Tar Baby in the Uncle Remus stories by Joel Chandler Harris—grab a handful and you can't let go. Soon both hands, then all of you is stuck, and stuck good!

Personally, while conceding the possibility of *some* possible excess in the total output of Civil War books, this writer is most thankful to those Civil War participants, researchers, historians, and other kinds of authors—*reliable* authors—who did write about the conflict in book or article form, since it is their work that I have relied upon for discovery of my best little ironies et cetera herein—and for the stories filling the first Civil War book my wife, Ingrid, and I put together, *Best Little Stories from the Civil War,* including Ingrid's "Varina: Forgotten First Lady."

Included with our ironies et cetera for this latest book in our Best Little series is Ingrid's "Mary Todd Lincoln: Troubled First Lady." And those two opposing first ladies indeed were two most fascinating women! But then so much of the Civil War and so many of its personalities are still fascinating to us today. Just check the numbers. Sixty thousand or more books, the man said, and many of them of recent vintage, too.

Sometimes, though, this writer must admit to feeling that a bit of the material found in the river of Civil War typeface is just too breathless and unquestioning. One doesn't always find a sense of the real tragedy involved, the really dead deaths involved, the real uselessness of so much killing, the real horror of friends, neighbors, even West Point classmates going at each other as they would go after a foreign army.

Was it all really necessary? Looking back today, one has to wonder. Couldn't the issues of slavery, states' rights, and economic imbalances have been settled some other way? Tough questions, to be sure . . . and of course by now strictly rhetorical. But still, outright war?

In any case, I am beholden to those who previously have trod the same paths I do in the book that follows, albeit in my own language and quite often with different viewpoint or interest in the outcome. Whether relying upon one source or stitching together the facts found in two or more accounts, I have tried to credit my sources in the text— but many apologies if in the turmoil of writing and assembling more than one hundred stories, someone's authorship or title was inadvertently left out. I owe thanks also to Primedia, Inc., publishers of *Military History* magazine, for permission to reprint in whole or in part four of my Best Little Stories columns that previously appeared in the magazine and are now found herein as the stories entitled "'Mudwall' for Governor," "He Lifted His Hat," "Custer Does a Favor," and "Love Found in Yankeeland."

Aside from giving credit where credit is due, I've tried to find a few cracks in the monolithic wall of knowledge built up by all those thousands of other books. If I have not in every case found the totally obscure, I hope at least to have offered most readers a new and different angle. Thus the material found herein will sometimes skip past the well known in favor of the lesser known. For instance, quite true, what greater irony in the entire Civil War than the story of the Wilmer McLean family, who in 1863 reluctantly moved away from the scene of the battles of First and Second Manassas (Bull Run), only to have the respective armies descend upon their peaceful retreat at Appomattox Court House two years later for Lee's surrender to Grant—right in the front parlor of the McLean home! Read about that ultimate irony in hundreds of Civil War books, but not in the pages to come. Even more than in our first Civil War book (which did point out the Wilmer McLean irony in passing reference), the emphasis herein is on the unexpected rather than the tried and true.

Meanwhile, is the following all about battles? No . . . just some of it. Is it all about causes? No . . . but a bit.

So what is it?

It's all about us. People. Only these people lived a while back, that's all. They jumped on a horse instead of slipping into a car or riding the bus or subway.

People. But there was a war, a terrible and grinding war, and they were caught up in it, like it or not. These are simply some of the things they did or said.

Ever wonder what we might do, caught in the same circumstances?

C. Brian Kelly

BEST LITTLE IRONIES, ODDITIES & MYSTERIES
of the
CIVIL WAR

★ Part 1 ★
Stage Setters

Too late, too late now. Part slave, part not, and so badly torn over that divisive issue, a still-expanding America by the 1850s was on a course leading to secession and then war, Civil War. At issue, too: Was the country merely a confederation of prideful states with rights all their own, or was it at core a federal union with the will to remain one rather than many? With ill winds fanning the embers of irresolvable dissent, who would emerge as the movers and shakers? As we take a look at a few, who can deny that fact really is stranger than fiction . . . that irony is as pervasive in real life as it is in the wildest of imaginations?

Stranger in Town

HE CAME TO TOWN IN 1837 to join an established local attorney as a partner, found a room above a general store and a roommate in the person of the store's co-owner, Joshua Speed.

So poor was the newcomer that he and Speed were forced to share the same bed for the next four years.

Three weeks after arriving in town the newcomer was so lonely that he wrote: "I have been spoken to by but one woman since I've been here and should not have been by her, if she could have avoided it."

The town itself had begun in the same inauspicious fashion. Founded in 1821, it was merely a village of six hundred souls a full nine years later. Its growth stayed slow . . . but only for a short while longer.

In 1837, a decision by the state legislature promised a quite different and far more flourishing future—the state capital would be moving to town by mid-1839! Hence the arrival of the new attorney, himself a member of that legislative body.

Despite such a sophisticated political position, he felt uneasy about going to church in his new surroundings, "because I am conscious I should not know how to behave myself."

Nonetheless, he was able to associate with the politically prominent—key among them was Ninian Wirt Edwards, son of a former territorial governor of the state. Through Edwards and his wife, Elizabeth, the newcomer met a young woman—Elizabeth's younger sister Mary—who was living with the Edwards couple.

He began courting her but soon encountered opposition from the Edwards pair. He thought after a time that he had won the young lady's hand . . . but then, in January 1841, their engagement suddenly fell apart. Who said what to whom is not really known today.

For his part, the lawyer-legislator was brokenhearted. Calling himself "the most miserable man living," he wrote: "If what I feel were equally distributed to the whole human family, there would not be one cheerful face on the earth. Whether I shall ever be better I can not tell; I awfully forebode I shall not. To remain as I am is impossible; I must die or be better, it appears to me."

He would not be miserable forever, as events turned out. After a year or more had passed, Mary and he reconsidered, reconciled . . . and made plans for their wedding November 4, 1842—in the home of Ninian and Elizabeth Edwards, of all places!

The newlyweds now moved into an inn, the Globe Tavern by name, boarding there for $4 a week.

In 1843 their first child, Robert, was born at the inn itself.

By now the new attorney in town was not so new, and he was earning and even saving money, enough to buy a house—the only home he ever owned—in 1844 for $1,200. There, at the corner of Eighth and Jackson Streets in the by now bustling new state capital, they would live until 1861. Meanwhile, for an added outlay of $1,300, they added a second floor in 1856.

In 1850 their second boy, Eddie, died of natural causes. Over the next few years, though, the couple would welcome two more sons into their family.

By 1855, as another spur to population growth and economic well-being, new railroad lines linked their town with key cities to the north, west, east, and south. By 1860, their little city's population had zoomed to almost ten thousand.

Meanwhile, in the two decades since his arrival in town, the attorney-legislator had gained such political prominence that he had served a two-year term in Washington as a U.S. House member. In 1858 he ran for the U.S. Senate but lost to incumbent Democrat Stephen Douglas. In 1860 he ran for another national office . . . and won.

That would mean another stay in Washington, complete with a new home provided for him, his wife, and their three surviving boys.

Preparing to leave his adopted home for the troubled nation's capital, no longer a stranger in town, he was able to address his fellow residents as "my friends."

As his cross-country train was about to pull out for the East on the day before his birthday in early 1861, he became deeply moved by the occasion. His parting words still can be found in the history books: "My friends—No one, not in my situation, can appreciate my feeling of sadness at this parting. To this place, and the kindness of these people, I owe everything. Here I have lived a quarter of a century, and have passed from a young to an old man. Here my children have been born, and one is buried. I now leave, not knowing when or whether ever I may return, with a task before me greater than that which rested upon Washington."

Whether ever he apparently did say. This was Abraham Lincoln's farewell to his adopted hometown of Springfield, Illinois, on February 11, 1861.

Off to West Point

YOUNG JIMMY, A COLLEGE STUDENT at Emory & Henry just north of Abingdon, Virginia, considered law, medicine, engineering, and "arms" as "hireling professions." Even so, with no land or financial legacies awaiting him, he chose one such profession—arms.

First, though, he did spend time, almost two years, at the small liberal arts college in southwest Virginia. He "got religion," the Methodist variety, his first year there, the result of a fervent religious revival at the Methodist school. Only fifteen when he started his college studies, he also got into occasional scrapes . . . fights.

Thus, he missed a crucial half-hour of a sacred history exam because he had suffered a bloody nose in one such scrape just before the exam period began. He was described by his recent biographer Emory M. Thomas as a sensitive youth who occasionally liked to write poetry . . . but who felt it necessary while growing up in strictly rural, rough-and-tumble Patrick County, Virginia, to hide any "tender" feelings and to stick up for himself with bravery and honor.

The occasional fights would continue over the next few years, but more important for the youngster just now was the goal of a complete education plus the choice of a future career. On both counts, he felt compelled to consider the U.S. Military Academy at West Point, New York. And why not? As biographer Thomas noted, "At the time a West

Point education was one of the best that could be had in the country, and it would provide James with training in one of the 'hireling professions' and leave him the option to pursue one of the others later."

His father, Archibald, a state senator and lawyer, had served a term in the U.S. House in the 1830s . . . and, lo, what's this? Good fortune? Here he was, in 1848, running for the House again. Would it be proper for him to nominate his own son for West Point? Was that ever a consideration for father and son at all?

Oddly, it's a moot point. Political Whig Archibald Stuart was defeated in his bid of 1848. But his rival, Democrat Thomas Hamlet Averett, the winner of the House race, promptly (some say as his very first action in Congress) appointed young James Stuart of Patrick County to the Point. Young James Ewell Brown Stuart, that is—the future Confederate cavalry leader *Jeb* Stuart.

Life Among the Lowly

FROM A HATER SOMEWHERE CAME the ear. Right in Harriet Beecher Stowe's mail—a black ear severed from the rest of a black person's body.

Her extremely controversial book, a bestseller from the start, of course was the reason. Even today, its sales figures would be regarded as impressive. In the first week of its appearance in book form in 1852, her previously serialized novel sold 10,000 copies. In ten months, 300,000. In onlooking England, 150,000. And by the time of the Civil War, more than one million copies had been sold.

Everybody, just about *everybody*, knew all about it, whether they approved or disapproved. Whether they had read it or not, they knew the story line and the central figures, whose names in fact entered the English language to stay . . . as unpleasant epithets.

Even today, most of us know what an *Uncle Tom* is, what a *Simon Legree* is, what *Uncle Tomism* is.

In the middle of the Civil War, in 1862, Southern diarist Mary Chesnut stopped all her various activities to read the book again. Sad little heroines, such as the book's "Little Eva," she commented, "are mostly in the heaven of Mrs. Stowe's imagination."

Now considered the Confederacy's foremost, most widely read diarist, Mary Chesnut made reference to Harriet Beecher Stowe and her book (or her also-famous brother, Henry Ward Beecher) nineteen times. In some cases Chesnut introduced the topic herself, but in many other instances she was simply reporting references to the book, its authoress, or its characters . . . allusions that popped up in conversations among Chesnut's Southern associates. In one case, she reported telling James Team, long-time slave overseer for her father-in-law, about the book. "We told him Uncle Tom's story as invented or imagined by Mrs. Stowe. [He] said he had not seen many [slaves] of that sort. If there was any, money could not buy 'em."

As part of his reaction, the veteran overseer said, "In all my life I have only met one or two womenfolk who were not abolitionists in their hearts—and hot ones, too."

He also touched upon an issue that would become a hot political controversy for the manpower-depleted Confederacy before war's end—the use of slaves to help fight the war. Perhaps surprising for us today, it was early in the conflict, 1861, when the veteran overseer from South Carolina said: "It [slavery] is a thing too unjust, too unfair to last. Let us take the bull by the horns. Set 'em free, let 'em help us fight, to pay for their freedom."

Oddly enough, the controversy occupying so many minds and tongues during the Civil War had erupted a full decade earlier with the first serialization of Mrs. Stowe's *Uncle Tom's Cabin* in the abolitionist magazine *National Era.* A Connecticut native and a resident of Maine, a committed abolitionist and, helpfully, a writer as well, she began her antislavery work after a brief visit to Kentucky, where she observed slavery in the flesh.

Who even today has not heard her book's basic story line, in whole or at least in part? With a bow to Southern gentility on the one hand, Stowe's story attacked the very concept of slavery with its sad tale of goodhearted Uncle Tom, that poor old slave devoted to his own white master . . . but flogged nonetheless by the vicious plantation owner Simon Legree for stubbornly keeping secret the hiding place of two runaway slaves, who happened to be women.

After Uncle Tom died, so in a while did Little Eva, the compassionate daughter of Uncle Tom's owner . . . but don't forget another

One of the evils of slavery was its breakup of families as one or more members were sold. In this photo, five generations of slaves appear together . . . at least for the moment.

important character—the young mulatto woman Eliza, who had to flee with her baby on often-depicted ice floes in the Ohio River to escape a slave catcher. Still, the chief villain of the book is the cruel Simon Legree. And . . . guess what? Simon Legree was a Yankee from Vermont, a Yankee gone south!

As for New Englander Harriet Beecher Stowe, daughter of one minister and wife of another, more writing and publication still lay ahead in her life, including a sequel to *Uncle Tom,* but nothing quite like the controversial antislavery bombshell she delivered in the last decade before the Civil War.

Uncle Tom's Cabin, by the way, carried a subtitle often forgotten today: *Or, Life Among the Lowly.*

Lucky Change of Heart

YOUNG TOM J., WHITE, just seventeen, an orphan pretty much on his own and already suffering stomach pains that would dog him for the next two decades, served as a constable in western Virginia's Lewis

County for ten months. As a result, he met all kinds of lowlife rough-necks, debtors, cheaters, even violent men.

While he was uncommonly young for the job, he was growing into his adult height of six feet, a full five inches above average for the time, and he knew how to use his head to solve the occasional problems that cropped up. When a local preacher failed to appear at the appointed time and place to hand over $10 he owed a local widow, Constable Tom's first response was to pay her out of his own pocket.

He then went about his business as usual, with no further comment . . . until the day the preacher came into the county seat on personal business, as surely he was bound to do *some*day. Tom soon heard about the preacher's presence and found him—mounted on his horse.

That was a situation that would have stopped most people—thanks to the era's unwritten "law" that a man seated on his horse could not be pulled off by force. But young Tom, undeterred in the slightest, simply took the reins and led the horse to the local black-smith's doorway—a low doorway.

Either the preacher would be knocked off his horse as Tom led the animal through, or he must dismount. Either way, the constable could confront the man on equal terms and demand satisfaction of the $10 debt. Which he did.

Other than Tom's demonstrated acumen for problem solving or his height, there was not much to remark about him. "He was quick in his movements but nothing remarkable in his appearance," said a local miller. "At supper he was a silent listener."

Suddenly, in 1841, the quiet listener was electrified to hear that his area's new congressman, Samuel L. Hays, was preparing to choose a candidate for appointment to West Point. For Tom, that sounded like the answer to all his ambitions—prestige, better health, good education, and a fulfilling career.

He went after the appointment with a vengeance, and in short time, the original field of four viable contenders came down to just two—Gibson J. Butcher, a deputy clerk from the Lewis County court, and young Constable Tom.

They knew each other well as former schoolmates and, now, as workers for the same court. Butcher was well versed in the written word, but of the two, Tom was the better athlete and probably the stronger student of mathematics, a subject at the core of studies at the Military Academy.

But the choice, announced in April 1842, went to Butcher rather than to young Tom Jackson. "The disappointment Jackson felt was crushing," wrote biographer James I. Robertson Jr. "He had lost perhaps the first thing he had ever wanted with all his heart."

Ironically, it was West Point that apparently had missed a golden opportunity, that had lost its claim to one of history's most famous military commanders . . . *almost* lost, that is.

Three months now had passed. In early June, Butcher arrived at West Point to take up his studies. That was on June 3, 1842. The next day, June 4, he was gone—"without even informing academy officials," he was on his way back to Weston, county seat of Lewis County. And there he told curious inquirers that he simply didn't like the Military Academy—further, the cold climate didn't suit his summer clothing. In short, one look and it clearly wasn't for him.

In Weston, friends of the spurned Tom Jackson began thinking, began talking, and soon got up a petition asking Congressman Hays to appoint Tom to West Point in Butcher's place.

They began their drive before young Tom even learned about Butcher's change of heart.

When informed, he went along with their plan guardedly—"after all," wrote biographer Robertson, "he was painfully familiar with disappointment." Still, his heart must have leaped at the news, and he did determinedly tackle all the complicated business of reapplying for admission to West Point and settling affairs at home and job.

Setting out for Washington to confront Representative Hays in person, Tom rode to Clarksburg in a "driving rain" to catch the stagecoach east, missed connections, then "galloped twenty miles through rain and mud until he caught up with the stage at Grafton." He rode the coach to a point east of Cumberland, Maryland, then took a train into Washington.

It was June 17 when he presented himself, unannounced, "mudsplattered and rumpled," before the congressman . . . who until this moment did not know about Butcher's return home from West Point. Tom showed him Butcher's letter of resignation "plus a small but impressive stack of recommendations in his own behalf."

But Hays, it seems, needed little persuading. Wrote Robertson: "He was from Lewis County and was familiar with [Tom] Jackson's background. Further, his first appointment to the Military Academy had reneged." The Congressman dashed off a quick letter to Secretary of War John C. Spencer asking him to appoint Thomas J. Jackson in place of Butcher. Spencer complied (subject to Tom's passing his entrance examinations) the very next day.

Wasting no time, Tom caught an overnight train to New York, and the next morning, Sunday, June 19, boarded a Hudson River ferry that carried him upriver to the boat landing below the academy at West Point.

He stayed overnight at the West Point Hotel, and on Monday, June 20, he reported at the academy adjutant's office to sign in. Among the first cadets to meet the newcomer from Virginia were fellow Virginians A. P. Hill and George E. Pickett.

As events turned out, he would stay, he would pass his exams (barely), and he would join an entering class of ninety-three plebes. So it was that West Point eventually could claim "Stonewall" Jackson as one of its own. (So it was, too, that Civil War scholar Robertson more than a century later would write his definitive biography, *Stonewall Jackson: The Man, the Soldier, the Legend.*)

Warship Plans Tabled

THE PROPOSAL FOR A NEW naval weapon submitted to the head of state by a foreign inventor sounded so unprecedented as to be out-landish—a futuristic pipe dream. But . . . if at all feasible, what a weapon it could be.

Imagine, a "vessel to be composed entirely of iron" and to be sitting nearly submerged in its watery environment! Steam-driven, yes, but that wasn't so mind-boggling a concept at a time when steam engines already were replacing sails. But almost all underwater, and all made of iron?

Then, too, above the single visible deck, would be a revolving cupola—a gun turret with an unimpeded, 360-degree sweep.

The deck, meanwhile, that protective shell of sheet iron three inches deep, would curl over the top edges of the hull and into the water at all points, with a special section eight feet in length protruding protectively over the rudder and propeller.

Boilers, engines, the propulsion system in general, plus most of the crew, would be below decks, below the water line.

The turret, naturally, would house the odd vessel's armament, and this is one area in which Swedish-born inventor John Ericsson stumbled ever so slightly. He suggested a steam-powered, breechloading gun. The steam gun would *not* be among the longer lasting of John Ericsson's lifetime total of nearly two thousand inventions, but another innovative weapon system he had in mind for his iron ship indeed would catch on . . . much later, in the twentieth century. That was his proposed system of underwater tubes that would fire off steam-powered "hydrostatic javelins," as he called them. We today call them torpedoes.

Regardless of detail such as armaments, it was his concept of a nearly submerged, iron-skinned, steam-powered ship that really caught the eye . . . and perhaps stirred more than a bit of derision among the experts in naval warfare. But then, what was *their* answer to events such as the disaster that overtook an ill-fated Turkish squadron of wooden ships at Sinope early in the Crimean War?

Thanks to the era's newfangled "shell gun" that fired penetrating, explosive-laden shells into the target, the rival Russian naval squadron at Sinope, nine ships, had sunk or captured ten of the eleven Turkish vessels on the scene. For the hapless Turks it was a massacre.

Like many others, Ericsson realized that at Sinope on November 30, 1853, naval warfare had undergone a dramatic and permanent change—wooden warships would be useless against the artillery of the future, against guns firing explosive shells. Unlike most interested parties, however, Ericsson thought he had the solution in hand—his very own "subaquatic system of naval warfare."

When the Crimean War soon widened to include France and Great Britain, the London-based Ericsson acted. He submitted the

The design of the USS Monitor *was the brainchild of John Ericsson, who had first tried to sell his naval designs in Europe before coming to America.*

BATTLES AND LEADERS

plans for his invention to a head of state . . . with expectations of prompt recognition.

Instead, he eventually received a note informing him that yes, "the Emperor himself has examined with great care the new system of naval attack that you have submitted to him," but adding that it was rejected. Rationale? Doubts that "the result to be obtained would be proportionate to the expense or to the small number of guns that could be brought into use."

What Napoleon III of France thus rejected was the plan for possibly the most revolutionary warship in history, the concept that less than ten years later would result in the Civil War battle of Hampton Roads, Virginia, between the Union's near-invincible ironclad, the USS *Monitor,* of John Ericsson's design and the Confederacy's only somewhat less-than-invincible ironclad, the CSS *Virginia* (formerly the Union frigate *Merrimack*), with neither ship emerging the clear-cut victor.

Real-Life "Eliza"

SHE WAS ELIZA IN Harriett Beecher Stowe's *Uncle Tom's Cabin,* but she really was Eliza, Eliza Harris in real life, too—her real life as a slave and thereafter.

And she really did flee, babe in arms, across the ice floes in an Ohio River stretch between Kentucky and Ohio. When pursuers descended upon her hideout, she really did burst out of a back door and run, holding her two-year-old. She did reach the water's edge, then began stepping from one cake of ice to another . . . some sinking into the icy water beneath her.

Levi Coffin, a Quaker originally from North Carolina, and his wife, Catherine, who were Indiana-based "stationmasters" in the "Underground Railroad," gave her the name Eliza Harris once she reached their home. Coffin later told her story in his *Reminiscences,* as did Harriett Beecher Stowe in *Uncle Tom.*

What an incredible story it was, too.

Nor was it fiction . . . made up.

As related by Coffin, the young slave woman originally belonged to a couple living on the Kentucky side of the river just below Ripley, Ohio. Her owners "were kind to her," but after suffering financial reverses, they prepared to "separate" her and her only child by selling one or both of them, it seems. With two children already lost to natural causes, this was a prospect the slave woman couldn't bear. She ran away with the child the night she discovered the couple's plan.

She approached the river at daylight, expecting to find it covered by a solid sheet of ice, as usually was the case that time of winter. But no, the ice was all broken up into floating, drifting cakes.

Afraid to try crossing, she found shelter for the day in a nearby home. "She hoped to find some way to cross the river the next night, but there seemed to be little prospect of any one being able to cross in safety, for during the day the ice became more broken and dangerous to cross," Coffin wrote.

That very evening, to make matters worse, "She discovered pursuers nearing the house."

Cornered, "with desperate courage she determined to cross the river, or perish in the attempt."

Carrying her child, she "darted out of the back door and ran toward the river, followed by her pursuers, who had just dismounted from their horses when they caught sight of her."

At the water's edge, she didn't even hesitate. "Clasping her babe to her bosom with her left arm, she sprang onto the first cake of ice, then from that to another and another."

And what to do when an ice floe sank beneath her weight? "Then she would slide her child on to the next cake, pull herself on with her hands, and so continue her hazardous journey."

Naturally, the young mother soon was soaking wet up to the waist. Her hands were numb from the cold. Still, "she felt that surely the Lord was preserving and upholding her, and that nothing could harm her."

On the far banks of the river, a man stood watching in amazement, "expecting every moment to see her go down," but apparently helpless, unable to go to her aid. When she finally reached the Ohio side of the river, however, he helped her up the embankment. After she caught her breath, he sent her to a house on the outskirts of nearby Ripley.

There she could only change into dry clothing and rest briefly before hurrying on to a station of the Underground Railroad a few miles inland. It wouldn't have been safe for her to stay at that first Ohio house for any length of time.

"The next night," wrote Coffin, "she was forwarded on from station to station to our house in Newport [Indiana], where she arrived safely and remained several days."

From there, newly named Eliza Harris by Coffin's wife, the mother—along with her child—was sent to Sandusky, Ohio, and then on to Canada, where they would live in a town named Chatham. According to Coffin's account, this really was the Eliza fleeing on ice floes in *Uncle Tom's Cabin* . . . the real, albeit newly named Eliza Harris. Indeed, he opened his account of her escape with these words: "Eliza Harris, of *Uncle Tom's Cabin* notoriety, the slave woman who crossed the Ohio River, near Ripley, on the drifting ice with her child in her arms, was sheltered under our roof and fed at our table for several days."

But how would Harriet Beecher Stowe, a resident of Maine when her novel was published in 1852, hear about the "Eliza story"? Simple—until just two years before, she had lived in Cincinnati, not far from Ripley and across the same Ohio River from Kentucky. Thus, as Wilbur H. Siebert wrote in a well-known nineteenth-century history of the Underground Railroad, she was well positioned to learn about slavery and its effects. "She numbered among her friends slaveholders on the one side of the Ohio River and abolitionists on the other," Siebert wrote in his *Underground Railroad: From Slavery to Freedom* (1898). "At the time of her first trip across the Ohio in 1833, she visited an estate, which is described as that of Colonel Shelby in *Uncle Tom's Cabin*." Further, the famous novelist's own home in Cincinnati became a "station" of the Underground Railroad.

As for her discovering the Eliza story, a more recent chronicler of the escape conduit for slaves, Charles Blockson, says this in his 1987 book *The Underground Railroad: Dramatic Firsthand Accounts of Daring Escapes to Freedom:* "Was there really an Eliza, an Uncle Tom? Indeed, Stowe had met the real-life 'Uncle Tom,' one Josiah Henson, who had told her of the real-life 'Eliza,' whom she encountered in Canada after Levi Coffin helped her escape there."

☆ ☆ ☆

Additional note: Visiting in Canada in 1854, the Coffins would meet Eliza once again. "At the close of a meeting which we attended, at one of the colored churches," Coffin wrote in his memoir, "a woman came up to my wife, seized her hand, and exclaimed: 'How are you, Aunt Katie? God bless you!' etc. My wife did not recognize her, but she soon called herself to our remembrance by referring to the time she was at our house in the days of her distress, when my wife gave her the name of Eliza Harris, and by relating other particulars. We visited her at her house while at Chatham, and found her comfortable and contented."

Epilogue: Should it be any surprise that the real-life Levi and Catherine Coffin also appear in *Uncle Tom's Cabin*—as the slave-helpers Simeon and Rachel Halliday? Harriet Beecher Stowe's not-so-fictional Eliza even stopped at a "Quaker settlement in Indiana" on her way to freedom via the Underground Railroad. In real life, added Blockson (himself the descendant of a slave), the Coffins of Indiana were so active in helping slaves escape north to freedom that their home was called "the Grand Central Station of the Underground Railroad."

West Point Buddies

A WILD FEW HOURS—minutes, perhaps?—spent with the wrong kind of woman, probably in New York, late in the summer of 1844 would cost this Virginia-born cadet, just eighteen years in age, his health, a future fiancée, and a year's hard work at West Point. If only he had thought first!

But he hadn't thought quite enough, and as a result, on September 9, 1844, he wound up a patient in the academy hospital. "Gonorrhea contracted on furlough" was the official finding. The supposition is that he stopped to investigate the fleshpots of New York on his way back to the Military Academy from a two-month summer furlough at home in Culpeper, Virginia.

For some patients, gonorrhea could be a passing illness that soon disappeared. But they were the lucky ones. With no cure for the venereal disease available until penicillin came along in the middle of the

U.S. ARMY MILITARY HISTORY INSTITUTE

The personal bonds between many commanders of the Civil War, North and South, began in the classrooms and on the parade grounds of the U.S. Military Academy at West Point.

twentieth century, others could and did suffer the effects of gonorrhea the rest of their lives . . . and future Confederate general Ambrose Powell Hill was one of those truly sad cases.

He felt gonorrhea's lasting sting almost immediately. Released from his hospital bed to begin classes, he began to suffer the disease's more unpleasant consequences—fever, difficulty urinating, and extreme pelvic pain. As he soon would learn, the pelvic pain sometimes could be so severe he couldn't take his seat on a horse.

Now suffering from the prostatitis that would come and go all his adult life, he was sent home in November on convalescent leave. In March of the next year, his family doctor had to report the young man still appeared to be "incapable of military and academic duties."

With his health finally improving by early summer of 1845, Hill prepared to return to West Point, only to be told he had lost so much time, he must repeat his third year. Not only would he have to repeat work done previously, he couldn't graduate with his friends and class-mates of three years' standing—many of them destined to become leaders in the Civil War. He never was fond of his classmate and fellow Virginian Thomas J. Jackson (the future "Stonewall"), but A. P. and his roommate George from their freshman year, George B. McClellan, had become close, close friends . . . an ironic situation later, since both of them would woo the same older officer's daughter and ask for her hand in marriage.

And then, of course, they would serve in opposing armies during the American Civil War.

But first, resuming his studies at the Military Academy in the fall of 1845, Hill formed a close friendship with three lower classmen who now were among his new classmates—cadets Ambrose Burnside of Illinois, Henry Heth of Virginia, and Julian McAllister of Georgia. They became "an inseparable foursome in their last two years at West Point," wrote Civil War historian James I. Robertson Jr. in his biographical *General A. P. Hill: The Story of a Confederate Warrior.*

As Hill's former classmates neared graduation in 1846, the Mexican War broke out, and "Hill watched with envy as his first Academy friends went south to seek military fame."

In his own senior year, Hill roomed with McAllister, and Burnside with Heth. "These four cadets, through practical jokes and boisterous conduct, became the social leaders—and hence the 'party managers'—of their class," Robertson wrote. Burnside, of course, would become famous, like McClellan, as a Union general. Heth would serve in the Civil War as a brigade commander under Hill himself . . . both famous Virginians, both Confederate, naturally.

After Hill's graduation from West Point came a brief period of combat in Mexico, followed by service against the Seminoles of Florida. During this period, Hill suffered his occasional bouts with prostatitis, but always managed to recover and resume normal duty.

In 1856, while assigned to the U.S. Coast Survey and based in Washington, D.C., Hill became engaged to Ellen Marcy, daughter of Maj. Randolph B. Marcy. She and her mother were staying at the Willard Hotel when Hill met her. She previously had been courted by one George B. McClellan, but he now was out of the country—assigned as an observer of the Crimean War in far-off Eurasia. Hill began escorting the fair Ellen to social functions in the capital city, and suddenly they were in love . . . but her parents were adamantly opposed to the proposed union, so much so that Mrs. Marcy apparently began gossiping about Hill's youthful bout with gonorrhea. How she found out about it is not known today.

The engagement fell through soon after. But Hill then met a young widow from Kentucky, Dolly Morgan, sister of future Confederate Gen. John Hunt Morgan. They married in 1859. Then, a year later, who should marry the winsome Ellen, Major Marcy's daughter, but McClellan, Hill's onetime West Point roommate, back from the Crimea.

He Began to Lie at Seventeen

DESTINED TO BECOME ONE OF the most famous men in American history, Phil, by his own later accounts, was born in the town of:

    a. Albany, New York
    b. Boston, Massachusetts
    c. Somerset, Ohio

As for his date of birth, that could have been the year 1830, 1831, or 1832, depending upon the variations to be found in his own and in other seemingly authoritative accounts.

Explanation?

According to Ezra J. Warner, compiler of the well-researched *Generals in Blue: Lives of the Union Commanders,* "Some historians believe he was born at sea en route to America on a vessel flying the British flag, others, that he was born in Ireland."

Perhaps Phil himself didn't really know, but either way, he "for obvious reasons wished it to be known that he was native [U.S.] born." What *obvious reasons?* Well, at one time in his life, based upon a highly successful military career, he would entertain presidential ambitions.

In any case, there seems no doubt that he was appointed to West Point from Somerset, Ohio, one of his possible birthplaces. In his own memoirs, Phil later explained that he was born in Albany on March 6, 1831, but his family moved to the frontierlike Ohio town of Somerset when he was only an infant.

He grew up there, obtaining a rudimentary education and then working as a clerk in a dry-goods store until receiving an appointment to West Point—thanks to the initial appointee's failure to pass the entrance examinations.

As he moved on to West Point, Phil gave his birthdate as 1830, incidentally. Years later, accepting his commission as a brigadier general in the Union army, he would change his birthdate to 1832. *Webster's American Military Biographies,* an authoritative source, says on the other hand that his birthdate was March 6, 1831.

Recent biographer Roy Morris Jr. offers a reasonable explanation for all the discrepancies in Phil's pedigree even while acknowledging that nobody today really knows the true facts. Wrote Morris: "He was born on March 6, 1831, somewhere along the wandering path his immigrant parents traced from their ancestral home in County Cavan, Ireland, to Somerset, Ohio, where he spent his childhood."

The U.S. Military Academy's own *Biographical Register of Officers and Graduates of the United States Military Academy* accepts Albany as the birthplace for Phil, but, Morris noted, "a case could also be made for Ireland, Canada, Boston, or the high seas en route to or from all those places."

Is it really possible that Phil himself did not know? "His mother, who presumably would have the final say in the matter, surprised the

Cadet Phil Sheridan (at center) with two of his original West Point classmates, George Crook (left) and John Nugen.

U.S. MILITARY ACADEMY ARCHIVES

general late in life by allowing that he had been born in the New York capital, not small-town Ohio, as he always had assumed," added Morris.

But she also would tell the Sheridan Monument Association, named and formed in Phil's honor, that her son was born at sea on the way to America from Ireland, "an account supposedly confirmed by parish priests."

Then, too, Phil Sheridan himself "showed little regard for hagio-logical niceties, variously claiming as his birthplace all the American locations and several of the conflicting dates," wrote biographer Morris in his *Sheridan: The Life and Wars of General Phil Sheridan.* "It has been suggested that he purposely obscured his foreign birth to pro-tect his putative presidential aspirations, in which case he must have been unusually ambitious, since by this reasoning he began to lie when he was seventeen, and unusually persistent, since he stood by the story in his posthumous[ly published] memoirs, long after he had passed beyond such transient glories. Probably, he just never knew. Such questions of provenance aside, he manifestly considered himself American, which in all things save possibly the place of his birth, indisputably he was."

Whatever the actual facts about his birth date and place may have been, Phil would have graduated from the U.S. Military Academy in 1852, but he was suspended for a year for fighting with cadet William R. Terrill of Virginia. As a result, future Union Gen. Phil Sheridan graduated in 1853 . . . in the bottom third of his class.

Additional note: That "fight" with fellow cadet William R. Terrill con-sisted of two serious altercations over a two-day period and could have ended with far worse consequences than Sheridan's one-year suspen-sion. The first of the two encounters came on September 9, 1851, as Cadet Sergeant Terrill ordered Cadet Private Sheridan to close up in the ranks with the man next to him.

Was it the way the Virginia-born Terrill said it? Who knows? What is known is that Sheridan's hot temper flared up. With an oath and the threat, "I'll run you through," he lunged at the senior cadet with his bayo-net, stopping just short of the other man. Sheridan then stepped back into line but continued to shout oaths and threats at the stunned Terrill.

The very next day, added Morris in his account of the affair, Terrill was sitting on the front steps of his barracks when along came Sheridan—"accidentally or not."

As Morris also noted, "Again something snapped." In seconds, Sheridan was screaming oaths again, and this time he even struck Terrill on the side of the head.

That was quite enough for the taller, heavier Virginian.

"The two slugged it out, the much-larger Terrill quickly gaining the advantage, until they were separated by a passing officer."

In the reprimands to come, Sheridan was lucky to avoid outright dismissal and an end to his military career before it really began. Even so, the relatively mild year-long suspension rankled. He called it "a very unfair punishment," but he did return to resume his West Point studies the next year.

Epilogue: Years later, in Louisville, Kentucky, just before the battle at nearby Perryville, the two men, both brigadier generals by now, bumped into each other for the first time since their unhappy encounter at West Point. Sheridan in the pending battle would be commanding an entire division, and Terrill only a brigade, but no matter. Noted Morris: "Now, allies again, they impulsively shook hands and buried their grudge." And barely in time, since Terrill would die just days later at Perryville.

Green Subdues Brown

ONE U.S. ARMY OFFICER, DRESSED in civilian garb, stood watching from a knoll forty feet away, while at a door to the small firehouse a younger colleague in a borrowed uniform coat signaled with his cavalry hat and lunged to one side, out of the way.

In seconds, a squad of U.S. Marines attacked the small building's two sets of double doors with sledgehammers, pounding for all they were worth—the lives of the hostages inside could depend on how fast they broke in.

Shooting erupted from inside, but the doors wouldn't yield.

BATTLES AND LEADERS

Inside the barricaded engine house at Harpers Ferry, Jeb Stuart and R. E. Lee found the fiery abolitionist John Brown, along with several cohorts and their hostages.

Lt. Israel Green, commander of the marine detachment, desperately cast his eye about the yard for another weapon, for inspiration . . . for anything that would provide quick entry to the barricaded structure. He spotted a heavy wooden ladder lying on the ground nearby and called forth more of his marines, telling them to assault the nearest set of doors with the ladder as a battering ram.

In seconds they hit the door with a stunning crash, but . . . nothing.

Again they lunged forward and delivered a second heavy blow to the door. This time there was the sound of a satisfying, splintering crash. Down near the ground on the right-hand side, part of the door had shattered under the blow.

As Green's men pulled back and extricated their battering ram, the leader of the hostage-takers inside fired a carbine at the disappearing ladder. The echo of the shot had hardly faded away before Lieutenant Green threw himself on the ground and thrust his head and shoulders through the hole. Barely able to see in the gloomy interior, he pulled himself all the way through and jumped to his feet.

One of the hostages immediately pointed to a bearded man kneeling close by—reloading a carbine. The leader and chief villain, obviously.

Green didn't yet know it, but his quarry inside the barricaded engine house at Harpers Ferry, Virginia, that October morning of

1859 was the fanatical abolitionist John Brown, already wanted for murder in Kansas. All Green knew was the obvious fact that the stranger before him could begin shooting again at any moment.

The officer didn't hesitate. Lacking a firearm of his own, he attacked Brown with his lightweight dress sword. One blow knocked the raider down and opened a gash on his neck but failed to incapacitate him. Green then tried a straight, bayonetlike thrust into the body, but the dress sword hit an unexpected hard object, possibly a belt buckle, and merely bent back. Desperate, the marine next rained blows upon his adversary's head with the hilt of the sword, until the man clearly was unconscious and no further threat.

By now, Green's men also had begun crawling through the small opening in the door. John Brown's companion raiders shot two of the marines as they struggled through the hole, mortally wounding one of them. Their fellow marines, however, made short work of the abolitionist's allies inside the engine house. Two of them were killed by bayonet on the spot, and two more quickly captured.

Still another two of Brown's followers had been killed earlier, before the marine assault, and so there were four bodies in all.

Important also, none of Brown's thirteen hostages had been harmed in the assault, which from start to finish had consumed all of three minutes, including the sledgehammer assault on the engine house. (All told, ten raiders had been killed.)

It appeared that Lieutenant Green and his marines were the heroes of the hour . . . and indeed they were. But the subjugation of John Brown and his followers in the attempt to seize the Federal arsenal at Harpers Ferry also resulted from the hasty plan developed during the preceding night by the civilian-clad officer looking on from the knoll forty feet away—U.S. Army Col. Robert E. Lee.

Crucial to the plan's success had also been the "hat signal" given by the officer with the borrowed uniform coat at the engine house door. He was Jeb Stuart, a former cadet under Lee at West Point and the future swashbuckling cavalry leader for the Confederacy. His assignment at Harpers Ferry had been to advance on the engine house with a flag of truce and deliver a note from Lee promising the raiders that no harm would come to them if they would surrender immediately.

When the door inched open in response to Stuart's call for a talk, he found himself looking into the eyes of the notorious John Brown, whom he had actually met earlier in Kansas. As Stuart biographer

Emory M. Thomas wrote in *Bold Dragoon: The Life of J. E. B. Stuart,* the still-young army officer also found himself looking "down the barrel of a cocked cavalry carbine."

But Stuart delivered Lee's message anyway—an ultimatum, really. Brown then kept demanding this condition and that condition as *his* terms, rather than accept Lee's surrender demand outright. At the same time, the anxious hostages behind the door shouted pleas to be more lenient in order to assure their safety.

One of the hostages, however, boldly shouted, "Never mind us, fire!"

Even from his vantage point forty feet away, Lee recognized the voice of Lewis W. Washington, a distant descendant of George Washington, biographer Thomas noted. Despite the crisis on his hands, Lee reflected aloud: "The old revolutionary blood does tell." (It was the same Lewis Washington, incidentally, who minutes later would point out Brown when Lieutenant Green pulled himself free from the hole at the bottom of the door.)

After a few moments of argument with Brown, meanwhile, "Stuart realized that Brown's wrangling and the conflicting calls from the prisoners were precisely what Lee wished to avoid," wrote Thomas. That was when Stuart waved his hat as the signal for the marine assault and lunged to one side, out of the way.

The attack by bayonet was deliberately carried out with no firearms issued to the marines, to keep any stray shots from hitting one or more of the hostages inside the small building.

Lee had been ordered to Harpers Ferry so hurriedly the day before that he hadn't had time to go home and don his uniform. Stuart, also on furlough, just happened to be visiting the War Department when the first rumors of trouble at Harpers Ferry drifted in. He eagerly volunteered to go with Lee to quell what turned out to be John Brown's raid on Harpers Ferry.

Additional note: While on the same visit to Washington, incidentally, Stuart had concluded an agreement with the War Department for the rights to his newly patented saber hook for cavalry belts—described by biographer Thomas as a device "that permitted a trooper rapidly to remove his saber and scabbard from his belt and attach it to his saddle." The brass hook thus "promised to spare a cavalryman some clanging awkwardness when he dismounted and simplified the temporary use of horsemen as foot soldiers."

Stuart's invention fetched him an outright $5,000 purchase price from the government. "In addition Stuart would receive a dollar for each device sold by the manufacturer," Thomas added.

Thus, as a result of his Washington visit in October 1859, Jeb Stuart had both earned a pretty penny and won accolades for his role in the capture of the notorious John Brown. For that matter, out of the various Federal and state troops (Virginia and Maryland militiamen) sent to Harpers Ferry, only Stuart had recognized the instigator of the raid as John Brown.

Epilogue: John Brown, convicted of treason, was hanged on December 2, 1859. Quite probably the infamous Free Soiler also would have been convicted of murder for his role in the slaying of five pro-slavery partisans at Pottawatomie Creek during the "Bleeding Kansas" troubles of the mid-1850s. Even so, his hanging after the affair at Harpers Ferry made him a martyr to many in the North. Ralph Waldo Emerson, for one, was moved to say that Brown's hanging would render the gallows "as glorious as a cross."

"God Alone Will Know"

A FRATRICIDAL WAR, WE say today? In general terms, yes . . . sometimes even specifically. Just ask (if you still could) the Terrill brothers, William and James, of still-tiny Warm Springs, Bath County, Virginia.

The sons of a prominent lawyer and state legislator, one, William, went to West Point and the other, James, to the Virginia Military Institute (VMI) in nearby Lexington, Virginia. Younger brother James graduated from VMI in 1858, the war clouds already scudding close, and became a lawyer like his father. Older brother William, after his graduation from West Point in 1853, became an artillery officer. Among other antebellum assignments he saw duty in both Florida and in the

Virginia-born brothers William Terrill, Union (at left), and James Terrill, Confederate, both became brigadier generals and both died in battle, but separately and two years apart.

troubled Kansas area. He also spent time as a mathematics instructor at West Point.

With the Civil War about to break out, it was a troubled older brother who went home to talk over his options with his father. While younger brother James opted to stay with his state and fight for the Confederacy, William chose to go the opposite way. He would loyally serve the Union . . . so long as he wasn't asked to fight in their home state of Virginia. His father counseled that he wouldn't be able to come back to Virginia except to die, but William stuck to his Union loyalties anyway.

Destined to be one of sixteen Union generals from Virginia, William never fought in the commonwealth, as events turned out. Instead, after brief recruiting and organizing duty in Washington, he was posted as commandant of a training camp in Kentucky. By early 1862 he became chief of artillery for the Second Division, Army of the Ohio, commanded by Don Carlos Buell. As such, it was said, he laid down such intense fire at Shiloh that wherever his battery turned its guns on the enemy "silence prevailed."

After Shiloh he served in the siege of Corinth, Mississippi, then joined the forces of Maj. Gen. William ("Bull") Nelson assigned to defend Kentucky from incursions by Braxton Bragg. Soon after the shellacking Nelson took at Richmond, Kentucky, Brigadier General Terrill would be among the officers stunned by news that Nelson had been shot and killed at the Galt House in Louisville, Kentucky, by a fellow Union officer, Brig. Gen. Jefferson Colombus Davis (similar name, but not to be confused with Confederate President Jefferson Davis). Terrill would be seen among those milling around in the lobby of the hotel and swearing vengeance on Davis, whose only punishment for the murder, the result of a petty quarrel, would be denial of promotion to major general.

Also in Louisville, Terrill bumped into his old adversary from West Point, Phil Sheridan, but instead of resuming their fisticuffs of earlier days, this time they would calmly shake hands.

Just days away, meanwhile, loomed the battle of Perryville, Kentucky. There, the night before meeting the enemy, Terrill, Thirty-third Brigade commander, and two fellow officers—Brig. Gen. James Jackson, Tenth Division commander, Army of the Ohio, and Col. George Webster, Thirty-fourth Brigade commander—speculated aloud that the odds were against their dying in battle.

The next day, ironically, all three perished in the battle of Perryville. Jackson died just minutes after being struck in the chest by two bullets. Webster was astride his horse and directing his troops when he was struck down. Terrill's death, however, was especially poignant.

Union Maj. James Connolly would live to describe Terrill's agonizing end. They were only five feet apart when a shell fragment whizzed across the battleground and tore away Terrill's chest. "He recognized me and his first words were, 'Major, do you think it's fatal?' I knew it must be, but to encourage him I answered, 'Oh, I hope not.' Then he said, 'My poor wife, my poor wife!' He lived until 2:00 the next morning."

Younger brother James Terrill, in the meantime, served his side in the Civil War with gallantry and efficiency as well. He too became a brigadier general. As commander of the Thirteenth Virginia, he saw combat at First Manassas (Bull Run), in the Shenandoah Valley, in the Seven Days' battles, at Second Manassas, Antietam, Fredericksburg, Chancellorsville, and Gettysburg before moving on to the battles of 1864—the Wilderness, Spotsylvania . . . until this point a remarkable record of survival.

This General Terrill commanded and fought so well as to elicit Jubal Early's pronouncement that Terrill's regiment "was never required to take a position that they did not take it, nor to hold one that they did not hold it."

But he also was destined to meet his end during the Civil War—in the small battle of Bethesda Church, Virginia, on May 30, 1864. He would initially be buried near the same spot . . . by his older brother's fellow troops of the Union.

At some point later, the family memorialized both brothers with a single headstone that said, "God Alone Knows Which Was Right."

Southern-Tinged Heroes

ONLY WEEKS BEFORE HIS MEN fired on Fort Sumter in Charleston Harbor, Pierre Gustave Toutant Beauregard ("Peter" to his friends) had been named superintendent of West Point. But, oops, since he was a known Secessionist, he held the position for only five days, less than a week—the shortest such posting at West Point ever.

Down at Charleston, South Carolina, meanwhile, an old acquaintance (some even say friend), a former instructor, fellow West Pointer, and Mexican War compatriot was waiting off-stage for his appearance under the spotlight of history. And who could have been more perfectly cast as "Southern-acceptable" than Maj. Robert Anderson? Just think, born in Kentucky (albeit a Border State), pro-slavery in his personal view, married to a Georgia woman, and having strong emotional attachment to the city of Charleston itself, where his own father had fought the British during the American Revolution.

And now, in April 1861, their two paths would cross once again. How did Central Casting come up with this combination—Beauregard, ousted West Point superintendent as newly named Confederate commander of Charleston Harbor, and Anderson, Federal officer in charge at Fort Sumter?

Months before, Beauregard, an aristocratic Louisiana Creole by birth, had run for mayor of New Orleans even while actively serving the army as its chief engineer officer in the area.

Defeated in his mayoral bid, he remained outspoken on political issues—he never was shy about speaking or writing in favor of secession. Oddly, he actively sought the post of superintendent of West Point.

Even more oddly, he was appointed, reportedly thanks to the influence of the Buchanan administration's pro-Southern secretary of war, John B. Floyd (also a former governor of Virginia and future Confederate general). But Beauregard only lasted for the period of January 23–28, 1861—five days in all. Washington belatedly realized it wouldn't do to have a known Secessionist in charge of the cadets learning how to defend the United States from all possible enemies.

Major Anderson, in the meantime, had been placed in charge of Castle Pinckney and Forts Moultrie and Sumter at Charleston, where his father not only had fought the British at Fort Moultrie but also had been held prisoner for nine months. Because of Anderson's various Southern ties, he was a "politically correct" choice to command an isolated Federal outpost in the sea of Secessionist fever that was Charleston in late 1860 and early 1861.

Unlike Beauregard, he would be absolutely loyal to the Union his father had fought to create—not for nothing was Robert Anderson born at a family plantation called Soldier's Retreat.

Both Anderson and Beauregard had served in the Mexican War of the 1840s with distinction, but it was the showy Creole who wrote a book about it: *Personal Reminiscences of an Engineer Officer During the Campaign in Mexico Under General Winfield Scott in 1847–48.*

Just weeks before firing on Fort Sumter—commanded by Union Maj. Robert Anderson (right)—Anderson's old friend and former West Point student P. G. T. Beauregard briefly was superintendent of West Point itself.

For both career army men, promotions had been typically slow over the years. Beauregard was still a captain in 1856, eighteen years after his graduation from the Military Academy. He considered resigning at that point, but acceded to the persuasion of his superiors and took on the New Orleans post instead. Anderson, meanwhile, was only a major by 1860 after an even longer stint of thirty-five years since he graduated from West Point, Class of 1825.

Stunned and angered by his abrupt dismissal in 1861 from the superintendency of the academy, Beauregard was on his way home to New Orleans when he received a telegram informing him that Louisiana had seceded on January 26. He needed hardly any urging to follow suit—he resigned from Federal service and obtained a quick appointment by Confederate President Jefferson Davis to brigadier general's rank, then he took his historic place as Confederate commander of Charleston Harbor.

As a result of all this, two Southern-tinged officers, both West Pointers, each well known to the other, were on a collision course that would culminate with the bombardment of Fort Sumter . . . the beginning of the Civil War.

For Maj. Robert Anderson, the older of the two men, Fort Sumter would be the climactic point of a long and honorable military career. No doubt he hated to see it end this way, but few could fault the major for surrendering his small garrison after thirty-four hours of bombardment by the far more numerous guns Beauregard brought to bear on the island outpost. Greeted in the North as a hero, Anderson would be forced to retire from the U.S. Army soon after the fall of Fort Sumter, due to illness, but not before the Lincoln administration used his good offices in Kentucky to help keep the Border State at least nominally on the roster of Union states.

Before his death while visiting the French Riviera in 1871, Anderson was destined to enjoy the symbolic triumph of raising the same flag over Fort Sumter in April 1865 that he had been forced to take down in April 1861.

Beauregard, widely greeted as a hero himself for the pummeling of Fort Sumter, remained colorfully active throughout the Civil War as one of the Confederacy's best-known generals—despite the mutual antagonism that he and early mentor Jefferson Davis developed toward one another. Thus, "Old Bory," as his men sometimes called him, would be on hand as second in command for the great Confederate victory at First Manassas. He would begin as second in command at Shiloh, then take over from the mortally wounded Albert Sidney Johnston and withdraw under Union pressure from both Shiloh and Corinth, Mississippi.

Sidelined temporarily by illness, Beauregard was unhappy to return to duty under the command of Davis's pet in the West, Braxton Bragg. From there, Beauregard moved to command the defenses of the Georgia and South Carolina coasts, especially of Charleston.

He returned to Virginia in 1864 as U. S. Grant pounded every wall erected by Lee's Army of Northern Virginia. During the last weeks of the war, Beauregard was in North Carolina with his former commander at Manassas, Joseph E. Johnston.

Once the smoke of battle cleared, he returned to New Orleans to serve as president of two railroads and as state adjutant general. He and fellow Confederate Jubal Early supervised the drawings of the Louisiana lottery. Beauregard died in New Orleans in 1893 at the age of seventy-four.

Boys in Confederate Gray

AFTER ATTENDING THE Milton Boarding School for Boys in Cockeysville, Maryland, young Wilkes, not yet fifteen, moved on to St. Timothy's Hall in Catonsville, a very "social" military school where in the early 1850s the boys wore gray uniforms—and demonstrated distinctly Southern sympathies.

The faculty members, on the other hand, were distinctly Northern in outlook.

The result was a bit of an insurrection, with Wilkes and his younger brother Joseph very much involved as participants. Someone, it seems, had killed a handful of school chickens. The faculty blamed the deed on students but didn't know which ones and imposed punishment upon the entire student body. The penalty, highly unpopular, was suspension of the school's weekly holidays.

A number of students, Wilkes and Joseph included, reacted by taking muskets from the school armory and marching off to a nearby woods. There the armed students bivouacked and refused to move until the holidays were restored.

They appeared quite ready to defend themselves, too.

After three days, the school administration gave in to their demand—the holidays were restored.

End of incident . . . except for the lasting impression on youthful minds that rebellious actions such as theirs could succeed. "It is not difficult to see why many of these young Southerners were ready and willing to fight the North eight years later," wrote M. Christopher New in the March 1993 issue of *America's Civil War* magazine. "In the minds of St. Timothy's alumni, they had already fought the North once—and won."

Epilogue: Leaving the military school in 1854 for the family farm in Bel Air, Maryland, Wilkes would *not* prepare himself for a military career, despite his own pro-Southern sympathies. Instead, he made plans to follow in the career footsteps of his late father and a highly successful older brother. The young man's pathway to fame soon would take him to Richmond, Virginia. There, from 1858 to 1860, in the city destined to become capital of the Confederacy, the Richmond Dramatic Star Company provided John Wilkes Booth the stage upon which to develop and polish his skills . . . as an actor.

Old Buck's Legacy

LIKE LINCOLN, HE WAS BORN in a log cabin. He was the fifteenth president. He owned a pair of bald eagles but kept them at home rather than at the White House. He was the only president never to marry.

Once, with the Prince of Wales visiting, so many guests, you know . . . he allegedly gave up his bed and slept in the hallway.

Like any president, he would leave a legacy of many facets, but most important, the first shots of the Civil War would take place on his watch.

Old Buck. Didn't do much, history says, but never to be forgotten because of the Civil War he handed off to his successor, Abe Lincoln. Old Buck, they called James Buchanan, former five-term member of the U.S. House, former U.S. minister to Russia, former U.S. senator; former secretary of state, former U.S. minister to Great Britain. With a résumé like that, could he have stopped it?

He might as well have stepped in front of a runaway train, but his vacillations didn't help, even if the Civil War might have been unstoppable by the time he took office in 1857.

The Democrat from Lancaster, Pennsylvania, in fact took office thinking the Supreme Court would take the steam out of the hot slavery issue by restricting its spread from the South into America's new western territories. Buchanan was so hopeful that he described the issue of slavery's spread in his inaugural address as "happily, a matter of but little importance."

He said the pending Supreme Court decision would settle the territorial issue "speedily and finally."

Even if Buchanan had been right in his expectation, even if the High Court had ruled that the nation's future states must be kept slave-free, slavery would have remained alive and well in the South— an evil cancer eating away at the soul of America.

As events turned out, however, two days after Buchanan's inauguration, the Supreme Court dashed his best hopes with its historic Dred Scott decision. That ruling in effect said Congress had no right to bar slavery from the territories.

The result, far from Buchanan's "matter of little importance," was outrage in the North and ever more heated argument between the nation's abolitionists and its proslavery advocates. Involved among the competing interests here were the obvious great moral problems, the issue of states' rights and, for many a plantation slave owner, a very basic question of economic survival.

For the slaves themselves, of course, the overriding consideration was freedom . . . their own personal freedom.

The nation plunged into political and sectional strife that was unprecedented, that no one seemed able to control. As one political factor, explains an official White House biography, "when Republicans won a plurality in the House in 1858, every significant bill they passed fell before the Southern votes in the Senate or a presidential veto."

Buchanan tried to have Kansas admitted to the Union as a slave state, but that move failed and only angered leaders of both political parties. In the meantime, proslavery and antislavery forces in that territory were engaged in an ugly guerrilla-type war.

Whether Buchanan liked it or not, the nation was headed for a violent showdown. But first, as the presidential election of 1860 approached, sectional feelings were so intense, his fellow Democrats divided into northern and southern wings, and each chose its own nominee for president. That meant an easy victory for the fledgling Republican Party's little-known and untried candidate for president, Abraham Lincoln. Kentucky-born but a Midwesterner by virtue of his residence in Illinois, he was not even listed on the southern ballots printed up for the election of 1860. Still, Lincoln won. And in the South, dismayed by the prospect of a Republican, presumably antislavery administration, the old slave states began to secede, led by the so-called fire-eaters of South Carolina.

The Palmetto State took its drastic step of severance on December 20, 1860. Mississippi, Florida, Alabama, Georgia, and Louisiana all followed in January 1861—by the time the Civil War was under way in earnest, the Confederacy consisted of eleven "secesh" states in all.

Buchanan at first did nothing about the devastating threat to the Union. In his view, the states had no right to secede, but then, the federal government had no right to intervene and stop them, either. *Stalemate.*

In early January, however, he did try to send reinforcements and supplies to the federal troops under Maj. Robert Anderson who were trapped at Fort Sumter in Charleston Harbor. The relief vessel the *Star of the West,* was turned away by cannon fire . . . from Southern-manned artillery. In effect, the first shots of the Civil War had been fired.

Buchanan still did nothing, and there matters stood until Lincoln took office on March 4, 1861.

Oddly, you might say, with his own presidency all over, Democrat Buchanan consistently, for the next four years, supported the Republican Lincoln administration in its prosecution of the Civil War.

☆ ☆ ☆

Additional note: How did a "mere" slave, with no apparent rights, bring about such a momentous Supreme Court ruling as the famous Dred Scott decision of 1857? Who was Dred Scott anyway?

You could argue—and *he* did argue—that he was a free black. But the Supreme Court ruled that he was a slave . . . worse, he was a nobody, a noncitizen.

The facts were these: Dred Scott first was a slave belonging to U.S. Army surgeon John Emerson of Missouri. Starting in 1834, he spent years with his physician master in the slave-free state of Illinois and in the slave-free part of the Wisconsin Territory that later became the state of Minnesota. In 1838, however, they returned to the slave state of Missouri, with grim implications for Dred Scott.

More unhappily, Emerson soon left Missouri without Scott, who not only was left behind, but was hired out and then sold to a second owner, John F. A. Sanford.

In 1846, Dred Scott went to a state court to sue Sanford for his freedom (and that of his family) on the grounds that his earlier residency in slave-free jurisdictions made him free. The first court he went to agreed, but then the state supreme court threw out the lower court's ruling. That meant Dred Scott would remain a slave.

Turning now to the federal courts, he took his case all the way to the U.S. Supreme Court . . . only to have it say after his decade-long battle that it had no jurisdiction in his case. As a slave, he was not a citizen either of Missouri or of the United States—practically speaking, he was a nonperson! Thus, he couldn't sue in the federal courts.

As for still being a slave, *his* central issue, he unfortunately had returned to the slave state of Missouri without protest. In effect, he had resumed being a slave.

Aside from rejecting Dred Scott's personal plea for freedom, the Democrat-dominated court also declared that the Missouri Compromise of 1820 was unconstitutional in its attempt to bar the spread of slavery into the territories. It was this part of the ruling that pleased the South, created furor in the North, and produced ugly strife over the slavery issue in the territories adjoining the traditional slave states.

Epilogue: Freed by a friend later in 1857, Dred Scott became a hotel porter and a minor celebrity in the St. Louis area until his death in 1858 . . . before the Civil War erupted. Born in the 1790s, he would have been in his sixties when he died.

★ Part 2 ★
1861

Embers to Hot Flame

It began, real war began, with the firing on Fort Sumter. Only two men died as a result, both accidentally. But that was only a beginning—before it was all over, more than 623,000 would become casualties. In 1861, the first big battles, starting at First Bull Run, would take place, would stun even the participants by the length of their casualty lists. But it also was a year of change and adjustment in government and society—two governments, two societies.

Where Was Mary Todd?

As a small but startling set of historical contradictions, please consider the burning issue of where Mary Todd Lincoln was on the drab, gray, and rainy morning of February 11, 1861, when her husband, Abraham, bade farewell to their hometown of Springfield, Illinois. Where exactly was the president-elect's wife as he entrained for Washington, D.C., for the presidency of the fast-fracturing United States, for posterity . . . and assassination?

The historical accounts of Mary's whereabouts that morning, even of her behavior, are surprisingly varied and diverse. And of course contradictory. To wit:

• In his book *The Life and Writings of Abraham Lincoln,* historian Philip Van Doren Stern cited "the story told" by an unnamed "New York newspaper correspondent" that Mary and Abraham had quarreled that early morning over "a political appointment she wanted him to make."

Worse and far more graphic to imagine as the poor man went off to an uncertain fate, "When the time for departure came, she was lying on the floor of her hotel room, screaming with hysterical rage that she would not leave for Washington unless her husband granted her wishes."

Thus, "The President-elect entered his carriage without his family."

Thus, too, he was driven to the railroad station in the dreary rain on what was "supposed to be his day of triumph, the auspicious beginning of a progress toward fame and success."

Thus again, some of his old friends who had gathered at the rail depot "doubtless inquired about Mrs. Lincoln, and the man whose heart was breaking at this miserable farewell to his own past had to parry off their questions and explain elaborately that she had changed her plans."

Thus (finally), no more mention of the missing Mary Todd Lincoln in this context. Lincoln gave his farewell speech, short and poignant—as all historical accounts agree—and then his train pulled out. It "moved off toward Washington, toward civil war and death."

• Another author, another version. In his *Lincoln,* David Herbert Donald, two-time winner of the Pulitzer Prize for biography, didn't shilly-shally around in *his* view of where Mary Todd was that crucial morning in 1861. As he succinctly stated his version of the facts (*her* place among them mentioned only in a parenthetical aside): "February 11 was cold and rainy, but a crowd of Springfield residents gathered at the Great Western Railroad depot to see Lincoln off. (Mary Lincoln had gone to St. Louis for additional shopping and would join her husband in Indianapolis.) The President-elect himself had roped the family trunks and labeled them A. LINCOLN, THE WHITE HOUSE, WASHINGTON, D.C."

• Moving on to yet another historical account, we find that Mary *was* there that morning after all! Right at the rail depot, buried somewhere in the onlooking crowd . . . and reacting emotionally as her husband said his farewells, especially as he mentioned their children and the burial of their little Eddie, victim of pulmonary tuberculosis. By this account, "One knows well that her tears came at the mention of Eddie's grave. Where they were going, there would be no one who had wept with them in that sorrow, no one who would remember. Mary's loving and dependent heart was torn even as her husband's."

So wrote Ruth Painter Randall, wife of noted Lincoln scholar J. G. Randall, in her *Mary Lincoln: Biography of a Marriage.* Mary, moreover, "heard that loved voice continue," heard her husband continue with "chilling suggestion of danger" as he said, "I now leave, not knowing when, or whether ever I may return, with a task before me greater than that which rested upon [George] Washington."

Interestingly, Mrs. Randall started in her study of Mary Todd Lincoln while helping her historian-husband in the research for two chapters in his two-volume work, *Lincoln the President, Springfield to Gettysburg,* published in 1945. It so happened that J. G. Randall's official research assistant at the time, also his later collaborator on the book *The Civil War and Reconstruction,* was the same David Herbert Donald mentioned above.

• Another historical work placing Mary Todd right at the scene of Abraham Lincoln's leave-taking that fateful morning of a grim February—the day before his birthday, by the way—is *Mary Todd Lincoln: Her Life and Letters,* by Justin G. Turner and Linda Levitt Turner.

The historical spotlight here again finds Mary in the crowd at the rail station as her husband "addressed the throng" with son Robert Todd Lincoln by his side. (By most accounts, Robert left Springfield on the train with his father that morning . . . no real dispute over that detail.)

By Ruth Painter Randall's account, one should imagine the tears that started in Mary's eyes at Abraham's mention of young Eddie's burial. But now, in the Turner account, "as the cars rolled eastward out of the Springfield depot, Mary Lincoln turned away, no doubt reflecting that this was the proudest moment of her life."

No doubt? But certainly, "there was sadness as well."

Surely also: "She was preparing to leave close friends and those who were of her own blood—people who understood, sympathized, who would remember her tragedies, and, in the end, forgive her shortcomings. Now the eyes of the nation would be upon her. Few people would understand and still fewer would be ready to forgive."

Wisely enough, it also might be said, the same book suggests that perhaps Mary Lincoln wouldn't go with Lincoln that day because of a quarrel . . . *not* about political appointments, but about the risks she and their remaining three boys might run by traveling with Lincoln. To wit:

> For months there had been threats on his life, ghastly effigies sent through the mail, dark hints that he never would live to be inaugurated. Because of the dangers all about, it was with some difficulty that Mary Lincoln persuaded her husband to allow her to accompany him on the long train journey to Washington; perhaps they had a real set-to on the subject, for she did not leave Springfield with him but joined him the following day in Indianapolis with Willie and Tad.

Then, too, just two pages earlier, the Turner duo noted a rumor at large in Springfield in the days or weeks before the Lincoln leave-taking that Mary had gone into hysterics over her husband's refusal of a political appointment she wanted him to make. Unlike historian Stern's version of a similar story, however, the Turners did *not* suggest that Mary was back in the Lincoln couple's temporary hotel quarters, lying on the floor in some kind of a hysterical fit while her husband went off to the rail station and said good-bye to the hometown folks alone.

• In somewhat similar fashion, meanwhile, Lincoln biographer Stephen B. Oates wrote (in *With Malice Toward None: A Life of Abraham Lincoln*) that Lincoln tried to talk his wife out of making the trip east in his train for two reasons. One indeed was the threat implicit in the assassination rumors. The other was simply to spare her the wear of a very public journey taking twelve days to complete. The plan—formulated by Lincoln's pending secretary of state, William Henry Seward—was to bolster Union morale by routing the president-elect's train through Ohio, Pennsylvania, New York, New Jersey, and Maryland on the way to Washington—sometimes even having the train shuttle back and forth within those states.

"Many of Mary's friends also said she should go to Washington later," biographer Oates wrote. "But Mary wouldn't listen to them. 'The plucky wife of the President,' said a reporter, announced that 'she would see Mr. Lincoln on to Washington, danger or no danger.' They [the Lincolns] finally agreed that Lincoln and Robert would leave today with Mary and the younger boys catching a later train and joining them in Indianapolis."

All well and good . . . but was Mary at the rail depot in Springfield to see her husband off or not?

According to Timothy P. Townsend, National Park Service historian stationed at the onetime Lincoln home in Springfield, now an officially designated National Historic Site, there is *no* rock-hard, bottom-line answer. Stated another way: "No specific reference to where she was."

But historian Townsend also threw cold water on suggestions that Abe Lincoln left his wife in hysterics on the floor of their hotel room or that she was out of town on a shopping expedition.

Whether she was in the crowd at the rail depot, however, remains a mystery . . . although it certainly didn't seem that way for the readers of the *New York Herald* the day after Lincoln's departure.

Quite contrary to the New York reportage cited by historian Philip Van Doren Stern, the *Herald* on February 12, 1861, reported: "The President-elect, *accompanied by his lady* [italics added] and a number of friends, left his hotel at half-past seven A. M., and rode up to the Great Western depot."

What came next was an emotional moment for all, it also seems.

"The president-elect took his station in the waiting room, and allowed his friends to pass him by and take his hand for the last time.

His face was pale, and quivered with emotion so deep as to render him unable to utter a single word."

At exactly eight o'clock, Lincoln was escorted to the waiting train, said the *Herald* with yet another reference to Mary Lincoln. "After exchanging a parting salutation *with his lady* [italics again added], he took his stand on the platform, removed his hat, and asking silence, spoke . . . to the multitude that stood in respectful silence and with their heads uncovered."

So there we have it—conflicting statements from both contemporary journalists and latter-day historians. Small mystery still unresolved.

Additional note: As for why Mary didn't accompany her husband and son Robert on *their* train out of Springfield that morning, National Park Service historian Townsend cited letters suggesting she was added to the Lincoln party traveling east only at the last minute, a delay to be blamed on concerns for her safety. Further, the train carrying the president-elect's party the morning of February 11 was a truncated one with no facilities suitable for Mary and her two other sons, Willie and Tad. They caught up with Lincoln in Indianapolis by the next day, then traveled with him until the night he left them behind to pass secretly through Baltimore in the sleeping car of a train running ahead of the official Lincoln train.

Oddly enough, Lincoln's two secretaries, John M. Hay and John G. Nicolay, wasted few words on the issue of Mary's whereabouts in the huge, ten-volume biography of Lincoln they produced many years later. A mere footnote in volume 3 of that meticulously detailed work states that she and the three Lincoln boys left Springfield . . . *on the train with Lincoln.* Keeping in mind that Hay and Nicolay didn't care much for Mary Todd, their offhand reference could be considered more an *indication* of her whereabouts than a fact etched in stone, according to Townsend.

Meanwhile, the reason for Lincoln's incognito arrival in Washington ahead of the official train was information that pro-Southern hotheads in Baltimore planned an assassination attempt as he passed through their state and city. While all the Lincolns on either train escaped harm in Baltimore, troops from Massachusetts weren't so lucky when they entrained for Washington via Baltimore in mid-April. They were greeted by a riotous mob, and several men were killed in the clash that resulted.

★

MYSTERY
What Did Lincoln Say?

★

WHAT EXACTLY DID ABRAHAM LINCOLN tell the hometown folks the day he left Springfield, Illinois, for his presidency in Washington? Good question, since there are versions and then versions—well, three in all.

As stated in an "Interpretive Bulletin" prepared by historian George L. Painter for the Lincoln Home National Historic Site in Springfield, the three are similar in overall thrust but vary in details such as phrasing.

Quite naturally, no tape recorders or video cameras were around to preserve Lincoln's every word when he said his touching, off-the-cuff good-bye to the home he had known for almost twenty-five years. Still, impromptu or not, it was a historic moment, and indeed attempts were made to preserve the president-elect's words for posterity.

One version, the version accepted by the National Park Service for display and dissemination at the Lincoln home, was "written down in pencil as the President-elect's train was leaving Springfield," reported historian Painter in the interpretive bulletin.

None other than Lincoln himself wrote down the opening words, while his secretary John G. Nicolay penned in most of the remainder of the short address—each one in handwriting recognizable to scholars. Each apparently went by his best memory of what Lincoln had said in that emotional moment just a short time before they began to commit his words to paper. Their combined account of what Lincoln said at Springfield the morning of February 11, 1861, now known as the "A Version," is this one:

> [In Lincoln's handwriting first] My friends—No one, not in my situation, can appreciate my feeling of sadness at this parting. To

this place, and the kindness of these people, I owe every thing. Here I have lived a quarter of a century, and have passed from a young to an old man. Here my children have been born, and one is buried. I now [here Nicolay's handwriting takes over] leave, not knowing when, or whether ever, I may return, with a task before me greater than that which rested upon Washington. Without the assistance of that Divine Being, who ever attended him, I cannot succeed. With that assistance I cannot fail. Trusting in Him, who can go with me, and remain with you and be every where for good, [Lincoln filled in the rest of this sentence] let us confidently hope that all will yet be well. To His care commending you, as I hope in your prayers you will commend me, I bid you an affectionate farewell.

The next version, the "B Version," is Lincoln's statement as reproduced in *Harper's Weekly* and a number of eastern newspapers the next day, February 12. The "B Version" text cited by Painter actually came from a broadside distributed four years after Lincoln's leave-taking from Springfield, in April 1865, by the American News Company of New York—according to Painter this version "is in all but a few marks of punctuation identical with that which appeared in *Harper's Weekly* and various eastern newspapers on February 12, 1861."

My Friends: No one not in my position can appreciate the sadness I feel at this parting. To this people I owe all that I am. Here I have lived more than a quarter of a century; here my children were born, and here one of them lies buried. I know not how soon I shall see you again. A duty devolves upon me which is, perhaps, greater than that which has devolved upon any other man since the days of Washington. He never would have succeeded except for the aid of Divine Providence, upon which he at all times relied. I feel that I cannot succeed without the same Divine aid which sustained him, and on the same Almighty Being I place my reliance for support, and I hope you, my friends, will all pray that I may receive that Divine assistance without which I cannot succeed, but with which success is certain. Again I bid you affectionate farewell.

Finally comes a "C Version," a text published in the *Illinois State Journal* the day after Lincoln's historic departure. The longest of the three, it may be the most accurate, many historians believe. "If this version was taken down as Lincoln spoke, this may be so," opined Painter. But he warned there is no proof that anyone did copy Lincoln's words

A beardless Abraham Lincoln, as seen in his U.S. Senate race of 1858 against Stephen Douglas . . . an old beau of Mary Todd Lincoln.

as he spoke. The "C Version," like the other two texts, begins with Lincoln noting what an extraordinary situation or position he faced on that February 11:

> Friends, No one who has never been placed in a like position, can understand my feelings at this hour, nor the oppressive sadness I feel at this parting. For more than a quarter of a century I have lived among you, and during all that time I have received nothing but kindness at your hands. Here I have lived from my youth until now I am an old man. Here the most sacred ties of earth were assumed; here all my children were born, and here one of them lies buried. To you, dear friends, I owe all that I have, all that I am. All the strange, chequered past seems to crowd now upon my mind. To-day I leave you; I go to assume a task more difficult than that which devolved upon General Washington. Unless the great God who assisted him, shall be with and aid me, I must fail. But if the same omniscient mind, and Almighty arm that directed and protected him, shall guide and support me, I shall not fail, I shall succeed. Let us all pray that the God of our fathers may not forsake us now. To Him I commend you all— permit me to ask that with equal security and faith, you will invoke His wisdom and guidance for me. With these few words I must leave you—for how long I know not. Friends, one and all, I must now bid you an affectionate farewell.

In all three versions, it should be noted, Lincoln made passing but feeling reference to the loss of his young son Eddie, the one member of the family who would not be making the journey to Washington . . . and the destiny that awaited the Lincolns there. Eddie had died in 1850 of tuberculosis.

Meanwhile, faced with these three choices, which one has history accepted as the most authentic of all?

At the Lincoln Home National Historic Site, Painter noted, the choice was the "A Version." That text, in fact, also is displayed at the railroad depot where Lincoln uttered his farewell words. It also was the choice for "the back of the Lincoln statue in front of the present [Illinois state] Capitol."

Inside the Lincoln tomb at Springfield, however, is a bronze plaque that carries another of the three versions. Here, for your information, the choice was the long "C Version."

Additional note: A short variation of sorts—hearsay, really, but interesting hearsay—can be found in a letter written the day after Lincoln's departure by Mrs. James C. (Mercy) Conkling of Springfield to her son Clinton, a schoolmate of Robert Todd Lincoln at the Phillips Exeter prep school.

"Truly!" she wrote to her son, "as Mr. Lincoln says, *'no President* ever was inaugurated under such trying circumstances.'"

Her letter also mentioned the emotions running rampant at the rail depot as their friend and neighbor from Springfield went off to his destiny. "Your Father described the scene at the [railroad] cars, as being very affecting, scarcely a dry eye in all the vast crowd."

Her husband, that same father of Clinton, then said much the same thing in a letter of his own, also written on February 12. "It was quite affecting," he wrote. "Many eyes were filled to overflowing as Mr. Lincoln uttered those few simple words which you will see in the papers. His own breast heaved with emotion and he could scarcely command his feelings sufficiently to commence."

Both parents of Robert Todd Lincoln's school chum expressed their fears and hopes for Lincoln's—or the country's—future. "Surely our prayers will follow him," wrote Mercy Conkling, herself an old friend of Mary Todd Lincoln. "God only can preserve him in times like these. We all feel greatly for him."

Added her husband in his own letter, "He [Lincoln] is now fairly on his way for weal or woe of the nation. God bless him and preserve him and nerve him for the terrible struggles and dangers which he may be called upon to meet and endure."

At the same time, added this practical father, "it may prove advantageous" for Clinton to keep in touch with "Bob," the president-elect's son, Robert Lincoln. "If you should visit Baltimore in the summer I should want you to go to Washington, provided all things are quiet and peaceful."

Epilogue: Of course, "all things" in the summer of 1861 would *not* be quiet and peaceful.

"What Is the Matter with Them?"

ODDLY, AS PRESIDENT-ELECT LINCOLN wended his way by whistle-stop train to Washington in February 1861, he several times made statements indicating that he had hardly any conception of the hard, anti-Union feelings already gripping the South.

Either that or he was trying to ease public fears of the conflagration that might (and did) come.

"For twelve exhausting days," wrote Stephen B. Oates in *With Malice Toward None,* "the train chugged through endless towns and villages, with crowds waving Union flags as the coach of the President-elect swept by. In the larger cities, Lincoln was obliged to attend receptions and give speeches—now from the platform of his coach, now from a hotel ballroom, now from the steps of a statehouse. And wherever he spoke, people wanted to know about secession and what he would do about the crisis. Trying to avoid any utterance that might ignite Virginia and the combustible [Kansas] border, Lincoln was extremely guarded in what he said now, assuring his audiences that he would make an explicit statement of policy in his inaugural address [on March 4]."

At Columbus, Ohio, Oates pointed out, Lincoln said, "There is nothing wrong. . . .We entertain different views on political questions, but nobody is suffering anything." All the country needed was "time, patience, and a reliance on that God who has never forsaken his people."

Turning up later at Pittsburgh, the gangly Illinois lawyer now said, "There is really no crisis except an '*artificial one*,'" to be blamed upon "designing" Southern politicians. Given "self-possession" among the people of both sides, the crisis would abate.

But why, he asked his audience in Cleveland, Ohio, was the South so upset? "Have they not all their rights now as they ever had? Do they not have their fugitive slaves returned now as ever? Have they not the same Constitution that they have lived under for seventy odd years? . . . What then is the matter with them? Why all this excitement? Why all these complaints?"

That was his refrain at stop after stop, noted Oates. "There was no real crisis. If the trouble in the South were left alone, it would take care of itself. Lincoln did not have to save the country; the country 'will save itself.' It was up to the people, not the President, to preserve the Union."

But Lincoln also did warn that if necessary, he, as president, would "put my foot down firmly."

With the firing on Fort Sumter in April 1861, he did. He surely did.

Additional note: Among those aboard the Lincoln "special" as it slowly wound eastward from Indianapolis—at a nonremarkable thirty miles an hour—were, in addition to the president-elect himself, his wife, Mary; their three sons, Robert, Willie, and Tad; Lincoln's two young secretaries, John Hay and John G. Nicolay; young Elmer Ephraim Ellsworth, organizer-drillmaster of a Zouave company famous for its prowess at marching; plus, as biographer Oates also noted, Ward Lamon, Virginia-born friend to Lincoln and fellow Illinois lawyer "who was loaded with guns as Lincoln's self-appointed bodyguard." In addition, noted Oates, "there was William Johnson, 'a colored boy' who worked as Lincoln's hired servant."

Epilogue: Ellsworth, unfortunately, was to become nationally famous soon after as an early, highly visible casualty of the Civil War. Leading his troops across the Potomac River from Washington and into the streets of Alexandria, Virginia, in the spring of 1861, he made for a hotel defiantly flying a Rebel flag. He and the hotel proprietor clashed on the stairs inside, and each was killed . . . each then becoming an instant martyr to his cause. Ellsworth, though, apparently the first Union officer killed in the Civil War, would be accorded the posthumous honor of lying in state in the East Room of the White House, an early and personally painful source of grief for the newly arrived Lincoln family.

And later: Here too, in 1862, would lie young Willie Lincoln, dead from a typhoidlike fever at age twelve; here Union troops earlier in the war period were quartered; and here, finally, after dreaming a dream of seeing his own casket in the East Room, Lincoln himself, in reality, would lie silent and still in April 1865 as thousands of people quietly shuffled through the room in two lines to say farewell to the assassinated president.

★

MYSTERY
Who Fired the First Shot?

★

IT'S AN OLD, SEEMINGLY IRRESOLVABLE mystery wrapped in lingering dispute and born in controversy—who fired the first shot of the Civil War?

There's no denying the first shots of the American Civil War were heard at Charleston, South Carolina. No denying they involved the Federal garrison under Maj. Robert Anderson stubbornly holding out, but trapped, at Fort Sumter, a man-made island in the middle of Charleston Harbor. And there's no denying that secession-minded Southerners were the first to open fire in the Civil War.

But who exactly? There is one, easy, simple, even unassailable answer, but historians and Civil War buffs alike still will argue into the wee hours of tomorrow over this old mystery . . . with their eyes fixed upon three *other* possible answers instead of the right one.

First on the list of some aficionados will be the fanatical graybeard from Virginia, Edmund Ruffin, plantation owner, agricultural pioneer, and dedicated Secessionist. And certainly he was there, in Charleston. He had been there for South Carolina's vote to secede in December of the previous year. He was there at an artillery battery in the still-black, early morning hours of April 14, 1861, as the very first 10–inch mortar round from the Confederacy arced over Fort Sumter and burst with a lightninglike flash of light and echoing boom announcing the war was on in earnest.

But Ruffin, while there on the scene in honor of his commitment to the Southern cause, wasn't at the right place at the right time to fire the first shot, ceremoniously or not. He was at Cummings Point, rather than Confederate Fort Johnson. The first shots came from the latter rather than the former, which, in fact, fired last in the first round of Confederate salvos.

No less an authority than Brig. Gen. P. G. T. Beauregard, commander of Confederate forces at Charleston Harbor, torpedoed Ruffin's claim to fame with this statement: "From Ft. Johnson's mortar battery at 4:30 A.M. issued the first shell of the war. It was fired, not by Mr. Ruffin of Virginia as has been erroneously supposed, but Capt. George S. James of South Carolina to whom Lt. Stephen Lee issued the order."

From this account, assuming Beauregard's memory was correct, it would seem that Captain James could make substantial claim to the "first-shot" title. A later account, published in the *Southern Historical Society Papers* of 1896, said that James first "offered the honor" to onlooking Col. Roger A. Pryor, a former U.S. congressman, also from Virginia, also a secessionist-minded fire-eater, but Pryor declined.

Whereupon, according to this account, another officer volunteered to fire the Fort Johnson mortar, only to have James say, "No. I will fire it myself." And, said the same article, "he did fire it."

Case closed?

Not really. Keeping in mind that Fort Johnson boasted two mortar batteries, that the first shot apparently issued from the East (or Beach) Battery, and that Lt. Henry S. Farley commanded that one, under the same Captain James, let's look at a competing claim. Writing in the *Charleston News and Courier* in 1906 and the *South Carolina Historical and Genealogical Magazine* of 1911 (quite a few years after the fact), Dr. Robert Lebby said he was there that fateful early morning, too.

Lebby admittedly was too far away to see who actually fired the first shot, but he quoted another eyewitness, another doctor in fact, W. H. Prioleau, as saying the mortar was sighted by Lieutenant Farley and Captain James gave the order to fire.

Unfortunately, Prioleau also had to admit that he did not actually see who pulled the lanyard to touch off the mortar round, according to the Civil War centennial booklet *The Civil War at Charleston,* published in 1966 by the Charleston *News and Courier* and *Evening Post* newspapers. But, said the booklet, Dr. Lebby, author of the 1906 and 1911 accounts, offered the opinion that Captain James "would not have given the order to himself."

How about a more direct statement, made by one of the two principals? There is one! Lebby cited a letter from Lieutenant Farley, written many years after the war, unequivocally stating that he, Farley, fired the first round at Fort Sumter. Asserting that the scene was still "fresh" in his memory, Farley gave this account: "Capt. James stood at my right with his watch in his hand and gave me the order to fire. I pulled the lanyard, having already carefully inserted a friction tube, and discharged a 13-inch mortar shell."

All well and good . . . except that the Confederate forces in Charleston in April 1861 could boast *no* 13-inch mortars, that is to say, *none,* according to the Charleston centennial booklet. Thus: "If Farley's memory tricked him as to the caliber of the weapon, did it also play him false in other parts of his statement?"

That point, raised by Warren Ripley, author of the "first shot" article in the centennial publication, certainly tends to muddy the waters of this old dispute all over again. "It's a puzzling question . . . one which no one has been able to solve conclusively," Ripley went on to say. "However, it seems fairly certain that the initial shot was fired by either James or Farley—and from there you can take your pick with the odds about even."

Again, all well and good . . . except that this begs the question: Who fired the first shot of the Civil War? And the answer is: *None* of the above.

For the real answer, go back to January 9, 1861. That was the day the steam-driven paddle wheeler *Star of the West,* normally a passenger liner, appeared in the main ship channel leading into Charleston Harbor. An unarmed, strictly civilian vessel, she was, on this one special occasion, carrying troop reinforcements for Maj. Robert Anderson's garrison at isolated Fort Sumter. The presence of soldiers on board was supposed to have been kept secret, but word had leaked out in advance—even into the newspapers and the streets of Charleston.

Still chagrined over Major Anderson's surprise move from vulnerable Fort Moultrie to the more-isolated Fort Sumter the month before (on December 26, 1860), South Carolina authorities were on guard against any more Federal "tricks." When the *Star of the West* nosed into the main ship channel the morning of January 9, the South Carolina guard ship *General Clinch* scooted ahead—"signaling the alarm with flares and rockets," the centennial booklet noted.

What followed shortly after was no mere shot across the bow. As the *Star* drew abreast of Morris Island, Lt. Charles J. Woods, commander of the relief troops on board the ship, was surprised to see a strange flag fluttering above an abandoned smallpox hospital building on the island—clearly in his view was the flag's white palmetto tree set against a red field (a symbol of South Carolina, the Palmetto State). No sooner had he spotted the flag, than "there was a puff of smoke from the dunes at the foot of the staff," reported the centennial booklet. "A swish and a splash announced the arrival of a shot across the bow."

But that wasn't all. Now came another round, actually crashing into the side of the ship itself. And then another. Also a hit.

Just ahead lay well-armed Fort Moultrie, its many guns covering the watery approaches to Charleston. And now, a loud boom announced that Moultrie was preparing a hot welcome of its own. In quick order, Fort Moultrie sent two more shots after the first. They were just a bit short on range, missed, but still signaled unfriendly intentions.

On nearby Fort Sumter, meanwhile, Anderson and his men watched in frustration . . . and hesitation. With no message from the War Department alerting him in advance, Anderson didn't know if the *Star* were coming to his aid or not. She did fly the American flag, but she was no military ship. When he tried to signal her with his flag, the halyards jammed. Just then, to avoid a nearly point-blank battering by the guns at Fort Moultrie, the *Star* began to turn away.

With no helpful response from Fort Sumter, Woods and the *Star*'s civilian skipper had decided the better part of discretion was to head out to sea again. As the passenger liner then did exactly that, the 24-pounders hidden in the dunes of Morris Island barked anew, several times. They missed this time, since the *Star* by now was steaming ahead too fast. "Soon she was beyond range."

A view of the Citadel, with Charleston Harbor seen in the background. The cadets who were trained here had a historic hand in the early proceedings.

And who did the shooting to open the day's action? The hurriedly erected battery of 24-pounders hidden in the dunes of Morris Island had been manned by forty cadets from the Citadel, the military school located at Charleston.

It's a matter of record that cadet G. W. Haynesworth fired the first shot the morning of January 9, 1861 . . . the first of the Civil War.

Additional note: Still another early, early "shot" of the Civil War sent a potentially lethal cannonball from Morris Island careening off the wharf at Fort Sumter, leaving a clearly visible white "scar" to mark the spot. That was on March 8, 1861, more than a month before the serious bombardment of Fort Sumter. But this shot was an accident committed by a green gun crew at artillery drill. It seems that a live round had been left in a cannon by mistake during a previous drill. Then came an exercise the next day with blank charges . . . only the live round was still in place. Boom! Apologies extended. No war on as yet.

The War's First Casualty

NO SOLDIER, SAILOR, OR MARINE of either side died during the unequal artillery exchanges that led to the surrender of Federal Fort Sumter to Confederate forces on April 14, 1861. Yet one man, Irish-born Pvt. Daniel Hough, Company E, First U.S. Artillery, did become a historic casualty before his U.S. Army brethren left the beleaguered island fortress that same day.

Quite accidentally, he became the Civil War's first known fatality . . . but not exactly due to combat conditions.

Others on both sides of course suffered various training mishaps and strictly ordinary accidents. In the Charleston area, for instance, a Rebel soldier "horsing around" with others in his barracks was stabbed in the eye with a bayonet and died as a result. Others on both sides suffered gunshot wounds, harmful falls, horseback mishaps, fatal illnesses and the like from time to time . . . and all before any real battles were fought.

But Private Hough, unfortunately, was in a class all his own. If there had been no bombardment of Fort Sumter, no surrender of the Federal outpost, he probably would have survived the day . . . and who knows how many more thereafter.

But the bombardment did take place, and he did die as a direct result, in a freak accident that only added to the gloom of the Yankees forced to surrender their holdout post in the middle of Charleston Harbor. The mishap occurred when Maj. Robert Anderson's artillery-men were firing a planned salute of one hundred guns to the American flag as it was being lowered for the formal surrender of the fort.

The thirty-four-hour bombardment of the island fort had ended about 1:30 the previous afternoon, with the rest of the daylight hours spent working out the surrender terms. The terms that Anderson finally agreed to at 7 P.M. April 13 included the ceremonial salute to the flag. The hour had grown so late, however, that both sides were willing to postpone the evacuation of the fort until 11 A.M. the next day, April 14. At that point, a Confederate vessel would carry Anderson and his small garrison to ships of the Federal relief fleet lying off the entrance to Charleston Harbor.

After one last night in possession of Fort Sumter, the major and his men assembled in the morning for the salute to the flag and their leave-taking. As his still-undamaged barbette guns began the unusually long series of salutes, they were firing into a strong incoming breeze. It's not known exactly what set things off, but Hough, a twenty-nine-year-old native of Tipperary, was loading a blank charge into the muzzle of the gun expected to fire off the forty-sixth round in the salute when the three pounds or so of black powder in the charge exploded with the force of nine to fifteen sticks of dynamite.

Severely burned, his right arm reportedly almost torn off, Hough died almost instantly. The young Irishman was described as prematurely gray, blue-eyed, and fair in complexion. He stood five feet, eight inches. A veteran of at least five years' duration by April 1861, he had reenlisted in the U.S. Army in December 1859, according to Rick Hatcher, historian at the National Park Service's Fort Sumter National Monument.

The explosion at Hough's gun apparently sent embers flying. One or more of them touched off a nearby stack of cartridges, with a hot, secondary explosion resulting—five more men were injured. The worst of these injuries—severe burns—were suffered by another Irish-born U.S. Army private, twenty-one-year-old Edward Gallway, also a member of the First U.S. Artillery's Company E. Transported ashore to a Charleston hospital, he died within hours.

Another of the Union men hurt in the accident also was treated ashore, then later allowed to return north. The remaining three injured in the second explosion were able to leave Fort Sumter with their fellow soldiers of the Anderson garrison.

First though, following what Anderson called the "unaccountable misfortune," the planned salute of one hundred guns was cut to just fifty. Then, too, there was a pause while Anderson and his men buried their compatriot, Hough, in the parade ground at Fort Sumter.

Because of the accident, the Federal evacuation of the fort had been so delayed that it was dark by the time Anderson's men boarded the Confederate vessel designated to carry them out of the harbor. It would be the next day, April 15, before the Federal troops were finally

U.S. ARMY MILITARY HISTORY INSTITUTE

The interior of Fort Sumter was photographed on the day after Anderson and his garrison departed. A fire ignited during the bombardment damaged the quarters in the left background.

transferred to the steamer *Baltic,* the ship that would carry them to New York.

Back at Fort Sumter, meanwhile, South Carolina state troops commanded by Col. Roswell S. Ripley moved in and raised both a Confederate and a state flag in the place of Old Glory. The South Carolina militiamen apparently placed a marker at Hough's burial site in the parade ground, with a few respectful words said in memory of the first casualty of the war.

The marker wasn't destined to last, however, and today the site of Hough's grave is unknown.

Additional note: The thirty-four-hour bombardment of Fort Sumter by the Confederate guns assembled and directed by Brig. Gen. P. G. T. Beauregard rained more than three thousand artillery rounds upon the tiny piece of real estate in Charleston Harbor. That pounding, however, was only an initial punishment for the same island fortress, only a fraction of what was yet to come in four years of war.

While held by Southern defenders of Charleston, Fort Sumter was destined to undergo eleven bombardments by Federal forces, beginning on August 17, 1863, and continuing intermittently until September 18, 1864. Those attacks dropped an estimated 43,380 rounds (3,500 tons) on the Confederate-held fort, with 309 Confederate defenders killed or wounded as a result. The island itself was reduced in size by two-thirds.

Even so, no matter how battered, the Confederacy's Fort Sumter never surrendered to the Union forces attacking it.

It finally fell into Federal hands—abandoned rather than surrendered—February 18, 1865, as Union Gen. William Tecumseh Sherman's march through the Carolinas outflanked the Charleston region. At that point, Confederate leaders abandoned not only Fort Sumter, but the entire city of Charleston in order to shift their dwindling forces inland to oppose Sherman in his path northward.

Policeman at Sumter

REMEMBER SGT. WILLIAM JASPER? That hero of South Carolina's Second Regiment who braved the enemy's artillery bombardment in Charleston Harbor to race outside his fort's walls and retrieve the regimental flag? Who then raised the brave colors once again at the end of an artillery sponge staff?

What a moment! What a hero!

But wait . . . what war?

Here's the telling clue: Jasper's heroics at Fort Sullivan (later, Fort Moultrie) came in 1776. And, yes, his war was the war for American independence fought against the British of the eighteenth century— the very conflict that established the union of former colonies to be called the United States of America.

Oddly, at another island fort in Charleston Harbor nearly one hundred years later, another hero of an artillery bombardment would emerge, again to raise the brave colors under withering fire. Like Jasper, this hero was basically a Union man . . . and again like militiaman Jasper, basically a civilian called to the colors.

The scene this time would be Fort Sumter in Charleston Harbor. April 1861. The artillery fire came from secessionist South Carolina and signaled the real start of the Civil War. The shells thus raining down on an isolated Federal outpost commanded by Maj. Robert Anderson.

Peter Hart had served under Anderson in the Mexican War of 1846–48 as a sergeant. While Anderson remained in the U.S. Army, Hart left the military life to become a New York City policeman.

Still, he was destined to be at Fort Sumter serving again under his onetime commander, Major Anderson . . . thanks to Anderson's wife. For it was she who contacted Hart and asked him to join Anderson and his troops in Charleston, where hostilities appeared imminent.

Hart promptly quit his job with the police department and traveled to Charleston with Mrs. Anderson, eager to join her husband and his Federal soldiers. When the authorities in Charleston refused to let him join the Anderson garrison as a newly sworn soldier, Hart simply "enlisted" as a carpenter in a work party going out to the island fort.

A volunteer all the way, he willingly stayed at Fort Sumter beyond the final ultimatums that preceded the artillery barrage launched by South Carolina. Acting the role of a sergeant again, Hart then led work parties putting out the fires started by the shelling.

On the second day of the thirty-four-hour bombardment, the garrison's American flag was blown down. And it was Peter Hart who responded by nailing the colors to a spar fastened to a gun carriage . . . who thus briefly raised the American flag over Sumter again.

Fittingly enough, Peter Hart again was with Brigadier General Anderson on April 14, 1865—four years to the day after Sumter surrendered in 1861—to take part in the symbolic raising of the American flag over Fort Sumter once again.

The flag in Peter Hart's hands on that April day in 1865 was the very same flag that had been lowered in surrender four years before.

★

PERSONAL GLIMPSE
"Colonel-Commander" John Taylor Wood

★

TALK ABOUT COMPETING FAMILY TIES! His maternal grandfather had been president of the United States. His father was a thirty-six-year veteran of the U.S. Army . . . and utterly loyal to the Union. But an uncle by marriage was newly installed Confederate President Jefferson Davis. Another uncle was future Confederate Lt. Gen. Richard Taylor, and this young U.S. naval officer's own brother already had signed on as a staff officer serving Confederate Gen. Braxton Bragg.

Small wonder that news of the Confederate firing on Fort Sumter rendered John Taylor Wood, an instructor at the U.S. Naval Academy in Annapolis, Maryland, "sick at heart."

Adamantly opposed to fighting his Southern brethren, Wood at first thought he could remain neutral by resigning from the U.S. Navy, but other, fast-moving events intervened. In quick order, Union troops occupied Maryland and even bivouacked on the Naval Academy grounds—the Naval Academy itself would be moving to Newport, Rhode Island. Wood in the meantime submitted his resignation, saw it denied, and then was stunned to receive papers saying he was dismissed . . . kicked out of the navy.

That did it—President Zachary Taylor's grandson, no longer on speaking terms with his father, joined brother Robert Crooke Wood Jr. as a warrior for the South, a decision destined to have punishing effect upon the Union navy that John Wood left behind.

A first hint of many exploits soon to come, newly sworn Confederate naval gunnery officer Wood helped to recruit and train the crew for the Southern ironclad *Virginia* (formerly the *Merrimack*). He and his men then more than ably served the *Virginia* in her historic clash with the Union's ironclad *Monitor* in Hampton Roads, Virginia, on March 9, 1862. Although the *Virginia* virtually destroyed five wooden vessels from the Union's James River Squadron the day before, the duel of two ironclads ended in a draw, with neither ship sunk.

Franklin Buchanan, captain of the Confederate ironclad and himself a former U.S. Navy officer (indeed, a founder of the Naval Academy), later reported: "Lieutenant Wood, whose zeal and industry in drilling the crew contributed materially to our success, handled his pivot gun admirably and the executive officer testifies to his valuable suggestions throughout the action."

Soon after, Wood distinguished himself in a land action—forced to ground, burn, and abandon the *Virginia* as Union forces seized Norfolk in May, Wood and his sailors found themselves manning Robert E. Lee's batteries atop Drewry's Bluff on the James River just south of Richmond. From there, they poured deadly fire upon three

Federal ironclads and two wooden gunboats advancing upriver upon the Confederate capital. "Later, they got credit for saving Richmond," noted historical writer Peggy Robbins in the *Civil War Times* of March 1998.

With the Federal fleet turned back from the upper James, Wood soon was involved in more action, more exploits and derring-do. As an unofficial naval observer for his uncle by marriage, Confederate President Davis (whose first wife was Zachary Taylor's daughter Knox), naval officer Wood had powerful backing for his innovative schemes. Soon commissioned a Confederate cavalry colonel in addition to his naval rank, Wood organized and conducted a series of bold raids against Northern merchantmen and naval vessels in the Chesapeake Bay region. Wood and his "horse marines," as they were called, hauled their shallow-draft raiding boats overland in wagons before taking to the water and boarding their unsuspecting prey.

So successful were the raids that the *Charleston Courier* called for "more Wood—John Taylor Wood." And there was no doubt that the publicity stirred by his exploits was good for Southern morale. No doubt, too, that the success of every mission emboldened Wood and his superiors to try ever more ambitious forays against the enemy.

In August 1863 Wood and a party of sixty men seized the Union gunboats *Satellite* and *Reliance* at the mouth of the Rappahannock River, capturing eighty Federals in the process. The next night, reported Robbins, "Wood's raiders went to the Chesapeake's eastern shore and captured three schooners, one a coaler from Philadelphia."

Now a commander (as well as a colonel), Wood next, in February 1864, led 150 men on a stinging raid against Union-occupied New Bern, North Carolina. The Confederate Congress reacted to this latest exploit by commending Wood and his men for "the capture [and destruction, actually] from under the guns of the enemy's works of the U.S. gunboat *Underwriter,* with the officers and crews of several vessels brought off as prisoners."

Even the Union navy's famous Adm. David Farragut was impressed. "This was rather a mortifying affair for our Navy, however fearless on the part of the Confederates," he wrote, while also noting that the "gallant expedition" was led by Wood.

Farragut in fact said, "It was to be expected that with so many clever officers who left the Federal navy and cast their fortunes with the Confederates, such gallant action would be attempted."

Could Wood's next blow have been "expected" as well? One has to wonder. Taking command of the Confederate commerce raider *Tallahassee,* he ran north from Wilmington, North Carolina, to Halifax, Nova Scotia, and back—a war patrol completed to the tune of thirty-three enemy vessels captured!

For all of John Taylor Wood's heroics, of course, the fortunes of war simply weren't ranged upon his side, and who would know any better than the very same naval-cavalry officer who was at the side of President Davis in the flight from Richmond in April 1865? Who was still by the Confederate president's side when he was captured by the Federals near Irwinville, Georgia.

But who saw no point in remaining a prisoner and so escaped by bribing a guard, then made his way to Florida and successfully set sail for Cuba in a small boat, "cheating death several times on the way."

Wood then, accompanied by his wife and two children, joined fellow Confederate expatriates in Halifax, where he lived out the rest of his life (until his death in 1904) as an insurance broker.

"He communicated occasionally with his father after the war, but only by mail," wrote Robbins. As for Wood's infrequent postwar visits to his native country, they were "mostly to attend Confederate veterans' functions, such as the 30th anniversary commemoration of the battle of Hampton Roads."

Lincoln's Oregon Connection

OREGON'S U.S. SENATOR EDWARD DICKINSON BAKER, the man who introduced Abraham Lincoln to the crowds attending Lincoln's first inauguration, once was a U.S. House member from Illinois and an old political rival of Lincoln's in that context. Yet they were such good friends that the Lincolns named their ill-fated son Eddie for Senator Baker.

'Tis said that the politically ambitious Baker cried as a child over the fact that he could never become president of the United States, because he had been born in London, England. Now, oddly enough, the solon from Oregon was introducing an old Illinois friend as president—the same Abraham Lincoln who once had been offered the governorship of the Oregon Territory and had turned it down.

Sadly for all concerned, Senator Baker was one and the same as the Union army's Colonel Baker appointed by Lincoln . . . and killed in the battle of Ball's Bluff near Leesburg, Virginia, October 22, 1861. Baker, about fifty, had written jokingly just four months before that he could become a "venerable martyr."

Senator Ewing's Other Fighting Son

NOT ONLY THEIR POLITICALLY POTENT father, but three Ewing brothers of Lancaster, Ohio, were destined to carve a niche for themselves in the history of America . . . in their case, in the history of the Civil War, too.

Moving through life with them, sharing many of the same experiences, was a foster brother who had moved into the Ewing home quite suddenly after his own father abruptly died. In that emergency situation, after all, he and ten siblings had to go *somewhere*.

In the Civil War to come later, each of the three Ewing boys would serve as generals for the Union. Each would serve with distinction and then move on to rewarding civilian careers . . . but then, wouldn't all that be expected of Thomas Ewing's sons? While himself too old to serve in the Civil War, he nonetheless had served his nation in his own fashion—as a U.S. senator from Ohio, as secretary of the treasury, as secretary of the interior. And now . . . weren't the sons of such a distinguished citizen bound to excel in their own fashions as well?

In the meantime, a bit older than the three Ewing boys, their foster brother grew up ahead of them and, with an appointment arranged by his foster father, entered the U.S. Military Academy at West Point. After that began an undistinguished U.S. Army career of thirteen years before he resigned his commission to represent a St. Louis bank in San

William Tecumseh Sherman was one of the most controversial generals of the war. By war's end he was praised in the North and vilified in the South, for he had fulfilled his promise to make Georgia howl during his March to the Sea.

Francisco, only to see that venture fail. Along the way, incidentally, he had married Thomas Ewing's daughter Eleanor.

As for the senator's sons, Thomas Jr., Hugh, and Charles, only Hugh, the middle brother, followed their foster brother to West Point. That was in 1844. Four years later, however, unable to make up a lack of credits in engineering, Hugh resigned just before his scheduled graduation from West Point.

He spent some time in California during the Gold Rush of 1849, but then entered the practice of law in St. Louis and Leavenworth, Kansas—with older brother Thomas and their foster brother, it so happened.

Thomas, in the meantime, at the age of nineteen, had served President Zachary Taylor as a private secretary. He then obtained his law degree and began practicing law in Leavenworth with his foster brother. A leader in the fight to bar the admission of Kansas to the Union as a slave state, "Free-Soiler" Thomas Ewing Jr. in 1861 became the first chief justice of Kansas.

Younger Ewing brother Charles went south for his more advanced education . . . to the University of Virginia. Also becoming an attorney, he, too, briefly practiced law in St. Louis.

Meanwhile, the law did not really suit the Ewing trio's foster brother, nor was he really a great success at it, either. He—"Cump," they called him—in 1859 drifted into a job as superintendent of the Louisiana State Seminary of Learning and Military Academy.

With the Civil War clearly looming in January 1861, Cump abandoned his Southern colleagues for a job at the helm of a streetcar company in St. Louis. Just a month after Fort Sumter, however, the West Point graduate rejoined the army—the Union army, of course—as commander of the Thirteenth U.S. Infantry, colonel in rank.

So that's where Cump was just before the hostilities of the Civil War erupted in earnest. As for his three foster brothers, Charles Ewing earlier that fateful spring had been busy at his law practice in St. Louis, Thomas was on the bench in the Kansas Supreme Court, and Hugh recently had returned to Ohio from the law practice in Leavenworth. But now all would be different. Their country was at war—at war with itself, and all three sons of Thomas Ewing Sr. soon emulated their foster brother, and thousands of other young men, in donning a uniform and siding with the Union.

Joining up as early as May 14, 1861—the same day that Cump reacquired *his* army uniform—Charles Ewing was appointed as a captain in Cump's Thirteenth U.S. Infantry. While the more experienced Cump soon was reassigned elsewhere, Charles Ewing was based uneventfully at Alton, Illinois, until the fall of 1862. At that point he was sent to Memphis, Tennessee, on the Mississippi River . . . en route, as events turned out, to the Union siege of Vicksburg downriver. He won notice for his exemplary conduct during an attack on the enemy, was shifted to William Tecumseh Sherman's staff, and named assistant inspector general.

Staying by Sherman's side for the remainder of the war, Charles was noted for his service at Chattanooga, in the Atlanta campaign, on Sherman's March to the Sea, and finally, on Sherman's march through the Carolinas. Before all the shooting was over, he was commissioned a brigadier general of volunteers.

Middle Ewing brother Hugh, in the meantime, also had joined the Union army in 1861, the year the war began. After serving on the staff of Ohio Gov. William Dennison, Hugh was posted with Gens.

George B. McClellan and William S. Rosecrans in Virginia for a period before becoming commander of the Thirtieth Ohio Volunteers in August 1861 with a colonel's rank. He fought with distinction at South Mountain and Antietam, moving up to brigade command, then was posted to Sherman's Fifteenth Corps in the long campaign against Vicksburg.

He earned his brigadier general's commission by the end of 1862 and, after the fall of Vicksburg in July 1863, assumed a division command, still under Sherman. At Chattanooga soon after, Hugh Ewing's division led Sherman's Fifteenth Corps in the difficult attack on Patrick Cleburne's Confederate right wing on Missionary Ridge.

After a posting at Louisville, Kentucky, Hugh Ewing in early 1865 joined Sherman for the wind-up of the Carolinas campaign. He left army service in 1866 with the brevet rank of major general.

Thomas, the oldest of the three brothers, left his seat on the high court of Kansas in late 1862 to form—and command—the Eleventh Kansas Cavalry, which then fought under James G. Blunt as infantry for the battles of Cane Hill and Prairie Grove, Arkansas. By March of the next year, Ewing had risen to brigadier general and taken command of the District of the Border along the long-inflamed Kansas-Missouri border that was noted for its guerrilla activity, cross-border raids, and bushwhacker warfare. There he issued a famous edict, infamous to some, his Order No. 11, intended to expel all residents of four Missouri counties along the boundary line.

He later defended against Sterling Price's raid into Missouri in 1864 and "distinguished himself at the battle of Pilot Knob and in the subsequent retreat of the Federal forces," reported Ezra J. Warner in his book *Generals in Blue.*

In fact, all three Ewing brothers at one time or another during the Civil War *distinguished* themselves, Warner also noted. They led exemplary civilian lives after the war as well. Charles resumed his practice of law, but now in Washington, D.C. Hugh, after a stint as U.S. minister to Holland, also entered law practice in the nation's capital then retired to a farm near the brothers' birthplace of Lancaster, Ohio, where a fourth Ewing, Philemon, practiced law. Thomas, the most publicly visible of the three, turned down President Andrew Johnson's offers to name him secretary of war or attorney general of the United States. Thomas Ewing Jr., also practicing law in Washington for a time, eventually returned to Ohio, only to reappear in Washington as a member of the U.S. House for two terms. He next ran for governor of Ohio but was defeated. He then, in his final career move, shifted his law practice to New York City.

Three brothers, three outstanding careers, both in the military and in civilian life . . . and yet it was their shared brother-in-law, Cump, who outranked all three, who today occupies page after page in the history books. Who indeed, all by himself, is the subject of entire books. Who emerged a major figure of the Civil War—their foster brother and fellow Union general, William Tecumseh Sherman.

Additional note: One of Thomas Ewing Jr.'s postbellum clients in Washington was a stagehand from Ford's Theatre who was accused of helping John Wilkes Booth escape from the theater after shooting Abraham Lincoln. Scene-shifter Edman or Edward Spangler apparently received a message from the well-known actor to hold the latter's horse at the theater's back door. But Spangler, with his stage duties to tend to, apparently placed the reins of the horse in the hands of "Peanuts John" Burroughs, a stage doorkeeper. When Booth fled after the shooting, broken ankle notwithstanding, he did run out the rear door and leap upon his horse, knocking down Burroughs in the process.

By that scenario, Spangler would appear entirely innocent of any part in the assassination plot. But the government produced a witness, Jacob Ritterspaugh, who testified that Spangler interfered as Ritterspaugh attempted to chase Booth. According to *The Abraham Lincoln Encyclopedia* by Mark E. Neely Jr., Ritterspaugh claimed Spangler struck him in the face and ordered, "Don't say which way he went."

The same source adds: "Thomas Ewing Jr., Spangler's lawyer, found witnesses who said that Ritterspaugh had changed his story after a month of imprisonment and intimidation by detectives. Immediately after the event he had said only that Spangler hit him and said, after Ritterspaugh insisted the escaping man was Booth, to shut up because he did not know for certain who the man was."

Despite Ewing's best efforts, however, Spangler was found guilty of helping in Booth's escape and was sentenced to six years at hard labor. He was serving his sentence at Fort Jefferson on the Dry Tortugas with Dr. Samuel Mudd when pardoned by President Andrew Johnson in

1869. Spangler, previously a drifter who normally slept right at Ford's Theatre, returned to Maryland to live with and work for Dr. Mudd, "to whom he had become attached during their imprisonment."

First Union Volunteer

AND NOW, A FEW THOUGHTS, please, upon another long-lingering historical question: Who was the first man to answer Abraham Lincoln's call of April 1861 for Union army volunteers? The very first out of Lincoln's first seventy-five thousand volunteers?

There is no doubt that Minnesota was the first state to stand in line, that Minnesota's First Regiment was the first of all regiments, the first volunteer unit of any kind. But first, before going any further . . . let's attach the word *apparently* to the foregoing, since it's always good to hedge a bit in the face of such grandiose claims.

To explain Minnesota's proud assertion is to accept an apparently reliable sequence of fairly haphazard events that placed the Gopher State first in line.

In Washington, D.C., on April 14, 1861, the morning Fort Sumter officially surrendered to the big guns of Charleston, South Carolina, was Minnesota Gov. Alexander Ramsey. Dropping into the Federal War Department, a short walk from the White House, Ramsey encountered Secretary of War Simon Cameron rushing out the door, his arms full of papers.

Ramsey explained he was there to make an advance commitment of a thousand volunteers from his state.

Cameron, saying he was just then on his way to confer with President Lincoln, told Ramsey to put the offer in writing and he would take it directly to the president. Ramsey did so, and that is how Minnesota became first among all the states of the Union to answer Lincoln's first call for volunteers, according to Vickie Wendell, educational programs director of the Anoka County (Minnesota) Historical Society.

Writing in the *Civil War Times* of August 1996, Wendell made it quite clear that the "1st Minnesota's claim to the title of 'first regiment' remains undisputed." As she also noted, however, settling upon the first volunteer *member* of the first regiment from the first state is a bit more difficult.

Helpfully, the issue boils down to a choice between just two claimants, it would appear.

One of them, Josiah King, is memorialized by a statue in the Minnesota capital of St. Paul honoring him as Minnesota's first volunteer recruit. "A variety of sources, including a letter written by King himself, state that he was the first person to record his name in a book of St. Paul militiamen willing to fight for the Union," wrote Wendell.

Conclusive? Not at all—there is still the small farming community of Anoka to be heard from. After all, the honor of first man in all the Union, added the Anoka Historical Society's Wendell, "could rightfully belong to Aaron Greenwald, a 28-year-old miller from Anoka."

How so? Well, here's the sequence of events bearing upon the Anoka-Greenwald claim:

First, Governor Ramsey in Washington informed Minnesota's adjutant general, William H. Acker, by telegram that morning of April 14 of the offer to provide a thousand Minnesota volunteers. Ramsey also fired off a wire to former governor Willis A. Gorman, an attorney just then plying his trade in an Anoka courtroom. He was defending a man accused of stealing ten bushels of cranberries and other items, Wendell explained.

Various court documents place Gorman at the court session at the right historical moment to make him a part of the "first man" scenario.

As events turned out, Gorman didn't receive Ramsey's message right away. The telegram could go only as far as St. Paul by wire; after that, a horseback messenger had to take over and carry it to Gorman in Anoka. Still, the delay may not have been all that crucial. "When the message arrived, the court recessed and Gorman took the opportunity to address the assembled people," added the Wendell account. Gorman also called for volunteers on the spot, "an act that would win him appointment as the first commander of the 1st Minnesota."

And then, the key moment of all, "After Gorman's impromptu speech, Greenwald became the first of seven Anokans to volunteer their services as Union soldiers."

Supposedly, too, "they made their offer in writing." That assertion came from Roe Chase, editor of the *Anoka Herald,* "who wrote about the matter in his newspaper near the turn of the century." Unfortunately, those written offers are nowhere to be found today. Still, Chase specifically said the Anoka Seven's enlistments "were taken shortly after 10 A.M. and that the St. Paul enlistments were not taken until that evening."

More than a bit contradictory, on the other hand, is a subsequent account by Greenwald's fellow First Minnesota enlistee James Groat. "That evening," he asserted, "a company of volunteers was organized in our village of Anoka." But Groat's memory at the time he wrote that assertion years after the fact possibly had become a bit fuzzy as to details. He, in fact, may not even have joined the same company as Greenwald. "Gorman raised one on the morning of the 14th, which Greenwald joined," wrote Wendell; "Marcus Q. Butterfield raised one that night, which may have been the one Groat joined."

Assuming that Aaron Greenwald really was the first of the Lincoln volunteers, what was his background . . . what was his ultimate fate?

Born in December 1832, he was a native of Weisenburg Township, Lehigh County, Pennsylvania, and married a Minnesota woman in 1858. They and their two sons lived in Anoka.

After enlisting with the First Minnesota, the first of all Union volunteers found his war quickly enough—at First Manassas (Bull Run). Surviving that Federal defeat, he went through another six battles before fate caught up with him in his eighth combat experience—at the third day of Gettysburg.

His volunteer regiment had fought at major battles such as the Seven Days', Antietam, Fredericksburg, and Chancellorsville before traveling to Gettysburg in the Union effort to stop Robert E. Lee. There, on the second day, the First Minnesota won hard-earned glory for a sacrificial charge that helped save Union positions behind . . . but cost the regiment 82 percent of its men.

Ironically, Greenwald's Company C had been detached elsewhere for the moment and thus was spared the carnage of the second day at Gettysburg. Not so, however, on the third and final day of the watershed battle.

This time, it was a Confederate charge—Pickett's famous charge—and it was the Union men trying to stave off the momentum of the enemy's rush forward. The men of Greenwald's Company C were right there, front and center. "The fighting was intense," wrote Wendell. "At one point the Minnesotans were locked in hand-to-hand combat with the Rebels, slashing with bayonets, using rifle butts as clubs, even throwing rocks and cobblestones."

Sometime during the fight, Greenwald took a bullet in the head and shoulder. He was left overnight on the battleground, untended, before being picked up and taken to nearby medical facilities on July 4. He died the next day, July 5.

Greenwald was buried nearby, but his father soon came from eastern Pennsylvania to retrieve his son's body for reburial in a family plot. A minister's wife wrote to Greenwald's young widow that his funeral drew a "large concourse of people," more than could fit into the church.

For the time being, that was the end of the "first volunteer" business. Peace came, although with holes rent in its cloth, and life went on . . . until some years later people in Minnesota began to ask who was the first volunteer. And now, Wendell reported, "St. Paul newspapers printed articles by men claiming the honor."

In 1911, though, the *Journal Press* of St. Cloud weighed in with a piece saying that while the official record seemed to substantiate Josiah King's claim to "this great honor," it also was the newspaper's "understanding that the first man in Minnesota and in the country to offer his services was the late Aron [*sic*] Greenwald of Anoka."

As real controversy over the issue developed, there were arguments over supposed irregularities in the Anoka enlistments that April morning. There were missing records, more claims, and counterclaims.

Silent on the issue for many years, meanwhile, was Greenwald's son William, who at last explained, "Father was dead, and the honor could do him no good."

On the other hand, "I knew what it meant to those old soldiers. And so I kept still. My father was gone. But they are all gone now, those claimants. I no longer hesitate to say that I am sure my father has the prior claim."

Anoka was sure enough also some years ago to create a Greenwald Park, just across the street from the site of the building where former governor Gorman had been trying his case the morning of April 14, 1861. Even so, the historical society's Wendell conceded, "the question of who volunteered first to fight for the Union likely will never be answered with certainty." Circumstantial evidence, noted the writer, points to both King and Greenwald, with no hard evidence—such as

Greenwald's enlistment documents—available to support his post-humous "claim."

In Anoka itself, of course, "There is no question."

Unsung Heroes I

NORTHERN VIRGINIA, EARLY IN THE hostilities, a Southern family's home behind Yankee lines . . . but Jeb Stuart and his cavalrymen had been there anyway, then set off on a raid elsewhere. As a result, the Yankees descended.

Where had Stuart and his troop gone? What direction did they take?

The master of the premises and a grown son were themselves absent, gone off to war. On the Confederate side, of course.

The man's wife, left behind to mind their home and the rest of the family, certainly would *not* divulge Stuart's plans, the visiting Yanks could tell. So they turned to two "Johnny Rebs" by her side.

Still the same question: Where had Colonel Stuart and his men gone? Still no satisfactory reply.

Then came the threats.

Even so, no information was forthcoming.

"Finally handcuffs and irons were brought," wrote Judith McQuire in *The Diary of a Southern Refugee,* published in 1867.

But still these two heroes remained adamantly unhelpful and silent as to Stuart's whereabouts. One had turned "pale as ashes," wrote Mrs. McQuire, a minister's wife. The other stood there "with his teeth clenched over his under lip, until the blood was ready to gush out."

And still, "not one word could be extorted, until, with a feeling of hopelessness in their efforts, they [the Yanks] went off, calling them cursed little rebels."

Not cursed, really, but *little,* yes. For they were their mother's two boys, eight and ten years old. Unsung heroes, they had kept silent the whole time.

Resources Inexhaustible

WAS HE RIGHT? Winfield Scott, aging veteran of the War of 1812, hero of the Mexican War, former presidential candidate, retiring general in chief of the Union army, good friend to Robert E. Lee, Virginia-born himself but loyal to the Union all the way, once had this to say on Southern soldiery (as reported by Southern diarist Mary Boykin Chesnut):

> He says we have elan, courage, woodcraft, consummate horsemanship, endurance of pain equal to the Indians, but that we will not submit to discipline. We will not take care of things or husband our resources. Where we are, there is waste and destruction. If it could all be done by one wild desperate dash, we would do it. But he does not think we can stand the long blank months between the acts—the waiting! We can bear pain without a murmur, but we will not submit to be bored, &c&c&c.

"Now," she added, "for the other side." *His* side, that is. "They can wait. They can bear discipline. They can endure forever—losses in battle [mean] nothing to them, resources in men and materials of war inexhaustible. And *if they see fit* they will fight to the bitter end. Nice prospect for us."

MYSTERY
Whose Portrait on the $10 Bill?

NO SOONER HAD THE CONFEDERACY formed itself, begun operations as a new nation, and then jumped into war with the North than the issue of money—Confederate money—came up.

Like the new nation itself, it had to be created . . . but not quite from scratch.

With the advent of hostilities, both the Union and Confederate governments turned to paper money rather than limit their official currency to the hard coin of the realm that prevailed as U.S. government issue before the Civil War. The paper money of old had consisted of private bank notes issued by various banks—with just about all printed by bank-note firms in the North, in New York City.

That unfortunate location presented Confederate Treasury Secretary Christopher Memminger with a major problem: He couldn't very well trade with the enemy by purchasing newly created notes from New York firms. Yet they had the equipment and the expertise to do the job.

He first tried having stone lithographers in Richmond prepare strictly Confederate notes, but the bills resulting from this outmoded process were greeted with an immediate outcry by Southern bankers. "Accustomed to handling beautiful, steel-engraved bank notes, they protested against the easy-to-counterfeit lithographs printed on cheap paper," wrote Brent Hughes in the *Washington Times* of December 16, 1995. "Memminger, himself a banker by profession, was humiliated by the criticism and took action."

Rather than trade with the enemy, he "borrowed" from the enemy, one might say. Through the good offices of Richmond stockbroker Thomas A. Ball, secretly sent to New York as the Confederate Treasury's agent, Memminger persuaded two expert engravers, Edward Keatinge and William Leggett, to relocate in Richmond and go into the note-printing business as Leggett, Keatinge & Ball.

This much accomplished by October 1861, Memminger ordered a supply of badly needed $5 and $10 bills. Rather than resort to the time-consuming process of steel-plate engraving, however, the engravers—with Memminger's permission—decided to adapt an existing plate provided by the Mechanics Savings Bank of Savannah, Georgia. "Leggett and Keatinge quickly removed the old lettering and replaced it with Confederate terminology," added the Hughes account. "They made no changes in the pictorial elements and simply appropriated them for their own use." They did add their own new company's name in one corner.

In short order, the Confederacy was the proud *issuer* of 20,333 $5 bills and 20,333 $10 bills, each with a hand-inscribed serial number and two handwritten official signatures.

As the notes then made their way through thousands upon thousands of hands, little attention was paid to the portrait on the $10 bill. "The Treasury quickly paid out the currency and, for the moment, the portrait was forgotten," wrote Hughes.

Wouldn't Memminger, Keatinge, Leggett, and company—along with a multitude of others throughout the Confederacy—all have been chagrined to learn that the portrait on the Confederate $10 bill was of an antisecessionist who was fully resolved to leave his native Southland and move to . . . New York City! Who, indeed, already had pulled up roots in anticipation of the war to come.

Certainly, they must have noticed in Savannah!

In any case, collectors appearing on the scene after the Civil War hoped to assemble complete sets of the notes issued by the defeated South before they disappeared. At this point, if not sooner, the question arose: Who was the man on the $10 bill?

One answer: "Someone mistakenly identified him as Williamson S. Oldham, a Confederate senator from Texas, and the error was accepted as fact for fifty years."

While that wrong answer held sway, the real model for the Confederate bill had briefly served the James Buchanan administration as U.S. minister to China, had settled his affairs in Savannah (for that indeed had been his antebellum home), and had removed to New York City, there to open a law office on Wall Street in 1866.

Years later, in 1915, historical researcher William West Bradbeer found a portrait of Confederate Senator Oldham that "bore no resemblance to the portrait on the Confederate note," reported Hughes.

Bradbeer should have stopped right there . . . but didn't. In short order, the researcher said the portrait really depicted a Confederate official named Edward C. Elmore.

But no, "Another historian, H. D. Allen, challenged this and became obsessed with finding the correct name." Allen went so far as to circulate a flyer depicting the Confederate note and offering a reward to anyone who could identify the man shown on the bill.

Meanwhile, the real model had long since gone to his grave, quite possibly unaware of the mystery that arose over his portrait. Possibly he didn't even know it had been used on a Confederate bill, although he certainly had known of the Savannah bank's original use of his image.

But Allen soon would be on his trail, in fact soon would be closing in on the former Savannah resident's identity. First, though, eight hundred or so persons responded to Allen's reward offer. None had the right answer.

An appeal then made through Southern newspapers bore more promising fruit—a Georgia respondent sent Allen an 1859 bank note issued by the Savannah bank. "Allen was stunned. The bill was almost identical to the Confederate note printed in 1861 by Leggett, Keatinge & Ball."

From there, the hunt became an easy one. Surely the portrait was of a well-known Savannah resident. An inquiry directed to Savannah newspaper editor Alexander A. Gardiner sent him into the old files of the *Daily Morning News,* where he found the final link closing out the mystery.

From the paper's issue of Saturday, December 2, 1854, came the information that the Mechanics Savings Bank of Savannah had opened for business the previous day; that its "beautifully designed and executed" bank notes carried a medallion portrait of a well-known Savannah political figure, one John E. Ward, a founding partner of the bank, mayor of Savannah, speaker of the Georgia legislature, and soon-to-be president of the 1856 Democratic National Convention (which nominated James Buchanan for president) . . . and, it also seems, at heart an antisecessionist who made it his business to leave Savannah and his native state of Georgia before the Civil War erupted.

PERSONAL GLIMPSE
"Beast" Butler

AFTER THREE MALE SLAVES FLED from their owner, a Confederate army colonel, and sought sanctuary at the Federal fortress, Fort Monroe, overlooking Hampton Roads in newly seceded Virginia, it wasn't long before their owner dispatched an underling with an amazing request. Basically, Col. Charles Mallory demanded, "Return my property."

If he had any expectations of compliance with his demand, however, he had picked entirely the wrong man to deal with. So prickly an adversary was Union Maj. Gen. Benjamin Franklin Butler that he

BATTLES AND LEADERS

Benjamin F. Butler's refusal to return a runaway slave opened the door for other runaways to seek refuge with the Federal army. Fort Monroe's position at the tip of the Virginia Peninsula made it a likely goal for huge numbers of slaves seeking freedom during the war.

soon, as commander of Federal occupation forces in New Orleans, would be known as "Beast" Butler.

For the moment, though, the general of Massachusetts volunteers was on good behavior—even on the side of the angels. So it was that he treated Colonel Mallory's emissary, a Major Cary, with calm, even-handed . . . well, it sounds very much like contempt.

As Butler himself later related in correspondence with Union Gen. Winfield Scott, the visiting Confederate major "desired to know if I did not feel myself bound by my constitutional obligations to deliver up fugitives under the Fugitive Slave Act."

Well, no, was Butler's reply, he didn't feel a bit bound, because "the Fugitive Slave Act did not affect a foreign country, which Virginia claimed to be."

By contrast, Butler also noted, a fugitive slave would be returned to his or her owner in nearby Maryland, a state that had *not* seceded from the Union.

Going a step further, Butler also assured the Confederate major that Colonel Mallory could reclaim his three slaves if he "would come to the Fortress and take an oath of allegiance to the constitution of the

United States." In that case, too, Butler would be glad to hire them for work needed done at Fort Monroe.

Needless to say, the slaves were not returned. In fact, with no objection registered by the Lincoln administration back in Washington, it seemed that Butler had given Southern slaves a green light to flee into Federal protection . . . and find freedom. At the same time, however, he also had said he would return fugitive slaves to owners who were loyal to the Union.

As part of the same episode in the spring of 1861, not so incidentally, Butler applied the term *contraband-of-war* to slaves escaping their Southern climes for refuge behind Union lines. The term *contraband* stuck for the duration and spread into general public usage.

All of which was just another of the many twists and turns in the political and military careers of the criminal lawyer and Democratic state legislator from the Bay State. The first major general of volunteers appointed by Republican Lincoln, Butler previously had attended the 1860 Democratic convention held in Charleston, South Carolina, and there had joined in fifty-seven straight votes in the vain effort to nominate Mississippi's U.S. Senator Jefferson Davis for president . . . of the United States, that is.

Butler later was all for Vice President John C. Breckinridge of Kentucky as the States' Rights nominee in the four-way presidential contest of 1860. After the war, by contrast, it was *Congressman* Butler, now a Radical Republican, who was very much a leader in the attempt to impeach President Andrew Johnson for being too lenient on high-ranking Rebel officials . . . such as Confederate President Davis and Secretary of War Breckinridge.

But all that, of course, was later, much later. In the interim, at the very start of the Civil War, Butler and his Massachusetts volunteers had become heroes of the hour by solving the "problem" of Baltimore. After rioting Southern sympathizers attacked Massachusetts troops passing through the city in April 1861, Butler bypassed the choke point on the north-south rail line by sending his men aboard ship to Annapolis, Maryland, and from there marching them into Washington. It was then, with the Federal capital no longer cut off from the North, that a grateful President Lincoln made Butler the Union's first major general of volunteers.

Little did Lincoln know at the time that the day would come when Butler himself would be touted for president, when Lincoln himself would offer Butler the vice presidential spot on the Lincoln ticket of 1864.

But first there was a war to fight, and now, with the Mallory "contraband" incident as fresh backdrop, General Butler turned to military affairs in earnest. On June 10, 1861, he led his men into battle . . . but into defeat at Big Bethel, Virginia, widely considered the first real engagement of the Civil War.

He next joined Flag Officer Silas H. Stringham in capturing two smallish Rebel forts at Hatteras Inlet, North Carolina, an action followed in 1862 by Butler's command of the land forces accompanying Adm. David Farragut in the Federal seizure of New Orleans. Then came Butler's controversial stewardship of the captured Southern city . . . so controversial that Jefferson Davis, now president of the Confederacy, branded the Union general an outlaw.

Never known for tact, patience, or kindness of heart, Butler ruffled the feelings of the city's diplomatic community and ordered a local man hanged simply for taking down the American flag at the customhouse. Then, too, stung by reports that local women openly insulted and even spat upon his men, Butler issued his infamous decree saying that any woman who displayed contempt or insult toward his Yankee soldiers would be treated as "a woman of the town plying her avocation."

Already ridiculed as the "American Cyclops" because of his cast in one eye, he now became known far and wide as "Beast Butler." Overlooked as Washington yanked him out of New Orleans and left him on the sidelines for the better part of a year was the fact he actually had done some good as military governor of the city. "As a career politician now serving as a civil administrator," wrote Thomas H. O'Connor in his 1997 book *Civil War Boston: Home Front & Battlefield,* "Butler demonstrated remarkable competence in improving living conditions in New Orleans. He suppressed lawlessness, constructed drainage systems, reduced the incidence of deadly yellow fever epidemics, and promoted commercial activity. For all his efforts, however, the Yankee general got little support and even less praise from Crescent City residents, who resented his heavy-handed version of martial law, and who accused him of lining his pockets by speculating in southern cotton." (Some also claimed he stole household silver!)

In the North, however, Butler still remained a name to be reckoned with . . . politically. With various Republican factions in argumentative disarray early in 1864, there was talk of running alternative candidates for the Lincoln White House, among them Treasury Secretary Salmon P. Chase . . . and Gen. Benjamin "Beast" Butler himself. "To forestall [a] possible candidacy by the Bay State's Ben Butler, but at the same time to capture any votes this canny lawyer-politician-general might deliver, Lincoln appeared to toy with asking Butler to run as his vice-presidential candidate," wrote O'Connor in *Civil War Boston*.

Lincoln even sent a delegation to ask if Butler was willing to do it, but Butler gambled and said no. As O'Connor noted, Butler shrewdly saw through Lincoln's game. "If he accepted second place on the ticket, Lincoln's renomination would be secure; without Butler, Lincoln's place on the ticket was in doubt."

Unfortunately for Butler's political aspirations, his military fortunes took a nosedive in 1864. As commander of the Army of the James, he presided over the Union defeat at Drewry's Bluff on the James River in Virginia and then was stalled at Bermuda Hundred across the stream while U. S. Grant's Army of the Potomac marched on Petersburg and Richmond. Then, too, Butler's planned amphibious assault late in the same year of 1864 against Fort Fisher, North Carolina, a venture to be shared with Adm. David Porter, also was a failure. Asserting the naval bombardment had failed to knock out the fort's formidable defenses, Butler refused the attempt to establish a beachhead with his men.

The result was a fiasco, with Butler being relieved from command early in 1865 by order of President Lincoln . . . a recently reelected President Lincoln at that.

Even so, neither that development nor the end of the war kept Butler out of the public eye. By 1867, as a Radical Republican, he was an elected member of the U.S. House of Representatives from Massachusetts, and he shortly was embroiled in the impeachment proceedings against Andrew Johnson as one of the House managers. Elected governor of Massachusetts in 1882 after four tries—as a Democrat once again—he even ran for president in the late 1880s at the head of the Greenback-Labor and Anti-Monopoly ticket.

Unsuccessful in his presidential bid, the mercurial New Hampshire native and long-time political figure from Massachusetts died in 1893. Fittingly in a way, his death occurred in Washington, D.C.

MYTH
Stonewall's Great Train Caper

IT MADE A GREAT STORY to tell over the campfire . . . or to the grand-children. How Stonewall Jackson, not yet famous or yet even "Stonewall," achieved the greatest haul of railroad stock in all four years of the Civil War by means of a simple trick.

The great railroad caper supposedly took place in May 1861, before the real fighting began. The Virginia Military Institute's professor Thomas J. Jackson was in charge of troops based at Harpers Ferry in today's West Virginia, just across the Potomac River from Maryland. Nearby, the Baltimore and Ohio railroad tracks were constantly busy with coal trains bound for Union supply depots.

At first, Jackson simply watched the nearby rail traffic, loath to take any aggressive moves that might dash Southern hopes that Maryland still might secede and join the Confederacy. On May 6, however, Maryland's leadership decided otherwise—the Free State would stand by the Union despite a citizenry deeply rent between Union loyalists and Southern sympathizers.

It turned out, Jackson was quite prepared for that eventuality . . . and tired of sitting still, like a hungry cat watching a mouse. According to the scenario later provided by his subordinate, Capt. (and later Brig. Gen.) John Daniel Imboden, Jackson complained to B&O president John W. Garrett that the eastbound night trains "disturbed the repose of his camps."

Everybody would be happier, suggested the wily Jackson, if those trains could run past Harpers Ferry between 11 A.M. and 1 P.M. instead of at night.

"Garrett complied with Jackson's request," wrote Imboden later, "and thereafter for several days we heard the constant roar of passing trains for an hour before and after noon."

So far so good, but that was only one half of Jackson's plan, it seems.

Once again to Imboden's account: "But since the 'empties' were sent up the road at night, Jackson again complained that the nuisance was greater than ever and as the road had two tracks, he must insist that the westbound trains should pass during the same hours as those going east. Mr. Garrett promptly complied again, and we had then, for two hours every day, the livliest railroad in America."

Now, of course, the cat would have no trouble pouncing upon the mouse—two mice at once, in fact.

In short order, Imboden reported, Jackson sent him and others into action blocking the double rail line at two points, east and west. "Thus he trapped all trains going east and west between these points."

The result was the capture of 56 engines and 380 railcars, the largest such seizure by either side during the Civil War and, of course, a great boon for the equipage-starved Confederacy.

But, oops . . . better revise that to say, *alleged* result, since, according to Jackson biographer James I. Robertson Jr., it never happened.

In his definitive 1997 biography *Stonewall Jackson,* Robertson minced few words in dismissing this "most intriguing anecdote in the first weeks of the war."

Said Robertson: "John D. Imboden manufactured it, Jackson biographer G. F. R. Henderson gave it credence, and writers over the past century have delighted in recounting it in detail."

But, added Robertson, "delightful as the story is, it is totally fictional."

For that matter, as Robertson's account would suggest, the story simply doesn't make good sense. "For Jackson to have severed the B&O," wrote Robertson, "would have been a large and direct act of war against civilian commerce. The struggle between North and South had not yet reached that stage."

Furthermore, "It is inconceivable that the B&O's brilliant and hard-working president, John W. Garrett, or its indefatigable master of transportation, William Prescott Smith, would not have immediately seen through such a transparent ploy as constricting the traffic schedule. Certainly neither official would have compromised his devotion to the B&O by agreeing to jam trains together for the benefit of the Confederates and to the detriment of the Union."

Additional note: A *train* story that Robertson did accept as fact explains how Stonewall Jackson acquired his famous horse, Little Sorrel. Personnel under Jackson's quartermaster officer, Maj. John A. Harman, did seize a train . . . an eastbound livestock train. "Four cars were loaded with beefs, the other car with horses."

Since Jackson at the time had no regular mount, Robertson explained, "he decided to purchase one of the horses from the Confederate government (to whom he had consigned the train and its contents)."

Sorting through the horses, Jackson first chose "a large and powerful gelding."

He also spotted a smaller horse, "a well-rounded sorrel gelding," and thought it would be perfect for his wife, Anna. He bought both horses, but then discovered the larger gelding "was skittish and had too hard a gait." The little sorrel, on the other hand, "showed a smooth pace, even temper, and, in time, extraordinary endurance."

In the end, Jackson kept both mounts for himself. "Because he had acquired the animal for his wife, Jackson initially named it [the little sorrel] Fancy, and he used that name thereafter. To everyone else, the horse was Little Sorrel."

The smaller mount, "gaunt, raw-boned," stood only fifteen hands high, but amazed one and all with its stamina. Staff officer Henry Kyd Douglas later wrote: "Such endurance I have never seen in horse flesh. We had no horse at Hd. Qrs. that could match him. I never saw him show a sign of fatigue."

Footnote Status Unsought

He didn't want to go. The night before leaving Richmond, he said, "They have sent me to my death."

How so? "They have not given me an adequate force," he complained. "I can do nothing."

Before the war broke out, as everybody apparently knew, he was reserved and cold to all. Even morose.

But not to his wife and child. "He adored them and cared for nothing else," wrote Southern diarist Mary Boykin Chesnut. Then came disaster. "One day he went off on an expedition. They were gone six weeks. It was out in the Northwest, and the Indians were troublesome. When he came back, his wife and child were underground. He said not one word. But they found him more frozen and stern and isolated than ever—that was all."

A Virginia native and West Point graduate, Confederate Brig. Gen. Robert Selden Garnett was a Mexican War veteran twice brevetted for bravery in that conflict. He was a major in rank and a respected career U.S. Army officer until he resigned in 1861 to become adjutant general of Virginia's forces, then commanded by Robert E. Lee. In effect, he became Lee's chief of staff, but not for long.

When Virginia joined the Confederacy, he transferred to Confederate service. Named commander of the Army of the Northwest, he left Richmond to lead Confederate forces in western Virginia—apparently feeling those forces were inadequate and that he was going to his death.

Mary Chesnut pronounced his epitaph: "He has been an unlucky man clear through."

His Rebel troops were withdrawing from a superior-sized Federal force at Rich Mountain and Laurel Hill, and Garnett was covering their retreat at Corricks Ford on the Cheat River when the last small store of his luck ran out.

It was July 13, 1861. As recalled by Ezra J. Warner in his book *Generals in Gray,* Garnett had deployed his rear guard near the ford. Then, "while directing the disposition of a skirmish line and awaiting the arrival of other troops which had been sent for, he was mortally wounded."

While it was a small, entirely forgettable action otherwise, Brig. Gen. Robert Selden Garnett would forever be footnoted, at the very least, as the first general officer of either side in the Civil War to be killed in battle.

Robert Garnett, incidentally, a native of Essex County, Virginia, was a cousin and West Point classmate of Confederate Brig. Gen. Richard Brooke Garnett, who was killed in Pickett's Charge at Gettysburg . . . and whose body was never found. In *Robert* Garnett's case, added the Warner account, "his body fell into the hands of the enemy, but was returned to his family and ultimately buried in Greenwood Cemetery, Brooklyn, New York."

But why would the Virginia-born Confederate officer be buried in Brooklyn? According to a footnote in Warner's book, the wife Garnett had so sadly lost shortly before the Civil War was the reason. "Garnett had married Marianne Nelson of New York in 1857," Warner wrote. "She died the year after and was buried in her father's lot in Brooklyn. After temporary internment in Green Mount Cemetery, Baltimore, the remains of Garnett were removed to the Nelson lot in August 1865."

Brothers at War

AT THE DAWN OF NOVEMBER 7, 1861, the greatest American fleet ever yet assembled stood off the wide mouth of Port Royal Sound, halfway between Charleston, South Carolina, and Savannah, Georgia. The greatest such armada, that is, except for a few vessels lost or delayed in storm-tossed waters off Cape Hatteras, North Carolina.

One of the great fleet's original vessels, now struggling to catch up, was Union Comdr. Percival Drayton's steam-driven gunboat, the *Pocahontas*—soon, as fate would have it, to be pouring her gunfire into a lightly defended Confederate bastion under the command of Drayton's older brother, Brig. Gen. Thomas Fenwick Drayton, Third Military District of the Department of South Carolina.

Local lore has it that the two brothers had met one last time at St. Michael's Church in nearby Charleston, their hometown, before going their separate ways, Union and Confederate. They had prayed together the entire night, side by side. And now, in the battle of Port Royal, they met in combat as enemies.

Fortunately, neither one was killed or wounded in the Union assault on the coastal area lying between Hilton Head Island and Beaufort, South Carolina. Even so, taking on a key role as the Federal armada assaulted two Rebel forts defending the entrance to Port Royal Sound, *Commander* Drayton's gunboat *Pocahontas* wound up shelling *General* Drayton's Fort Walker on Hilton Head Island from a virtually unanswerable flanking position.

At the same time, Union Flag Officer Samuel DuPont's heavier warships attacked the fort head-on, administering one pounding after another.

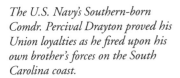

The U.S. Navy's Southern-born Comdr. Percival Drayton proved his Union loyalties as he fired upon his own brother's forces on the South Carolina coast.

But there was quite a story behind the arrival of the fleet—and that of Commander Drayton's steam-driven screw sloop, *Pocahontas.*

On the way south from its original assembly point at Hampton Roads, DuPont's fleet ran into a hurricanelike gale off Cape Hatteras. Not all of the seventy ships gathered for the assault on Port Royal were the ultimate in seaworthiness. The "armada" was led by DuPont's modern steamer *Wabash*—forty-six guns, true, but his fleet's vessels ranged from the strictly sail-driven sloop *Vandalia,* circa 1830, to untested, hastily built gunboats, to an army "fleet" of twenty-five transports contained within the navy fleet, and an old passenger steamer, the *Governor,* carrying six hundred marines.

The gunboat *Pocahontas* herself was a bit suspect as a former merchantman with limited coal capacity.

The storm struck late on Friday, November 1, and still was blowing so savagely the next day that by dark the *Governor* had been beaten into a crippled hulk floating about at the mercy of the heavy seas. Fortunately, the frigate *Sabine* came across the old coastal steamer and managed to rescue her crew and all but seven of the marines before she rolled over and disappeared.

When the storm clouds finally cleared, supply ships *Peerless, Belvedere, Union,* and *Osceola* all were gone, too. The transport *Winfield*

U.S. ARMY MILITARY HISTORY INSTITUTE

Union Naval Comdr. Drayton's older brother, Thomas Fenwick Drayton, was the Confederate brigadier general in charge of defending Hilton Head Island.

Scott had survived by dumping her cargo overboard, while the *Isaac Smith,* a makeshift "warship," had accomplished the same end by dumping her eight cannon.

Like many of his fellow Union skippers, Percival Drayton found himself alone on the ocean as Sunday, November 3, dawned bright and clear. His little ship, armed with one 10-inch gun, four 32-pounders, and a rifled piece that didn't always fire properly, had ridden out the storm with no real damage.

Drayton hastily resumed course for Port Royal Sound, well aware of two problems. One was his dwindling supply of coal. Just as important, Drayton knew that he, himself, was somewhat suspect in "Yankee" eyes because of his South Carolina ties. If he missed the fight ahead for lack of coal, such suspicions would only linger.

Then, too, there was the question of his own brother's whereabouts as the Federal fleet approached. But no matter, no choice, all such worries aside, Comdr. Percival Drayton, USN, had to hurry on.

By daybreak November 7, with DuPont's fleet already at the mouth of Port Royal Sound, Drayton and his crew could see the Tybee Light at the mouth of the Savannah River, below Hilton Head. Then, looming just ahead in the early morning mist, was one of the Federal fleet's colliers!

Wasting no time, Drayton took the coal supply ship under tow and pushed ahead, even while restocking his coal bins.

Approaching the mouth of the sound soon after, he and his crew heard booming cannon fire ahead. Clearly, the fight for Port Royal was already on. Abandoning the collier, the *Pocahontas* dashed forward, just in time to find DuPont's *Wabash* and her companion warships circling beyond range of the batteries at Fort Beauregard to the south and trading blows with the guns at Fort Walker on the Hilton Head side.

It was an unequal exchange, since the Federal ships carried so many more guns than the poorly equipped Confederate bastion. "Before the day was over, some 3,500 shells plunged into [both] Confederate positions, 900 of them from the *Wabash*," reported Roger Pinckney in the *Civil War Times* of March 1999.

To be sure, the overwhelmed Rebel gunners occasionally scored a hit in retaliation, but they obviously wouldn't be able to hold out long. In fact, Fort Walker displayed a naked flank that soon attracted Federal attention, too. "Left out of the fiery circle DuPont was tracing in the *Wabash,* the *Pocahontas* took station on the flank of Fort Walker," wrote Arthur M. Wilcox in the Civil War centennial section of the *Charleston Post-Courier.* "There she poured in a cross fire."

For those inside the beleaguered fort, it was a day of sheer hell. The fort's surgeon, Dr. George Buist, had been decapitated, his body falling to the ground with a bandage still held in his hand. "Dismembered corpses and pools of blood littered the ground," reported Pinckney.

General Drayton, in charge of the area's defenses, was present for most of the deadly bombardment, leaving only briefly to round up a few reinforcements and then return with them. But, as events turned out, not to stay.

"After more than five hours of shelling and with his brother's shells repeatedly finding their mark," wrote Pinckney, "Thomas Drayton knew the battle was lost. 'No alternative was left but to leave the island and concentrate upon the mainland,' [General] Drayton reported, 'where we would be enabled to fight the enemy on more equal terms should he venture beyond the protection of his fleet . . .' Drayton left Colonel William C. Heyward of the 11th South Carolina Infantry in command at Fort Walker while he [Drayton] rushed to ready the infantry to cover the Rebel retreat."

Also falling into Federal hands that day was the even weaker Confederate stronghold Fort Beauregard, located opposite Fort Walker at

Bay Point, two and a half miles away. As a result of the brief battle of Port Royal, the way was opened for the U.S. Navy to seize the sound and control it for the remainder of the Civil War.

It was a victory that would have far-reaching psychological and practical implications for the Union.

"The battle of Port Royal, occurring a little less than seven months after the fall of Fort Sumter, was of surpassing value in its moral and political effect, both at home and abroad," recalled future admiral Daniel Ammen, whose gunboat *Seneca* took part in the action also. "It gave us one of the finest harbors on the Atlantic Seaboard, affording an admirable base for future operations; and, by the establishment of coaling stations, shops and supply depots, made it possible to maintain an effective blockade within the entrances of the whole coast from Charleston to Cape Florida."

So far as is known, meanwhile, the brothers Drayton had no reason to cross paths in combat again. For one thing, older brother Thomas—a close friend and West Point classmate of Jefferson Davis—next was stationed far inland as a brigade commander in James Longstreet's corps of the Army of Northern Virginia.

Confederate General Drayton was criticized, however, for moving his brigade too slowly at Second Manassas (Bull Run). In the eyes of his superiors, he then failed to redeem himself at South Mountain and Antietam—as a result, his brigade was broken up, with its regiments parceled out to other commanders in the field. He spent the rest of the war "employed in minor departmental command and on boards of inquiry in the Trans-Mississippi Department," reported Ezra J. Warner in his book *Generals in Gray.*

Union naval officer Drayton, for *his* part, was commended for his role in the battle of Port Royal. Once the gunfire had died down on that November 7, Drayton steered his gunboat for DuPont's *Wabash,* to be greeted by DuPont's voice booming across the water between ships. Supposedly the fleet commander's welcoming words for his Carolina-born officer were: "Drayton, I *knew* you would be here."

By some accounts, he said, "*Captain* Drayton," rather than *Commander.* In any case, for his part in the great Union victory at Port Royal, and at his own brother's expense, Percival Drayton indeed was promoted to captain's rank. He remained in good favor throughout the Civil War—so much so that in the later battle of Mobile Bay (August 1864), he was captain of Adm. David Farragut's flagship, the

Hartford, while also serving as Farragut's fleet captain (West Gulf Blockading Squadron).

It was aboard the *Hartford,* not so incidentally, that Farragut at a critical point in the battle climbed into the rigging above deck and shouted the famous refrain attributed to him ever since (or words close to it): "Damn the torpedoes! Full speed ahead!"

Transferred to Washington in 1865 as chief of the navy's Navigation Bureau, a desk job, Southern-born Percival Drayton, fifty-three, died there in August of that year. Older brother Thomas, meanwhile, a long-time survivor of the Civil War, became a farmer in Dooly County, Georgia, and, later, an insurance agent in Charlotte, North Carolina. He also served as president of the South Carolina Immigrant Society before dying in 1891 at the age of eighty-two.

★ Part 3 ★
Generally Speaking I

As in life generally, the Civil War was rife with ironies, oddities, and mysteries great and small, with tragedy . . . and triumph, too. But all were concentrated in a short, short time span.

He Fought on Both Sides

BELIEVE IT OR NOT, Frank Crawford Armstrong, born an army "brat," finished exemplary service in the Civil War as a Confederate general . . . *after* first fighting the "Johnny Rebs" as a Union captain.

Just for good measure, for many years after the war he served the United States as a *Federal* government official.

Born in late 1835 at the Choctaw Indian Agency in today's state of Oklahoma, where his army officer father served as the Choctaw agent, young Frank Armstrong remained an army brat even after his father died—the boy's mother then married Mexican War hero Persifor Frazer Smith, a general.

The youth once, in 1854, accompanied his stepfather on a military campaign in New Mexico. He then graduated from Holy Cross Academy in Massachusetts and by 1859 was a first lieutenant with the regular army's Second Dragoons. A captain by summer 1861, he led his regiment's K Company at First Bull Run (Manassas) on July 21 just outside of Washington, D.C.

As is well known, the enemy, the Confederate army, carried the day at Manassas. Not so well known was the transfer of the young captain from one army to the other within weeks of the battle. Armstrong's resignation from the Union army officially took effect on August 13, 1861—but he already had joined the Confederacy's Gen. Benjamin McCulloch as a volunteer aide present for the battle of Wilson's Creek, Missouri, on August 10, three days before.

The second great Confederate victory in this early stage of the war, Wilson's Creek took place west of the Mississippi and southwest of Springfield, Missouri. Led by Brig. Gen. Nathaniel Lyon, 5,400 Federals took on 11,000 Confederates under Generals McCulloch and

Sterling Price. The somewhat disorganized Rebels at first gave ground to the Union attack, but then rallied and mounted three spirited charges. All were repulsed, but General Lyon was killed in the fighting. Deprived of their commander, the Federals withdrew from the field, thus granting the South a large chunk of Missouri real estate.

Armstrong then served as a staff officer for both McCulloch and Gen. James McQueen McIntosh, a West Point graduate and himself a former regular army officer.

At the battle of Pea Ridge, Arkansas (Elkhorn Tavern), in March 1862, Armstrong was standing only a few feet away when McCulloch was fatally wounded in the chest by a Union sharpshooter. Minutes later, leading a cavalry charge, McIntosh also went down, shot in the heart.

After surviving the same withering Federal fire, Armstrong was elected colonel of the Third Louisiana Infantry. Noted next for his performance in the siege of Corinth, Mississippi, he was given command of the cavalry units serving Gen. Sterling Price, still in the western theater of the war.

As a brigadier general, he then commanded a brigade under Nathan Bedford Forrest for the battles of Tullahoma and Chickamauga. He also served under Joseph Wheeler, Stephen Lee, and James Ronald Chalmers. Service with Wheeler, incidentally, could be especially dangerous work, since Wheeler's cavalry took part in so many skirmishes and battles that thirty-six staff officers were cut down by his side, while sixteen of Wheeler's horses were shot out from under him.

Frank Armstrong finished his wartime service to the Confederacy early in April 1865—under Forrest at Selma, Alabama, where the legendary Forrest finally met defeat at the hands of Union Gen. James Harrison Wilson.

After the war, Armstrong worked for the Overland Mail Service in Texas, then became a U.S. Indian inspector and assistant commissioner of Indian Affairs. Living until 1909, he remained unique as the only general-grade officer of either Civil War army who had fought on both sides.

Additional notes: In a similar case, West Point graduate Richard K. Meade Jr., a Virginian, was serving as a U.S. Army engineer officer at

Fort Sumter during its bombardment by Confederate forces, the action that opened the Civil War. Switching sides soon after, he became an engineer officer with Lee's Army of Northern Virginia.

A volunteer officer moving in the opposite direction early in the war was North Carolina planter Oliver H. Dockery of Wake Forest, who first served the Confederacy as an officer in the Thirty-eighth North Carolina but then became a Unionist.

Her Father Was Black

SLAVE CHILD PRISCILLA'S MOTHER was white—the missus of the plantation herself: Ann Liza Joyner, wife of Ricks Joyner. Priscilla never saw her real father, a black man who left the Joyners' farm in Nash County, North Carolina, the day that Anna Joyner gave birth to her brown baby child . . . the very day.

The golden brown child who came of the illicit union, black man and white woman, never knew her father; she thought maybe he was the carriage driver, "whose duties took him in and out of the house, day and night." She admitted, "It's just the idea that got into my head about the coachman."

In any case, the master of the plantation, Ricks Joyner, was . . . well, away a lot. His wife, apparently a young woman of some means, had married him and "set him up on her farm" long before Prissy came along. The white couple had two children, Morning and Margaret. But the master wasn't much of a farmer—or husband and father, it appears.

"He wouldn't plant in time, nor supervise the slaves, nor even stay on the place. He used to go away for months at a time and come back in rags, without a cent in his pocket."

Then, adding injury to insult, the white master took two of his wife's slaves to Rocky Mount and sold them. They had been "given" to her with the farm property, as those things went *before* the Civil War. Apparently taking a firm stand, "Miss Ann Liza" then told her husband to stay away until he brought the two slaves back with him.

That was when Prissy was conceived, and who knows under what desperate, loving, impulsive, or passionate circumstance? The child was born on Robert E. Lee's birthday, January 19, in 1858. Her unknown father, apparently a slave, waited only for the final moment before he bolted . . . perhaps, for all, quite wisely.

"Whoever my father was, he waited to find if I and my mother were all right. Then he left the place, never to come back no more. She never did let him see me, my mother told me later."

So, in the final years before the outbreak of the Civil War, when slaves were slaves, and women, even white women, were expected, sometimes even forced, to keep their "place," here was a white Southern missus awaiting the return of her wastrel husband with news of a child in the house that wasn't his, that was half black, that was fathered by one of their own slaves. And it was no secret, either.

"The colored people knew all about it and wanted to take care of me in the quarters, but my mother refused—told them that I was her baby, and she was going to raise me herself."

And Ricks Joyner did come home, and his wife did present him with the new, brown baby. As Prissy heard when growing up years later, "those must of been troublous days." *Troublous!*

But the white husband, even then, was at some disadvantage—financial disadvantage. "Old Ricks didn't have nothing—everything was in my mother's name." He wanted his wife, his white wife, to do something about this brown baby in their house. It was enough to learn of her shocking infidelity, her crossing of the line, we can only suppose, but then to be asked to "accept" the presence of a child of color in the cream-white household as a daily reminder . . . well, obviously, as Prissy herself later said, that "must of been enough to try anybody, 'specially since they already had two white ones."

But the husband and wife managed to strike a "deal" . . . of sorts. Ann Liza could keep her brown baby, and Ricks wouldn't have to pay her for the two slaves he had sold.

Meanwhile, the husband and wife somehow found enough peace, sporadically at the least, to return to their own connubial bed together, for they soon had two more children, both boys—Robert and Jolly. The antebellum household now consisted of father, mother, and five children, four of them white and one in her own racial no man's land somewhere in between things. It was happy for little Prissy, yet it wasn't.

"So here was five of us children, all having the same mother, living in the same house, and me different from the other four." And now some years passed. "It was a long time before I knew that I was any different from the others. All of us children used to play and eat together. The only difference was Morning and Margaret had one room, Robert and Jolly had another, and I had a room all to myself."

But it wasn't long before the specter of racial differences and slavery itself arose to forever change the setting as Prissy knew it. The children were playing "house" in the yard one day; Morning took the role of the father, and little Jolly was the make-believe family's baby. That was when Margaret suddenly looked at her sister Prissy and said, out of the blue, lines that Prissy never forgot:

"Prissy, you can't stay in here with us. You have to stay in the slave quarters. Papa says that's where you belong, anyway."

So now Prissy, about four or maybe five, knew. She cried, naturally, and ran to her mother (where else?). And her mother called all the children together, tried to repair the damage that could not be repaired, and said, "We were all brother and sister and must play together without fussing." But change, irrevocable as the pall in the Garden of Eden, had come, and now all was different . . . forevermore. That night, "Miss Ann Liza" slipped into Prissy's room, gathered up the child and held her in her arms and cried and cried, even if Prissy didn't quite know what the matter was with her white mother. That was the first of many nights they had visits together, their own little secret.

"I remember that I always felt comforted when the other children tormented me, because I knew that my mother would come in that night. I never let on to the other children. It was our secret, and I promised her not to tell."

Meanwhile, Ricks Joyner clearly was doing his best to "poison the minds of his own children against me." The girl Morning was three years older, and Margaret about two years ahead of Prissy. And now, the older they became, "the harder they made it for me."

But the Civil War had been raging for three years by this time, and Ricks never had gone off to battle at the side of his Southern brethren. They now came for him and "made him join up." In a month, though—"they tell me," said Prissy—he deserted. He tried to make his way back to the plantation but was caught and returned, quite possibly not to the ranks of the Confederate army. "It was the last Miss Ann Liza ever saw of him. Some say he was shot for being a deserter; others say he was killed during the fighting at Newbern [New Bern]. Whichever it was, I don't think Miss Ann Liza cared one way or another."

With the master of the house gone, the war soon over, and slavery officially banished in America, things did not really improve that much for the young, racially mixed girl. "Robert and Jolly were growing up and sometimes it was all I could do to keep all four from jumping on me." Jolly, the youngest, was Prissy's favorite of her half brothers and sisters, however. "He hadn't been old enough when his father lived to understand any of the things he was told about me," Priscilla Joiner explained so many, many years later. Her recollections appear in notes written by a Federal government researcher who interviewed her in the 1930s. They appear among more than one hundred interviews with Virginia ex-slaves published in the book *Weevils in the Wheat*, edited by Charles L. Perdue Jr., Thomas E. Barden, and Robert K. Phillips.

Still, the brown child of the household was "pretty unhappy most of the time." Her only real comfort was when her mother came to her at night. "One night, she stayed up with me until daybreak. While she was talking and stroking my hair, I fell asleep, and when I awoke, she was still holding me. Then she told me, crying all the while, that she was sending me away to school in Rocky Mount."

And so came the harbinger of Prissy's new and longest-lasting life— "with my own people." But her mother first told her, that same early morning, "how I must not forget that I was as good as anybody else— how much she loved me—and how I was always to remember that this is my house." In fact, "Miss Ann Liza" not only told Prissy she would "be taken care of," but "the house and this place will be yours some day, and you are going to have the biggest share of my money."

Prissy was twelve when Jolly Bowen, "one of the colored men who stayed with the Missus after freedom," loaded a trunk containing Prissy's belongings into a buggy and drove the child to Rocky Mount. It was 1870, and Mrs. Joyner had placed the girl with Mrs. Harriet Glenn Dancy of Tarboro, North Carolina. And that fall, Prissy began going to school in Rocky Mount. Way behind at first, she soon caught up with her schoolmates; she attended the school for four years. She heard from her mother every month and always replied with news of school and how well she was "getting along." And for a while, at Christmas every year, Jolly Bowen came to fetch Prissy and take her "home" for the holiday—"but it wasn't home anymore for me."

The other children, she recalls, "were all very polite to me—used to admire my starched dresses and hair ribbons, and so on." It was, for a time, "a regular family reunion each Christmas." As Prissy says, however, she had been "getting to live with and understand my people." In fact, "I used to look forward to going back less and less."

Then, in 1874, when her mother wrote about the annual visit, Prissy sent back word that she couldn't go . . . no particular reason. One reason, though, was that she simply didn't want to. Another was "well, because I had a beau." He lived in Tarboro, too, and he wanted her to stay for Christmas. He lived just across a creek from Mrs. Dancy's house. His name was Lewis . . . Lewis Joiner (or Joyner), in fact, but no "relation so far as I know." Then, the following June, they were married. Prissy was seventeen by then.

They moved to Suffolk, Virginia, because he was offered a job there. They lived "happily" for thirty-nine years, until his death in 1924, and they had thirteen children over those years, seven of them still living when Mrs. Joiner was interviewed in the late 1930s. One daughter's name was Ann Liza.

And what of the first "Ann Liza," Prissy's mother? The last time they saw each other was soon after World War I and shortly before Prissy's husband died. Prissy went to Rocky Mount for a visit. Her half brother Robert came to pick her up and take her back to the old plantation, where their mother now was bedridden by some unnamed illness.

The older woman hadn't been able to leave her bed for more than a year, in fact, and she made Prissy stay in the room with her for practically the entire time of the visit. She "insisted that was the last time she'd see me because she knew she was dying."

It became quite a scene. "She cried and sobbed and told me how much she regretted the wrongs she'd done me, but she was going to try to make up for it by leaving her estate to me. I told her I didn't need nothing, and that she didn't owe me a thing. I told her how happy I'd been with Lewis and my children and that it had been the best thing in the world for me to be put with my own people."

Naturally, too, Prissy still wanted to know who her father really was. She always had wanted to know . . . his name, at least. And what harm now, so long after?

But Prissy's mother just closed her eyes and turned her head away. "It's best not, Prissy," she said finally. "There's no need of even thinking about it. All I can tell you is that he's dead. I know that he's dead. He was a good man, Prissy, and you're a lot like him. Just remember that I'm your mother, and I love you as much as any mother ever loved her child."

They said good-bye, with the older, obviously dying woman hugging Prissy and crying over her, and finally the daughter had to just pull herself away. Robert drove her back into Rocky Mount . . . "and I was glad to get away."

The two half brothers had been "very kind and friendly" during the visit, Prissy also recalled. It was their wives and children "who didn't have anything to say to me."

Not long after, Jolly, once Prissy's "favorite," wrote to say their mother had died. "She didn't leave no will, he wrote, and outside the house and farm, there wasn't no property. Mother had transferred the farm to Robert and him a long time ago, he told me."

Once, Prissy's son Frank, down on a visit from New York, told her she ought to show that letter to a lawyer and see if "Miss Ann Liza" hadn't really "left me that place." But Priscilla Joiner didn't. "I never worried none about it. If it's mine, and they want it, they can have it. I have my own place here and my flowers. What more could an old woman want?"

Forgotten Veep

IN THE SEVERAL WEEKS AFTER winning the fledgling Republican Party's nomination for president in the 1860 election, Abraham Lincoln was besieged by well-wishers, vilified by many others, and already sought out by favor-seekers hoping for his election to the presidency in the fall.

One key individual, however, had not yet been heard from—his ticket-mate and candidate for vice president, Sen. Hannibal Hamlin, a former Democrat from Maine.

Finally, Lincoln sat down and wrote his new compatriot a short letter saying, "My Dear Sir: It appears to me that you and I ought to be acquainted, and accordingly I write this as a sort of introduction of myself to you."

Lincoln went on to say that they might have met when Lincoln served his single term in the U.S. House, but in any case, "I shall be pleased to receive a line from you."

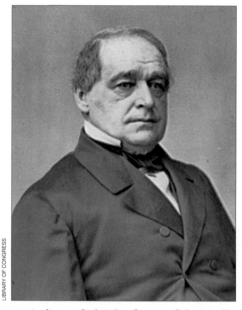

Hannibal Hamlin, the legislator from Maine who served as Lincoln's first—and now largely forgotten—vice president.

Oddly enough, Lincoln and his first vice president would not meet until more than two weeks *after* their election to office that November. Was there a problem, some hostility between them? Probably not. By all accounts, when they finally met in Chicago late in November 1860 for three days (at Lincoln's behest), their discussions were entirely cordial. The focus of their talks, not only with each other but also with other Republican leaders, was to develop a list of candidates for Lincoln's cabinet.

Since Hamlin, an attorney by occupation, hailed from New England, he was given four names to consider for a single New England cabinet post. He chose Gideon Welles to become secretary of the navy. Welles, a Connecticut newspaper editor, once (in the 1840s) had been head of the navy's Bureau of Provisions and Clothing.

Hamlin again was visible at the first Lincoln inauguration in March 1861, but after that, like many vice presidents before and after, he slowly sank from sight. He supported the administration's firm stand in provisioning Fort Sumter that spring, but by 1862 he complained to a friend that he wasn't being consulted in administrative actions.

"He was often absent from his job as president of the Senate and spent considerable time in Maine," wrote Pulitzer Prize–winning historian Mark E. Neely Jr. in his *Abraham Lincoln Encyclopedia*. "For two months in 1864 he even served a tour of garrison duty with the Maine Coast Guards."

Known to be antislavery on moral grounds but unsympathetic with abolitionism, "he thought the President too slow to move against slavery and claimed that he had been the first to be shown Lincoln's Emancipation Proclamation," added Neely's account. "When the proclamation was issued, he complimented the President for the 'great act of the age.'"

In fact, twenty years after their joint inauguration of 1861, Hamlin labeled Lincoln "one of the most distinguished [men] of all times and all nations."

Hamlin apparently did not blame Lincoln for the Republican Party's decision in 1864 to put forward a new candidate for vice president, Andrew Johnson of Tennessee. It took only one ballot at the party's convention in Baltimore to dump the Maine legislator in favor of "War Democrat" Johnson.

As for Lincoln's possible role in the changeover, Neely wrote, "Many would agree with Ward Hill Lamon's recollection that Lincoln wanted . . . Johnson but worked for his nomination only secretly in order not to give offense to New England."

Regardless of what *he* may have thought or known, Hamlin dutifully campaigned for the Lincoln-Johnson ticket that fall.

A year later, now president due to the assassination of Lincoln, Johnson made Hamlin collector for the Port of Boston. But Hamlin disagreed strongly with Johnson's Reconstruction program and soon left the appointive post to others. In 1869 he returned to politics and once more was elected a U.S. senator from Maine. (He previously had served Maine as a state legislator and governor, as well.)

Elected in 1875 to a third and final term in the Senate, he left elective politics to become U.S. minister to Spain, thanks to the appointive powers of Secretary of State James G. Blaine, himself a veteran of the political scene in Maine.

Evening an Old Score

A IS FOR ADAMS, Daniel and William, both Confederate generals. D is for duel . . . and sometimes for death. B is for brothers, and I for irony.

T could be for that . . . for *that,* unhappily, was their story.

William Wirt Adams was born in Frankfurt, Kentucky, on March 22, 1819. Two years later, along came younger brother Daniel Weisiger

Adams, born in May or June 1821. Same town. Their father was federal district judge George Adams and their mother the daughter of Kentucky pioneer Daniel Weisiger.

The Adams brothers spent a few formative years in the Kentucky capital, but the family moved on to Natchez, Mississippi, in 1825, the Civil War then a mere mote smoldering on the horizon. Older brother Wirt (who went by his middle name) served in the army of the independent Republic of Texas in 1839, then rejoined the civilian world as a Mississippi planter, banker, and state legislator.

Daniel, in the meantime, read the law and joined the Mississippi bar. He practiced his attorney trade both in Mississippi and in Louisiana, but mostly in the latter. He attracted a bit of attention in those antebellum days when he challenged a newspaper editor to a duel. The editor had been rash enough to print comments critical of Judge Adams, father of the Adams brothers. The editor, unfortunately, would write no more. He was killed in the duel.

Life went on anyway—duels were not all that uncommon. Daniel, in fact, was officially acquitted of a murder charge stemming from the contretemps over hot words, pride, and honor. With the Civil War soon erupting, the unhappy encounter was more or less forgotten as the two Adams brothers stepped forward to take their respective places in the ranks of Confederate officers.

By now, Wirt Adams had established himself as a leading citizen of his adoptive state—so much so that newly installed Confederate President Jefferson Davis (also from Mississippi) offered him a cabinet post as postmaster general of the Confederacy. But Wirt said no, he would rather fight. And fight he did. Raising the First Mississippi Cavalry Regiment and leading it as a colonel, he at first ranged more or less freely against Union forces in Mississippi and Tennessee, but then was kept busy by the battles of Iuka and Corinth, as well as the Vicksburg campaign.

After Vicksburg finally fell to U. S. Grant in 1863, Wirt was promoted to brigadier general. Continuing to serve as a cavalry commander, he led his horsemen in campaigns almost exclusively in Mississippi and Louisiana. But the end of the Civil War found him serving under Nathan Bedford Forrest in a desperate attempt to repulse Union Gen. James Harrison Wilson's raid on Selma, Alabama.

Younger brother Daniel, in the meantime, also had risen to prominence in the years immediately before the Civil War—so much so that

Louisiana's governor asked him to serve on a three-member board charged with preparing the state for the oncoming war. Then, with the opening of hostilities in 1861, Daniel Adams led the First Louisiana Regulars, initially as lieutenant colonel and later as colonel.

Less fortunate than his older brother, he was destined to be wounded three times in the fighting that lay ahead. He and his regiment distinguished themselves in the battle of Shiloh, but that was where he lost his right eye. He was promoted to brigadier general in 1862—a year before his brother earned a general's rank.

Despite the limitation of one eye, Daniel Adams served on . . . and on. As commander of the Louisiana Brigade, he fought at Perryville, Kentucky; Murfreesboro, Tennessee; and Chickamauga, Georgia. Having suffered a second wound at Murfreesboro, he was cut down a third and final time on the second day of battle at Chickamauga, where he also was captured.

After another recovery period and an exchange freeing him from prisoner status, he spent the latter months of the war in command of central and northern Alabama. He was called into real action one more time—like older brother Wirt, Daniel was thrown into the futile Southern struggle against Wilson's march into Alabama and Georgia.

By now, of course, the war had been irretrievably lost. Daniel Adams next embarked upon a different sort of recovery period—he left the country for a sojourn in England.

Disinclined to spend the rest of his life there, however, he soon returned to his law practice in New Orleans, where, after only a few short years, he died in 1872 at the young age of fifty-one.

Wirt, after also distinguishing himself in battle, lived until 1888. Once again taking the role of a leading citizen, he served the state of Mississippi as its revenue agent for a few years, then accepted a federal appointment as postmaster of Jackson, the state's capital city.

Wirt, though, more than two decades after the Civil War, was destined to die violently. He quarreled with one John Martin, and when they met on the street in Jackson one day, Martin killed General Adams, then sixty-nine.

Oddly enough, John Martin, the man who killed the older of the two General Adamses, was—like the victim of Daniel Adams's antebellum duel—a newspaper editor.

M Y T H
Creator of Baseball

OLIVER WENDELL HOLMES SR. (Harvard, Class of 1829) recalled that he played the game quite frequently during his college days. A bit earlier (in 1787), the overly exuberant boys at Princeton were enjoined against playing "with balls and sticks" on the college common. Even as early as 1778, Continental army soldiers wintering at Valley Forge with George Washington were known to take part in a bat-and-ball game called "playing at base."

It may all go back, at the very least, to a book published in England in 1744, *A Little Pretty Pocket-Book,* and its references to a game featuring batter, pitcher, base hits, and runs scored. Then, too, early nineteenth-century tomes cited the English game called rounders—with batters hitting pitched balls, then rounding the three bases in a diamond-shaped infield and scoring by returning to the batter's original place of business. Miss the infield, and it was a foul ball. Three strikes, and you were out. A caught fly ball, and again you were out.

In the United States they called that game, alternately, goal ball or base ball (two words).

One big difference from today's game of baseball: The base runner could be "tagged" out by nailing him with a thrown ball!

With all this known history behind the game, with all the spread of baseball before, during, and of course, *after* the Civil War, how is it that a single Civil War general of the Union variety would be given credit far and wide for "inventing" the game of baseball, when, in provable fact, he didn't?

He was, of course, Abner Doubleday, and it was the highly respected Spalding Commission that labeled him the creator of modern baseball because he had developed the game's basic rules while teaching at a military prep school in Cooperstown, New York, during the summer of 1839. As noted by the *Encyclopedia Britannica,* among various sources, that was the reason the National Baseball Hall of Fame and Museum was situated in Cooperstown, "although it was later proved that Doubleday was not in Cooperstown in 1839."

Union Maj. Gen. Abner E. Doubleday, who did not really invent baseball . . . was at Fort Sumter, Antietam, Gettysburg, and other "hot spots" of the Civil War.

U.S. ARMY MILITARY HISTORY INSTITUTE

Doubleday's absence or presence in Cooperstown aside, "The Spalding Commission's finding that the national game was of purely American origin was discredited by subsequent inquiries confirming baseball's evident connection with the English game called rounders, feeder or base ball."

But then . . . what about Doubleday's reputed connection with the national pastime? The fact is, the upstate New York native apparently did attend school in Cooperstown before going off to West Point in 1838 and graduating from the Military Academy in 1842, with future Confederate generals James Longstreet, D. H. Hill, and Lafayette McLaws listed among his classmates. He then, like many fellow West Pointers, served in the Mexican War of 1846–48 (as an artillery officer) and in the mean little Seminole War in Florida during the 1850s.

Doubleday achieved quick notice in the Civil War by commanding the artillerymen at Fort Sumter who fired the first Union salvos in response to the Confederate bombardment of the Federal fort in the Charleston Harbor.

He emerged from the war with the rank of major general of volunteers (temporary) after taking part in the battles of Second Manassas (Bull Run), Antietam, Fredericksburg, and Gettysburg, all of which were major engagements. Somewhere along the line, he picked up the nickname "Forty-Eight Hours" for his reputation of moving his forces very *s l o w l y.*

After the war, Doubleday wrote a book (*Reminiscences of Forts Sumter and Moultrie in 1860–61*) about his Civil War experiences but apparently did not make any claims himself to having creating the game of baseball. According to history professor George B. Kirsch in the *Civil War Times* of May 1998, Doubleday in fact "possibly never even visited Cooperstown."

The Spalding Commission (sometimes also called the Mills Commission) that credited Doubleday with the origin of organized baseball was chaired by Abraham Mills, head of professional baseball's National League in 1907. According to the Kirsch account, "Mills had known Doubleday ever since the men served together in the Civil War, but his friend apparently had never said anything about his supposed brainstorm in Cooperstown."

So where did the *originator* story come from? "The tale rests entirely on the testimony of Abner Graves, who recalled playing ball with Doubleday as a boy in that bucolic town in upstate New York," wrote Kirsch in his magazine adaptation of material from his 1989 book, *The Creation of American Team Sports: Baseball and Cricket, 1838–72.*

If that seems rather a thin reed to lean on, consider also the fact that Graves was an elderly man recalling "an event that occurred 68 years earlier." Then, too, Doubleday, who had died in 1893 after retiring from the army in 1873, obviously was in no position to offer corroboration—or refutation. And finally, a few years later, Graves was packed off to an insane asylum after shooting his wife.

Case dismissed!

Bees Being Bees

IN THE SOUTH, A WOMAN living in a one-room log cabin had a sure-fire way of discouraging Yankee foragers the moment they approached. Her secret lay with the bees—with the beehives placed in her front yard. The hives, that is, and the length of cord she had fashioned from cotton fabric and attached to the hives.

"When she saw the blue coats coming," related her granddaughter, Mrs. Clint Bearden of Georgia, many years later, "she turned the hive over with the cord[,] which she had pulled through a hole in the door."

Bees being bees, they were upset at having their home so unceremoniously upset. No matter that the approaching Yankees were entirely innocent parties. "Several times the horses and men got stung badly. The horses would sometimes throw their riders and hurt them. But the men always left her home without bothering her or what little food she had!"

Who Wrote "Taps"?

APPARENTLY NO TRICK, NO HOAX, no falsehood is attached to another icon of American life ascribed to a Union Civil War general, and that is the purely sweet, heart-rending bugle call today known far and wide as "Taps."

Apparently, because for some time many historians questioned the story. Perhaps some still do. But others today seem quite willing to credit the composition of "Taps" to Maj. Gen. Daniel Butterfield, Medal of Honor winner thirty years after the fact for rescuing the fallen colors of a Pennsylvania regiment in the battle of Gaines's Mill outside Richmond in 1862. As a brigade commander in the battle, he had lost six hundred or so men when he took up the Pennsylvania regiment's flag and, under heavy fire, urged the scattered troops around him to gather 'round again and continue the fight.

Wounded in that action, he later became chief of staff to Joseph "Fighting Joe" Hooker and fought at Chancellorsville, served with George Meade at Gettysburg until laid low by a piece of flying metal, resumed his place on Hooker's staff at Chattanooga, and then commanded a division in the Atlanta campaign.

It was while Butterfield was engaged in the Peninsula campaign of 1862 against Richmond that he began experimenting with bugle calls for his Third Brigade, First Division, Fifth Army Corps, Army of the Potomac. As one thing led to another at his brigade encampment at Harrison's Landing, Virginia, the story goes, he ended up composing "Taps" to replace the tradition of firing three rifle volleys at the end of a soldier's burial service.

The new bugle call also would replace the French "Tatoo," traditionally used to signify "lights out," wrote Kathryn Shenkle, a historian

Union Maj. Gen. Daniel Butterfield, Medal of Honor winner now fully credited with composing "Taps" about the time of his heroics during the Peninsula campaign of 1862.

at Arlington National Cemetery, in *Soldiers* magazine (May 1995). "Butterfield's bugler, Oliver W. Norton of Chicago, was the first to sound the new call," she reported. "Within months, 'Taps' was sounded by buglers in both Union and Confederate forces."

According to the Arlington historian also, Butterfield's bugle call "is sounded during the 2,500 military wreath ceremonies conducted at the Tomb of the Unknowns every year." "Taps" is also played at the military funerals conducted with honors each weekday at Arlington National Cemetery, usually about fifteen a day, to say nothing of the hundreds more veterans' funerals conducted throughout the nation every day.

Then, too, every night at U.S. military installations around the world "Taps" still is heard at ten o'clock to signal "lights out."

After the Civil War, incidentally, Butterfield returned to a busy business and social life, complemented by world travel. When he died in 1901, Butterfield, a non–West Pointer, was buried at West Point, courtesy of a special ruling issued by the War Department. Buried, of course, to the sweet, wavering notes of his own "Taps."

A Husband Pardoned

IN RICHMOND, THE WHITE-FACED WOMAN begging—nay, desperately pleading with—Varina Howell Davis, wife of Confederate President

Jefferson Davis, wailed on and on. "He only intended to stay one day, but we coaxed and begged him, and then he stayed and stayed, and he was afraid afterward to go back. He did not mean to be a coward or to desert."

As the piteous woman explained, too, the army would be coming close by their home. And . . . again from Mary Boykin Chesnut:

> Poor little Suzie had just died, and the boy was ailing. Food was so scarce and so bad. They all had chills. She was so miserable. The negroes had all gone to the Yankees. There was nobody to cut wood, and it was so cold. They were coming so near. "I wrote—and I wrote—if you want to see the baby alive, come. If they won't let you, come anyhow. *You see, I did it*—if he is a deserter."

Of course, he was. And he had been found out, and now he was going to be shot for it. But Varina Davis left the room, left the white-faced woman alone with Mary Chesnut, endlessly repeating her story, for "ever so long," then came back "smiling."

"Here it is," she said. "All that you want."

A pardon for the husband.

U. S. Grant Capitulates

Ulysses S. Grant, "Ulys" to his intimates, was noted during his Overland campaign of 1864 for pounding his enemy with sledgehammer blows, one after the other, despite the horrendous casualty rate among his own troops—despite critical cries from fellow "Yankees" upset by so many casualties.

Earlier in the war, he set the tone of events to come with his stern demand for absolutely unconditional surrender by the Confederates holding Fort Donelson, Tennessee.

Needless to say, the stubborn Grant was not one to give in to pressure from friends or enemies. Surrender—on his own part—was not a part of his vocabulary.

Normally not, that is. For there did come a time, on an issue arising from the Civil War and very much involving the Confederate enemy, when he did back down, did surrender his stand to another—to his wife, Julia Dent Grant.

The issue was Union treatment of a single Confederate prisoner of war, Capt. Jack Govan. Julia, protesting that the prisoner was ill, wanted her husband to grant the Rebel officer a parole. But her Ulys said no; under new rules issued from Washington, he could not do that. He blamed a recent action by Confederate President Jefferson Davis for the current Union crackdown on parole rules . . . and he was adamant in saying he must follow the new Federal mandate in regard to prisoner paroles.

The issue came up when Grant was visiting his wife in temporary quarters at Memphis early in his Vicksburg campaign. A pair of emissaries had arrived to ask for resumed parole for Govan.

"I know what they came for," Ulysses told Julia. "It is to have Captain Govan put on parole again."

Julia was surprised. "I thought he was already on parole."

"Yes," said her husband the general, "but Jeff Davis has published a very severe order and, in retaliation, an order has come from Washington to place every man on parole under strict surveillance."

Grant asked his wife to see the two emissaries, one of them a bishop, but to make no promises.

She did . . . and gave only her own personal promise. "I had become much interested in this family . . . especially in Captain Jack, who was in very poor health," wrote Julia in a memoir published in 1975 (*The Personal Memoirs of Julia Dent Grant*). She promised to relay their request and expressed hope that her husband would grant it.

Ulysses S. Grant, who began the Civil War as a colonel of volunteers and wound up as commander of all the Union armies.

Then it was time to face her husband and present her plea. "Ulys," she said, "of course you will continue Captain Govan's parole."

"No, I will not," he said. "I cannot."

"Oh! Ulys, you can, you will," she protested. "Captain Govan is a very sick man." Adding that Govan was as sick as the brother Grant recently had lost, she asserted that it would "kill" the prisoner to keep him confined.

"He is too ill to do any harm to anyone," was her final argument.

But Grant was adamant. "I cannot help it. The order is imperative."

Julia now unlimbered her heaviest artillery. "Ulys, I ask it as a personal favor."

Even that personal plea failed to reduce Grant's defenses. "You have no right to ask a personal favor in this matter."

"You refuse to grant this to me?"

"Yes."

So the conversation ended—for the moment. Grant remained impregnable—for the moment.

Julia wrote that she at this point "turned to the window and shed bitter tears of disappointment." She took other measures to undermine her husband's stand as well.

"I seated myself at some distance from the general and occupied myself with a book, never looking towards him. People were coming in and going out for two hours."

Apparently, though, the bombardment of her silence was taking its toll. "At last, when a card was brought in to the General of a Mr. Hiller, saying it was for Mrs. Grant, the General glanced at it, arose, brought it to me, and said in a low tone, 'If he comes in behalf of Captain Jack Govan, I will place him on parole.'"

And exactly he had. Victory! The walls were breached, Grant had conceded! To Hiller, Julia said sweetly, "Do you come in behalf of Captain Jack Govan?"

"I do," he said.

Smiling with delight, Julia was able to say: "The General has just now told me he will place him on parole."

Thus, added Julia's memoir, Hiller "did not linger, but hastened with the glad news to Captain Govan's friends and took the parole with him."

For once, Ulysses S. Grant had capitulated.

Yankee Dentist in Napoleon's Court

AS A YOUNG DENTAL STUDENT, Philadelphia-born Thomas Evans had but one goal, a lofty one at that—to serve "all the crowned heads of Europe" as their dentist. And he did achieve his aim in part . . . as French Emperor Napoleon III's personal dentist.

But events evolved in such a way that Evans also became an agent-lobbyist for the Union during the Civil War, after serving the self-proclaimed emperor of France as a spy . . . of sorts. To Evans, as one result, goes much of the credit for keeping Napoleon's France neutral in the war between the American North and South.

Who would have thought . . . when young Evans arrived in Paris in December 1847 to become a dental assistant to a fellow American, an older dentist, officially serving the court of King Louis Philippe of France? Who could have expected the king's sudden departure just two months later, as the revolutionary fervor of 1848 swept Europe? And then the older dentist's return—in effect, retirement—to America?

In the meantime, in 1850, rebellious Louis Napoleon Bonaparte, nephew and step-grandchild of Napoleon Bonaparte, was elected president of France. When time approached to seek election again, he instead, in 1853, staged a coup d'état to seize the helm of France and call himself Napoleon III.

By that time he and young Evans already had met and had become fast friends—at first as patient and dentist, for Evans indeed had assumed his former associate's dental practice. In 1853 Napoleon III officially appointed Evans surgeon-dentist to the imperial court, but there was more, much more, to their growing camaraderie.

As explained by Ernest O. Grab in *Military History* magazine (October 1995), the "frank and honest" American offered a friendship free of political innuendo and palace intrigue. Napoleon III, as penalty for his own plots against the throne, had been both an exile and a long-time prisoner for many years before King Philippe's denouement. As a result, he had few political associates he could trust. Added Grab: "Distrustful of his cabinet ministers he developed a mania for clandestine diplomacy. Evans agreed to work for him as a secret agent. Using his profession as a 'cover,' he traveled among the courts of Europe and soon found himself drawn into the shadowy world of political intrigue."

While Evans thus was living his onetime dream in part, he was appalled by the primitive approach he found in the medical care afforded in Europe to soldiers wounded in battle. He enlisted the support of Napoleon III for more enlightened treatment of the wounded, but received little cooperation from the French army's medical corps.

When the American Civil War broke out, Evans assumed a new mission—apparently without being asked. And what a boon for Washington! Imagine, a little-known American dentist taking on the role of an agent for the Union! Even more startling, he frequently met with the emperor in a small room off the emperor's study to plot the movements of the Union and Confederate armies on a large map.

Evans, well aware of the French cabinet's pro-Southern leaning, took those opportunities to argue against French recognition of the newly formed Confederacy. While the French leader held off any such move, he at first was openly skeptical of Lincoln's hopes of restoring the secession-rent Union.

Even before Lincoln took office, Evans had decided upon bolder, more direct action. "What Napoleon III needed, the dentist decided, was a direct communications link with Washington, D.C., outside normal diplomatic channels—himself," Grab reported. Evans wrote the War Department's chief clerk, James Lesley Jr., to the effect that Napoleon III was willing to take a wait-and-see attitude for the time being, rather than rush into sudden acceptance of the Confederacy.

While that must have been welcome news, Evans soon was busy scouring Europe for war-making supplies. "As a private citizen, but armed with the consent of Napoleon III, he purchased arms and ammunition from a French munitions firm for use by the U.S. government. Obtaining a swatch of Union blue, he contacted a firm making uniforms for the French army and had [it] dye the material and cut it to American specifications."

In the meantime, though, Confederate agent John Slidell was doing his best to influence the French government, too. He finally arranged an audience with Napoleon III in August 1862, after which the French emperor proposed an armistice that would stop the fighting in America for six months. During that period, France, Russia, and Britain would do what they could to help the warring parties settle their differences peaceably.

But Union authorities saw the proposal as a foot in the door leading to recognition. Worse, Evans on November 15 "was disturbed to note that when discussing the war, the emperor's replies were vague." The American had to wonder if Napoleon III were edging toward a change of heart . . . the *wrong* change of heart.

They were in the small war room, the dentist and the emperor. Evans decided to risk all on a throw of the rhetorical dice. What was Napoleon III's candid assessment of events in America at that point, and what about the proposed armistice as well? "Napoleon III replied that the North did not seem capable of putting down the rebellion."

Alarmed, Evans "objected vigorously" and pointed to recent Union gains on Napoleon's map. The emperor "countered with descriptions of the brutal conduct of Union General Benjamin ('The Beast') Butler toward the citizens of New Orleans, especially the women." The Frenchman was influenced also by Democratic Party gains in the congressional elections of 1862.

Their discussion continued until the emperor at last fell silent, "still except for an occasional twitch of his mustache." Finally acknowledging that Evans had made a good case, he gave the dentist permission to "transmit their remarks to President Abraham Lincoln and Mr. [Secretary of State William] Seward, but in strict confidence."

Evans immediately did so. As one result, he was recognized at home as "the only American in Paris capable of obtaining the information the administration needed." Thus he became the confidential link between Washington and the emperor.

Soon, however, the ever-dubious Napoleon III withdrew his mediation offer, in part blaming the refusals of Russia and Britain to join in his peacemaking effort. Even after the Union victory at Gettysburg and during the siege of Petersburg, with the Confederacy staggering under the burden of war, the French leader still questioned the possibility of ultimate Union vindication.

In the end, Evans offered to visit Lincoln and Seward and report back on the situation in Washington, if the emperor would only hold off on making any commitment to the struggling South. Napoleon III agreed: "I don't think I shall recognize the Confederacy until you have had the opportunity of communicating to me the results of your visit."

Assured of Napoleon III's remarkable trust in him, Evans and his wife embarked for the United States from Liverpool, England, on August 1, 1864. After visits with both Lincoln and Seward, this unusual ambassador-without-portfolio spent five days observing U. S. Grant's tightening siege lines in the area of Petersburg and Richmond.

"In a letter to Napoleon III, he detailed his findings, convinced the emperor would agree that ultimate victory would belong to the North." By the time Evans returned to Paris in November (after observing conditions in Union field hospitals), little doubt remained that the North indeed would win the Civil War. Recognition of the Confederacy had become a dead issue.

In France, meanwhile, other riveting events soon would come to the fore and engage Napoleon III's fullest attention—foremost among them being the Franco-Prussian War of 1870 that led to disaster for France, riots in Paris, and the emperor's capture by the Prussian enemy and the loss of his throne. In all the tumult, the American dentist again played a crucial role—he "spirited the empress to safety in England."

Some years later, after the emperor's death in 1873, Evans wrote a book castigating French political figures who had plotted against Napoleon III and even sought defeat for the French army in order to see the emperor deposed. Still a traveler, still "welcome in royal circles," Evans then spent more years carrying "letters and parcels that allowed Europe's royalty to communicate with each other free from the prying eyes of officialdom."

Evans, briefly a widower, died in 1897 . . . in Paris, but of course.

Mrs. Lee's Mysterious Cousin

IT WAS A QUIET AFTERNOON in early May 1861. Mrs. Robert E. Lee was in her room at Arlington House, working on a portrait of her son Rob, when a handsome young U.S. Army officer interrupted with news she had been dreading for days—Federal troops were coming to occupy her stately home the very next day!

The bearer of the bad news was Orton Williams, a distant kinsman of Mary Custis Lee, a young man who had been a frequent visitor, even an intimate of the Lee family for years. As an officer on the staff of Winfield Scott, "general in chief" of the entire army—Union army, that is—young Orton surely would know what he was talking about.

And he did, except that he had to return the next morning to report that the occupation of the Lee home would not take place that day after all. No matter, he warned, Mrs. Lee certainly ought to pack up and secure the family valuables anyway—the Federal troops would be coming soon.

As a small, lingering mystery even today, it still is not known if perhaps Winfield Scott himself suggested the warning visit . . . or if the impetuous Orton took it upon himself to alert the Lees. Mrs. Lee always did suspect that General Scott, her husband's former commanding officer and good friend, had a hand in Orton's visit.

Either way, Orton would have needed little urging, since Arlington House had become a second home to him and older sister Martha "Markie" Williams after they were orphaned not many years before. Their father, Virginia-born Capt. William George Williams, had been killed in the Mexican War. Their mother, America Peter Williams, a first cousin to Mary Custis Lee, had died soon after. The Williams couple were survived by three children in all, Markie, Orton, and Lawrence, the last a cadet at West Point while R. E. Lee served as the Military Academy's superintendent in the 1850s.

The Lee home that both Markie and Orton came to know so well during the same period was a grand estate on the brow of a hill across the Potomac River from Washington, D.C.—its columned façade at the Virginia end of Memorial Bridge still highly visible today. Seized by the Union in 1861, exactly as Orton Williams had warned, it today is best known as the capstone of Arlington National Cemetery, the burial ground for war dead begun by the Union in the Civil War.

In those last peaceful days before the war broke out, Markie especially had been a constant visitor, so much so that Lee daughter Mary's room became known as "Mary and Markie's room," recalled Mary P. Coulling in her 1987 book *The Lee Girls*.

As a teenager attending boarding school, Orton, too, was a frequent visitor on his vacations—one of the Arlington House bedrooms sometimes was called "Orton's room." Meanwhile, it soon became evident to

When Union forces occupied Arlington in the summer of 1861, the home of R. E. and Mary Lee fell into Federal hands. In the years that followed, the front steps of the mansion became a popular setting for many photographs of Union officers.

one and all that Orton and Lee's daughter Agnes, born third of the four Lee girls, had grown quite fond of each other.

When Orton first came to visit, of course, none could have foreseen the sometimes dark and mysterious turns his short life would take.

As young adults, he and Agnes never did make marriage plans. She may have said no. In fact, she never did marry anyone, but Orton's name was on her lips moments before she died—young, in her thirties.

By then, Orton himself long since was dead, young himself and a victim of the Civil War—no battlefield casualty, but victim, more specifically, of a mysterious spy mission gone terribly, terribly wrong. He left behind a story of many gaps, coupled with the odd fact he changed his name at one point, coupled also with the ugly story that he had shot a fellow Confederate soldier in a fit of temper at the battle of Shiloh.

And, yes, he had gone over to the Confederacy soon after his two warning visits to Arlington House. Within days, in fact, he had tried to resign from the U.S. Army and cross the lines to join the other side, like so many other Southern sympathizers before him. But Orton Williams ran into unexpected difficulty—he was arrested by Federal authorities who feared he knew too much about Union war plans by virtue of his position on Scott's staff.

Sent to Governor's Island off Manhattan in New York, he was granted parole on his word that he wouldn't go south for a month. At that point, he did go, he did join the Confederate forces as, first, a lieutenant on the staff of Leonidas Polk, then as a captain and assistant chief of artillery for Polk's superior, Braxton Bragg.

Orton initially had traveled to Richmond to visit with General Lee, future commander of the Army of Northern Virginia. It crossed Lee's mind to appoint Orton to his own staff, but, as Lee later informed the family, he realized the Northern press was likely to stir up fresh allegations of Orton's "intended betrayal of Gen. Scott's plans." According to Mary Coulling's book, it was Lee who "made sure the young man was sent to Tennessee to serve with General L. Polk."

Then, so far as the Lee girls were concerned, silence. For months, no word from Orton. Not even when Agnes wrote him a long letter toward the end of September 1861. Finally, on December 1 of the same year, an obviously hurting Agnes wrote that she had been hoping "ever since I sent my last long letter written the 29th of Sept . . . to have a response in due time."

Now feeling that "hope told a flattering tale," she added: "I have been tempted to believe you have forgotten your old Virginia friends generally, me in particular, but ashamed of this skepticism in regard to 'our brave defenders' I am going to do what I rarely ever do—write again."

The troubled young woman closed with a plea: "Remember to take care of yourself. . . . I pray daily dear O His blessing may be upon you, & how I wish your own voice may ascend as often for your self."

She signed off, "Your friend, Agnes L."

Then came the terrible year of 1862 for the Lees—second daughter Anne Carter Lee, twenty-three, died October 20 in North Carolina of typhoid fever, and son Rooney Lee's newborn baby girl died in December—the second child he and his wife, Charlotte, had lost.

Hearing about Annie's death, Markie Williams sent condolences through Agnes and also lamented that she hadn't heard from Orton for more than a year. She, too, was "tired of writing" him with no response. But still she cared. "When you write, Agnes, tell me if you hear from my dear dear Brother & how & where he is," Markie wrote. "Tell me everything you know of him."

What *had* Orton been up to? Not a whole lot of good, unfortunately. He had served bravely enough in the battle of Shiloh, it seems, but he also had shot one of his own soldiers who was slow to obey his commands. Orton's troops then turned against him so vehemently, he was assigned to General Bragg's command . . . and somehow escaped being brought up on charges.

It was at this point that he changed his name to Lawrence Williams Orton, borrowing in part from his older brother Lawrence.

Now, too, he surprised the Lees by appearing at Hickory Hill, the Virginia home of Rooney's in-laws, the Wickhams, to spend Christmas with them while on leave from temporary cavalry duty with the Army of Northern Virginia. But the visiting Orton was a man changed in demeanor as well as name, Mary Coulling wrote in *The Lee Girls*. "In his uniform the young man was handsomer than ever," she noted. "But in other ways Orton Williams had changed. His finely chiseled features seemed to have coarsened, as if he had been drinking heavily."

He had brought gifts for Agnes, and they spent considerable time together on "long [horseback] rides in the woods." But "the end of the visit was not a happy one."

After they secluded themselves in the parlor one day for a long, earnest conversation, Orton abruptly left. "Still aching from the loss of Annie," wrote Coulling, "Agnes was not ready for the temptuous kind of love Orton was offering." Sadly, "Orton no longer seemed the boy she had cared for, the young man whose welfare in the army she had prayed about."

Now Orton disappeared again into the maw of war. For months nothing more was heard from him. The fact is, he had returned to Bragg's command as a cavalry officer. But no one around Agnes, not even her father, made mention of Orton or his whereabouts.

Then came the shock . . . June 13, 1863, in the *Daily Richmond Examiner* for all in the capital of the Confederacy and its environs to see. They had his name wrong, thanks to his own, self-initiated change, but the news was harsh and unequivocal. The Federals had captured Orton. They had tried him as a spy and they had hanged him and a fellow officer, all in less than twenty hours.

It happened in Tennessee, near Franklin. In the twilight hours of June 8, a foggy night, two riders, strangers dressed as Union officers, appeared at the headquarters of the Eighty-fifth Indiana. When they explained they were Col. Lawrence Orton and a Major Dunlop, U.S.

Army "inspectors," the regiment's commander, Col. J. B. Baird, was so taken by their story of an ambush and robbery by Confederate bush-whackers that he lent "Colonel Orton" $50.

The two strangers somehow managed "to keep" their credentials, which upon examination Baird also found convincing. When he invited them to stay overnight, however, they said they had to push on to Nashville and rode on out of his command post into the thickening fog. We may never know what their real plan was, for an officer on Baird's staff was far more skeptical of the strange pair's story than his superior.

Quickly voicing his doubts, he alarmed Baird, who then "sent a soldier rushing after them in the fog." Brought back to camp, Orton and his companion were placed under guard while Baird checked further. His query went by telegraph to James A. Garfield, a brigadier general on the staff of Gen. William Rosecrans and a future president of the United States. Garfield in short order wired back: "There are no such men as Inspector General Lawrence Orton, colonel U.S. Army, and Assistant Major Dunlop, in this army, nor in any army, so far as we know. Why do you ask?"

Ominously for Mrs. Lee's mysterious cousin, other developments had already taken place. A search of the two prisoners revealed all—except the object of their mission. Baird's men found more than $1,000 hidden on Orton's person. Both his saber and hatband gave his real name and rank in the Confederate army. Dunlop, too, was revealed as bogus by similar evidence.

The pair then acknowledged their real identities and allegiance—the second man was Orton's own cousin (on his mother's side), Walter Gibson Peter, also an officer in the Confederate army.

Now came the sad denouement that the Lees never could forgive, that Robert E. Lee later would brand "an atrocious outrage." Once again contacting his headquarters at Murfreesboro for instruction, Baird received a chilling message: "The two men are no doubt spies. Call a drum-head court-martial to-night, and if they are found to be spies, hang them before morning, without fail."

Beginning at three o'clock in the morning, the "trial" was over in less than a hour—the two Rebel officers were found guilty of being spies. Baird again messaged Garfield for instruction. "Must I hang him?" he asked, while also saying he would like to have the hanging take place elsewhere. Obviously rattled and loath to proceed, Baird added that if he didn't hear anything further, "they will be executed."

He did hear further, though—he received a specific and peremptory reply: "The general . . . directs that the two spies, if found guilty, be hung [*sic*] at once."

And so the die was cast. A Union chaplain ministered to the condemned pair. Both took Communion and then wrote letters.

Oddly, after being apprehended in a Union uniform and admitting he was actually a Confederate officer, Orton wrote a denial to his sister Markie. "Do not believe that I am a spy," he wrote, "with my dying breath I deny the charge."

By this time, the end was close at hand. Coulling's book provides the final details. "As infantry and cavalry troops stood at attention, Orton Williams and Walter Peter were escorted to the scaffold. By nine-thirty in the morning of June 9, 1863, it was all over. Orton was dead at the age of twenty-four."

While the news came as a blow to the Lees, especially Agnes, they did have other worries on their collective mind. For one, Rooney Lee had been wounded in the cavalry battle at Brandy Station, Virginia, that June 9, the very day of Orton's death. In just seventeen days, he would be snatched up, convalescent bed and all, at wife Charlotte's Hickory Hill plantation and carried into captivity by a Union raiding party. About that time also, R. E. Lee was leading his Army of Northern Virginia northward through Maryland for his fateful confrontation with Union forces at a small town in Pennsylvania known as Gettysburg.

Despite such distractions, neither the Southern nor the Northern press were quite ready to drop the mystery story attending Orton's capture and death. Newspapers on both sides of the Mason-Dixon Line openly wondered what Orton's mission possibly could have been. In the North, too, there were questions as to the harsh treatment he and his cousin received. A Detroit reporter wrote, incidentally, that he had interviewed the two Confederates and found Orton to be "one of the most intellectual and accomplished men that I have ever known." In the South, the *Richmond Examiner,* for one, called the hanging episode outright "murder."

The Lincoln administration's secretary of war, Edwin Stanton, finally was moved to draft and to make public a telegram to General Rosecrans saying, "Your prompt action [in the Orton Williams affair] is approved."

Agnes, quite naturally, had been staggered to hear of her once-dear Orton's fate. Charlotte Wickham Lee's young brother Harry later said it was a shock "from which she never recovered." He also said, "She became very quiet and pensive in after life. I do not recall hearing her laugh, and when she smiled it seemed to me that she was looking beyond."

The next Christmas passed sadly, and soon after, Agnes received a letter from Markie recalling their happier times at Arlington with Orton . . . but also revealing another woman's claim that she and Orton had become engaged shortly before his death.

"Markie and her brother Lawrence had met the woman after Orton's death and were convinced that she was 'deranged,'" wrote Mary Coulling. They did believe she cared for Orton but, inexplicably, at the time of the engagement, "she was married to another man who subsequently was killed in action."

Poor Agnes! Still another blow, another mystery about Orton.

In the years after the Civil War, his drumhead trial and execution by hanging were just added seeds of bitterness for the daughter of the defeated Confederacy's best-known general. When the Lees moved to Lexington, Virginia, and the campus of tiny Washington College (today's Washington and Lee University), Agnes "was consistently friendly and kind," wrote Coulling, "but to many young men she seemed aloof and reserved." Young Harry Wickham, now a frequent visitor at college president Lee's home, "was convinced she was still grieving over the lost Orton Williams."

And most likely so. Only a few years later, in 1873, she lay on her deathbed—due to "a debilitating intestinal disorder." Only thirty-two years in age, she said, "I never cared to live long, I am weary of life."

In her final hours she roused herself at one point to order her Bible given to Markie. "You know," she said, "Orton gave it to me." Those were among her very last words.

First Medals of Honor

THE KNOCK OFTEN HEARD ABOUT Medals of Honor given out for gallant service in the Civil War is that the service wasn't all that remarkably gallant after all . . . that the medal sometimes was handed out wholesale and even indiscriminately.

In some instances, reviewed later, that proved to be the case. Even from the citations that survived that official review of 1916–17 you cannot always tell what the honored recipient did to deserve the Nation's top award for bravery. Irish-born Sgt. Maj. Augustus Barry, Sixteenth U.S. Infantry, for instance, was honored in 1870 for "gallantry in various actions during the rebellion." No further detail furnished.

Then, too, English-born Pvt. Philip Baybutt, Company A, Second Massachusetts Cavalry, was vaguely cited for "capture of flag," no other explanation, except to say the action took place September 24, 1864, at Luray, Virginia.

Other citations, however, are chock full of convincing detail, the very kind of detail that might well have qualified their recipients for the medal under the most stringent criteria imposed by the U.S. armed forces of today.

Sailors Gurdon H. Barter of Williamsburgh, New York, and David L. Bass, a native of Ireland, both from the USS *Minnesota* and both taking part in the amphibious assault on Fort Fisher, North Carolina, in January 1865, were honored for going ashore with the troops, then staying with the remnants of their landing party even after two-thirds of their companions "became seized with panic and retreated on the run." Barter and Bass stayed with the remaining one-third of the landing party until after dark, at which time "it came safely away, bringing its wounded, its arms, and its colors."

If supply officers sometimes are vulnerable to bad jokes about their lack of risk, that wasn't the case with Lt. Col. Richard N. Batchelder of Manchester, New Hampshire, chief quartermaster officer for the U.S. Second Corps. He won the medal for successfully moving his supply trains on "a continuous day-and-night march" in northern Virginia October 13 to October 15, 1863, without military escort and while under attack. Arming his teamsters, says his citation, Colonel Batchelder bulled his way through, "against heavy odds" and "without the loss of a wagon."

It was during the Civil War, not so incidentally, that the medal was created and first bestowed upon brave soldiers and sailors—all Union of course. While the first Medal of Honor created by act of Congress was intended for enlisted men of the navy and Marine Corps, the army soon was allowed to follow suit . . . and in fact was able to claim the first official Medals of Honor actually bestowed. No longer restricted to enlisted men only, those went to the nineteen Union raiders, all volunteers, who plunged deep into the Confederacy in April 1862 to sabotage its rail lines, commandeered the locomotive *General* at Big Shanty, Georgia, then led their pursuers on the famous, ninety-mile Great Locomotive Chase.

All nineteen raiders, disguised as civilians, were captured, and eight were executed. Almost a year later, in March 1863, six raiders who had been paroled from Southern captivity were presented the first Medals of Honor ever bestowed on American fighting men or women. Edwin Stanton, the secretary of war, personally presented the medals in a ceremony held in Washington. The remaining thirteen medals later were awarded to the other raiders, some, of course, posthumously.

In a development right afterward that temporarily cast an unwelcome shadow upon the medal's reputation, Lincoln himself authorized presentation of the medal to any man of the Twenty-seventh Maine Volunteer Infantry willing to reenlist after the regiment's enlistment expired in June 1863. Lincoln's intent was to keep the regiment available for duty, and 309 men did reenlist, whether in response to his inducement or for other reasons.

Still, even in the award's early, trial period, simply reenlisting wasn't sufficient reason to earn a Medal of Honor. Then, too, to make matters worse, a clerical error "awarded" the medal to the men of the Twenty-seventh Maine who actually had turned their backs on Lincoln and gone home in defiance of his inducement to stay and fight. The Twenty-seventh Maine's 864 Medals of Honor, as matters turned out, made up the bulk of the 910 medal awards that were officially nullified in 1917 by a review board composed of five general-rank officers.

Among the forty-six additional Civil War participants stripped of their medals, incidentally, were one William F. "Buffalo Bill" Cody and Dr. Mary Walker, a woman who had served as a surgeon in the field and suffered four months of captivity in the Confederate capital of Richmond. She went to her grave protesting the loss of her medal . . . and in 1977, far too late to be of any comfort to her personally, her award was restored by order of Clifford Alexander, secretary of the army.

As for those Civil War participants allowed to keep their Medals of Honor, the Union army could claim 1,200 of them, the navy 310, and the marines 17, for a total of 1,527.

Would all those citations stand up to today's officially prescribed scrutiny? In some of the more vaguely stated actions, perhaps not, unless supporting documentation were available and convincing. In many other cases, however, judging by the actions described in the citations, it would seem difficult to deny the recipient's eligibility. A few examples:

• Sgt. George Banks, Fifteenth Indiana Infantry, twice wounded, nonetheless was the first color-bearer of eight in his brigade to plant a flag on the enemy works at Missionary Ridge, Tennessee, on November 25, 1863. Likewise, Sgt. Nathaniel Barker, Eleventh New Hampshire Infantry, grabbed up and carried the two flags of his regiment throughout the battle of Spotsylvania, Virginia, in May 1864 after six other regimental color-bearers were killed.

• Then, too, Sgt. Thomas Plunkett, Twenty-first Massachusetts Infantry, was cited because he seized the regimental colors from a felled bearer at Fredericksburg, Virginia, on December 11, 1862 "and bore them to the front where both his arms were carried off by a shell."

• Also based upon a soldier's seizure of the regimental colors, but a switch from the norm, was the medal awarded to Pvt. Solomon J. Hottenstine, 107th Pennsylvania Infantry, for taking up the *enemy's* fallen colors near Petersburg, Virginia, in August 1864, and with it tricking Rebel soldiers into following him past the nearby Union lines and into captivity.

• A general's leadership at the head of a charge at Fair Oaks, Virginia, June 1, 1862, by the Sixty-first New York Infantry cost him his right arm . . . but led to the Medal of Honor. He was Brig. Gen. Oliver O. Howard, a fire-eating abolitionist later destined to be routed at Chancellorsville by Stonewall Jackson; to be credited by Congress (some say wrongly) for selecting Cemetery Hill and Ridge as the key Union fallback position at Gettysburg; and to be noted for his role in establishing both Howard University in Washington, D.C., and Lincoln Memorial University in Harrogate, Tennessee.

• A sailor awarded the medal was Third Class Boy George Hollat of New York, cited for his steadfast courage when his navy ship the *Varuna* attacked Forts Jackson and St. Phillip on the Mississippi River, April 24, 1862. He stayed at his battle station, "despite extremely heavy fire and the ramming of the *Varuna* by the rebel ship *Morgan,* continuing his efforts until his ship, repeatedly holed and fatally damaged, was beached and sunk," his citation says.

• One of the most colorful—and detailed—of all the Civil War citations for the Medal of Honor describes the actions of Sgt. Maj. William B. Hincks, Fourteenth Connecticut Infantry, at the crest of Cemetery Ridge, the third and crucial day of battle at Gettysburg, July 3, 1863. "During the highwater mark of Pickett's charge," the citation says, "the colors of the 14th Tenn., C. S. A. [Fourteenth Tennessee, Confederate States of America, same number as that assigned to Hincks's own Connecticut regiment] were planted 50 yards in front of the center of Sgt. Maj. Hinck's regiment. There were no Confederates standing near it but several were lying down around it. Upon a call for volunteers . . . to capture this flag, this soldier and two others leaped to the wall. One companion was instantly shot. Sgt. Maj. Hincks outran his remaining companion running straight and swift for the colors amid a storm of shot. Swinging his saber over the prostrate Confederates and uttering a terrific yell, he seized the flag and hastily returned to his lines. The 14th Tenn. carried 12 battle honors on its flag. The devotion to duty shown by Sgt. Maj. Hincks gave encouragement to many of his comrades at a crucial moment of the battle."

Additional notes: While each side in the Civil War could claim its share of heroes, only the Union offered its soldiers and sailors a Medal of Honor. The Sons of Confederate Veterans in recent years has sought to make up for the South's lack of a parallel award by establishing an after-the-fact Confederate Medal of Honor intended to give belated recognition to the Confederacy's most deserving heroes.

How Some Died

THE GLORY OF WAR? Some glory. Just consider how some participants died in the American Civil War.

• At the battle of Big Bethel, Virginia, Union Maj. Theodore Winthrop, a promising author, climbing to the top of a fence to urge his men on . . . was shot through the heart.

• North Carolina Pvt. Henry L. Wyatt, one of the very first Confederate soldiers killed in the Civil War . . . also at Big Bethel, was shot in the forehead while moving ahead of the Rebel line to clear out Union sharpshooters.

• Confederate Capt. Dabney Carr Harrison, Fifty-sixth Virginia, a Presbyterian minister in civilian life and former chaplain at the University of Virginia, was fatally shot in the right lung during the battle of Fort Donelson, Tennessee. (Also from the Fifty-sixth Virginia, a bizarre and painful wound . . . Lt. Col. Philip Peyton Slaughter was leading a bayonet charge in the battle of Gaines's Mill, Virginia, when a shell shattered his field glasses and drove pieces into his groin. He survived the war but never fought again and died young, at age fifty-four.)

• On the Union side, leading his brigade at one of the many battles over control of Winchester, Virginia, Brig. Gen. David Allen Russell fell on the spot after a shell fragment entered his heart. Lingering for a day after a fatal wound, on the other hand, was Brig. Gen. William Price Sanders, a Union cavalryman. Wounded while dismounted in the battle of Knoxville, Tennessee, he was carried to the bridal suite in the city's Lamar Hotel, where he died the next day.

• Then, too, there was no warning for Confederate Brig. Gen. Lewis Henry Little as he sat on his horse at the battle of Iuka, Mississippi, talking with the ranking Rebel general on the scene, Sterling Price, and two other generals. Quite unexpectedly, out of the Union ranks some distance away, came a ball that coursed beneath Price's arm and hit Little in the forehead. He was killed instantly. Buried by torchlight that night in a nearby garden, his remains were later permanently interred in his native Baltimore.

• On the Confederate side also, the youngest West Point graduate to attain the rank of major general was Stephen Dodson Ramseur, shot through both lungs at Cedar Creek, Virginia . . . and taken prisoner. At Phil Sheridan's Belle Grove headquarters the next morning he died among the enemy. No, not quite . . . make that among friends—classmates from his West Point days.

• Perhaps Confederate Brig. Gen. Martin Edwin Green had to take a quick look at the work of Union sappers sixty yards from his Rebel parapet at Vicksburg, perhaps not. In any case, it was a Union sharp-shooter who took down this soldier with a rifle ball to the head.

And, yes, it is a grim roll call. As Sherman so famously indicated, war is hell. As he might also have said, however, war is no respecter of any person, any rank, any exalted station in life . . . not even an Episcopal bishop such as Confederate Lt. Gen. Leonidas Polk, killed by cannon fire at Pine Mountain, Georgia, outside Atlanta. Nor is war the least bit sympathetic to the throbs of the human heart. Ramseur learned only the night before his death in friendly captivity that he was a father. More ironic you might say, fellow West Pointer John Pegram, a Confederate brigadier at an early age, was married at a Richmond church in January 1865. Three weeks later, he was buried after services at the same church, the victim of a musket ball that tore into his chest at Hatcher's Run, Virginia.

• William Dorsey Pender . . . remember him? Brilliant young Confederate major general who led well at Seven Pines, the Seven Days', and Chancellorsville, only to suffer a leg wound from a flying shell fragment at Gettysburg. Followed by infection. Followed by amputation. Followed by death sixteen days after he was hit.

• A Rebel who went to his death as the result of a careless personal mistake was Brig. Gen. Felix Kirk Zollicoffer, who inadvertently rode his horse into the midst of an advance Yankee line at Mill Springs, Kentucky. He was killed by an entire volley of rifle fire.

• Speaking of volleys, in real battles and even some skirmishes the air was filled with flying pieces of metal, some light, some heavy, but all potentially lethal. In the unusually fierce November 1864 battle of Franklin, Tennessee, thousands of men were struck and killed by those metal bits. Among the dead were six Confederate generals. Yes, six, and, if you harken to local historian Thomas Cartwright, no wonder. "It was said that when a cannon fired here, you'd hear two sounds: first the firing of the cannon, then the snapping of bones. One Confederate officer said, 'How could a just God allow this to happen to us?'"

One of the generals killed was the popular, Irish-born Patrick Cleburne. After losing two horses to the shot and shell whizzing through the air at Franklin, he was seeking a third mount when struck below the heart. He was killed instantly.

Another of the generals felled at Franklin was States Rights Gist, "shot first in the thigh and then through a lung," reported battleground visitor John Dunlap in the *Washington Times* of November 27, 1999. Dunlap wrote after touring Civil War battlefields in search of the paths his great-grandfather, Confederate Col. John Calhoun Dunlap, had followed as a Civil War participant.

Shot in the foot earlier in the war, Colonel Dunlap was severely wounded at Franklin—serving in Gist's brigade. He was shot in the neck, back, and leg but somehow survived.

Franklin was such a vicious fight, local historian Cartwright told the colonel's descendant, "men were clubbing, clawing, stabbing, stomping, shooting, and biting each other in hand-to-hand combat."

Cartwright, director of the Carter House Museum at Franklin, pointed to a nearby field. The Confederates back in 1864 marched across the field, "right toward us here at Carter House," he said. "The Rebel soldiers getting ready to go across the field called it 'The Valley of Death' before they even fired the first shots, since they knew they were on a suicide march."

On that march, Confederate Colonel Dunlap's Forty-sixth Georgia Infantry "was caught in fire that came from three directions—front, left and right," wrote Dunlap after his visit. "It was a hellish place to be, and he quickly fell wounded."

• Meanwhile, disease also was no respecter of persons. A wealthy planter, a former congressman in the Texas Republic and then Texas state senator, Confederate Brig. Gen. Joseph Lewis Hogg lived long enough to sire a son, James Stephen Hogg, who one day would sit as governor of Texas . . . but Confederate General Hogg did not live long enough even to don a Confederate uniform. He died of dysentery soon after reporting with his men to Corinth, Mississippi.

And again, yes, this is a *long* and grim roll call of the dead . . . .and yet it is only a minute fraction of the more than 623,000 men who died in the Civil War. Soldiers not only shot by minié ball or mowed down by cannon fire, but sailors who drowned at sea or were scalded to death by exploding boilers, soldiers crushed to death by falling horses, men badly wounded then burned where they lay by brushfires, as happened in the battle of the Wilderness.

• No way was a good way, but William Yarnel Slack, another Rebel brigadier, must have thought, *Oh no, not again!* because . . . after recovering from one severe gunshot wound to the hip in one battle, in another battle he was struck in the same hip, only an inch away from his first difficult wound. This time, twice moved about to avoid capture by the Yankees, he failed to recover and died two weeks later.

• But then . . . when is war ever fair? Call war sometimes even-handed . . . and yet so often random in its punishment. Consider the day, September 17, 1862, that seventy or so girls, fourteen to sixteen in age, became casualties of the war. And no, they were *not* frontline Union soldiers fighting at Antietam that same day to blunt Lee's first thrust out of Virginia and into the North. 'Course not! They and a few teenage boys all died in Pittsburgh when a horse's iron shoe—or perhaps a fragment of iron from a wagon wheel—struck the stone pavement outside a large building . . . struck stone in such a way as to create a spark, which in turn ignited loose gunpowder on the same cobbled pavement and thus blew up the entire building, an arsenal producing ammunition for the Union armies.

Killed in the three explosions that destroyed the Allegheny arsenal's main laboratory structure were a total of seventy-eight persons, most of them teenage girls busy making bullet molds and small-arms cartridges in tiny crowded rooms.

Ironically, the battle fought at Antietam Creek near Sharpsburg and South Mountain, Maryland, on that same date produced the worst single day's combined casualty toll, North and South, of the entire Civil War . . . while to the north, the triple explosions at the Pittsburgh arsenal ranked as the worst civilian accident of the war period.

A similar arsenal explosion occurred in the South, killing thirty girls and young women in Richmond, Virginia, on Friday, March 13, 1863. Still another munitions mishap occurred in the North on June 17, 1864, in Washington, D.C., and killed twenty-one young women.

• Finally, and again on the Union side of the grim ledger, Irish-born Brig. Gen. Thomas Alfred Smyth had the misfortune to become a historical footnote—as the last of the Union's 583 generals to die. In April 1865 the Federals were close behind Lee's shattered Army of Northern Virginia as it staggered toward Appomattox after the fall of Petersburg and Richmond. On a skirmish line near Farmville, Smyth was shot through the mouth by a Confederate sharpshooter. One of his cervical vertebrae shattered by the deadly ball, Smyth lived for another two days before dying on April 9, 1865, the same day as Lee's surrender.

☆ ☆ ☆

Additional note: While the Union lost more men, overall, to the Civil War than did the Confederacy, the Confederacy lost more generals both in total number and in ratio to the total number serving than did the Union. Stated another way, the Union saw 47 of its 583 generals killed or fatally wounded in action, while the South lost 77 of its 425 generals to combat.

Percentage-wise, that meant the Union lost 8 percent of its generals to combat, while the Confederacy's percentage loss was a much greater 18 percent. The two sides were close together in the number lost to disease: 18 percent for the Union, 15 percent for the Confederacy, but other comparative figures show how desperately short of qualified leaders the South was compared to the North. Or, stated in reverse, how rich the North was in its supply of generals.

Just consider: The North allowed 110 of its general officers to resign at one time or another during the war, compared to the South's 19. Further, 6 Northerners were allowed to retire to 1 Southerner. Finally, 22 Northern appointments to general's rank were canceled, compared to just 5 such cancellations in the Confederacy.

Guard Boat Going Out

HE BEGAN LIFE AS A slave, became a Civil War hero, served several terms in the U.S. Congress, and for a time wore the stars of a major general in the South Carolina state militia. Among his efforts as a nineteenth-century congressman, he supported legislation guaranteeing equal accommodations for blacks and whites on public conveyances.

In twentieth-century terms, that would mean nobody, black or white, would be relegated to the back of the bus.

South Carolina's Robert Smalls won all those achievements and many others, starting with a spectacular escape launched in Charleston Harbor.

It is nighttime, May 12, 1862 . . . down at Southern Wharf, hard by the headquarters of Confederate Brig. Gen. Roswell S. Ripley,

Robert Smalls, hired-out slave and pilot of a Confederate dispatch boat at Charleston . . . until he commandeered his craft and bolted for freedom with a party of fellow slaves.

Charleston District army commander, seven dark figures pass, one at a time, along the dock to the berth of Ripley's dispatch boat, the *Planter.*

Reputed to be the fastest vessel moored at Charleston, she is a twin-engine steamer 147 feet in length. Her skipper is C. J. Relyea, and normally his pilot is a "hired-out" slave—Robert Smalls. Raised in the area of nearby Beaufort, Smalls belongs to one Henry McKee but works for others, with his "salary" going to his owner.

On this night of May 12, Relyea is *not* among the seven men going aboard the *Planter* one by one, but Smalls is . . . as the leader in this bold attempt at escape from bondage.

Since the *Planter* normally comes and goes at various times of day and night, the sentries at General Ripley's headquarters pay little attention to the men openly, casually, walking to the vessel on Southern Wharf. At about 3 A.M., all his cohorts now aboard, Smalls passes the word to fire up the boilers. At 3:30 or so the lines are cast off and the inland steamer slips into the night—quite visible, actually, in the bright moonlight. Still, the closest sentry has no reason to question the vessel's leave-taking. Surely her skipper is aboard, surely her black deckhands and firemen all are performing their normal duties under his supervision.

Surely not, though, on this occasion!

Passing upriver, the *Planter* makes an unusual stop . . . by the side of the steamer *Etowah.* Here, oddly enough, more mysterious figures have been waiting. With barely suppressed excitement, they now step aboard the speedy *Planter,* too. The new group consists of another male slave plus the wives and children of various of the remaining men intent upon escaping from slavery.

But now, the *Planter* steaming onward in earnest . . . now comes the most crucial moment for them all.

To reach safety out there, with the Federal fleet patrolling just beyond the bar, the *Planter* and her consignment of escaping slaves must slide by Fort Sumter and its guns without provoking dangerous inquiry. A full-speed dash in the semidarkness would be foolhardy, Smalls knows—those guns can come to bear all too quickly, can reach out and pummel his little steamer before it can race out of range. No, far better to appear normal. Better to approach the fort in the confusing half-light of approaching dawn boldly, at deliberate speed.

It won't be at all unusual for the steamer to pass the harbor fortress, since the dispatch boat often follows the same course on the way to Morris Island. Normally she would proceed some distance past Fort Sumter, then turn in the direction of Morris Island and its fortifications.

As a further stratagem to make the *Planter's* mission appear all the more routine, Smalls has donned Captain Relyea's well-known and distinctive hat. From a distance the sentries probably won't be able to tell that the face beneath is black instead of white.

At least, that is the hope of Smalls and his fellow slaves. A fervent hope, too. To be captured now, even to become unnerved and voluntarily go back, would be equally disastrous for them all, especially their ringleader, Robert Smalls.

Onlookers did not realize the guardboat Planter, *with slave Robert Smalls at the helm, was making a dash for the line of Federal warships blockading the entrance to Charleston Harbor.*

He now is standing in full view of the sentries as the steamer draws abreast of Fort Sumter. There is the sudden shriek of a whistle . . . it could be startling to the crowd aboard the *Planter,* except that Smalls himself has signaled with the whistle. Perfectly normal. In fact, absolutely required if the *Planter* is to appear on a normal outing.

At the fort, the whistle, the sight of the small steamer, indeed does stir up activity. A sentinel on the parapet alerts the corporal of the guard. But it is a perfectly normal notice that is taken: guard boat going out. And now the same information is passed to the officer of the day. No action is taken. None appears needed, since it is not unusual for the "guard boat" to pass by at that hour.

The *Planter* plows ahead now as the water roughens, then reaches the turning point for Morris Island.

But now . . . oh-oh, what's this? Surely, they are wondering back at Fort Sumter. The general's dispatch boat, the guard boat, is plowing onward *without* turning. She's pointed straight ahead, toward the sea . . . toward the line of blockading Federal ships out there. And yes, she is *bolting* for the sea, it now appears . . . charging ahead at full speed.

And now look, so distant, too, she's taken down her Confederate Stars and Bars and raised a makeshift flag of white, an ordinary sheet!

This is far from normal.

Among the Federal vessels beyond the bar, meanwhile, at least one noticing the inland steamer's curious approach has called the crew to quarters and is prepared to open fire.

But no, wait! That white flag of truce or surrender is clear to see.

A boarding crew is sent over the waves to investigate.

Then comes discovery of the escape of Robert Smalls and fifteen fellow slaves.

End of story? Not really . . . the *Planter,* highly useful for cruising coastal waters because of her shallow draft, was a valuable acquisition for the Union forces blockading and soon besieging the Charleston area. Also a prized gain for the Union, a painful loss for the Confederacy, was Robert Smalls himself. First, he was a font of intelligence about the disposition—and in some aspects, the intent—of Confederate forces in the Charleston area. Then, too, in no time at all, he was serving as a highly knowledgeable pilot aboard the same *Planter* again. No, make that captain! And all on behalf of the Union, of course.

Came the end of the war, and the *Planter* was sold in Baltimore. Back in South Carolina, now under Reconstruction, Smalls was a natural for politics. Explained the bicentennial booklet *The Civil War at Charleston*: "The *Planter* episode had made him the darling of the Northern conquerors. His moderate views and kindness toward the family of his former master made him, to the Southern whites, the least objectionable of the freedmen entering politics. Moreover, the fact that he was the pet of the Yankees led other former slaves to believe he was the smartest Negro in the state. These were an unbeatable combination during the Reconstruction era."

In short order, Smalls served as a delegate to the state Constitutional Convention of 1868, then, the same year, won a two-year term in the South Carolina House of Representatives. At the end of that time, he moved on to the state senate and served there through the session of 1874.

Now Smalls, a slave just twelve years earlier, was elected to the U.S. House—he would serve there from 1875 to 1887, except for a two-year gap, 1880–81.

According to the Charleston centennial booklet, his career in Congress was notable for thwarted ambitions: "His most important speeches were attacks on the election tactics of South Carolina Democrats and in support of a bill to provide equal accommodations for the races on interstate public conveyances. He also made an unsuccessful attempt to have $30,000 voted to him as additional compensation for the *Planter* abduction."

Before going to Congress, Smalls also squeezed in twelve years (1865 to 1877) as a Reconstruction-era leader of the state militia. A major general before leaving that activity, Smalls during the same period was "a conspicuous figure" at the Republican National Conventions of 1872 and 1876. As still another entry for his résumé, Smalls was appointed collector of customs for the port of Beaufort in 1888—he would hold that job on and off until 1913.

In the interim, he suffered a disappointment especially galling for a former slave who had achieved so much, who had made such gains for himself and his race—as a delegate to the state Constitutional Convention of 1895, "he made a vain effort to prevent the disenfranchisement of members of his race." Good for some, bad for others, Reconstruction was over.

Nonetheless, reported Warren Ripley in the centennial booklet, "the last twenty years of his life were spent quietly at Beaufort, where he apparently enjoyed the confidence of both races. He died in February 1915 at the age of seventy-six."

Travels of a Southern Lady

THE SHACKLIKE CABIN GREETING Sara Rice Pryor in Virginia one day late in the Civil War as her latest wartime "home" was so tumbledown, so long unused, that the wasps had to be smoked out before she and her children could move in.

The former general's wife just didn't have many other options. And no surprise, either. In the South during the Civil War, women and children often had to struggle along with few of life's basic necessities, to cope with problems of comfort, possibly even survival, that would have been totally foreign to their counterparts in the North.

Their would-be country, after all, was cut in two after July 1863, was invaded (or at least threatened with invasion) from all quarters, was strewn with battlegrounds (more than two thousand in Virginia alone), was largely cut off from supply by sea . . . for four long years was a doormat for restless armies marching back and forth on Southern soil.

If the menfolk gone off to fight the war's battles had to grapple with pure survival, so did their families at home . . . in terms of food and a roof over their heads. They often found themselves living in territory occupied by the enemy, or they had to flee their homes, permanent or temporary, to avoid occupation rule.

On a higher level, Robert E. Lee's wife, Mary Custis Lee, once was caught behind the Federal lines as Union forces moved up the York and Mattaponi Rivers toward Richmond. In a gentlemanly gesture by Union commander George B. McClellan, she was allowed to pass through the lines in order to take up residence in Richmond—McClellan's campaign goal, ironically.

More famously, Union forces in the meantime had taken over the Lee family's Arlington estate overlooking Washington from the southern banks of the Potomac River. They soon turned it into a hospital then a burial ground. The Lees never got it back, and today their once happy home is the focal point of Arlington National Cemetery.

Like so many other Southern women financially able to keep on the move, the arthritic Mrs. Lee visited various family estates, relatives, friends, even a country spa in the mountains, and made a home in Richmond after leaving Arlington House to the Yankees. Sara Pryor, wife of former congressman Roger Pryor, younger and more aggressive in her intents, was even more often on the move during the war.

She started out planning to be with her husband in the field. "I steadily withstood the entreaties of my friends and determined to follow my husband's regiment through the war," she wrote later. "I did not ask his permission. I would give no trouble. I should be only a help to his sick men and his wounded."

With her husband appointed colonel of the Third Virginia Infantry and posted to Norfolk and then Smithfield, Virginia, she busied herself rounding up a field stove, bedding tick, blankets, and a camp chest with tin utensils. She figured they could "always" obtain a tent from his quartermaster officer. She hardly had arrived in Smithfield, however, before her husband was off to serve in the Confederate Congress in Richmond.

"Installed," as she put it, in a comfy private home with her children, she could only wait until he returned. She thus had been left alone, she wrote, not as "child" of the regiment but as a regimental "mother" hearing every day "from all the sick men in winter quarters and ministering to them according to my ability."

Still, Smithfield was an idyll that would end all too soon, as events turned out. She one day received her colonel's "peremptory" order to leave town before daybreak the next morning. "My colonel had returned suddenly," she explained later in her memoir *My Day: Reminiscences of a Long Life*. "When I, in an open wagon, was on my way next morning at sunrise to the nearest [railroad] depot, he and his men were *en route* to the peninsula." Specifically, in early May 1862, to the battle of Williamsburg, Virginia.

While Pryor was busy earning plaudits—and promotion to brigadier general—at Williamsburg, Sara had repaired to the Exchange Hotel in Richmond—"that I might be near headquarters and thus learn the earliest tidings from the peninsula."

She read about his apparent promotion in local newspapers but wasn't sure it was true until they, together again, attended a soiree given by Confederate President Jefferson Davis and his wife, Varina, at the Spotswood Hotel.

As recalled by Sara Pryor, in Richmond, this is the conversation in the highest political circles of the wartime capital of the Confederacy early in the war:

> A crowd gathered before the Exchange to congratulate my husband, and learning that he had gone to the Spotswood, repaired thither, and with shouts and cheers called him out for a speech. This was very embarrassing, and he fled to a corner of the drawing room and hid behind a screen of plants. I was standing near the President, trying to hold his attention by remarks on the weather and kindred subjects of a thrilling nature, when a voice from the street called out: "Pryor! *General* Pryor!" I could endure the suspense no longer, and asked tremblingly, "Is it true, Mr. President?" Mr. Davis looked at me with a benevolent smile and said, "I have no reason, madam, to doubt it, except that I saw it this morning in the papers," and Mrs. Davis at once summoned the bashful colonel: "What are you doing lying there *perdu* behind the geraniums? Come out and take your honors."

But Richmond itself soon had to tremble—a bit—at General McClellan's slow, almost majestic approach up the peninsula toward the capital city. Now came the battles of Fair Oaks, Mechanicsville, Gaines's Mill, Frazier's Farm, Malvern Hill, with *General* Pryor fully engaged in each . . . with his wife, Sara, still in Richmond, now fully engaged in nursing the wounded. "Every linen garment I possessed, except one change, every garment of cotton fabric, all my table-linen, all my bed-linen, even the chintz covers for furniture—all were torn into strips and rolled into bandages for the soldiers' wounds."

Then came the day, the fight over and McClellan withdrawing his mighty host, that "a gray, haggard, dust-covered soldier entered my room, and throwing himself upon the couch, gave way to the anguish of his heart—'My men! My men! They are almost all dead!'"

And to think, still more battles, many more months of war, yet to come!

Sara Pryor, meanwhile, had nothing but praise for her fellow women of Richmond . . . and for the people she knew as slaves. The women she praised for "heroic fortitude and devotion." She described them as "delicate, beautiful" and said, "Not once did they spare themselves, or complain, or evince weakness, or give way to despair."

As for the blacks, "One beautiful memory is of the unfailing kindness and loyalty of the negroes. In the hospitals, in the camps, in our own houses, they faithfully sympathized with us and helped us."

The fighting outside Richmond soon was followed by Second Manassas (Bull Run), up in northern Virginia, and that major battle was succeeded by Lee's incursion into Maryland, a bold advance producing the battle of Antietam. General Pryor was on hand for both conflicts.

Left to her own devices, Sara Pryor repaired to "a little summer resort, 'Coyners,' in the Blue Ridge Mountains on the line of the railroad." There she was in the company of recently wounded Confederate Maj. Gen. Arnold Elzey and his wife, his doctor, his young aide, a Captain Contee, and the latter's new bride—"who had crossed the Potomac in an open boat to join him and redeem her pledge to marry him."

Also on hand were Brig. Gen. and Mrs. Louis Trezevant Wigfall and their daughter, plus Dolly Morgan Hill, wife of Maj. Gen. A. P. Hill and sister of Brig. Gen. John Hunt Morgan. The setting apparently was idyllic—

"The small hotel spanned a little green valley at its head, and stretching behind was a velvet strip of green, a spring and rivulet in the midst, and a mountain ridge on either side. I had a tiny cottage with windows that opened against the side of the hill (or mountain), and lying on my bed at night, the moon and stars, as they rose above me, seemed so near I could have stretched a long arm and picked them off the hilltop!"

But it wasn't paradise after all. Not only did thoughts (and fears) of the distant war intrude inescapably, but "the vexed questions of precedence, relative importance, rankled in the bosoms of the distinguished ladies in the hotel," wrote Sara Pryor years later. "One after another would come out to me: 'I'd like to know *who* this Maryland woman is that she gives herself such airs'; or, 'How much longer do you think I'll stand Dolly Morgan? Why, she treats me as though she were the Queen of Sheba.'"

To such complaints, Sara later asserted, perhaps with tongue in cheek, "I could only reply with becoming meekness: 'I'm sure I don't know! I'm only a brigadier, you know—the rest of you are major-generals—I'm not competent to judge.'"

As another intrusion, typical of the Civil War era, her son, "my little Roger," fell desperately ill with typhoid . . . "and for many days I despaired of his life."

Roger did recover, they moved on to Charlottesville, a prewar domicile for Sara and her husband, but there Little Roger suffered a relapse and "was ill unto death for many weeks."

Sara's husband, meanwhile, had been assigned to the Suffolk, Virginia, area. Once her son had recovered, Sara resolved to follow her husband with her camp gear and three of their boys. "General Pryor did not dream I would come to his camp," she wrote. He thought she would "find quarters among my friends," but the fact was, "I had now no home."

So off she went to the farthest point eastward on the rail line south of the James River that her train could go without running afoul of Union lines. She and her boys disembarked alone, at twilight, one house in sight beyond their small depot–post office, the surrounding land "a dead, bare level, as far as the eye could reach, and much, very much, of it lay under water."

They were near Dismal Swamp, in a region dotted with swamps, and the only noise to be heard was "a mighty concert" from millions of frogs. Her husband's encampment still some miles away, she found overnight lodging with the postmaster on the scene, "and the next day my general, at his invitation, made the house his headquarters."

As 1862 faded into 1863, Pryor's men fought sporadic battles in the Suffolk area, but he then was ordered back to Richmond on an indefinite basis, his next assignment unidentified. "As for myself," recalled his wife, "the camp chest and I and the little boys took [to] the road again. We wandered from place to place, and at last were taken as boarders, invited by a farmer, evidently without the consent of his wife. There I was, of all women made most miserable. The mistress of the house had not wanted 'refugees.' Everything combined to my discomfort and wretchedness, and my dear general, making me a flying visit from Richmond where he was detained on duty counselled me to go still farther into the interior to an old watering place, the 'Amelia Springs' kept by a dear Virginia woman, Mrs. Winn."

Unfortunately, as soon as Sara and her sons joined a number of "refugee women" at this latest resort, the boys came down with whooping cough "and were strictly quarantined in a cottage at the extreme edge of the grounds." By now it was summer, and she spent "long sultry nights" nursing her three boys through their agonizing coughing fits.

Sara had good company this time, but there was no happiness to speak of. "The little hotel and cottages were filled with agreeable women, but everything was so sad, there was no heart in any one for gayety of any kind." This, of course, was the summer of Confederate defeat at Gettysburg and Vicksburg.

Meanwhile, with that episode at last behind her, Sara Pryor decided to try living with her "people" back in Charlotte County, Virginia, where a fourth son, Theo, and two daughters had been staying all along, out of harm's way. "But repeated attempts to reach my country home resulted in failure. Marauding parties and guerrillas were flying all over the country . . . I positively *could* not venture alone."

That meant trying to find boarding rooms in some private home in her husband's hometown.

Not so easily done, it turned out. She reached the town in the autumn of 1863 "and wandered about for days seeking refuge in some household," she recalled. "Many of my old friends had left town. Strangers and refugees had rented the houses of some of these, while others were filled with the homeless among their own kindred. There was no room anywhere for me, and my small purse was growing so slender that I became anxious. Finally my brother-in-law offered me an overseer's house on one of his 'quarters.'"

It was "hardly better than a hovel," she found, and full of those wasps that had to be smoked out with a "smudge" before she and the children could move in. The "smoke-blackened" kitchen offered no windows, the first floor was made of loose planking with the dirt below visible through openings between the planks, and the single upstairs room was so small that when she pulled out the trundle bed from beneath the regular bed there would be no standing room left.

"This would be my winter home," Sara wrote. Then, too, just to make arrangements more interesting, she was in an advanced state of pregnancy!

She did have neighbors—a black woman named Mary and her husband who lived in a cabin nearby, a white couple who had a cow and sent her a "print" of butter and buttermilk biscuits every morning, plus occasional treats such as stewed dried peaches. The distaff half of the white couple, incidentally, Lucy Henry Laighton, was a grand-daughter of Patrick Henry. "Her talk was a tonic to me. It stimulated

With warring armies marching back and forth through their homeland, many a Southern family had to take to the roads as refugees carrying what they could of their personal belongings.

me to play my part with courage, seeing I had been deemed worthy, by the God who made me, to suffer in this sublime struggle for liberty."

As for help, "I had a stout little black girl, Julia, as my only servant; but Mary had a friend, a 'corn-field hand,' 'Anarchy,' who managed to help me at odd hours."

The days of fall faded, and a day or two before Christmas 1863, "a great snow-storm overtook us." The toy cupboard was basically bare, but her children made no complaint. Then, with the snow falling "thickly" on Christmas Eve, Sara herself "suddenly became very ill."

Mary's husband rode into town, three miles away, to fetch a doctor. "I was dreadfully ill when he arrived, and as he stood at the foot of my bed, I said to him: 'It doesn't matter much for me, Doctor! But my husband will be grateful if you keep me alive.'"

With that, she passed out . . . only to awaken hours later and find the doctor still at her bedside. And next to her on the bed, "a little warm bundle." It was her seventh child, a girl.

Urging her to summon all her strength and courage, the doctor said he couldn't come again, he had too many sick people to take care of. Her Julie had to leave, so she hired Anarchy to help her nights for

$25 a week. "But her hands, knotted by work in the fields, were too rough to touch my babe. I was propped up on pillows and dressed her myself, sometimes fainting when the exertion was over."

Sara was still in bed three weeks later, she wrote, "when one of my boys ran in, exclaiming in a frightened voice, 'Oh, Mamma, an old grey soldier is coming in!'"

Then the old gray soldier was in the room with her, looking at her, leaning on his saber. He was furious.

"Is this the reward my country gives me?"

It was, she realized at hearing his voice, her husband.

And he really was furious to find her in need in so many ways. In minutes he had sent off his manservant, a hired slave named John, to sell his horses and buy provisions with the money. Before the end of January he had moved his family into a real house in town—"one of my brother-in-law's houses having been vacated at the beginning of the year."

Roger Pryor still had to report for duty at his military headquarters, but at least he could take comfort in knowing his wife and children now were living under vastly improved conditions.

Neither Roger Pryor nor his wife, Sara, quite knew, of course, that in just a few months his hometown of Petersburg, Virginia, would fall under a Federal siege, complete with repeated artillery bombardment and lasting for nearly a year—the longest siege ever undergone by any American city.

Note to readers with Internet access: An electronic edition of Sara Rice Pryor's memoirs can be found on-line as part of the University of North Carolina's Web site, *Documenting the American South*—specifically at: http://metalab.unc.edu/docsouth/pryor/pryor.html. This is the source for the Sara Pryor materials in this book.

★ Part 4 ★
1862–63

High-Water Mark Reached

Perhaps . . . up to the double blow of Gettysburg-Vicksburg in the first days of July 1863, just perhaps some of the Confederacy's best hopes could have been realized, through victory on the battlefield, through negotiation from position of strength. When it was not to be, however, the fighting went on anyway.

His Bosom Still Warm

IT WAS AN EVENING AT Shiloh when the unauthorized visitor, a tall and handsome woman, appeared at Union Gen. U. S. Grant's headquarters on the Tennessee River. She had arrived just in time to see the general himself ride up with his staff . . . to see that he was unable to dismount from his horse because of an injured leg.

"He was helped off his horse and almost carried into his dispatch boat," said the onlooking woman later.

Under those circumstances, clearly enough, it wouldn't be easy to penetrate the Union commander's inner sanctum. "I was told that I could not enter. The General was ill."

That stopped her for a moment. But a moment only. Martha Canfield was absolutely determined, indeed desperate, to visit her husband, Lt. Col. Herman Canfield of the Seventy-second Ohio, just then lying wounded in a field hospital some distance downriver.

"I hesitated, but at last my intense anxiety to go to my husband overcame all else, and I boldly entered the boat. The orderly on guard said, 'You cannot enter,' but I passed on and entered."

Inside the cabin, she found doctors cutting off the boot on Grant's badly injured and swollen foot. They told her his horse had stepped on a loose rock while the general was reconnoitering the night before. Stumbling, the horse then fell heavily on Grant's leg.

Now Grant himself spoke up to explain a bit further. "He said he had not felt it all day until he went to dismount and was quite astonished to find his leg quite swollen and numb."

But Mrs. Canfield still had her husband foremost in mind. After all, she told Grant's wife, Julia, some days later, that's why she traveled to Shiloh in the first place. Despite the well-known orders "that no women should be allowed to come up the river," she had felt "impelled" to go.

"When I arrived," she told Julia Grant, "it was the evening of the first day of that dreadful two days' fight. I was told on my arrival at Shiloh—as I felt all the time it was so—that my husband, Colonel Canfield, was among the wounded and was then lying in a hospital I had passed a few miles down the river."

Emphatically warned she could not go to him, she was "in despair." It was just then that Grant's entourage appeared, with Grant unable to dismount from his horse. Now, inside the cabin of his dispatch boat, she pleaded with him for permission to see her husband— "General, he has been wounded and they tell me I cannot go to him. Do, for God's sake, allow me to proceed!"

Grant, the future commander of all the Union armies, didn't hesitate a moment, it appears from Julia Grant's version of the story, published in her posthumous *The Personal Memoirs of Julia Dent Grant* (1975). He could write his report on the day's military activities while she waited, he told Mrs. Canfield, and then she could travel downriver again on the dispatch boat carrying his report. She simply would have to wait about an hour while he composed the report.

"Paper and ink were brought," Martha Canfield related to Julia, "and the General sat rapidly writing, not once stopping until his report was finished; then folding, addressing and sealing it, he rapidly wrote an order to pass me on the dispatch boat, and that I should be permitted to visit the hospital in which my husband was, kindly bidding me goodbye with the hope that I would soon meet with Colonel Canfield. All this so kindly, so gently, so full of sympathy."

Sadly, it was a "tall, handsome" woman in widow's weeds, "clad in deepest mourning," who found Julia Grant some days later at the home of her father-in-law in Covington, Kentucky, across the Ohio River from Cincinnati. Martha's husband had died of his wounds.

She did reach the field hospital, and she did find him in his cot, she explained. "I was too late, too late," she sobbed before the general's wife. "I was conducted down the aisle between the cots in the hospital, and my escort paused and pointed to a cot, the blanket drawn up so as to cover the face. He was dead—my beloved, my noble husband. I thrust my hand into his bosom. It was still warm, but his great heart had ceased beating."

If only she had reached his side sooner, she sobbed. He might have lived—"my husband only needed the services of a kind nurse."

There and then she pledged before Julia Grant to devote her time for the rest of the war to the wounded. "And," added Grant's wife in her later memoir, "this gentle, lovely woman did go, and for three long, weary years devoted her entire time to the hospitals, nursing and caring for our wounded and sick soldiers."

Julia once again saw the widow Canfield when the triumphant Union armies marched up Pennsylvania Avenue in Washington in 1865 to celebrate their victory over the Confederacy. As the commander of those armies, Grant was in the reviewing stand, and beside him was his wife.

"How magnificent the marching! What shouts rent the air!" wrote Julia Grant later. And in the midst of it all, "when all this was passing," she saw Martha Canfield, "the soldier's widow, the soldiers' nurse."

Unmistakably, it was she . . . and yet she had changed since the days she appeared before first one Grant then the other back in 1862. "She, yes, she had grown older in these three long, weary years, for her hair showed threads of silver, her fair face and brow were furrowed and browned by care and exposure, her mourning robes looked worn and faded, as did the flag of her husband's old regiment as it passed on that glorious day up Pennsylvania Avenue."

Epilogue: Mrs. S. A. Martha Canfield also organized an orphanage in Memphis for black children. And finally, during U. S. Grant's presidential administration of eight years, she was given a job as a clerk in the Federal Bureau of Education.

Death of the Twenty-second Indiana

ALL'S FAIR IN LOVE AND WAR? How about in war, at dusk one day, going across the lines and telling the commander of the enemy troops that your men and his are all on the same side and, so, please quit firing? Then, as his guns fall silent up and down the line, going back to your side . . . and opening fire all up and down the line? With a real slaughter of the enemy's troops resulting?

It happened.

To be sure, it wasn't exactly planned that way, but such was the fortune of the officers and men of the hapless Twenty-second Indiana Infantry at Perryville, Kentucky, on October 8, 1862. By order of Confederate Maj. Gen. Leonidas Polk, a West Point graduate and an Episcopal bishop, it did happen . . . but largely by accident.

Here's the scenario: Late in the day, Confederate Brig. Gen. St. John Richardson Liddell was ordered to advance with his Arkansas brigade. Looking for the "hottest place" in the fighting just ahead, he moved right, toward the Yankee left. He encountered fellow Confederate Benjamin Cheatham, a major general, who excitedly told Liddell: "General, you can save the fight! Go on and save it!"

But it was so dark Liddell hesitated. "Come and show me your line," he requested. "It is now getting too late to distinguish colors clearly. I might fire by mistake upon your men."

"No," said Cheatham, "go on and save the fight. You will find the line."

Across the frontlines, meanwhile, Union Col. Michael Gooding had been ordered that afternoon to move up with his Thirtieth Brigade, Ninth Division, in support of Maj. Gen. Alexander McDowell McCook's fast-crumbling First Corps. Gooding's Thirtieth Brigade consisted of two Illinois regiments and the Twenty-second Indiana.

Gooding found McCook's men "badly cut up and retreating" while being "hotly pressed by the enemy." As his brigade joined in the fray, the lines surged back and forth. Late in the day, "Gooding ordered the 22nd Indiana to move in support of his Illinois troops on the left, where the fighting was the hottest," wrote Stuart W. Sanders, assistant director of the Perryville Battlefield Preservation Association, in the *Civil War Times* of October 1999.

On the Confederate side, Liddell was moving up his own brigade. "Suddenly," he later said, "we confronted a dark line hardly more than twenty-five paces off the crest of the elevation we were ascending."

As his men opened fire, the "dark line" started shooting back . . . but men also were yelling, "You are killing your friends!" and, "For God's sake, stop!"

Confused, Liddell ordered a halt to the firing. Just then General Polk rode up. Liddell said he was afraid his men had fired upon fellow Rebels.

"What a pity," said Polk. "I hope not. I don't think so. Let me go and see."

With that, General Polk told Liddell to open his ranks and let him ride through, which he did . . . all the way across a road and into the dark, silent line beyond.

There Polk somehow found a colonel in charge, "and demanded to know why he was firing upon friendly troops," wrote Sanders.

The colonel, though, wasn't quite ready to agree. "I don't think there can be any mistake about it," he said. "I'm sure they are the enemy." (How right he was, too!)

According to Sanders, Polk turned huffy. "Enemy!" he exclaimed, "Why I have only just left them myself."

In rapid-fire order he then said, "Cease fire, sir! . . . What is your name, sir?"

The Union officer identified himself as Squire I. Keith and then demanded for his part, "Who are you?"

This is when it dawned upon Polk he was in the enemy camp.

Deciding that in the dark his uniform might not be too obvious, Polk realized he could only try to "brazen it out." According to Sanders: "Polk shook his fist in the Yankee colonel's face and growled, 'I'll show you who I am. Cease firing at once!' Then, mustering all his courage, the general boldly rode down the Union line, shouting for the men to cease fire."

Amazingly, his bluff worked! Polk rode on, feeling, he admitted later, "a disagreeable sensation like screwing up my back" and "calculating how many bullets would lie between my shoulders every moment." But he safely reached some trees and galloped off . . . back to his own line.

There he told Liddell, "General, every mother's son of them are Yankees. I saw the colonel commanding the brigade [regiment, actually] and looked closely at the dark clothing of the men and am sure of not being mistaken."

Then came the fateful order. "You may get up and go at them."

And Liddell's men did. "A tremendous flash of musketry for the whole extent of the line for nearly one quarter of a mile in length followed," he later reported. "It continued for some fifteen minutes."

Colonel Keith's Yankees of the Twenty-second Indiana never knew what hit them. The Rebel muskets "blazed as one gun," Polk later said, adding, "I assure you, sir, that the slaughter of that Indiana regiment was the greatest I had ever seen in the war."

To be sure, the stunned Yankees fired back for a time, a short time. When their sporadic fire died out, the Confederates moved forward. Liddell reported finding that "the ground before my line was literally covered with the dead and dying."

Among the dead: Colonel Keith. Among the prisoners now taken: brigade commander Gooding. Of the Twenty-second Indiana's three hundred personnel, nearly two-thirds were dead, wounded, or captured—"mostly during the final encounter with Liddell's troops," wrote Sanders.

On a larger scale at Perryville, Braxton Bragg withdrew his outnumbered Confederate forces, giving the Union's Don Carlos Buell overall victory for the day. Still, there would be no victory parade for the Twenty-second Indiana.

Oddly, just before his troops were committed to the fight, Liddell had watched an advancing Union line, the familiar Stars and Stripes waving up front. The setting sun had caught the Union flag, the *American* flag, in such a way that it looked like "a flame of fire." Liddell had "the sudden misgiving that the Union flag would yet consume the Confederacy."

Waiting to go into action, he couldn't help but reflect that "our ancestors had given us this right by helping to make this flag for our own protection." He thought, too, "Perhaps it would have been better for us to fight for our rights in the Union under the same flag."

Just then, at 5:30 P.M., interrupting his ruminations, came the order to advance, the order that led to the decimation of the Twenty-second Indiana. Such is war. Not always fair.

Additional notes: Life, too, can be unfair. St. John Richardson Liddell, a plantation owner from Louisiana, survived the war only to be murdered five years after the hostilities ended. Having fought at Perryville, Murfreesboro, and Chickamauga, he also took part in the Red River campaign and the defense of Mobile Bay. He was captured at nearby

Fort Blakely on a historic day—April 9, 1865, the day that R. E. Lee surrendered his army at Appomattox.

"Some years later," wrote Ezra J. Warner in his *Generals in Gray,* "on February 14, 1870, differences between himself [Liddell] and a neighboring planter, Charles Jones, late lieutenant colonel of the 17th Louisiana Infantry, resulted in Liddell's death on board a Black River steamboat at the hands of Jones and his two sons."

Leonidas Polk, in the meantime, had *not* survived the Civil War—he was killed instantly by cannon fire at Pine Mountain, Georgia, not far from Atlanta, on June 14, 1864.

Benjamin Cheatham, destined to be accused by John Bell Hood of allowing Union Gen. John M. Schofield's trapped army to slip out of Spring Hill, Tennessee, and take up an unassailable position at neighboring Franklin, survived both the war and Hood's wrath. The Nashville native, sixty-five, died in 1886, after serving as head of the Tennessee state prison system and as postmaster of Nashville.

Of all the general-rank officers directly involved in the shattering experience of the Twenty-second Indiana Infantry, Union Gen. Alexander McDowell McCook enjoyed the longest lifetime. One of the North's famous "Fighting McCooks," he survived the war but was assigned part of the blame for the Union defeat at Chickamauga. Still, he remained in the U.S. Army and steadily advanced in permanent rank until he retired in 1895 as a major general. The following year, he represented the United States at the coronation of Nicholas II as czar of Russia. McCook lived to the age of seventy-two before passing away in 1903.

A Brave Courier's Fate

"DEAR MOTHER," HE WROTE. "O how painful it is to write you! I have got to die to-morrow—to be hanged by the Federals."

True enough, sadly enough, young Sam Davis, captured in uniform six days before, was about to die because a Yankee court-martial had condemned him as a spy.

If only he would talk, explain how he came to be carrying Federal fortification plans, or reveal who the mysterious scout leader "Captain Coleman" was, he might, he just might, be spared the gallows.

The morning came, and as Sam was trundled to the hanging site atop his own coffin, Yankee soldiers along the bumpy wagon road shouted out their entreaties for his cooperation, which would spare them all the grim sight of his execution.

The Yankee general in command sent one more message offering a reprieve if the captured Confederate would divulge his secrets. At one point or another, the general even offered a new horse and an escort to the Confederate lines. But Pvt. Sam Davis, intelligence courier in Confederate service, only twenty-one, still said no.

In a brave reply reminiscent of Nathan Hale of the Revolutionary War a few generations earlier, Davis said, "If I had a thousand lives to live, I would give them all rather than to betray a friend or the confidence of my informer."

It was late November 1863, and Davis, a native of Tennessee's Rutherford County, had been in Confederate service since the Civil War started in the spring of 1861. Then an eighteen-year-old cadet at the Western Military Institute in Nashville, he had wasted no time in signing up as a private in the First Tennessee Volunteer Infantry. His regiment marched off to war first at Cheat Mountain, next in the Shenandoah Valley, then at Shiloh and Perryville.

Wounded slightly at Shiloh, Davis suffered a real wound at Perryville, but soon was in a very active saddle as a courier for Coleman's Scouts, who roved Middle Tennessee under the stewardship of a mysterious Rebel leader sought by the Union troops of Maj. Gen. Grenville Dodge's Sixteenth Corps.

Unfortunately, it was Davis who was found and captured first— near Minor Hill, Tennessee, on November 20, 1863.

Although he wore a makeshift Confederate uniform, it might be noted, his two Yankee captors themselves were dressed as Confederates. When they first approached, they said they were conscripting additional soldiers for the South. "Davis replied that he was already a Confederate soldier and showed them his pass," says an Internet historical sketch from Giles County, Tennessee, scene of his capture and later execution. "The soldiers led him to their commanding officer, who took his gun. A search revealed papers in the soles of his boots and [in] his saddle."

The various items his captors quickly discovered included maps and descriptions of Federal fortifications in the area, a report on the Union army dispositions in Tennessee, plus a few personal toiletries for delivery to Confederate Maj. Gen. Braxton Bragg at Chattanooga—soap and toothbrushes. Along with everything else was a letter of introduction and a pass intended to clear his way into Bragg's headquarters.

The pass was signed by Captain E. Coleman.

Confined in the Giles County jail at Pulaski, young Davis was the center of attention for General Dodge and his staff for several days. So exacting was the material Davis carried on Federal fortifications in the area, that Dodge felt sure someone in the high command at Nashville must be divulging Union secrets.

According to an article appearing in the *Confederate Veteran* in 1895 (vol. 3) and written by Joshua Brown, a Confederate scout in Tennessee with Sam Davis, Dodge later said that he tried his utmost to persuade his captive to cooperate and save his own life.

"I plead [*sic*] with, and urged him with all the power I possessed to give me some chance to save his life," Dodge told Brown years later, "for I discovered that he was a most admirable young fellow, with the highest character and strictest integrity. He then said: 'It is useless to talk to me. I do not intend to do it. You can court martial me, or do anything else you like, but I will not betray the trust imposed in me.'"

Another *Confederate Veteran* article (vol. 9, 1901) asserted that Davis was often the courier delegated to collect intelligence information from Miss Robbie Woodruff—information gleaned from a Union officer who had fallen in love with her while recovering from an illness in her sister's home, just south of Nashville. Apparently she or a younger brother, William, often left the information for Davis in a hollow tree.

Meanwhile, while Dodge was busy with Davis, little attention was paid to another Rebel ensnared shortly after Davis's capture, Capt. Henry B. Shaw, even though he also was held at the Pulaski jail. (So, in fact, by his later account, was Joshua Brown, who had been captured bearing intelligence information to the Bragg headquarters in Chattanooga as well. He, fortunately, carried his information in his head . . . no incriminating papers.)

When Sam Davis continually refused under interrogation to divulge the secrets he so obviously knew, Dodge at last ordered a court-martial to try the young man for espionage. The outcome was conviction . . . and the sentence of death by hanging.

The night before his scheduled execution, Davis wrote the farewell note from the Pulaski jail to his mother in Smyrna, Tennessee. "Mother, do not grieve for me," he urged. "I must bid you good-bye forevermore. Mother, I do not fear to die. Give my love to all."

There was a postscript for his father, too, according to Joshua Brown's article. "Father, you can send after my remains if you want to do so. They will be at Pulaski, Tenn. I will leave some things with the hotel keeper for you." (What he meant by "hotel keeper" is unclear. *Jail* keeper, perhaps?)

He went to his hanging the next day just as bravely, even telling General Dodge's apologetic provost marshal, a Captain Armstrong, the officer in charge of the hanging, "I do not think hard of you; you are doing your duty."

Thus Sam Davis went to his death with never a look back.

And he never did betray his friend and compatriot, the key man he left behind in the Pulaski jail, Capt. Henry B. Shaw . . . alias "Capt. E. Coleman."

Additional note: Many years later, former Confederate 1st Lt. P. H. Benson, Company I, Twenty-third Arkansas Infantry, reported that he was a prisoner with the same Captain Shaw, an "old steamboat man," at the Johnson's Island Union prison camp. "One day I called upon Capt. Shaw," Benson wrote in the *Confederate Veteran* in 1901 (vol. 9), "and found him reading a paper—the Pulaski *Citizen*—and I noticed tears running down his cheeks."

By way of explanation, Shaw handed Benson the newspaper and pointed out the article that so deeply affected him. "It was an account of the execution of Sam Davis."

The newspaper story mentioned the conditions offered to Sam Davis "whereby he might have stopped the execution."

When Benson had finished reading the article, Shaw "told me that he was the man they were after."

Epilogue: Whatever became of Captain Shaw? According to the same *Confederate Veteran* article, the "old steamboat man" died after the war aboard a steamboat. Ironically, he and Sam Davis's older brother John had gone into the steamboat service together, with $12,000 in purchase money furnished by the Davis family. Both John and Shaw were killed and their steamboat was destroyed in a boiler explosion.

Note: Sam Davis is still remembered in Tennessee today—at the Sam Davis Home, Smyrna, Tennessee; at the Sam Davis Museum, erected at the site of his hanging in Pulaski, Tennessee (both open to the public); and by various memorials, including a statue on the grounds of the Tennessee state capitol at Nashville.

Wasp's One Sting

THIS SIXTY-ONE-YEAR-OLD CONFEDERATE navy officer about to enter a historic battle at Hampton Roads, Virginia, began his U.S. Navy service as a midshipman at fourteen and later served as the first superintendent of the U.S. Naval Academy at Annapolis, Maryland.

Gray-haired and balding, Como. Franklin Buchanan faced the upcoming battle as commanding officer of the CSS *Virginia*—converted into a hulking ironclad at Norfolk, Virginia, from the Federal navy's sunken frigate USS *Merrimack.*

Refusing to wait until every last widget was in place, Buchanan gave orders on a bright Saturday in March 1862 for his refitted, iron-plated behemoth to nose out of her berth on the Elizabeth River and push into the vast harbor of Hampton Roads. His intent was to break through the Federal naval blockade that had bottled up the James River, normally a highway of commerce to the edge of Richmond, far inland. And no, not merely to break through, but to shatter the flotilla of Federal ships, all wooden, maintaining the Union guard in the Roads.

With the former *Merrimack* sheathed in iron, "Old Buck" felt he had the very weapon to accomplish his ambitious goal.

But he must act quickly, before the Union could complete work in Brooklyn, New York, on its ballyhooed ironclad of John Ericsson's radical design, the USS *Monitor,* and send it down to Hampton Roads to defend the blockading line.

As his *Virginia* steamed out, crowds on the shoreline waving and cheering, his initial prey would be two Union frigates so antique that

The Confederate ironclad Virginia, *captained for her first fight in Hampton Roads by Commodore Buchanan, previously was the Union frigate* Merrimack, *a traditional wooden ship now covered with iron.*

they were powered by sail only—the *Cumberland* and the *Congress,* anchored close together off Newport News. And of the two, he pointed first for the *Cumberland.*

With crowds of Union soldiers and other onlookers also gathering—along the Federal-held shoreline opposite Norfolk—Buchanan's heavily armored, boxlike craft advanced upon the two frigates gradually but inexorably. As slow as Buchanan's vessel was, the two Union ships had neither the time nor the maneuvering room to set sail and escape. But would it matter? These, after all, were heavily gunned frigates of the U.S. Navy.

But then, as the first shots from a Union escort and even the *Cumberland* bounced harmlessly off the *Virginia's* thick new skin, it appeared that perhaps a greater effort at escape would have been wise.

Buchanan initially did not return fire. His strange and monstrous-looking vessel simply plowed onward at an undeviating six knots. Shells now lobbed at him from Federal shore batteries also had no visible effect upon his *Virginia* as she moved relentlessly toward the *Cumberland.*

While Commodore Buchanan held his fire, his more traditional escort, the single-gun *Beaufort,* did open fire with her 32-pounder. No great results noted.

Finally, though, when less than a mile from the *Cumberland,* Buchanan gave the terse order for his gunners to commence firing as well. The ironclad's 7-inch Brooke rifle bow gun at last spoke. Its very first shot struck home on the *Cumberland* and killed several marines. When a second round from the *Virginia* impacted, an entire gun crew aboard the *Cumberland* was killed or maimed, all but the powder boy. The *Cumberland*'s thundering broadsides fired in response had no visible effect.

Still the *Virginia* came on . . . and on. And as she did, few could have guessed that Buchanan's real plan was to ram the vessel before he turned on the neighboring *Congress*—quite possibly the first such ramming to take place in a major naval battle since the days of Greek and Roman galley fleets a thousand years earlier.

Nothing the *Cumberland* tried made the oncoming iron-covered vessel swerve or slow in the slightest. On she came until, at three hundred yards, the *Congress,* too, was loosing one broadside after another upon the Rebel craft, but again with no seeming effect. Buchanan's long forward gun continued to fire . . . but as he drew abreast of the *Congress,* the *Virginia*'s heretofore-idle guns at starboard, 9-inch Dahlgrens, suddenly had a target.

Thus, it now was the *Virginia*'s turn to fire a broadside, and the result was absolute havoc aboard the *Congress*—gun crews decimated, hull holed, fires springing up aboard the wooden ship and threatening her powder magazine.

And still the *Virginia* held to her steady course for the broad side of the *Cumberland.*

The Federal frigate's pilot, A. B. Smith, saw the approaching ironclad as something "like a huge, half-submerged crocodile."

A Boston journalist described the Confederate vessel as "weird and mysterious, like some devilish and superhuman monster, or the horrid creation of a nightmare."

It was about this time that pilot Smith became aware of the deadly ram cutting through the water ahead of the *Virginia*'s bow. As he later said, he could see "the iron ram projecting, straight forward, somewhat above the water's edge, and apparently a mass of iron." Oddly, when the ram tore into the hull of the *Cumberland,* the jolt wasn't all that noticeable to the busy crewmen aboard either vessel.

Still, as the iceberg did to the *Titanic,* the ram did its fatal damage, noted naval historian James Tertius deKay in his 1997 book *Monitor.*

Even if the impact were "almost lost in the noise and activity of the ongoing battle," he wrote, the great mass of iron "tore into the side of the *Cumberland* below the waterline, leaving a gaping hole large enough to drive a horse and cart through."

With water pouring through the seven-foot gap, the *Cumberland* began to sink. This, of course, was just what Buchanan had hoped to achieve, but suddenly, unexpectedly, his own craft was in its greatest peril of the historic day. The ram was entangled with the sinking *Cumberland*, which now threatened to take the *Virginia* below with her. Try as he furiously would over the next few minutes, Buchanan could not break free the great iron protuberance and pull his ship away.

But fate dealt him a winning hand after all—the shifting tide of early afternoon turned the ironclad almost parallel to her victim, hull to hull, rather than bow-first. Unasked but supremely welcome nonetheless, the twisting action saved the *Virginia* by breaking off her ram and leaving it embedded in the sinking *Cumberland*. Said the *Virginia*'s chief engineer, H. Ashton Ramsay, later: "Like the wasp, we could sting but once, leaving the sting in the wound."

Even now, though, the *Cumberland* kept up the fight. "For nearly half an hour after the ramming she remained afloat," added naval historian deKay, "and during that time, she and the *Virginia* traded close-range broadsides of terrible ferocity, which produced, in the case of the *Virginia*, sickening slaughter aboard the Yankee ship, and in the case of the *Cumberland*, a heartbreaking, pointless waste of lives."

Aboard the neighboring *Congress*, meanwhile, purser McKean Buchanan, sixty-two, normally the shipboard paymaster, had received his skipper's permission to serve at a battle station.

Both he and his captain of course knew who commanded the dangerous Southern ironclad threatening their ship with destruction—McKean's younger brother, Franklin.

The *Cumberland* finally was abandoned by its captain and crew after a fight so brave that Confederate Lt. John Taylor Wood of the *Virginia* later said, "No ship was ever fought more gallantly." To this, the *Virginia*'s executive officer, Catesby ap Rogers Jones, added, "She went down bravely, with her colors flying." Lost with the Federal frigate were 121 of her crew.

The *Congress* all the while had not been entirely idle. Stunned by the sight of the ramming, her skipper decided against running the risk of a repeat performance and ran his ship, bow-first, aground close to the Union shore batteries. He didn't realize Old Buck had lost his ship's stinger, but no great matter—the wooden *Congress* wouldn't fare any better in a straight-on gun battle with the *Virginia* than had the *Cumberland.* The *Congress* for that matter had already been grievously wounded by the ironclad's broadside guns.

As the unwieldy *Virginia* now took the time to turn, with the help of the escorting *Beaufort* and *Raleigh,* the crew of the *Congress* enjoyed a brief respite . . . but not for long.

Unfortunately for the second of the *Virginia's* victims that afternoon, the beaching had left the *Congress* pointing straight into shore, her stern sticking out seaward . . . exposed, vulnerable, with only two guns able to bear on the approaching enemy. A parallel beaching allowing broadside salvos would have been a far better defense for the *Congress* . . . although, against the *Virginia,* there would have been little to gain anyway.

Well aware of his brother's presence on the doomed sailing ship ahead, Franklin Buchanan nonetheless brought his ironclad to a point two hundred yards away and pounded the sailing ship with his starboard guns. In no time the *Congress* surrendered, her skipper by now killed and 135 of her 434 crewmen either dead, wounded, or missing.

With the appearance of her white flag of surrender, Commodore Buchanan of the *Virginia* ordered his shallow-draft escorts, *Beaufort* and *Raleigh,* forward to rescue survivors (officers and the wounded). But now the rescuers were subjected to unremittent fire from the Yankee shore batteries (which had *not* surrendered) and riflemen. By some accounts, too, it appears that loaded cannon were set off by fires aboard the stricken ship, with a number of the well-meaning rescuers killed and wounded as a result.

To all this, Old Buck reacted vehemently. "Vile treachery!" he is said to have shouted. And to have ordered Lt. Catesby ap Rogers Jones: "Burn that damned ship, Mr. Jones! She is firing upon our boats under a flag of surrender."

Telling Jones to pour hot shot (red-hot cannonballs) and incendiary shells into the hapless ship before them, deKay recounted, the outraged Buchanan himself "clambered to the top deck of the Virginia and began furiously firing a carbine toward shore."

Predictably, his pop-gun efforts didn't last long—he soon was brought down by a sharpshooter's minié ball to the thigh. As next in line, Jones assumed command of the *Virginia* and took her to an anchorage out of harm's way for the night—but first there would be a brief pounding by the *Virginia* and her two escorts of a third Union ship, the steam frigate *Minnesota,* which had become grounded earlier in the afternoon.

Late that same night, with a series of terrific booms, the powder magazine of the *Congress* finally gave in to the fires aboard—the ship exploded "into smithereens," said deKay.

Meanwhile, McKean Buchanan was one of those fortunates who survived the terrific punishment the *Virginia* had imposed upon both wooden sailing ships. Franklin Buchanan would eventually recover from his leg wound. He would command in battle again and spectacularly so—taking on the entire Union fleet in the battle of Mobile Bay as skipper of the lone Rebel ironclad *Tennessee,* and no dishonor to him that he finally had to surrender at the end of that punishing attack. The galling aspect of his wounding at Hampton Roads was that he was forced to give command of the *Virginia* to Jones, just in time for battle—an even more historic battle—the very next day against the Union ironclad *Monitor.*

Unknown to either Jones or Buchanan, the *Monitor* had slipped into Hampton Roads just hours after Buchanan's rampage against the Federal blockaders. When Jones brought out his ironclad the next day to finish off the Federal flotilla, he and the *Virginia* were confronted by the *Monitor*—and so it was Jones, rather than Old Buck Buchanan, who would go down in history as the Confederate commander in the famous duel of the ironclads *Virginia* and *Monitor* in Hampton Roads on March 9, 1862, basically a draw as events turned out . . . but salvation for the Union's wooden ships on hand.

If Franklin Buchanan were disappointed, and understandably so, the fact is he had won a great (albeit easy) victory the day before the clash of ironclads. He not only destroyed two Union frigates outright; his *Virginia's* very appearance in the waters of Hampton Roads had sent the *Minnesota* and the sloop of war *St. Lawrence* aground, while the steam frigate *Roanoke* scurried for cover at Fort Monroe.

All in all, Buchanan's victory the day before the clash of ironclads had been "a remarkable victory for the Confederacy," observed deKay. "In a little over four hours of action, the CSS *Virginia* had handed the United States Navy the most humiliating defeat it ever had been forced to endure. It would not suffer a worse one until the Japanese attack at Pearl Harbor, on December 7, 1941."

Confederate Como. Franklin Buchanan is seen here in his antebellum U.S. Navy uniform.

Unlike many brothers who fought on opposite sides during the Civil War, the Buchanans not only survived the war but remained close until they died in their seventies.

Franklin might even have fought alongside his U.S. Navy officer brother in the Civil War but for the hardening attitudes that prevailed just before full-scale warfare broke out between North and South. Thinking that his native Maryland would secede, Franklin had submitted his resignation from the U.S. Navy after forty-seven years of service. When Maryland didn't secede, after all, Franklin sought to withdraw his resignation but was turned down by no less a personage than the Lincoln administration's newly installed navy secretary, Gideon Welles. The hot-tempered Buchanan then joined the Confederate navy, even though he reportedly once complained the war was "the most unnatural, useless, fratricidal war ever known."

Additional note: While news of the *Virginia's* great success on March 8, 1862, prompted an alarmed President Lincoln and his cabinet to meet in Washington the very next day, a Sunday, the wounded Buchanan took a couple of days to draft an after-action report on both battles in the Roads and dispatch it to his own navy secretary in Richmond, Stephen Mallory—along with the rolled-up flag taken from the battered *Congress*. Excited, Mallory escorted Buchanan's messenger into the presence of Confederate President Jefferson Davis and some of *his* cabinet members.

"After providing a detailed account of the action," wrote deKay, "the officer dramatically unfurled the captured flag, only to discover it was saturated with blood."

The sight "put a momentary damper on the celebration," since everyone in the room "had at one time or another sworn allegiance to the same flag."

The unhappy reminder "was quickly rolled-up again and sent to Mallory's office for safekeeping." Whereupon it disappeared, its later whereabouts and ultimate fate unknown today.

MYSTERY
The Issue Was Bodies

DURING THE CIVIL WAR, Atlanta was burned. Columbia, capital of South Carolina, was burned. Richmond, capital of the Confederacy, went up in flames as well. And then there was the Winchester Medical College.

Burned to the ground . . . but why—"who done it?"

Winchester, you know, at the north end of the Shenandoah Valley, changed hands between North and South an astounding seventy-two times.

On one of those occasions, in the evening it was, and with the dreaded Yankees in town, the innocuous little medical school at the corner of Boscawen and Stewart Streets burst into flames.

The fire department responded with three engines, none motorized, of course.

As the local firemen advanced on the burning building, wrote Jerry W. Holsworth in the *Washington Times* of December 2, 1995, "a Union officer stepped forward to stop them."

Stop the firemen at their natural-born work?! Was he confused . . . or what?

Not at all, but simply following orders—the orders of Union Gen. Nathaniel Banks. And now the locals could only watch as their tiny medical school turned into ashes before their eyes, never to rise again.

Oddly, too, "several observant residents also noticed that Union soldiers had buried several bodies behind the building before it was consigned to flames," wrote Holsworth, a seasonal ranger at Antietam National Battlefield.

Shades of John Brown's body! What was this all about?

It was, in fact, all about the fanatical abolitionist John Brown, who, with twenty-one followers, had seized the Federal arsenal at Harpers Ferry in 1859, not far from Winchester itself. As U.S. troops—led by Robert E. Lee and Jeb Stuart, it so happened—stormed the arsenal and freed Brown's hostages, ten of Brown's followers were killed, including two of his sons. Brown himself was later executed.

His body was buried in North Elba, New York, but "normal" burial arrangements were not quite the case for all those killed on the spot at Harpers Ferry.

None of which would seem likely, at first glance, to be intertwined with the operations of a small medical school in Winchester with an unspectacular past. Founded by three local doctors in 1826 as the first medical school in Virginia, the small facility had shut down just three years later—"when most of the professors were lured to other schools."

In 1847, however, Dr. William P. McGuire led a drive to reopen the school, which then turned out seventy-two fledgling doctors before the events of the Civil War shut it down permanently. The school's graduates included "Doctor William's" own son, Hunter McGuire, best known as Stonewall Jackson's doctor (and later as a president of the American Medical Association).

Before the Civil War erupted, the single-structure school served as a local hospital, while also giving its students access to lecture rooms, an operating room, a laboratory, and a dissecting room.

But then, on the eve of the Civil War, came John Brown's abortive raid on Harpers Ferry, a dramatic event sealing the fate of the little medical school in nearby Winchester. In a word, the issue that now arose was . . . *bodies.*

According to Holsworth: "Subjects for the dissecting room were hard to find. Students had to be creative to come up with bodies for study." The older Dr. McGuire himself once said, "In those days, if a student knew where [he] could get hold of a body not long since from this mortal coil, the body was obtained, whether by fair means or foul."

The shootout at Harpers Ferry, together with the casualties resulting, brought his eager students running—by train, that is.

They apparently scooped up "several" of the dead, "crammed" their bodies into barrels and hustled back to the medical school in Winchester.

When General Banks and his men occupied Winchester in March 1862, a Union soldier named Tom Graham "rushed into headquarters very much excited," wrote a Union staff officer. Graham told of "wandering into the medical college and of seeing terrible sights."

A quick search of the medical facility revealed "the body of a young black male on the dissection table and a skeleton labeled 'Old John Brown,'" wrote Holsworth.

While it could not have been the real John Brown, since he was known to be buried in New York, it could have been one of his three sons. But which one? Owen, Oliver, or Watson?

Owen, in actual fact, had escaped, eventually to reach safety in California. That left Oliver and Watson as the only possibilities. A wartime diary left by Mrs. Hugh Lee, a Winchester resident who had known the Doctors McGuire well, asserted the skeleton was Oliver Brown's. But Holsworth wrote that "most believed it to be Watson Brown, whose body was separated from the other raiders at the time of his death in the raid."

The fact that it apparently was any one of John Brown's sons "enraged" General Banks and his soldiers, many of whom considered Brown and his raiders to have been heroes. Banks "ordered the bodies buried and the college burned."

Why it took from the time of the gruesome discovery of the cadavers in March until mid-May to burn down the school is not clear.

Meanwhile, Holsworth wrote also, abolitionist professor James Monroe traveled from Oberlin College in Ohio "to recover the body of John Copeland . . . a black man [who] had participated in the raid and had been tried and executed." Monroe later asserted the medical school personnel confirmed that Copeland's body was in their possession. He also said he saw the remains of Shields Greene, a second black man who had accompanied John Brown.

Still, Monroe returned to Oberlin empty-handed, without either man's body. "They probably were buried by Union troops with Watson (or Oliver) Brown in the rear of the former medical college," added Holsworth's account.

☆ ☆ ☆

Additional note: In Alabama, toward the end of the Civil War, quick thinking by another Southern doctor—and an outright falsehood—managed to save both his town and his home from the possible depredations of Union raiders.

Who more likely to convince raiding enemy soldiers than a local doctor riding out to the edge of town to warn them of a smallpox epidemic raging through the community?

That was the story—entirely false—told by Dr. C. C. Reese when Union cavalry under Brig. Gen. James H. Wilson, nemesis of Selma, Alabama, approached the doctor's hometown of Lowndesboro. As a result, the Union force bypassed the town . . . and Dr. Reese's own home, nowadays a historic structure called Marengo Plantation and the home of a successful restaurant.

Built in 1835 in Autauga County, the home had already developed an unusual history by the time of the Civil War. Its original owner, a doctor named Howard, moved both the two-story house and his practice to Lowndesboro in 1847. Slaves did much of the work, dismantling the structure, piling the pieces on oxcarts, taking them across a river by barge, then reassembling the entire house all over again.

According to Art Moody of Montgomery, who with family members operates the restaurant in the house, "This house until modern times was occupied primarily by medical people, as opposed to planters."

And now, as a facility owned by the Lowndesboro Landmarks Foundation, the antebellum home is a mecca for history- (and dinner-) minded tourists.

Coincidentally, the old medical college grounds in Winchester, Virginia, in recent years was the site of a similar mecca—the Northwestern Trail Tourist Home.

A Smile on His Face

IN COLLEGE THEY WERE GREAT friends . . . buddies. Allen, Gates, John, and Cliff. To that bunch, add Bill, another John, Frank, and Robert as Allen's classmates. They all knew one another, shared the college life at Miami of Ohio.

Before the war came.

Only Allen—Joel Allen Battle Jr.—was from a southern clime. He had come north to Ohio from Tennessee to pursue his college studies. He made many friends. "He seemed indeed an ideal type of young American manhood, and [was] beloved by all his associates," said classmate Gates—future Union Gen. Gates P. Thruston.

Graduating from Miami, young Allen married in Ohio. Said his pal Gates later: "We expected him to settle permanently in the state."

But no, came the secession crisis, came the war, he hurried on home to Tennessee and there joined the regiment his father had organized on June 21, 1861, the Twentieth Tennessee Infantry. "Joel A. Battle, Sr., Allen's father, was named colonel," explained Jerry Holsworth, a seasonal ranger at the Antietam National Battlefield. Writing for the Civil War page in the *Washington Times* of January 13, 1996, Holsworth added, "The younger Battle was appointed adjutant."

To the north, back in Ohio, so many of his old buddies and classmates were joining up, too—in Union outfits. Not only Gates Thruston, but Allen's college roommates John C. Lewis and Cliff Ross. Not only those two, both adjutants like Allen, but classmates Bill Chamberlain, John Chamberlain, Frank Evans, and Bob Adams.

Came March 1862, and Gates Thruston, stationed near Nashville, risked both life and reputation to pay a visit to Allen's family behind Confederate lines. A mutual friend, wrote Holsworth, enabled the Union officer to pass through the Rebel lines to spend an evening in the Battle home with Allen's wife and sisters.

Although they viewed the war differently, wrote Holsworth, "the Battle family extended a warm reception." The friendship of college days between Gates and Allen still "bridged sectional differences."

At that early stage of the fighting, too, both the Union officer and the Battle family were relative innocents "still naive about the war," added Holsworth. They even "joked about what would happen if the men ever met on the battlefield." It was a bad joke.

Shiloh was only weeks away (April 6 and 7), a bloodbath that would shock relative innocents in both the North and South. Young Allen Battle's Twentieth Tennessee was there, as part of John C. Breckinridge's division. His college roommates John Lewis and Cliff Ross were there, too, with the Forty-first Illinois and the Thirty-first Indiana, respectively. Also taking to the field at Shiloh—with the Eighty-first Ohio—were classmates Bill and John Chamberlain, Frank Evans, and Bob Adams.

After the fighting died out April 7, it fell to old roommates John and Cliff to come across Allen's body on the littered battleground. His right hand extended, he appeared to have been pointing ahead when struck down. Oddly, there was a smile on his face.

He had been killed on that second day of fighting, his body left behind during the Confederate withdrawal.

John and Cliff immediately spread the word, then stood guard over the body until they could arrange a fitting but quick burial for the Rebel in their old crowd. Hurrying to the scene from the ranks of the Eighty-first Ohio were the Chamberlains, Lieutenant Bill and Sergeant John, plus Major Frank and Captain Bob.

Making do with the only materials at hand, the Miami alumni fashioned a coffin from wooden cracker boxes. They dug a grave next to a large black oak, "close to where he had fallen," wrote Holsworth. "No marker was placed over the grave, and the earth was beaten flat so that it could not be found or disturbed."

Before they all left the scene, John Chamberlain chopped a marker into the side of the oak so they could find Allen's burial place later. "None, however, returned, and [Allen] Battle's grave remains unknown."

All six members of Allen's impromptu burial party did survive the war, as did Gen. Gates Thruston. Capt. Robert Adams reached the rank of brigadier general before it all was over. Frank Evans remained a major, while the Chamberlains, William and John, advanced to the ranks of captain and lieutenant, respectively. John Lewis and Cliff Ross remained adjutants of their respective regiments.

Unfortunately for the Battle family, there was even more bitter news to come from Shiloh. Joel Allen Battle Jr.'s brother William had been killed during the Confederate attack the day before, April 6.

Their father went searching the battlefield for both young men, his sons, once the fighting died down . . . only to be captured on the spot.

To the Rear, March

IT TOOK ABRAHAM LINCOLN HIMSELF to save the good name of Union Brig. Gen. Joseph Warren Revere, grandson of Paul Revere, after

Revere turned his troops to the rear just when they were desperately needed up front during the May 1863 battle of Chancellorsville.

Another Revere grandson, on the other hand, Paul J. Revere, served the Union in heroic fashion—wounded and captured at Ball's Bluff, exchanged and then wounded at Antietam, and yet ready to serve once again as commander of the Twentieth Massachusetts at Gettysburg.

As fate would have it, Paul, the *heroic* Revere grandson, would *not* survive the war, whereas grandson Joseph would.

They had come to the upheaval known as the Civil War by very different routes, at very different ages.

Joseph Warren Revere, born in 1812 in Boston and named for Revolutionary War hero Dr. Joseph Warren, began a lengthy, colorful, and varied military career in 1828—as a globe-circling officer in the U.S. Navy. Serving in that branch of service until 1850 and rising from lowly midshipman to lieutenant's rank, he resigned to settle briefly in California, then joined the Mexican Army as an artillery officer, now with colonel's rank.

Wounded while engaged against revolutionary forces, he returned East in 1852 to take up civilian life in Morristown, New Jersey, for almost a full decade. When the Civil War broke out in 1861, he tried to join the navy again but was not immediately embraced by his former seagoing peers. He found quicker acceptance in the Union army as colonel of the Seventh New Jersey Infantry.

His regiment served in the Peninsula campaign of 1862 as part of the Third Corps, with regimental commander Joseph Revere present and at the lead during the Seven Days' battles. He also served at Second Bull Run (Manassas) that summer. By the end of the same year, Revere had gained the rank of brigadier general and was commanding the Third Brigade of Daniel Sickles's division, still under the Third Corps, at Fredericksburg. His brigade, however, was not directly involved in the fighting at Fredericksburg, a debacle for the Union forces.

Then, in the spring of 1863, came Revere's own personal debacle—Chancellorsville. His divisional commander, Maj. Gen. Hiram Berry, was rushing his men forward the early morning of May 3 to fill the gap created by Stonewall Jackson's nighttime flanking march against the Union right . . . but Berry, himself the grandson of a Revolutionary War soldier, was mortally wounded. The command of the division then devolved upon Revere.

Surprised or simply overwhelmed by the sudden responsibility thrust upon him, he ordered a march rearward instead of following Berry's intended mission of providing desperately needed relief for the collapsing Union front. Revere later explained he withdrew his men— a full three miles, by some accounts—"for the purpose of reorganizing and bringing them back to the field comparatively fresh."

He asserted his (Berry's) division was so badly scattered that he had to pull back to reorganize its various remnants.

The result, though, was relief from command and an embarrassing court-martial verdict calling for his outright dismissal. That is when Lincoln stepped forward and offered Revere a chance to resign before he could be booted out of the army.

While Joseph Revere was undergoing his Civil War trials, meanwhile, the far-younger Revere grandson, Paul J. (born in 1832), also found combat in the Civil War to be a trying experience. For young Paul the downside of war began early, with the day he was wounded and captured early in the war—in the Union defeat, October 21, 1861, at Ball's Bluff near Leesburg, Virginia.

This was the fight on the bluffs of the Potomac River, thirty-three miles northwest of Washington, D.C., in which Capt. Oliver Wendell Holmes Jr., future U.S. Supreme Court justice, was hit twice in the chest. But he was only one among the many men from three Massachusetts regiments left dead, wounded, or taken prisoner in the futile attempt to take the heights on the Confederate side of the river. In all, 50 Union men were killed, 158 were wounded, and 714 listed as missing—most of the latter had been taken prisoner, among them Maj. Paul J. Revere of the Twentieth Massachusetts. And most of the prisoners were wounded, with Revere to be counted among that number, too.

"News about the casualties at Ball's Bluff brought sadness to families all over the state [Massachusetts], and resulted in a call for a congressional investigation," noted historian Thomas H. O'Connor in his 1997 book *Civil War Boston*.

The wounded Paul Revere for a time became a hostage held as insurance for appropriate treatment of Southern privateers held prisoner by the Union. At last returned to his Twentieth Massachusetts and eventually advanced to the rank of colonel, he overcame his second wounding—at Antietam—before finding himself at Gettysburg in early July 1863 . . . now in command of his old regiment.

Paul Revere's third and final wounding came on the second day of battle at Gettysburg. He died two days later, barely past his thirtieth year of life. His brevetted promotion to brigadier general as of the day he was wounded (July 2, 1863) was posthumous.

Joseph Warren Revere the very next month would see his resignation from service become effective (on August 10). He then retreated to a civilian life of frequent travel abroad, despite declining health. He published memoirs of his experiences and lived until 1880. He died at Hoboken, New Jersey, and was buried in Morristown.

MYSTERY

Murderer's Fate?

A MURDER UNAVENGED? He was convicted of murder, he was sentenced to death . . . but was he ever executed? *Was it really murder?*

The story begins with an open carriage carrying an ailing Union general and moving eastward in Tennessee on August 5, 1862. The passenger was Brig. Gen. Robert Latimer McCook, thirty-four, one of the famous "Fighting McCooks" of Ohio. (Fourteen sons of two McCook brothers fought for the Union, and five of them rose to general's rank.)

General McCook, a lawyer in civilian life, had fought in West Virginia and in January 1862 had distinguished himself at Mill Springs, Kentucky, as a brigade commander but suffered a wound there. By the late summer of 1862, his brigade was a part of Union Gen. Don Carlos Buell's forces moving through Tennessee.

McCook was so ill that he rode on a bed placed in the open carriage. He and a small escort were about three miles ahead of the brigade when they stopped at a private home between the towns of Winchester and Decherd, Tennessee, to discuss the possibility of setting up camp somewhere nearby. Shortly after their stop, a party of Confederate cavalry and partisans swooped down on the small Union band, attacked and scattered McCook's men.

His carriage driver tried to make a run for it, whirling around for a dash in the direction of the brigade, but too late. He and the general were quickly surrounded and brought to a halt. Gunfire broke out. The patient in the bed was struck in the abdomen. It was a fatal wound— McCook died twenty-four hours later in another private home.

The Union reaction to the helpless officer's violent death was pure outrage. Investigation established a Capt. Frank Gurley as the guilty party. The soon-captured Gurley previously had been a Confederate cavalry officer, but on the day in question he "held an appointment from General E. Kirby Smith as captain of partisan rangers," according to Ezra J. Warner's book *Generals in Blue.*

Oddly enough, Gurley could be convicted of murder largely because under Confederate law only President Jefferson Davis held the authority to appoint officers of partisan rangers, Warner also reported. It was a Union military court that found Gurley guilty of murder and recommended execution.

But was he ever executed? While he was a prisoner of the North, Gurley was exchanged in March 1865—by mistake. He next appears in the historical record after the war . . . arrested in Huntsville, Alabama, and again held for execution.

In November of that year, however, President Andrew Johnson, Lincoln's successor, suspended the sentence "until further notice," Warner reported.

From that point, Gurley disappears from view.

Additional note: An amazing patriarch who, himself, would give his life to the Union cause, Daniel McCook Sr. of Carrollton, Ohio, would send eight sons into the Civil War, five of them destined to become generals. And from brother John McCook's "tribe" came still another five officers in Union cloth—all together, including Daniel Sr., fourteen "Fighting McCooks."

Attorney Daniel McCook Sr. left his native Pennsylvania for Ohio and subsequently settled in Carrollton. He is memorialized by a monument marking the area where he died (in the battle of Buffington Island) as a colonel in the Ohio militia opposing Confederate raider John Hunt Morgan's foray into Ohio in 1863.

All told, three of Daniel's sons also died in the Civil War, including Gurley's victim, Robert L. McCook, and seventeen-year-old Charles (the only McCook who was not an officer), killed at First Manassas (Bull Run).

Daniel Sr.'s third son to die was Daniel Jr., a brigade leader selected by his old law partner, William Tecumseh Sherman, to lead the Union charge on Kennesaw Mountain near Atlanta on June 27, 1864. "McCook, recognizing the adverse odds, had recited Horatio's speech to his men just before the zero hour," wrote Warner. "He reached the Confederate works[,] where he fell mortally wounded."

On a happier note, among the McCooks who survived the hostilities, John McCook's son Edward, also of general's rank during the war, was so successful in his postwar business interests that he "at one time [was] the largest taxpayer in Colorado," Warner also noted. In earlier years, Edward McCook served as territorial governor of Colorado, after spending three years as U.S. minister to Hawaii.

Note: The McCook House, the large brick home that Daniel McCook Sr. built in Carrollton, is open to the public certain days of the week during the summer months as an Ohio historic site. (Call 800-600-7172 for hours and other information.)

Woman at the Lead

No ordinary color-bearer, this one wore a distinctive uniform consisting of a loose, long-sleeved blouse and Union army trousers surmounted by a short skirt wrapped by a red sash with a tassel. Since color-bearers were a prime target to begin with, was this sensible attire for a color-bearer attached to a Union company of sharpshooters?

For a time, it worked out just fine for Kady McKenzie Brownell, official Union color-bearer, South African–born daughter of a Scottish soldier in the British army, wife of Pvt. Robert Brownell of the First Rhode Island Detached Militia.

Just fine for a time even in combat . . . combat such as First Bull Run, a Union debacle from which she had to be pulled away despite her own protests. Separated from her husband in the rout, fearing that he might have become a casualty, she was assured of his safety by future division commander Ambrose Burnside.

Prior to Bull Run, she had carried her company's colors at Fairfax Court House. Before that, she had "joined" the regiment as wife of her newly enlisted husband. She became a "daughter of the regiment," or *vivandiere,* which meant she would be expected to serve as a combination cook, laundress, and nurse. Somehow, though, she had won official appointment as a company color-bearer.

After Bull Run, her husband mustered out of the First Rhode Islanders only to reenlist with the Fifth Rhode Island. Soon both Brownells set off—under Burnside again—on the Carolina campaign of 1862 resulting in the Union capture of New Bern, North Carolina.

Brave Kady Brownell once more faced a storm of enemy fire while carrying the colors in the lead of Union soldiers ranged behind her.

This time, though, both Kady and her husband came up casualties. Of the two, it was Robert who was the more seriously hurt. After a long hospital stay, with wife Kady acting as his personal nurse, he was discharged from the army in 1863. They returned for a time to Providence, Rhode Island, but later made their home in New York.

Widowed in time, Kady could thank Burnside for the pension she received for her army service. She also had been allowed to keep her sword and the colors she had carried under enemy fire . . . as a real-life *heroine.*

A Footnote Only

NEARLY EVERY HISTORY OF THE Civil War (sixty thousand such works published so far) will mention the capture of Robert E. Lee's eldest son, Brig. Gen. William Henry Fitzhugh "Rooney" Lee, at his wife's family home in Hanover County, Virginia, shortly after being wounded in the great cavalry battle of Brandy Station in June 1863.

Those histories will mention the Rooney Lee episode, and that is as it should be. But there is a little-known footnote to the story.

*Robert E. Lee's Harvard-educated son,
Rooney, was wounded at Brandy Station
then seized by a Union raiding party.
He never saw his wife, Charlotte, again.*

First, though, more detail from the capture of young Lee: Before the eyes of his pregnant wife, Charlotte Wickham Lee, and his mother, Mary Custis Lee, he was carried off, convalescent mattress and all, by a Union raiding party that had come ashore from rivercraft nosing into White House Landing on the Pamunkey River, a river estate belonging to the Lee family.

While Rooney Lee did eventually recover from his wounds, the sad story is that both Charlotte Lee and her unborn child died during his long months of captivity. He was held prisoner nearly a year as a hostage against Confederate threats to execute a pair of Union naval officers. R. E. Lee's eldest son was finally exchanged in March 1864.

The footnote rarely mentioned in Civil War histories is the story of the Union officer for whom he was exchanged—Brig. Gen. Neal Dow—who also suffered greatly for his wartime commitment, in his case to the Union cause. A Quaker and former mayor of Portland, Maine, Dow was expelled from his pacifist church for becoming a soldier and taking part in the war. Then, too, like Rooney Lee, he was severely wounded in battle—at Port Hudson, Mississippi. While still convalescing, he was captured by Confederate forces and sent to Libby Prison in Richmond. There, reported POW Lt. James M. Wells of Michigan, Dow "treated us now and then to temperance lectures, which, in a practical view, seemed to be quite unnecessary, as food was very scarce and intoxicating drink, absolutely out of the question." Dow spent several months as a prisoner there before he was exchanged for Rooney Lee.

Unlike Lee, he wasn't well enough to return to active duty. Returning to Maine, he resumed his antialcohol campaigns of old, going so far as to run for president in 1880 as the Prohibitionist Party candidate. Years before, in 1838, he had organized the Maine Temperance Union. Then, at the outset of his stint as mayor of Portland (from 1851 to 1858), he wrote and helped to assure passage of Maine's state prohibition law of 1851. "His Maine Law of 1851," says the *Encyclopedia Britannica,* "presaged national prohibition in the United States."

Rooney Lee, by contrast, resumed his role as a Confederate cavalry officer after the exchange. Lee became a major general before the war ended. He then was chiefly a farmer, but he also served in the Virginia state senate and in the U.S. Congress.

Born in 1837, Lee died in 1891, not yet sixty. His exchange "partner" Dow, born in 1804, lived until 1897 before dying at the age of ninety-three. Dow's autobiography, *The Reminiscences of Neal Dow,* appeared in print the next year.

"Mudwall" for Governor?

WELL, HE WASN'T "STONEWALL," AND he didn't achieve first fame at Manassas in Virginia. Instead, he was Cousin "Mudwall," and a key battle in *his* career was Bulltown, also in Virginia (sort of, anyway) . . . and that is no bull!

The battle that *didn't* really make this Confederate General Jackson's career was a botch from start to finish, as unhappy events turned out.

His "Jackass" artillery battery (so named by the troops since it was carried, in pieces, by mules) didn't use the right kind of shot against the dug-in Federal troops.

His pincer arm no. 1 began the battle *before* pincer arm no. 2 took its assigned position in support . . . and thus alerted the sleeping Union men in time for them to take to their rifle pits.

In the end, a relative handful of Federals held out all day long against an attacking Confederate force vastly superior in number.

In the end, too, there were embarrassing stories that the Rebels, on their march to remote Bulltown in the rough terrain of "northwestern" Virginia, had come across a whiskey still and happily partook of its nefarious product.

To be fair, that charge was never proved, and Mudwall Jackson—a kinsman of Stonewall Jackson—was to some degree a victim of sheer bad luck. It wasn't entirely his fault that the commander of pincer arm No. 1 didn't wait for his colleagues to reach their appointed positions.

Further, the Federals did not cover themselves in glory at every step of the way, either. Before the action even began, they lost one set of pickets to Confederates who approached—and disarmed—them in captured Federal uniforms. Another twenty-five Union pickets, it is alleged, simply melted into the forest—deserted—when confronted by the Rebels.

None of which, Federal or Confederate actions notwithstanding, is to suggest that William Lowther "Mudwall" Jackson, cousin of Thomas J. "Stonewall" Jackson, was anything but a fine officer and gentleman by anyone's standards. Indeed, Judge Jackson, as William L. also was known, was an established, highly regarded, and even popular Virginian of distinction at the time of the Civil War. At age thirty-six, he had been a lawyer for some years, a judge, and, for that matter, lieutenant governor of the Old Dominion.

As the war clouds descended over the land, he left the Elysian fields of law and politics to join the Confederate army as a mere private. For a man of his abilities and reputation, however, such lowly rank wouldn't do for very long—he soon was an officer, first a lieutenant colonel, Thirty-first Virginia, serving in western Virginia, and later a full colonel.

Mudwall Jackson for a time had served as a volunteer aide on the staff of his more famous cousin Stonewall—they were together during Stonewall Jackson's Shenandoah Valley campaign and for the Seven Days' campaign outside of Richmond, at bloody Antietam and at Second Manassas. Civil War historian James I. Robertson, in his monumental biography of Stonewall Jackson, mentioned Cousin Bill only three times, but one of those allusions was to a moment when both Jacksons rode off together, alone, as Stonewall prepared to lead his troops into yet another battle. Presumably, they were close.

By October 1863, however, Stonewall Jackson was dead, victim of a stray shot fired by one of his own men at Chancellorsville the previous May. Cousin Bill, on his own now, was back in the Greenbrier River Valley as commander of a cavalry regiment, the Nineteenth Virginia.

His territorial responsibility as a Confederate officer stationed in western Virginia was that truly nettlesome mountainous region—

then of Virginia in theory, now of West Virginia in fact—where brothers and neighbors were often divided in their loyalty to South or North, where local partisans roamed and raided, often to settle old scores unrelated to the war itself. Where, also, Union troops were stationed in part to defend rail and other vital supply lines running westward from the East and in part to provide protection from partisan raids.

One such Federal outpost in the fall of 1863 was Bulltown in today's Braxton County, West Virginia, a tiny village at the juncture of the Little Kanawha River and the Weston and Gauley Bridge Turnpike. And here, in the second week of that October . . . came a partially mounted column of six hundred to eight hundred Rebels winding its way on obscure trails through the tough hills, with Mudwall Jackson in command.

Ahead, the night of October 12, Union Capt. William H. Mattingly and an estimated 150 effectives were bedded down in log cabins erected among two strings of rifle pits on a bluff overlooking the Little Kanawha, their pickets carefully flung out according to standard practice.

As we have seen, however, the pickets proved no use whatsoever—not a one gave warning of Jackson's arrival. As the Union men within Mattingly's thin fortifications slept on, Jackson had ample time to split and dispose of his forces. One detachment would attack from the northeast, the other from the southwest, and both would leap off with the first boom of Jackson's mule-packed artillery at 4:30 A.M.

The detachment assigned to the northeast post did exactly what Jackson ordered . . . almost. It launched an attack at 4:30 A.M., precisely. The trouble was, the second detachment and the artillery were not yet in position—that meant no support, no artillery signal. Worse yet, one of the attacking detachment's officers foolishly shouted, "Charge!" and fired his pistol, fully alerting Mattingly's men. The Federals quickly took to their rifle pits and held off the Confederate attack with a hail of fire.

As the totally insignificant battle of Bulltown then became a stalemate lasting twelve hours, one bizarre turn followed another. Not a great deal of history has been written about it, but among the bits and pieces that are available today, notes a booklet by regional historian Richard L. Armstrong (*West Virginian vs. West Virginian*), the capture and abduction of a pet bear cub the Federals kept in a log cabin became one objective of the attacking Rebels.

Capture a bear cub? Well, be that as it may, it is fairly well established that Jackson twice demanded a Federal surrender. He was turned down, but there did come a time-out in the shooting, notes Armstrong. The laudable intent was to allow a Confederate army surgeon to treat Union Captain Mattingly's upper thigh bone, shattered by a Rebel shot. At the same time, the Confederates were able to recover their dead and wounded.

During the two-hour truce, the men on both sides casually visited among the opposing lines. After all, many knew each other as neighbors or relatives.

They "very freely" mingled, reported onlooker and participant James Neil, a Union lieutenant, "laughing and talking just as we were the best of friends." Neil noted: "Some of Company G of our regiment [Sixth West Virginia] had brothers and fathers in the fight. They shook hands and talked of old times. The boys of the 11th [West] Virginia knew nearly all the rebels. A great many had friends and relations among them, and it was good for curious reflection to see them meet and talk."

As soon as the truce period ended, Neil recalled, "they would be shooting at each other again." And for a while, they indeed were.

At some point that day also, a local farmer, Moses Cunningham, excited by the battle taking place on and around his land, was wounded when he appeared between the lines shouting a hurrah for Jefferson Davis. Both he and Captain Mattingly survived. Late that afternoon, his designs on the Federal outpost thoroughly thwarted, Mudwall Jackson withdrew his force. With little accomplished and a handful of casualties on each side, the battle of Bulltown was over.

Mudwall became a brigade commander and a brigadier general and fought on during the Civil War. He was present for the defense of Lynchburg and the battles of Monocacy, Third Winchester, Fisher's Hill, and Cedar Creek, also in the Shenandoah Valley. He refused to surrender at war's end—he instead disbanded his command and himself repaired to Mexico. Later, he reconsidered, returned to Kentucky, and again became a judge.

Thought for the day: If there had been no Civil War, would Stonewall Jackson have remained an obscure (and rather eccentric) professor at Virginia Military Institute (called "Tom Fool Jackson" by many of the cadets, incidentally), while his popular cousin Mudwall

Jackson moved on in politics from lieutenant governor to become a famous and historically significant governor of a much larger Virginia?

Additional note: Oddly, the Confederacy produced a second Gen. Mudwall Jackson—Tennessee-born Alfred Eugene Jackson, who picked up the nickname "Mudwall" while commanding an infantry brigade in East Tennessee that captured the Union's 100th Ohio Infantry at Telford's Station (alternately, Depot) on September 8, 1863.

Before the war, this Mudwall also had been a highly successful man in his field, which was business. Using wagons and riverboats, he shipped and traded goods all over the South, noted Ezra J. Warner in his book *Generals in Gray.* "His various enterprises, which included stores, mills, manufactories, and farms, ranged at one time from North Carolina to the Mississippi River."

Reduced to poverty status by the Civil War, he had to begin all over again, now farming rented land in Washington County, Virginia— "with his own hands," noted Warner's book.

Jackson's postwar prospects gradually did improve, however. "He was subsequently issued a special pardon by President Johnson [himself an East Tennessee resident] for kindnesses shown the latter's family during the war. His [Jackson's] estates were gradually restored to him, and he was able to take up residence at Jonesboro, Tennessee, where he died, October 30, 1889, in his eighty-third year, and where he is buried."

Death of a Reputation

PERHAPS IT WAS THE YOUNG Union general's youth and inexperience. Perhaps it was a heady combination of champagne and too strong a whiff of an obliging woman's perfume . . . and perhaps she had been sent to entrap him. Whatever the exact cause, Edwin Henry Stoughton, a brigadier general at the age of twenty-four, certainly was caught napping one night when Confederate raider John Singleton Mosby came acalling. In just minutes, Stoughton was routed from bed and carried off into captivity.

Mosby, the "Gray Ghost of the Confederacy," said a Union deserter reported a break in the Union picket lines close to Fairfax Court House in northern Virginia. As a result, Mosby and twenty-nine of his men were able to slip into town the night of March 8, 1863, and make off with West Point graduate Stoughton and thirty-two other prisoners, plus fifty-eight horses.

It was the loss of perfectly good horseflesh that seemed to bother the boy general's higher-ups the most. "I can make new brigadier generals," Abraham Lincoln remarked, "but I can't make horses."

Allegedly, too, alcohol and womanizing were elements of the young general's lifestyle. By some accounts, he went to bed at a house known as the Rectory that night of March 8 after a merry party at a nearby home, then awoke to hear a stranger by his bedside asking if he knew about Mosby. The inquirer, it turned out, was Mosby himself.

Another of the stories swirling about the Stoughton capture credited a young woman named Antonia Ford with encouraging his consumption of champagne that evening—and letting Mosby know where to slip past the Federal lines. Mosby, on the other hand, insisted he obtained his information on the gap in the Union picket lines from the deserter, a man named Ames who had been attached to the Fifth New York Cavalry.

But forget the details. In essence Mosby's feat was accomplished despite the nearby presence of thousands of Union troops, most of them undoubtedly asleep. Confederate cavalry commander Jeb Stuart called Mosby's Fairfax Court House raid "a feat, unparalleled in the war."

Stoughton, taken to Libby Prison in Richmond, was exchanged two months later, but he did not regain command of his brigade of fellow Vermonters assigned to the outer ring of Washington's defenses. He never regained command of anything, in fact. His brigadier's commission expired four days before his capture, and he simply was not reappointed to Union ranks at all.

For the rest of his short life, Stoughton was a civilian, a resident of New York City practicing law with an uncle. At one time in the 1860s the youngest general officer serving the Union, he now was destined to be outlived by many an older man who survived the war itself. He died on Christmas Day, 1868, at the age of thirty. His reputation, unfortunately, had died five years before him.

Additional note: Antonia Ford, the woman often linked with Stoughton's capture, was so notorious as an informer for the Confederates that Jeb Stuart himself pressed Mosby to deny she had had a hand in the Stoughton raid—which came after a party at her family's home near the Rectory. And Mosby did deny that she played any role whatsoever in that particular escapade.

That Stuart might jump to such a conclusion would have been perfectly reasonable, since he once gave her a strictly honorary "commission" as a major as reward for valuable information she had furnished the Rebels on a Union battle plan. As he knew also, she often did furnish Mosby with useful information picked up from Union officers staying at her father Edward Ford's large brick home in Fairfax.

The Federal authorities clearly came to the same conclusion as Stuart—they arrested her four days after Stoughton's disappearance into the night with Mosby and his men. She then was held in prison so long, subject to such a poor diet, that even her enemies became concerned. A campaign in her behalf, led in part by Union officer Joseph C. Willard (co-founder in 1850 of the famous Willard Hotel in Washington, D.C., today known as the Willard Inter-Continental Hotel), finally secured her release, but she was left in a frail condition widely blamed for her early death in 1871 at age thirty-two.

First, though, she found a moment of happiness . . . by marrying the Union officer who helped win back her freedom.

Unsung Heroes II

EAGERLY JOINING COMPANY K, First Michigan Sharpshooters, in mid-1863, they were craftsmen, farmers, and clerks. Their eager recruiter was a schoolteacher, linguist, and musician in civilian life. And all were American Indians, chiefly of the Ottawa tribe.

Noted for their sharpshooting skills, most of them were recruited by schoolteacher Garrett A. Gravaraet, son of an Ottawa chief but only part Indian himself. Gravaraet's Indian father, Chief Mankewenan, also joined up . . . as Sgt. Henry Gravaraet.

Off they then marched to war . . . except that at first they were employed as prison guards at Camp Douglas outside Chicago. Not exactly what they were hoping for.

Then came the spring of 1864 and transfer to the Army of the Potomac as Ulysses S. Grant initiated his sledgehammer campaign in Virginia that saw the Union forces drive their Confederate foes into Richmond and Petersburg. "Company K stood out because of its distinctive appearance, highlighted by an unusual battle flag, a large live eagle that preceded the company on a six-foot-high pole," wrote Roy Morris Jr., editor of *America's Civil War* magazine, in its July 1996 issue.

Even now, however, even in the ensuing battles of the Wilderness and Spotsylvania, the sharpshooters were not put to their most effective use. "Instead," wrote Morris, "like virtually all the soldiers in . . . Grant's army, the men were fed into a giant meat grinder whose only intent was to wear down the outnumbered Confederates of General Robert E. Lee."

The largely Ottawa Company K did see plenty of action, but basically as regular infantry. At Spotsylvania, the entire First Michigan pushed through "a heavy and destructive fire of musketry, grape and cannister" to close within fifty yards of the Rebel lines and then repel two counterattacks, only to back off in the end.

In a week's time, sadly, thirty-four regimental personnel were killed, including thirteen from Company K. Among them was Chief Mankewenan, Gravaraet's father.

After more battles on the way southward came the fighting around Petersburg in June 1864. On June 17, the regiment was briefly surrounded by the enemy but fought its way free . . . with more casualties.

A letter to Gravaraet's mother announced that he was one of the wounded and that he had been shipped north to Washington for surgery. Writing the letter himself, he explained almost cheerfully that he had been wounded in the left arm and it had been amputated below the shoulder.

"I think I shall be discharged before long and come home if my arm does well," he wrote. "The Dr. thinks it will do well. Don't be discouraged about me."

Unfortunately, two weeks later, due to "mortification of the heart," it was his fallen father he joined rather than his mother back in Michigan. Added Morris: "A hospital administrator told Gravaraet's mother that he was 'a good soldier and was liked by all.'"

Mystery of a Missing Limb

UNION COL. ULRIC DAHLGREN'S FATHER, Adm. John Dahlgren, may have acted a bit too quickly when he embedded his wounded son's amputated right leg underneath the cornerstone of a new building at the Washington Navy Yard . . . although, true enough, his son was close to death after being wounded in a post-Gettysburg skirmish. Quite true as well, possibly to save Ulric's life, the leg was amputated, always a desperate and dangerous medical procedure in those Civil War times.

The limb then came to the Navy Yard in a box covered with the American flag . . . somewhat like a mini-casket for a fallen hero.

It then was buried beneath the cornerstone of Building 28, in 1863 a new foundry and more recently the site of a sheet-metal shop, according to Stephen M. Forman in his 1995 book *A Guide to Civil War Washington*.

The admiral, famous in his day as inventor of the Dahlgren smoothbore gun and at the time chief of the Union navy's Bureau of Ordnance, also ordered up a plaque for the Navy Yard's new foundry. It said: "Within this wall is deposited the leg of Col. Ulric Dahlgren, USV, wounded July 6, 1863, while skirmishing in the streets of Hagerstown [Maryland] with the Rebels after the battle of Gettysburg."

As Admiral Dahlgren prepared to lay the cornerstone for his new foundry in 1863, his son Ulric was still fighting for his life. At that grim moment, the admiral apparently hoped the plaque would serve

Union Rear Adm. John A. Dahlgren was determined to memorialize his wounded son, Ulric, with the young man's amputated leg.

as both a memorial for his son and inspiration for others. He felt "that a proper tribute to the bravery and courage exemplified by his young son would be a tablet on the corner of the foundry, where those who built the guns of war would be reminded that through the ages, men had always been willing to fight and sacrifice for what they believed was right," wrote historian Forman in his guidebook.

After Admiral Dahlgren's son managed to survive the amputation of his leg and then to learn to walk with crutch and wooden leg, there seemed, so far as the public knew, little reason to remove the tablet or to change its wording . . . especially when Ulric died less than a year later in an abortive and controversial cavalry raid on Richmond, a martyr to the Union cause after all.

The controversy, not so incidentally, stemmed from papers allegedly found on his body and allegedly stating that one purpose of the raid was to kill Confederate President Jefferson Davis and members of his cabinet. In short, to assassinate the leaders of the Confederacy.

While the true purpose of the Dahlgren raid may be one lingering mystery of the Civil War, another—albeit somewhat lesser—riddle has to do with the younger Dahlgren's amputated leg. The fact is, it disappeared.

According to Forman, "When the original [Navy Yard] building was demolished to make way for a new one, the leg could not be found." How could that be? Well, Forman could only relay the most obvious speculations: "Some say that Confederate sympathizers opened the wall and removed the leg; other people believe that it was removed and buried with Dahlgren's body."

That event—Ulric's burial—also involves a story of some complexities, since he was first buried in Virginia's King and Queen County, where he was killed in early March 1864 . . . but buried only for the moment, thanks to the Union's Richmond-based spy Elizabeth Van Lew. She, it seems, gathered some helpers and arranged for Dahlgren's body to be disinterred for reburial on a farm near Richmond until the end of the war.

Additional notes: To continue with a macabre subject matter, Ulric Dahlgren's leg was not the only severed human limb to become a memorialized artifact of the Civil War. Stonewall Jackson's amputated left arm still lies (presumably) below an obscure and hard-to-find marker in a corner of the Chancellorsville battleground where Jackson was fatally wounded by his own troops firing blindly in the dark. Jackson himself is buried in Lexington, Virginia.

Robert E. Lee, it may be recalled, referred to Jackson's amputation in the famous quote: "He has lost his left arm; but I have lost my right arm."

Then, too, controversial Union Brig. Gen. Daniel Sickles, wounded at Gettysburg, also survived the amputation of his right leg, just like Dahlgren. That severed limb—or parts of it—can be seen today by visitors to the Armed Forces Medical Museum, Walter Reed Army Hospital, in Washington, D.C., while Sickles himself is buried at Arlington National Cemetery.

Who Was He?

KNOWN ONLY TO FAMILY AND friends in life, Amos Humiston became famous in death . . . and only because nobody knew who he was.

His friends, fellow members of the 154th New York Infantry, known as the "Hardtack Regiment," last saw him moments after their line gave way before an overwhelming Confederate surge at the center and right flank the first day at Gettysburg. Sergeant Humiston was trying to reach the safety of Union lines at Cemetery Hill, the hotly pursuing Rebels close behind.

And no wonder he had to flee. Only four officers and fifteen men of the regiment were still standing that same night.

But not Humiston.

A local woman came across him a few days later. Came across his body, that is. He was holding an ambrotype of his three children. Mortally wounded, quite obviously, he had taken out the picture and died looking at it.

But there was no identification on the body. The question arose, which soon made the newspapers of the day: Who was he? And the answer at first became "The Unknown Soldier of Gettysburg."

Still, somewhere in the land, in the North anyway, those children lived and were waiting, waiting for their father. Their mother, his wife, now his widow and unaware, was waiting.

Dr. Francis Bourns of Philadelphia, who told the newspapers about the local woman's grim discovery, developed a publicly announced system. Every time he received an inquiry about the Unknown Soldier, he would send back an inexpensive *carte de visite* version of the children's photo. Surely someone in the world beyond Gettysburg would write, obtain the picture copy, recognize the children, and so realize who their father was.

For five months, however, despite all the publicity, Amos Humiston continued to go unrecognized. Bourns continued to send out his responses to the inquiries that came to him by mail . . . eventually one of his *carte de visites* wended its way to an inquirer from Portville, New York, a woman named Philinda, who was the mother of three.

The children in the picture were a bit younger, but she knew them all right, knew their father. The Unknown from Gettysburg was her husband, Amos Humiston, former whaler, former harness maker, Union soldier who had fought at Chancellorsville and then Gettysburg. His regiment had just missed Fredericksburg a bit earlier.

Arriving at Gettysburg July 1, 1863, the Hardtackers had taken position before Kuhn's brickyard and then tried to withstand the onslaught of attacking Confederates under Maj. Gen. Jubal Early. Mark H. Dunkleman's book *Gettysburg's Unknown Soldier* tells the Amos and Philinda Humiston story in detail.

Part of that story is the unexpected sequel to the discovery of the Unknown Soldier's name—and family. After Bourns and friends established a foundation financing a Gettysburg orphanage for the children of deceased soldiers, Philinda Humiston and her children moved to town from their home in Portville—moved *into* the orphanage, where she had been given a job making clothes for the orphans as their wardrobe mistress.

Her late husband remained buried close by, and in 1993 he was recalled once again by the dedication of the Amos Humiston Memorial, said to be the only monument in the historic Gettysburg battlefield commemorating an individual enlisted man.

Disappearance of a General

OUT OF A CLOUD OF fire and gunsmoke came the general's terrified, bleeding horse. Galloping and riderless.

Years later, Confederate Brig. Gen. Richard Brooke Garnett's sword turned up in a Baltimore pawnshop.

But where was the general himself?

Last seen in broad daylight, with hundreds—nay, thousands—of onlookers swirling around Cemetery Ridge on the third day at Gettysburg, Garnett and his brigade of Virginians had been in the front ranks of Pickett's Charge.

Last seen just twenty or so yards from the Union line, he disappeared into the smoke and fire. Moments later, his horse galloped out of that same maelstrom, its saddle empty.

Garnett was never seen again by any who knew him.

And while that much is true—never seen again, alive or dead—another scenario compiled by historians has his horse found on the ground, wounded, dying. By this account, there was no steed galloping out of the smoke and tumult.

Still, the dying animal was a horse—his horse—without a rider.

All told, the three-day battle of Gettysburg exacted fifty thousand casualties on both sides. "Of fifty-two Confederate generals, seventeen, or almost one third fell in the battle," noted historian Jeffry D. Wert in his 1993 biography, *General James Longstreet.*

With so many killed or maimed—just in Pickett's Charge alone—men did "disappear," their bodies blown apart by explosives, accidentally buried, or crushed beyond recognition. Or, more often, simply stripped of identifying insignia, side arms and other accouterments, such as Garnett's sword. They, in the case of Confederates, then were buried in a mass grave with other unidentified dead, for possible reinterment at a later date in the South.

So it may have been with Richard B. Garnett, West Point graduate and a veteran of the Seminole campaigns in Florida and long years of duty in the far West.

His had not been a spectacular career in the "old Army" of pre–Civil War times, but he came to the Confederacy as a seasoned and knowledgeable officer. He then served as commander of the Stonewall Brigade, but after the battle of Kernstown ran into a tempest—and court-martial—fostered by Stonewall Jackson. That matter never resolved before Jackson's death at Chancellorsville in 1863, Garnett next served as a brigade commander in George Pickett's division, a part of James Longstreet's corps, at South Mountain and Antietam.

Then came Gettysburg . . . and its third, final day, also in 1863. Like Longstreet and many, many others, Garnett did not like the look of the planned assault up the slopes of Cemetery Ridge to a grove of oaks at the top. "This is a desperate thing to attempt," he said upon viewing the hilly approach to the line of Federal artillery batteries and masses of infantry.

Like his fellow Confederate officers, however, Garnett would do as he was ordered, even though he was ailing that day. "General Garnett, buttoned to the neck in an old blue overcoat and much too ill to take the field, mounted his great black horse and rode out in front of his column as it sprang into line," wrote Douglas Southall Freeman in his classic biography of R. E. Lee.

Garnett would be leading the five Virginia regiments that made up his brigade. He and his men held down the left half of Pickett's front in the advance up the hill, first at a measured walk, finally at a flat-out run.

It may be that he did *not* ride the "great black horse" cited by Freeman. He instead was aboard a bay gelding, "his best horse," because his "dark bay mare" had already been killed, wrote historian Robert K. Krick in the book *The Third Day at Gettysburg & Beyond.*

It seems that the bay gelding went down only twenty-five yards or so from the Union infantry massed behind a stone wall. Garnett went down with his horse, said Krick's account.

Who could say, though, second by second, what happened to any single man in the swirl of action just before the Union line? Of Garnett's thirteen hundred men who started up the hill with him, more than nine hundred joined their leader as casualties. And *they* were only a relative few of the thousands who took part in Pickett's Charge and also went down that day. "The carnage had been frightful," noted Freeman. "From Pickett's division only one field officer had found his way back to the [Rebel] lines. All the others had been killed or had been wounded and captured."

As in the case of many others also, there had been no shirking on the part of Garnett. He had been "our cool, gallant, noble brigade commander," recalled a survivor from Garnett's command, Maj. Charles Stephens Peyton of the Nineteenth Virginia. Himself felled by Federal fire during the historic charge, Peyton elaborated: "Never had the brigade been better handled. . . . There was scarcely an officer or man in the command whose attention was not attracted by the cool and handsome bearing of General Garnett, who, totally devoid of excitement or rashness, rode immediately in rear of his advancing line, endeavoring, by his personal efforts . . . to keep his line well closed and dressed."

Cited in Krick's detailed account, Peyton apparently was one of the last to see what happened to Garnett in the bloody climax of the charge. "He was shot from his horse while near the center of the brigade, about twenty-five paces of the stone wall," Peyton claimed.

Another eyewitness cited by Krick, Lt. Col. Norborne Berkeley, "lying wounded and awaiting capture," reported seeing both the general, dead, and his dying horse next to him, "unable to move from the spot."

And yet, like an earthquake changing the shape of the land, the fury of the still-raging battle atop Cemetery Ridge somehow swallowed up and hid Garnett's remains. "Astonishingly," adds the Krick account, "Dick Garnett's body disappeared. He had been the cynosure of thousands of eyes on both sides as he led the dramatic attack on horseback and as he fell, but no one ever identified his remains." Not even, it seems, when an old Union army friend, Gen. Henry J. Hunt, the next day "made diligent search[,] in person, for Garnett's body."

There was only the discovery many years later—by fellow Confederate Brig. Gen. George H. Steuart (a Gettysburg survivor, it so happened)—of Garnett's inscribed sword in a Baltimore pawnshop. In the meantime, said Krick, "Dick Garnett's bones doubtless went back to his native state after the war, together with thousands of other unidentified bodies from Gettysburg, for burial in Richmond's Hollywood Cemetery."

Additional notes: In more recent years, in 1991, specifically, Krick wrote, a monument to Garnett's memory was dedicated in Hollywood Cemetery by "interested historical students." In another twentieth-century development the historian cited, Garnett's descendants and others asserted that a photograph for many years considered a picture of Richard Garnett in fact was not. Showing a man with a short beard, it instead was a photo of his cousin, Confederate Brig. Gen. Robert S. Garnett, first general of either side to be killed in the Civil War. The General Garnett killed at Gettysburg, Richard, was beardless. To add to the confusion, Richard Garnett's family apparently was left no known photograph of the slain general.

Bitter News to Impart

CORRESPONDENT SAM WILKESON WROTE HIS dispatch for the *New York Times* from Gettysburg, a dead Union soldier beside him. In the midst of a bird's "warbling," he wrote, "a shell screamed over the house, instantly followed by another and another, and in a moment the air was full of the most complete artillery prelude to an infantry battle that was ever exhibited. Every size and form of shell known to British and American gunnery shrieked, moaned, whirled, whistled, and wrathfully fluttered over our [Union] ground." In a trice, "houses at twenty and thirty feet distant were receiving their death, and soldiers in Federal blue were torn to pieces in the road and died with the peculiar yells that blend the extorted cry of pain with horror and despair."

So severe was the Confederate barrage, "not an orderly, not an ambulance, not a straggler was to be seen upon the plain swept by this tempest of orchestral death thirty minutes after it commenced."

A somewhat earlier death was that of the young Federal lieutenant who lay next to him—Lt. Bayard Wilkeson, the newspaperman's son. And since he was, *had been,* his son, no wonder that Sam Wilkeson also wrote: "Who can write the history of a battle whose eyes are immovably fastened upon a central figure of transcendingly absorbing interest—the dead body of an oldest born, crushed by a shell in a position where a battery should never have been sent, and abandoned to death in a building where surgeons dared not stay?"

No Happy Ending

WHEN CONFEDERATE CAPT. WELDON EDWARD DAVIS was wounded trying to escape Union captors at Kelly's Ford, Virginia, in November 1863, his right leg badly broken, a Union officer came galloping up to the fallen man, handed him a canteen, and said: "Captain, I am sorry to see you so badly wounded. Have something to drink; it will help you."

Davis gratefully did partake of his kind enemy's offered canteen . . . but no happy ending was the result for either man. A shot rang out from among the freshly captured (but not yet disarmed) Confederates looking on, and the helpful Yankee fell exactly by the wounded man. He, in turn, was carried to a Union hospital in Washington, D.C., where army surgeons amputated his right leg. But infection set in and he died two weeks later.

From General to Private

ODD, ISN'T IT, THAT ANY one man could serve his state, Virginia, as an antebellum congressman, serve also as a Confederate congressman, voluntarily go from Confederate general's rank to Confederate private during the Civil War, and yet wind up years later as a member of the Supreme Court of New York? Along this roller-coaster lifetime path, the same Roger A. Pryor endured an accidental poisoning at Fort Sumter, reportedly survived various duels, served bravely in several battles, endured capture by the Yankees and, in his eighties years later, reportedly beat off a would-be mugger in a New York subway with an umbrella.

Lawyer, newspaper publisher-editor, politician, general, private, or judge . . . he at one time or another was all those, but his wife, Sara Agnes Rice Pryor in her memoirs liked best to call him "the general" or even "my dear general."

They met about the time he was a student at Hampden-Sydney College in Virginia. Taking a law degree at the nearby University of Virginia in 1848, he set up shop as an attorney but had to quit that often-oratorical vocation due to a throat ailment. He turned to newspapering in his native Petersburg, Virginia, area as editor of the *South Side Democrat,* then went to Congress as a U.S. House member. The Civil War now looming, Pryor became widely known for his secessionist writings and fiery speeches (his throat ailment apparently no longer an impediment to his oratory).

But he didn't wish for war, according to Sara. Addressing the House as the crisis worsened, "he entreated for a pacific settlement of our controversy," she wrote years later in her *My Day: Reminiscences of a Long Life.* "'War,' he urged, 'war means widows and orphans.' The temper of the speech was all for peace. He made a noble appeal to the North for concession. He prophesied (the dreamer) that the South could never be subdued by resort to arms!"

He didn't wish for war, but he resigned his seat in the Federal Congress on March 3, 1861, and was in Charleston for the firing on Fort

Sumter a month later as a volunteer aide to P. G. T. Beauregard. Offered the historic opportunity to fire the first shot, he declined.

He did make history, footnotable history, as a member of the Confederate party sent out to the island fortress to negotiate the Federal garrison's surrender. Seated at a table inside the dark dispensary, he helped himself to a drink from a nearby container, apparently thinking it was merely water. But it wasn't—the black bottle held iodide of potassium, a potentially lethal chemical compound.

The garrison's doctor, later a combat commander and major general, Samuel W. Crawford, had to pump Pryor's stomach clear of the toxic fluid.

Unbowed by that potentially embarrassing experience, Pryor soon won election to the Provisional Confederate Congress but then resigned to become colonel of the Third Virginia Infantry. After commanding his regiment in the battle of Williamsburg in April 1862, he was promoted to brigadier general and led a brigade in the Seven Days' campaign outside of Richmond, at Second Manassas, and at Antietam, where he briefly led a division as well.

According to Roger W. Tatum Jr., writing for the Civil War page in the *Washington Times* of August 17, 1996, Pryor as a regimental commander "gained a reputation as a harsh disciplinarian." Many of his men "refused to re-enlist and serve in his regiment." The problem eased when he took over a brigade encompassing his Third Virginia and regiments from other states. His command "fought well," and "Pryor himself was noted on several occasions for his leadership and bravery."

He then was sent to the Suffolk, Virginia, area, south of the James River—"to collect forage and provisions from counties near the Federal lines," explained his wife in her memoir. The need for that tiresome duty may have been great, but the effect was to place her general in a thankless backwater of the war.

Had he failed in some respect, stepped on someone's toes? Or did they need someone reliable in that inglorious post?

According to his obviously adoring wife, he and his men at the Blackwater River stood "in front of a large Federal force to keep it in check while the [Rebel] wagon trains sent off corn and bacon for Lee's army." Said she also: "This was accomplished by sleepless vigilance on the part of the Confederate general [her husband, General Pryor]. The Federal forces made frequent sallies from Suffolk, but were always driven back with loss. It is amusing to read of the calmness with which his commanding officers ordered him to accomplish great things with his small force."

In one response to his pleas for reinforcements, Brig. Gen. Raleigh E. Colston said, "It is almost useless to make such requisitions, for they remain unanswered." Since added manpower simply wasn't available, Colston urged Pryor "to deceive the enemy as to your strength, and [said] you must hold the line of the Blackwater to the last extremity."

Another general, Northern-born Samuel Gibbs French, also pleading an inadequacy of forces, called upon Pryor to "annoy the villains all you can, and make them uncomfortable. Give them no rest. Ambush them at every turn."

While Pryor did his best in the southeastern corner of Virginia, big changes were pending for Robert E. Lee's Army of Northern Virginia— a reorganization of regiments and brigades by state. Somehow, despite all kinds of solicitous comments by his superiors, Pryor came out of the shuffle—a "general upheaval," his wife would call it—with no brigade.

"He was positively assured of a permanent command," said Sara later. According to her account, Lee himself seemed to give such assurance. "I regretted," he wrote in late November 1862, "at the time, the breaking up of your brigade, but you are aware of the circumstances which produced it were beyond my control. I hope it will not be long before you will be again in the field, that the country may derive the benefit of your zeal and activity.'"

Time passed, considerable time, as Pryor waited in Richmond for the promised command. But he waited in vain despite repeated pleas for action. By April 1863 he had carried his appeals all the way to the top—to Jefferson Davis.

Reported Sara Pryor: "The President wrote courteous letters in reply, always repeating assurances of esteem, etc., and continuing to give brigades to newer officers."

Finally, in the late summer of 1863, Pryor paid a quick visit to his wife and children at Amelia Springs, "an old watering place." He came with startling news. "He had resigned his commission as brigadier general and was en route to join General Fitz Lee's cavalry as a private."

Unsurprisingly, "It was a bitter hour for me," she recalled. She "implored" him to stay with her and their children.

But he of course said he couldn't. "I had something to do with bringing on this war," he said. "I must give myself to Virginia. She needs the help of all her sons."

If the Confederacy had "too many" brigadier generals, he also declared, "certain it is there are not enough private soldiers."

With that he was off to his new duties as a private under Lee's nephew, Maj. Gen. Fitzhugh Lee.

The cavalry commander, for his part, was bemused if not non-plused by Pryor's voluntary change in rank. Welcoming Pryor, Fitz Lee wrote: "Honorable, General or Mr.: How should I address you? Damn it, there's no difference! Come up to see me. Whilst I regret the causes that induced you to resign your position, I am glad that the country has not lost your active services, and that your choice to serve her has been cast in one of my regiments."

Lee and his subordinate commanders didn't exactly treat Pryor as an ordinary private. Assigned to the Third Virginia Cavalry, Pryor apparently acted with some independence of movement as a courier and scout. "He worked on special assignments for many senior Confederate officers serving near Petersburg, including . . . Lee, who clearly appreciated Pryor's talents for intelligence work," wrote Tatum in the *Washington Times*.

The roof fell in when Pryor was captured in late November 1864 during the siege of Petersburg. He was at that moment trying to exchange newspapers with his Union counterparts opposite a Rebel battery, according to Tatum's account. Since *Private* Pryor was still armed with "connections," generals got in touch with generals, and soon a plea for his parole from captivity at Fort Lafayette in New York City reached the desk of Abraham Lincoln. "Lincoln was pressured on Pryor's behalf by Southern delegates to the February 1865 peace talks in Hampton Roads, by Horace Greeley and other Northern newspapermen, and by some of Lincoln's Senate friends," wrote Tatum also.

Granted parole to his home in Petersburg by the end of February, Pryor "remained there quietly during the closing days of the war."

Now would come chapter 2 (3 perhaps? 4?) in the lifetime of Roger Pryor . . . in New York City.

Initially "associated with" the city's *Daily News,* according to Ezra J. Warner's *Generals in Gray,* Pryor soon returned to his original field of law. Unable to move his family north with him for a time, he eked out a limited income at first—it was a big day when he could send his wife a couple of hundred dollars. Gradually, though, his growing reputation as a skilled attorney brought him bigger cases and larger fees.

His family of course eventually rejoined him in New York, where many of their friends were onetime Union generals Pryor had fought in the recent Civil War, in theory if not in person. Still intrigued by politics, he openly backed former Union Maj. Gen. Winfield Scott Hancock in the latter's failed presidential bid of 1880 against James A. Garfield (also a former Union general).

Recognized in time as an outstanding lawyer, Pryor was named to the New York Court of Common Pleas as its chief judge, then to the New York State Supreme Court. Attending a dinner in his honor one night in 1890, even before his prestigious bench appointments, were Grover Cleveland, Mark Twain, Thomas Nast, and former Union Gens. Daniel Sickles and William Tecumseh Sherman, among others of note.

"Laying his hand on my husband's shoulder," wrote Sara Pryor, "General Sherman said: 'We would have done all this for him long ago, but he had to be such a rebel'!"

Sherman's good-natured sally would make a good "last word" for a brief glimpse at the remarkable career of Roger Pryor, who died in 1919 at the age of ninety . . . except that his wife, the widow Sara Rice Pryor, provided better ones at the end of her memoir when she wrote:

> The war had left him with nothing but a ragged uniform, his sword, a wife, and seven children—his health, his occupation, his place in the world, gone; his friends and comrades slain in battle; his Southern home impoverished and desolate. He had no profession, no rights as a citizen, no ability to hold office. That he conquered the fate which threatened to destroy him—and conquered it through the appreciation awarded by his sometime enemies—is a striking illustration of the possibilities afforded by our country; where not only can the impoverished refugee from other lands find fortune and happiness, but where her own sons, prostrate and ruined after a dreadful fratricidal strife, can bind their wounds, take up their lives again, and finally win reward for their labors.

★ Part 5 ★
Generally Speaking II

People, real people, filled the homes and landscape of the Civil War era . . . they had their moments of joy and laughter, along with the sorrows and miseries of a war tearing at their vitals. People just like us today . . . only they did have that war on their doorstep.

A Tale of Two Horses

THEIR NAMES COME DOWN THROUGH history. Generals. Political figures. Battlefield heroes of all ranks. Famous spies. Plus . . . two horses of note!

Traveller and Little Sorrel—Lee's mount and Jackson's, too. Just horses . . . yet these two steeds are probably better known by name today than anyone among either Confederate general's own family members. That may have been the case, or close to it, in their own time as well. In an age, in a war, when a man's horse was his best way to get around the countryside, was his trusty companion, was an integral part of his overall persona, these two mounts became icons just like their two owners.

Oddly, each horse would figure, directly or indirectly, in separate accidents resulting in painful injuries to both generals on the eve of the battle of Antietam.

But that didn't come about until the fall of 1862. In the meantime, each general found and came to rely upon his favorite mount of the Civil War period.

Traveller came from the mountains of western Virginia, today's West Virginia . . . and very nearly did *not* fall into Robert E. Lee's hands. In the late spring of 1861, while engaged in his first Civil War campaign, and a rather unsuccessful one at that, Lee was at Sewell Mountain—he came across a gray stallion, four years old, named Jeff Davis. He talked to the owner about buying the horse, but nothing came of their discussion at first.

Reassigned to the defenses of the Georgia, Florida, and South Carolina coasts that fall, Lee did purchase the handsome steed, then named Greenbrier, for $200. "Lee renamed him Traveller, rode him

203

for the rest of the war, and raised him to the pantheon of warhorses," wrote Emory M. Thomas in his biography of Lee.

Stonewall Jackson, in the meantime, found his famous Little Sorrel in the late spring of 1861 also—among the horses his troops unloaded from a train captured near Harpers Ferry. Insisting on paying the Confederacy for the sturdy little gelding, as well as for a larger gelding, he originally planned to give the smaller horse to his wife, Anna, and named the animal Fancy. When the larger horse didn't work out as a satisfactory personal mount, "the little sorrel" intended for Anna became Jackson's own mount until the time of his fatal wounding at the battle of Chancellorsville in May 1863.

He in fact was riding Little Sorrel when he was struck by three bullets fired by his own men, wounds leading to the loss of his left arm and later to his death.

For most of the two previous years, though, Little Sorrel was his faithful and constant companion in battle and in transit to battle. Soon famous among Jackson's troops for its stamina and endurance, Jackson's small sorrel, only fifteen hands high, seemed in an odd way to almost take care of its brilliant if a bit eccentric—and always fatigued—rider.

At the time of the March 1862 battle of Kernstown in the Shenandoah Valley, for instance, Jackson was riding at the head of his column. "Little Sorrel," wrote Jackson biographer James I. Robertson Jr., "navigated without any pull on the reins for its rider was lost in thought."

As time went on and Jackson's Valley campaign continued, accomplishing the impossible in logistics and mobility again and again, his weary soldiers came to picture him and his horse as one, really.

At the battle of Winchester two months after Kernstown, an artillerist in Dick Ewell's division caught a glimpse of the legend-in-process and later wrote, "Yonder, in a faded gray coat, on Old [*sic*] Sorrel, came Stonewall himself, his cap in his hand, his eye bright with victory, his hair fluttering in the wind, the very cyclone of battle, followed by his panting staff."

Another onlooker, also an artilleryman, was equally moved, saying later: "As he came the men pressed in shoals to the road-side and waved their hats enthusiastically. It was deafening. . . . I never saw a more thrilling scene."

The same remarkable reception by the troops occurred more and more frequently as Jackson's reputation grew. On another day in 1862, after the battle of Antietam, a Georgia sergeant serving under James Longstreet heard cheering "down the road in our front." As also reported in Robertson's biography of Jackson, this young sergeant wrote that "sure enough, it was Gen. Jackson galloping along the road with his escort."

The Georgia soldier also said: "He passed us with his cap off and the cheering continued down the line as far as we could hear. The boys claim that he is getting tired of the army because Longstreet's men keep him bareheaded so much. . . . He certainly creates more excitement than all the rest of the officers put together."

The fact was, such adulation embarrassed the humble and deeply religious general. But . . . did his horse somehow understand that? Also according to Robertson: "By that stage of the war, Little Sorrel had learned its master's embarrassment at the cheers from the soldiers. Whenever Confederates raised loud and friendly noise, the horse would break into a gallop and carry its rider speedily away."

Unfortunately, right before the battle of Antietam, Little Sorrel disappeared. Jackson's favorite mount somehow became lost or was stolen. As Lee's army struck across the Potomac River and entered Maryland—his first "invasion" of the North—a Marylander presented Jackson with a large gray mare. Needing a good horse, Jackson accepted the gift, albeit "somewhat embarrassingly."

He tested the horse that evening, and all appeared well. But not the next morning. When his new horse at first refused to move, Jackson "touched her with a spur." That was a mistake!

The gift horse reared up with Jackson clinging to the saddle, lost her balance, and "fell heavily to the ground." So did her precious rider.

Both stunned and bruised, the general stayed there for thirty minutes or so while doctors checked him out for any broken bones. No permanent injury was evident, but the shaken Jackson for a few hours "rode ingloriously in an ambulance." He would be hurting for days to come.

Oddly, Robert E. Lee also progressed toward Antietam after being both shaken and slightly injured in a horse-related mishap. It happened on the heels of his victory at Second Manassas (Bull Run)—on a rainy day, August 31, 1862. Dressed in his "rubber suit" of overalls and a poncho, Lee was standing with his staff, Traveller's reins on his arm, when someone shouted, "Yankee cavalry!" Just then, said a witness later, a line of Union prisoners under escort suddenly appeared at the brow of a nearby embankment.

Spooked, Lee's horse reared up. The general grabbed for the reins but tripped over his awkward overalls and fell. "Instinctively he broke his fall with his hands and in the process broke a bone in one of them and sprained them both," wrote Thomas in his Lee biography.

As a result, the general soon to lead Confederate forces into the North couldn't ride his horse, set pen to paper, or even dress without help for several weeks.

So it was that the absence of one general's horse and the display of nerves by the other sent both Confederate leaders into a critical battle in less than ideal physical shape. Then, too, Longstreet joined them at Antietam wearing a slipper on one foot due to a blister on his heel.

A little more than eighteen months later, in the battle of Spotsylvania in the spring of 1864, Traveller more than made up for any earlier transgressions—you could even say that Traveller on this occasion saved Lee's life! According to long-time Longstreet aide Moxley Sorrel, Traveller reared up at one point with Lee in the saddle just when a cannonball streaked their way. With Traveller on his hind legs the "cannon ball whizzed beneath the horse's girth," wrote Thomas. "Had Traveller not been on his hind legs the ball would surely have hit and likely killed the general."

Traveller and Lee together survived the remaining battles of 1864, the siege of Petersburg, and for some years the peace that followed Lee's surrender at Appomattox. Lee's famous horse remained with his master through the latter's years as president of little Washington College in Lexington, Virginia (later Washington and Lee University). Traveller was still there when Lee died in 1870 . . . and he was there for the funeral procession that followed. Lee's famous mount of course was a featured part of the procession.

Meanwhile, by unlikely seeming good fortune, Jackson was reunited with Little Sorrel shortly before the guns spoke at Antietam. Just how that came about is not clear. Biographer Robertson's years of research on Jackson could only establish that "sometime during September 6–8 [1862], Little Sorrel was returned to the general." We apparently know the dates because "a field correspondent noted near the end of the Frederick [Maryland] encampment [on the way to South Mountain, Sharpsburg, and Antietam Creek] that Jackson was on 'his old horse.'"

That "old horse" was destined to disappear once again . . . but for fully understandable reasons. The evening of May 2 at Chancellorsville both horse and rider mistakenly came under fire from friendly troops in the scrub woods nearby. Skittish, Little Sorrel "wheeled away" from the first burst of gunfire. More and more shots rang out and Jackson was hit by three .57-caliber bullets, two of them in the left arm.

"For the first and only time, Little Sorrel bolted from the sound of gunfire," wrote Robertson. "The horse dashed obliquely toward the northwest as Jackson reeled in the saddle. An oak limb struck him in the face, knocked off his cap, and all but unseated him."

Jackson somehow managed to stay in the saddle until two members of his escorting party were able to sandwich his mount between them and hold the horse still. In the dark and the confusion, with others—both men and horses—also shot in the errant volleys, it took a few minutes for Jackson's two companions to ease him to the ground. "Little Sorrel, meanwhile, could comprehend nothing but fear. When [Pvt. William T.] Wynn released the reins, the horse galloped wildly toward the enemy lines."

That was the last that Jackson, soon fighting for his life, would ever see of his wartime mount. After suffering the amputation of his left arm and seeming to regain his strength, Jackson contracted pneumonia and, on May 10, died.

Once again, however, Little Sorrel reappeared! According to biographer Robertson, "Private Thomas R. Yeatman of [Jeb] Stuart's horse

Stonewall Jackson's favorite wartime mount, Little Sorrel, outlived his master by many years, most of them at the Virginia Military Institute where Jackson once taught.

VIRGINIA MILITARY INSTITUTE

artillery is generally credited with recapturing Little Sorrel a few days later. Ironically, word was sent to Jackson of the recovery of the horse on the day the general died." But it was too late for a reunion.

Unfortunately, too, the little sorrel wasn't recovered in time for Jackson's funeral—another horse he recently had ridden, named Superior, took part in the funeral procession that wound through Richmond's Capitol Square. Little Sorrel did spend some time afterward with Jackson's widow, Anna, but then was sent to Virginia Military Institute (VMI), also in Lexington, Virginia, where Jackson once had taught. There the horse became an institution, living to the ripe old age of thirty-six.

So it was, ironically, that both horses lived out their remaining years in the same small Virginia town after the Civil War, although Little Sorrel stole a march on Traveller by "living on" for years more with his hide mounted for display at the VMI Museum.

★

PERSONAL GLIMPSE
"Extra Billy"

★

FIVE TIMES A U.S. CONGRESSMAN, once a Confederate congressman, twice governor of Virginia, five times wounded in battle, two kinds of Confederate general, William "Extra Billy" Smith was extra all right . . . extra in many ways.

Uniform for battle? He wore a high beaver hat and carried a blue cotton umbrella at Chantilly, Virginia, on a rainy day during the Second Manassas campaign. He had joined the Civil War fighting after becoming involved in a running gun battle in nearby Fairfax Court House a year earlier. Pure chance had placed the former governor on the scene as a troop of Union cavalry attacked the town. With the Confederate commander, Capt. J. Q. Marr, killed, Extra Billy took command of the defenders.

That done, he soon took over the Forty-ninth Virginia Infantry as its colonel. He also was elected to the First Regular Confederate Congress, meeting in the Confederate (and Virginia) capital of Richmond,

Onetime mail carrier, Confederate general, and Virginia governor William "Extra Billy" Smith.

U.S. ARMY MILITARY HISTORY INSTITUTE

and for a time attended its sessions between battles and campaigns. He became noted for his disdain of formal military tradition—he favored commonsense decisions over rigid adherence to by-the-book tactics.

His nickname, however, had nothing to do with his political career or his Civil War experiences. It came instead from his long-time operation of a postal service between Washington, D.C., and the capital of Georgia at the time, Milledgeville. He made extra mail deliveries on the side for an extra fee. Thus, Extra Billy.

As a politician later, he proved no friend to emancipation of the slaves—he many times proposed that all free blacks be ousted from Virginia.

A man with no military training or experience, Smith certainly didn't let his political career stop him from soldiering on and on after that first skirmish at Fairfax Court House. He fought in the Peninsula campaign, in the Seven Days' battles, at Antietam, and even Gettysburg. Wounded five times in all, he suffered three of those injuries at Antietam but remained in command of his newly assigned brigade until it had fulfilled its role in that major battle.

Recovering, he was promoted to brigadier general. Smith resigned his congressional seat, accompanied Lee's Army of Northern Virginia to Gettysburg (and survived), was promoted to major general, and was elected governor of Virginia for a second time—all in the same year, 1863.

Now Smith did give up soldiering to take office as governor in early 1864 and serve in that post until the end of the Civil War. The great conflict's denouement of course was an especially trying period for Virginia, the scene in 1865 of the Confederate government's collapse and Lee's surrender at Appomattox.

His own stewardship of Virginia taken over by a Union military governor, Gen. John McAllister Schofield, Extra Billy returned to farming at his family estate and birthplace, Marengo, in King George County. Some years later he briefly reappeared in the Virginia state legislature.

All this from a man born in the century before the Civil War period—a man born, in fact, two years before the death of George Washington. You see, William "Extra Billy" Smith was born in 1797. He was sixty-four when he joined the firefight at Fairfax Court House. He was sixty-seven when he attended his second inauguration as governor in 1864. He was eighty when he briefly returned to the Virginia House of Delegates. He was eighty-nine years old when he died at Marengo in 1887.

Men of Iron

Will the union's real Iron Brigade please stand up?

And no, it wasn't that hard-fighting, hard-marching Wisconsin outfit also known as the Black Hat Brigade. Well, at least not at first it wasn't, although, true, sometime *after* Antietam in 1862 Brig. Gen. John Gibbon's black-hatted brigade really and famously *did* become known far and wide as the Iron Brigade.

According to oft-repeated legend, that particular christening scenario took place at the battle of South Mountain, basically the opening round of the struggle known as the battle of Antietam (or Sharpsburg) during the first Confederate invasion of the North. The story here was that Maj. Gen. George B. McClellan, commander of the Union's Army of the Potomac, and his First Corps commander, Maj. Gen. Joseph Hooker, were discussing the Confederate stranglehold on the heights overlooking Turner's Gap *early in the battle*. McClellan allegedly told Hooker, "If I had an iron brigade, I could pierce the enemy's center by taking that gorge on the pike." And Hooker supposedly said, "General, I have that brigade in my command."

By another variation of the frequently stated story, McClellan somewhat later in the day asked Hooker whose men were those fighting on the same pike, and Hooker identified them as Gibbon's brigade from Wisconsin.

McClellan then said, "They must be made of iron."

To which Hooker supposedly rejoined: "By the Eternal, they are iron! If you had seen them at Bull Run as I did, you would know them to be iron." The Hooker reference, not so incidentally, was to *Second* Bull Run, in the summer of 1862, not to First Bull Run of a year earlier.

It all comes together as a colorful story, but Civil War scholar Tom Clemens asserts it just wasn't so. Writing in the first issue of the Civil War quarterly *Columbiad* in 1997, Clemens knocked one prop after another from under the Iron Brigade tale. According to Clemens . . .

• McClellan and Hooker did *not* study the terrain at South Mountain together. "Hooker's report clearly states that McClellan sent him ahead to scout the terrain, and did not accompany him," wrote Clemens.

• Since the fighting began at 9 A.M. that day and Hooker did *not* arrive until "the early to mid-afternoon," and McClellan did *not* show up until even later, they could *not* possibly have scouted Turner's Gap (together or separately) early in the battle, as often alleged.

• Furthermore, Hooker at Second Bull Run was with Third Corps as a division commander, rather than First Corps, and therefore was unlikely to have seen Gibbon's men in action in another part of the battleground. "He [Hooker] . . . had no real contact with Gibbon's men, and probably had no opportunity to observe their fighting there."

But here, in reference to what Hooker possibly *did* see at Second Manassas, is another possibility—"At best, he may have seen them grudgingly give ground to Brig. Gen. John Bell Hood's Confederates on the 30th of August, as the Union army retreated to Washington."

So where or how did such a factual mix-up come about? According to the Clemens article, blame one W. H. Adkins for the original story giving McClellan credit (sort of) for renaming the Wisconsin Black Hat Brigade (so named for the regular army's dress hats the men wore instead of the familiar field or forage cap). Adkins was author of a piece that appeared in the Union army veterans' newspaper *National Tribune* in 1904. He, in turn, said *his* source was a letter from onetime

Capt. John B. Callis of the Seventh Wisconsin, one of the Black Hat–Iron Brigade regiments. And Callis allegedly was relying upon a postwar conversation with "Little Mac" McClellan himself at a convention in a Philadelphia hotel.

In sum, postulated Clemens, "the Adkins/Callis account is pure fiction." The story, upon "careful examination," is fraught with "several improbabilities and internal inconsistencies." Further, "It's hard to determine who is responsible for the inaccuracy: Adkins, Callis, McClellan, or a combination of all three. Adkins did not publish all of Callis's letter, but only quoted from it. By the time Adkins wrote his article, Callis, McClellan, Hooker, and [Ambrose] Burnside [also at Antietam] were all dead, so there was no one to refute Adkins's version."

Still, no one can dispute that from *some* point in 1862 (or, it turns out, 1863) to the end of the Civil War, the Wisconsin outfit certainly was known as the Iron Brigade—and widely admired as such on both sides, North and South. How and why this came about also is not entirely clear today. General Gibbon himself wrote in 1886: "I do not know who first suggested the name Iron Brigade. . . . I believe it was started soon after the battle of Antietam."

As Clemens also pointed out in *Columbiad,* however, Gibbon's Wisconsin men were *not* the only or even the first "iron men" to be found among the formidable array of Union forces. Gibbon's Fourth Brigade of Abner Doubleday's division, in fact, may have acquired the nickname from the same division's all–New York First Brigade, apparently—now hear this!—the *original* Iron Brigade. The Wisconsin men replaced the New Yorkers as the First Brigade in the same division upon their mustering out of the army . . . *in the spring of 1863.*

Nor was the new Iron Brigade the only one to appear in the Civil War—to the contrary, the Union boasted several iron brigades and the Confederacy at least one, wrote Clemens, while offering quotes from soldiers' letters home and even the New York brigade's "Iron Brigade" badge as evidence of the popular nickname's usage. Indeed, three infantry regiments from New York adopted the term "iron" for their nicknames: the 176th "Ironsides," the 136th "Ironclads," and the 115th "Iron Hearted" regiments. As for the Confederates, South Carolina boasted its "Iron Scouts" cavalrymen under Wade Hampton, while the Confederacy's very own "Iron Brigade" served in Brig. Gen. J. O. Shelby's hard-riding cavalry command in Mississippi.

Obviously enough, the term appealed to both sides and appeared in many variations, including those *iron*clad fighting vessels often associated with the American Civil War.

An odd coincidence, also noted by Clemens, was that three of the Union's iron brigades took part in the battle of South Mountain, "within a mile or two of one another, and participants' accounts from all three make reference to using or acquiring the name there or soon afterwards."

Said Clemens: "None of these commands can conclusively be shown to be the one and only 'Iron Brigade.' Indeed, we can irrefutably prove that there were several 'Iron Brigades.' The 'Black Hats' are certainly the most famous, and through their conduct in battle they earned every honor they have received. But they were not the first or the only 'Iron Brigade.'"

Additional note: John Gibbon, commander of Wisconsin's Black Hat–Iron Brigade in 1862, could claim no real ties to the Badger State. He was born in Philadelphia, Pennsylvania, but grew up in North Carolina, then returned north to attend the U.S. Military Academy at West Point, New York.

Graduating in the same class as the future Confederacy's A. P. Hill and the Union's Ambrose Burnside in 1847, Gibbon stuck by the Union when the Civil War erupted—contrary to three brothers who entered Confederate service instead.

As a brigadier general of volunteers, he led a brigade at Second Bull Run and in the fighting at South Mountain and Antietam. Then assigned to command of the Second Division of First Corps late in 1862, he suffered a severe wound at Fredericksburg. Recuperating some weeks later, he took over the Second Division of Second Corps, only to be felled again at Gettysburg.

In 1864, once again recovered, he joined U. S. Grant for the Overland campaign taking Union forces southward through Virginia from the Wilderness west of Fredericksburg to the gates of Petersburg. Promoted to major general in mid-1864, Gibbon took charge of the Twenty-fourth Corps, Army of the James, early in 1865 and at

Appomattox was one of the Union officers charged with officially receiving the surrender of Lee's army.

With the hostilities then ended, Gibbon remained in the army, chiefly as an Indian fighter. It was his command that rode to the aid of George Armstrong Custer at the Little Bighorn . . . but arrived only in time to rescue the handful of survivors and to bury the dead. Gibbon later campaigned against the Nez Perce Indians and earned brigadier general's rank in the regular army.

He retired in 1891 and died in 1896. His *Personal Recollections of the Civil War* appeared in 1928. Appropriately enough, he once said, "At the Judgment Day I want to be with Wisconsin soldiers."

His old brigade, originally the Black Hats, indeed was predominantly composed of Wisconsin men—from the Second, Sixth, and Seventh Wisconsin Volunteers—but it also included a few "outsiders"—from the Nineteenth Indiana Volunteers and the Twenty-fourth Michigan Volunteers.

Often considered the most famous infantry brigade in the Army of the Potomac, the Midwestern brigade fought all the war's most significant battles in the East from August 1862 to Lee's surrender at Appomattox in April 1865. An indication of its constant exposure to combat, the Black Hats–Iron Brigade recorded the greatest percentage of battle deaths suffered by any infantry brigade fighting for the Union. In the first day of battle at Gettysburg alone, the brigade counted 1,212 of its 1,883 men, or 65 percent, as casualties, reported Alan T. Nolan in the second (summer 1997) issue of *Columbiad.*

It was a brave but significantly outnumbered brigade that stood in Lee's way west of Gettysburg that first day. "Its dogged and desperate fighting helped protect the strategic high ground south of the village and purchased time for the Army of the Potomac to concentrate and deploy," wrote Nolan. "From that hard-won high ground the Federal army defeated the Confederates over the next two days, but the Iron Brigade's effort had been desperately costly."

Added Nolan: "Fragments of the Iron Brigade, supplemented by Eastern units, fought on to Appomattox and kept their proud name alive, but that first day at Gettysburg effectively destroyed the original unit." Even so, the record will show that of the twenty Medals of Honor won by Wisconsin soldiers overall, six went to Iron Brigade members.

West Pointers All

THEY WENT TO WEST POINT . . . and more than a few ironies, oddities, conflicts, and coincidences later emerged.

For instance, as odd juxtaposition, take the Class of **1846.** *George* B. McClellan, commander of the Union Army of the Potomac for the Peninsula campaign, ranked second in the class, while ranking fifty-ninth and last was *George* E. Pickett, famous for Pickett's ill-fated charge at Gettysburg . . . ill-fated but not really his fault.

Then, too, in the Class of **1847:** two future opponents named *Ambrose* . . . future Confederate general *Ambrose* P. Hill (A. P. Hill in most historical accounts) and future Union general *Ambrose* Burnside.

Earlier, much earlier, the Class of **1827** produced the future war's only fighting bishop of the Episcopal Church, plus a general-rank officer who upset even his own compatriots by his use of antipersonnel land mines. Both Bishop Leonidas Polk and Gabriel Rains would emerge as Civil War generals of the Confederate persuasion. Polk, a good friend of Jefferson Davis, Class of **1828,** was destined to be killed in 1864 by an artillery shell at Pine Mountain, Georgia, near Atlanta. Rains, a self-taught explosives specialist, used his expertise to invent the antipersonnel mine, "which he sowed in the roads in large quantities, causing not a few Union casualties," according to Ezra J. Warner in his book *Generals in Gray.*

Wrote Warner also: "This hitherto unknown mode of warfare excited much comment and criticism from Federals and Confederates alike. General Longstreet forbade its further employment as 'not proper.' By the end of the war, however, even its most violent opponents were converted to its use."

Appearing in the Class of **1840,** meanwhile, were the Confederacy's future generals Richard S. Ewell, Bushrod R. Johnson, Thomas Jordan, James Green Martin, and William Steele, plus the Union's outstanding future generals William Tecumseh Sherman (ranking sixth in the class) and Virginia-born George H. Thomas ("the Rock of Chickamauga"). Classmate William Hays, also Virginia-born and destined to become a Union general, saw his army career ruined after everyone at

How much could these members of West Point's Class of 1860 have known, or even guessed, of the momentous events awaiting them less than a year after their graduation?

his headquarters was found asleep at 6:30 A.M. just three days before Lee's surrender at Appomattox.

Oddly, classmates Bushrod Johnson and William Steele were born in Northern states but became Confederate generals. Then, too, future "Reb" Thomas Jordan was Sherman's roommate at West Point.

Incidentally as well, "Old One Wing" James Green Martin, as he was called by his men, entered Confederate service and became a notably courageous combat leader despite the fact he had already lost his right arm in the Mexican War fifteen years before. Richard Ewell, for that matter, lost a leg at the Civil War battle of Groveton but continued in active Confederate service anyway . . . on a wooden leg.

Confederate leaders Jubal Early, Braxton Bragg, and John Pemberton all graduated from West Point in 1837, along with future Union foes John Sedgwick and Joseph Hooker. But here was another West Pointer caught napping—their classmate and fellow general E. Parker Scammon, reported *Harper's Weekly,* was "gobbled up" one night early in 1864 by Confederate guerrillas who found him asleep on a steamboat.

From the Class of 1844 came future Union general Winfield Scott Hancock, wounded hero of Gettysburg . . . and many years later, the presidential candidate who lost to fellow Civil War veteran James A.

Members of the Class of 1862 expected an early baptism of fire as young officers thrown into battle against older graduates of the same academy who had opted to fight for the South.

Garfield, a non–West Pointer. Hancock ranked eighteenth in a class of twenty-five. His classmates included Simon Bolivar Buckner, future Confederate general and governor of Kentucky, and Alexander Hayes, future Union general and good friend to U. S. Grant until killed in action in the battle of the Wilderness, May 5, 1864.

Rarely recalled but a product of West Point's famous Class of **1841** was Schuyler Hamilton, grandson of Revolutionary War leader Alexander Hamilton, first secretary of the treasury. But why *famous?* Because the class produced a total of twenty general-rank officers for the opposing sides in the Civil War. Among them was the Union's Don Carlos Buell, number thirty-two in a class of fifty-two.

Not far behind the Class of **1841** as a contributor of Civil War generals was the Class of **1842** with its crop of seventeen general-rank officers. Among them was the Union's John Pope, a collateral descendant of George Washington and related by marriage to Mary Todd Lincoln.

Ranking third in the Class of **1839**, meanwhile, was the future general in chief of the Union forces, Henry Wager Halleck, once dismissed by Lincoln as of no more weight than a good clerk . . . brother-in-law, by the way, to Schuyler Hamilton (Halleck married a granddaughter of Alexander Hamilton).

Ranking first, it *must* also be mentioned, in the benchmark Class of 1843 was William Buel Franklin, future Union general blamed by Burnside for contributing significantly to the disastrous Federal defeat at Fredericksburg. More enduringly, Franklin was also construction supervisor for the Capitol dome in Washington, D.C., and the capitol of Connecticut in Hartford. But why *benchmark* class? Well, ranking twenty-first among the graduates of 1843 (and chiefly noted for his superb horsemanship) was the Union's preeminent Civil War general and a future U.S. president as well, Ulysses S. Grant.

The same Class of 1843, thirty-nine members in all, provided the North with ten Civil War generals and the South three, not counting brevet (temporary) promotions.

Moving on, first in the Class of 1851 was little-known George Leonard Andrews, future civil engineer, Civil War general, Mississippi planter, U.S. marshal . . . and later (talk about a career change!), a professor of French at West Point.

In the Class of 1825 was Robert Anderson, future Union general . . . also the officer who withstood Confederate bombardment of hapless Fort Sumter for thirty-four hours before surrendering the Federal outpost in Charleston Harbor on April 14, 1861, at the outbreak of the Civil War. Four years later to the day, he also would be the Union officer who once more raised the Stars and Stripes at Fort Sumter, now (April 14, 1865) back in Union hands.

Ranked fifth in his Class of May 1861, meanwhile, future Union general Adelbert Ames was destined to win the Medal of Honor, serve as a Reconstruction governor and U.S. senator from Mississippi . . . and die in 1933 as the last surviving full general from either side of the Civil War. Ranked dead-last in the Class of June 1861, incidentally, was George Armstrong Custer. (Obviously success on the battlefield did not depend on success in the classroom.)

Just missing the status of permanent classmate to Ames and Custer was the future Confederate general Thomas L. Rosser, a Virginian who resigned from Federal service just two weeks before the May graduation day of 1861 . . . and then, during the war that followed, was destined to lose to former classmate and fellow cavalryman Custer in the battles of Woodstock and Cedar Creek, Virginia.

Out of forty-three members in the Class of 1852, it may also be noted, future Indian fighter and Union general George Crook ranked number thirty-eight.

From the Class of **1853** came John Schofield, future Union nemesis to classmate John Bell Hood at Franklin and Nashville, Tennessee. Number seven in their class, Schofield later would serve as the Military Academy's superintendent, the nation's secretary of war, and the regular army's commanding general. It was he who suggested establishing a U.S. naval base at Pearl Harbor in the Hawaiian islands. (Schofield Barracks, remember?) Not to be forgotten, of course, two more Union luminaries from the same class were Philip Sheridan and James B. McPherson; the latter was killed during the Atlanta campaign.

Also a member of the Class of **1853** was future Union general Joshua Woodrow Sill, ranked number three in his stellar company of cadets. At the battle of Murfreesboro, by odd coincidence, he picked up classmate Phil Sheridan's coat by mistake when leaving the latter's tent one night . . . and was killed the next morning still wearing Sheridan's uniform coat. Fort Sill, Oklahoma, is named for him.

Let it be known, too, that another future superintendent of West Point emerged from the same Class of **1853**—third-ranking Thomas Howard Ruger, also a future Union general.

Returning to the class of the two Ambroses, **1847**, it might interest some to know that bottom man of all thirty-eight class members was future Confederate general Henry Heth.

Many years before that, future Union general Charles Ferguson Smith, Class of **1825**, became a widely loved commandant of cadets—a position he held when both Grant and Sherman passed through West Point as cadets. He in fact was an idol to both of them, especially to Grant.

During the Civil War, ironically, an aging General Smith served under Grant in the storming of Fort Donelson. But then, just before the battle of Shiloh, he sharply banged his shin jumping into a rowboat. The bruise produced an infection that would not go away and he soon lay dying.

He lay dying, in fact, at Grant's headquarters at Savannah, Tennessee, just close enough to hear the sound of battle in the distance as his two former cadets, Grant and Sherman, pressed home their victory (with Buell's timely help) over the Confederates at Shiloh—against still another West Pointer, Albert Sidney Johnston. Johnston, it's worth noting also, graduated from the Military Academy just a year (**1826**) after Smith himself. Sadly, too, wounded in the leg at Shiloh, Johnston kept to his horse and slowly bled to death before the battle's end.

Meanwhile, achieving the highest grades ever given at West Point until Douglas MacArthur came along at the turn of the century (Class of 1903) was William Henry Chase Whiting, Class of 1845. At first a star in the Confederate firmament, this Mississippi native from Biloxi was promoted to brigadier general on site at First Manassas—by no less a personage than Jefferson Davis. After supervising the construction of Fort Fisher at the entrance to the Cape Fear River near Wilmington, North Carolina, unfortunately, Whiting was accused of being drunk on alcohol or other drugs at Petersburg, Virginia. Returning to Fort Fisher in time for its seizure by Union forces in January 1865, he was severely wounded and taken prisoner. Confined at Fort Columbus on Governor's Island off Manhattan Island, New York, Whiting died there in March 1865, due to the lingering effects of his wounding two months earlier.

Last but far from least in any accounting of the Civil War, the Confederacy's preeminent general, Robert E. Lee, also graduated from West Point—as second-ranking man in the Class of 1832. Remarkably, he sailed through his four years at the Military Academy without incurring a single demerit. He later would serve as superintendent at West Point, and his eldest son, George Washington Custis Lee, would follow as a member of the Class of 1854. The very same class of '54 also produced one J. E. B. Stuart—the dashing, highly colorful future major general of Confederate cavalry, Jeb Stuart. To continue with the Lee family saga, however, not far behind them would be the elder Lee's nephew, Fitzhugh Lee, Class of 1856. Both younger Lees would serve the Confederacy as generals, too. (As for R. E. Lee's other son of general's rank, William Henry Fitzhugh "Rooney" Lee, future cavalry officer and major general, he spent his college days at Harvard. Youngest Lee son Rob, also destined to serve as a Confederate officer, did not achieve general's rank . . . or attend West Point.)

When the Civil War ended, some of the West Pointers who had opposed one another during the hostilities resumed old friendships. Case in point: At Appomattox shortly after the surrender documents had been signed, recalled Evan Connell in his book *Son of the Morning Star,* George Custer (Class of 1861 and Union, of course) and Fitz Lee (1856, Confederate) "embraced and fell to the ground, wrestling like schoolboys."

☆ ☆ ☆

Additional notes: George Crittenden, Class of **1832**, served the Confederate cause as a general, while his non–West Pointer brother, Gen. Thomas Leonidas Crittenden, served the Union. So did their father, U.S. Sen. John Jay Crittenden of Kentucky.

Other West Pointers of more than passing interest: Pierre Gustave Toutant Beauregard, Class of **1838**, ranked second; Barnard Elliott Bee, Class of **1845**, killed at First Manassas . . . but not before he gave Thomas J. Jackson (Class of **1846**) his famous nickname "Stonewall."

Then, too, hailing from the Class of **1860**, Stephen Dodson Ramseur would become the youngest major general in Confederate service. Fatally wounded and captured at Cedar Creek late in the war, as stated earlier, he died among friends . . . among fellow West Pointers, and all Union, of course. A relative oldster who hailed from Albert Sidney Johnston's Class of **1826** was future Union general Samuel P. Heintzelman, who at least twice, in two different battles (First Bull Run and Seven Pines), went to notably heroic extremes trying to rally his retreating men . . . but to no avail.

As a final note, from an even earlier class, **1817**, came Ethan Allen Hitchcock, grandson of the legendary Ethan Allen, leader of the Green Mountain Boys of the Revolutionary era. Hitchcock, reported Ezra J. Warner in his book *Generals in Blue,* later became an intimate of Abraham Lincoln and Secretary of War Edwin Stanton. Further, Hitchcock was "one of only a half dozen West Point graduates born in the eighteenth century who became general officers during the Civil War."

Showing the Way Home

A SOUTHERN WAGONER OFTEN DELIVERING goods behind Union lines, Joshua Moon Jr. was able to help escaping Confederate prisoners both day and night . . . on his way home "down South." By night, they could ride his otherwise empty wagon in the relative safety of the dark. By day, though, any interested Union soldier could look and see what was in the wagon, other than wagoner Moon and his young son Columbus.

In most cases, the Yankees taking a look at the wagon paid little attention to the tree boughs laid out on the wagon bed. Only once did an inspecting Yankee even ask, and he was easily put off by Moon's reply that the branches were just a "fool notion" of his son.

Their real purpose was quite different. The Moons, father and son, were using the tree boughs to mark the route home for Rebel compatriots following on foot during the daytime as best they could. To avoid detection, the escaping prisoners clung to the woods along the roads as much as possible, but they at least knew where they were going, thanks to the wagoner and his son. That was because at crucial turns and forks in the road, the Moons dropped off the tree boughs to point out the proper pathway leading South.

Strife Among Generals

IN THE CONFEDERACY OF 1861–65, many were the disputes and hard feelings among principal figures. Not so much aimed at the enemy, the powerful and implacable North, but among themselves.

Most visibly, President Jefferson Davis despised Joseph Eggleston Johnston, a hero of First Manassas and the full general who commanded the Army of Northern Virginia before Robert E. Lee. Johnston fully despised Davis in return.

Johnston, moreover, was in dispute with Lt. Gen. John C. Pemberton over who truly should take the blame for the loss of Vicksburg in early July 1863.

Famously also, many of Braxton Bragg's subordinates despised him, with rough-tough Nathan Bedford Forrest once going so far as to physically threaten Bragg, his superior officer, to his face.

Then, too, division commander George Pickett of Pickett's Charge fame never did quite forgive Robert E. Lee for ordering the terribly costly assault against Cemetery Ridge on the third and final day of the battle of Gettysburg. For that matter, corps commander James Longstreet openly questioned Lee's strategy at Gettysburg and was slow to comply with his commanding officer's orders.

Lee, it may also be recalled, was most unhappy with Jeb Stuart's initial absence from Gettysburg. Stuart was engaged on a raid elsewhere in the Pennsylvania countryside, but the fault may have been Lee's own unclear orders. And Longstreet's as well.

The kindly, widely revered Lee on another occasion had harsh words for South Carolina's proud cavalryman Wade Hampton. When Hampton one time complained that Stuart had transferred one of Hampton's horse brigades to Lee's nephew Fitzhugh Lee, the elder Lee, obviously irritated, snapped, "I would not care if you went back to South Carolina with your whole division."

This bit of gossip is according to well-known Southern diarist Mary Boykin Chesnut, whose husband, James, was an antebellum planter, a Confederate senator, general, and aide to Jefferson Davis.

By her account, too, Hampton found Lee's manner in making the remark "*immensely* mortifying."

Her diary entry for March 15, 1864, goes on to say: "It seems General Lee has no patience with any personal complaints or grievances. He is all for the cause and cannot bear officers to come to him with any such matters as Wade Hampton came."

But that contretemps was only a minor tempest by comparison with the widely known enmity that existed between Jefferson Davis and Joseph E. Johnston—a situation attributed in large part to the

In the Confederacy, it was widely known—and discussed—that President Jefferson Davis (left) held no love for Gen. Joseph E. Johnston (right). Nor did Johnston care much for Davis.

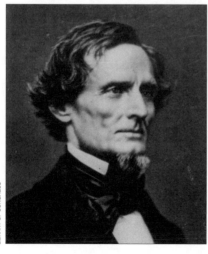

Confederate president's designation of Johnston and four other officers as full generals but with three of them (Robert E. Lee included)
outranking Johnston despite his seniority in the U.S. Army. When
Johnston remonstrated by letter soon after the designations became
known in the summer of 1861, Davis brushed off the complaint as
"one-sided," "unfounded," and "unbecoming."

With those uncharitable words was born a feud that would
become the talk of military campfires and drawing rooms throughout
the Confederacy. Chesnut, for instance, repeated the gossip that Johnston's wife once changed her description of first lady Varina Howell
Davis from "a western belle" to "woman" instead of "belle."

Two years later, with Johnston now in command of the Department of the West, the diarist still was reporting the damaging effects of
the feud. On the heels of a visit to Johnston's command, her husband
advised Davis that Johnston was popular with his subordinates. General Chesnut told Davis that "every honest man he saw out west
thought well of Joe Johnston," wrote Mary Chesnut.

She in fact went on at some length:

> He [her husband] knows that the president detests Joe Johnston for
> all the trouble he has given him. And General Joe returns the com-
> pliment with compound interest. His hatred of Jeff Davis amounts
> to a religion. With him it colors all things.
>
> Joe Johnston, advancing or retreating, I may say with more truth,
> is magnetic. He does draw the goodwill of those by whom he is sur-
> rounded. Being such a good hater, it is a pity he had not elected to
> hate somebody else than the president of our country. He hates not
> wisely but too well.

The Johnston-Pemberton feud, for that matter, was but a tribu-
tary to the river of ill-feeling between Johnston and Davis. When
Vicksburg, the Confederate "Gibraltar" on the Mississippi, finally fell
to Union siege by U. S. Grant in July 1863, much of the blame was
placed upon the Davis-Johnston schism. As Ezra J. Warner reported in
his book *Generals in Gray,* "In 1863 Johnston was in the anomalous
position of attempting to retrieve the situation at Vicksburg, while the
city's commander, General Pemberton, was receiving contrary orders
from Richmond."

As commander of the Department of the West at the time, Johnston had no real army at his personal disposal—he was dependent

upon Pemberton and Braxton Bragg, then commanding the Army of Tennessee (and later to request his own replacement after losing Chattanooga, also to U. S. Grant).

The same situation made things all the more difficult for Pemberton as well. "He was hampered by conflicting orders from the outset," wrote Warner. The unhappy denouement of Vicksburg for the Northern-born Pemberton was to step down from his high general's rank and accept an appointment by President Davis as a lieutenant colonel of artillery, Warner also noted.

Meanwhile, the Davis-Johnston feud simmered on, so far beyond all reasonable bounds that in 1864 Jefferson Davis, as commander in chief, was somewhat gingerly ordering Johnston to "do what you can" in assisting Lt. Gen. Leonidas Polk to halt Union Maj. Gen. William Tecumseh Sherman's advance from Vicksburg in February 1864.

Johnston, in response, did nothing. Now in command of the Army of Tennessee, he did not wish to dilute his preparations for a possible Union assault upon Atlanta. The Confederate president kept on suggesting that Johnston send some of his troops to Mississippi, still with no response.

Finally, on February 17, Davis gave an outright, unequivocal order to send the troops. Johnston still had not complied by February 23, by which time it was clear that Sherman was falling back upon his base at Vicksburg. No help would be needed. Temporary end of crisis.

Ironically enough, just months later, the same Sherman besieged Atlanta, rolled over its Southern defenders, and occupied the city. Thoroughly fed up with Johnston's withdrawals before the advancing Sherman monolith, Davis on July 17, 1864, replaced Johnston with John Bell Hood while Sherman's armies were poised at the very gates of Atlanta, although many analysts then and later thought Johnston had performed brilliantly under obviously adverse conditions as he tried to stem Sherman's advance. "During the retreat of the army from Dalton [Georgia] to Atlanta," wrote Warner in his compendium of Confederate generals, "Johnston demonstrated himself to be at least the equal of Lee as a defensive tactician."

Come to think of it, how had Johnston reacted earlier to Lee's taking his place as commander of the Army of Northern Virginia? Severely wounded at the battle of Seven Pines (Fair Oaks) outside Richmond in May 1862, Johnston really had little choice in the matter—somebody had to take his place, and immediately at that. But the fact that the as yet unheralded Lee then became the brightest star in the Confederate firmament may have rankled. On this point, please note remarks by diarist Mary Chesnut once again. "Johnston," she wrote, "can sulk, too [like Gen. P. G. T. Beauregard, mentioned in the paragraph before]. He is sent west, he says, that they may give Lee the army that Joe Johnston trained. Lee is reaping where he [Johnston] sowed. But then he [Johnston] was backing straight through Richmond when they stopped his retreating." And, quite true . . . with Union commander George B. McClellan's Peninsula campaign threatening Richmond at the time, Lee had begun a series of aggressive attacks against the ever cautious "Little Mac." In the Seven Days' battles that ensued, Lee managed to drive off a numerically superior Union army, save the Confederacy's capital city of Richmond from capture and, not so incidentally, launch his own legend as the chief hero of the Confederate cause.

In the final weeks of the Civil War, as these tangled events turned out, Robert E. Lee, now himself commander in chief of Confederate forces, assigned Johnston to stop Sherman's march northward from Georgia into the Carolinas. In the end, two weeks after Lee's surrender at Appomattox, Johnston surrendered his army to Sherman in North Carolina. That was it. Except for a sporadic skirmish here and there, the Civil War was over. The South had lost.

As yet another irony of sorts, Joe Johnston years later would march bareheaded in the funeral procession for a fellow Civil War warrior, catch cold, it is reported, and himself die just days later. The fellow general whose funeral he attended in March 1891 was William Tecumseh Sherman.

Additional notes: Not all the wartime disputes among Confederate officers remained in the realm of hard feelings alone. John Austin Wharton, a lawyer and native of Nashville, Tennessee, for instance, rose to the rank of major general and fought with distinction at Shiloh, in Kentucky, at Murfreesboro and Chickamauga, and in the Red River campaign. The cavalry officer survived it all, including a wound suffered at Shiloh, only to meet with a squalid death in a Houston hotel room.

The story is that he and Col. George W. Baylor of the Second Texas Cavalry argued over "military matters." They met on April 6, 1865, just days before the war would end, in a room at the General Magruder in Houston. According to Baylor, the survivor of their encounter, Wharton called him a liar and slapped him in the face. Baylor then shot and killed Wharton on the spot. Added Ezra Warner's book on the generals of the Confederacy: "The general was later found to have been unarmed."

Lincoln's Lady Adviser

WHO SUGGESTED THE UNION'S HIGHLY successful western campaign of 1862 along the Tennessee and Cumberland Rivers, rather than the more obvious Mississippi? Who on behalf of the Lincoln administration inspired this campaign that made Ulysses S. Grant's reputation virtually overnight?

According to Anna Ella Carroll, Union pamphleteerist, early feminist idol, and perpetual gadfly, all the credit belonged to . . . well, Anna Carroll herself!

According to many others, however, not so. According to those many others, Carroll did have surprising access to figures in the Lincoln administration, but she at the same time was shamelessly extravagant in her claims of influence. While many a nineteenth-century feminist defended and extolled Carroll, various critics called her a sham and a fraud—a neurotic, self-aggrandizing woman at best.

In the face of such contradictory views, what are the facts?

As a Carroll from Maryland, Anna came from a blue-blooded slaveholding family of considerable social and political power. Unlike most women of her era, however, she was not content simply to exert quiet influence over her menfolk from a dignified parlor setting—she instead plunged into the outer world as a political activist and propagandist, a controversial one at that. She first became a public figure in the 1850s, as an apologist for the Know-Nothing (or American) political party in Maryland.

With the coming of the Civil War, she freed her slaves and became an apostle of the Union and the Lincoln administration. She wrote pamphlets defending Lincoln in regard to the Constitution and his war-making policies. She had high-level contacts within the administration—Attorney General Edward Bates for one, Assistant War Secretary Thomas A. Scott for another.

Abraham Lincoln himself once wrote that he appreciated one of her political works—"Like every thing else that comes from you I have read . . . [it] with a great deal of pleasure and interest," he wrote.

But Lincoln balked at her notion of going to Europe and carrying on a propaganda campaign there to the tune of $50,000. On the other hand, perhaps the $50,000 was a bill submitted for tracts she wrote extolling Lincoln policies. Historical accounts differ.

They all agree, however, that her most significant—or outrageous—claim of all was her insistence she was the inspiration of the Union's Tennessee River campaign of 1862.

Fact or fiction? Both logic and various facts go far to undermine her assertion. First of all, Union military strategists hardly could have missed the possibility of pursuing an invasion of the South by way of the Tennessee. Further, historians say the pieces were set in place before the date she later gave for her original suggestion on the strategy. Finally, the Confederates obviously thought of the same strategy, else why fortify Forts Donelson and Henry along the invasion route?

Was she simply a bit mistaken? Not in the eyes of historian William C. Davis, who has called her claim "pure bunk." Writing in the *Civil War Times* of August 1996, Davis minced no words as he pointed out that planning for the Tennessee campaign "had been underway for months" before the date of her "supposed" suggestion by letter. Davis said there is no record of such a letter's existence. He then noted that Anna Carroll six months later wrote to President Lincoln, "claiming she was due 'a substantial and liberal reward' for her suggestion."

In sum, "Like a host of other charlatans and crackpots who proposed ideas that were already obvious to the military, she wanted money, and a lot of it."

Nor did Carroll give up easily. "Nothing came of her claims during the war, but years later Carroll's megalomania resulted in a series of congressional hearings commencing in 1870, during which she pressed her claims aggressively and backed her stance with a few influential men whose support she could secure. . . . As late as 1890, she was still suing for money from Congress—and being turned down."

About that time, too, her cause had been adopted by early feminists. One, Sarah Ellen Blackwell, told Carroll's story in *A Military Genius,* published in 1891. Also in the late nineteenth century, the women's magazine *Godey's* gave cover treatment to "The Woman That Saved the Union: Anna Ella Carroll, Secret Member of Lincoln's Cabinet."

According to Davis, her case, unbelievably, "was still being argued in the press, on television and even in the courts, as late as the 1950s, with those refusing to acknowledge the justice of her claims being labeled by her defenders as, among other things, 'communists.'"

All that fuss, it would appear, over a woman whose story "was rooted in her own self-delusion, opportunism, and instability!"

But then, of course . . . what a story there was in her story!

State Pride at Stake

TALK ABOUT AN EVOLVING, ESCALATING situation! First it was just a few excitable young men, but then company-sized groups joined in the exchange of missiles from either side of a large ravine down in Georgia.

It quickly became a battle of parochial pride . . . the men of one state against those of the other.

In short order, the conflict spread, drawing more and more men into its vortex.

"The news spread like wildfire throughout the two camps that an engagement of major proportions was shaping up," wrote William G. Bentley in the September 1999 issue of *Civil War Times*. With fresh recruits pouring into the battle zone by the minute, nearly two thousand men soon had joined in the contest. And then even more. In the end, nearly five thousand.

Over the next few hours, the tide of battle washed back and forth rather sporadically. "During the various charges many prisoners were captured, but in the wild excitement of another swooping charge they would make their escape and rejoin comrades in the battle."

Thinking ahead, some of the participants built up stockpiles of ammunition, but those "large mounds" quickly became targets of the charges by the enemy camp.

The situation had evolved without orders or immediate notice by the high command on either side. But it wasn't long before the men from one state entreated a popular colonel to mount his favorite horse and "lead them in the attack."

"Accepting the invitation, the colonel mounted his horse, grabbed a flag that one of the soldiers had made from an old bandana, and came galloping out to the battlefield to take his place at the head of his troops."

From his side of the ravine came "a tremendous roar" of approval.

No sooner had he appeared than the opposing side produced a mounted officer of its own, and he also was greeted by a rousing cheer.

Now the fat was in the fire. One side had to win, the other to lose. State pride was at stake here.

"Excitement was now at fever pitch; not only were two large forces lined up in battle formation, but hundreds of noncombatants had assembled on the surrounding hills to watch. Enlisted men scrambled for good seats, and general officers and their staffs were either mounted on their horses, or were seeking higher ground to watch the action."

Ordering his ordnance officers to bring plenty of ammunition and to follow close behind the men up front, the mounted colonel signaled a general charge by his Tennesseans.

More deep-throated roars echoed over the land and hundreds of missives clogged the air as the colonel's men swept across the ravine, but many became casualties. "Men stumbled and tripped over one another in their attempts to dodge out of the way. Others were knocked down by direct hits. Hardest hit of all were the colonel and his horse in front of the charge."

The Tennesseans charged so fiercely, however, that they could not be denied. In seconds they had broken through the enemy's center and rolled up each of his flanks. Not yet satisfied, the Tennesseans now pursued through the enemy camp "and into the woods behind."

So was reaped on the spot a harvest of black eyes and broken arms . . . but little else.

So ended the hours-long battle of Dalton, Georgia, of wintertime, 1863–64, the morning after a heavy snowfall . . . so ended the *snowball* battle of Dalton . . . with not a Yank in sight, since the fight was strictly a Confederates-only affair, Tennesseans versus Georgians, and all of them members of Joe Johnston's Army of Tennessee.

War's Most Amazing Escape?

FOR BROTHERS GEORGE, MICHAEL, AND MARTIN TUCKER, plus cousin Michael Real and friends Robert Burke, Albert Patrick, and Emery Behen, all of them Union soldiers, all recently captured prisoners of the Confederacy, the outlook in the spring of 1864 was not good, not good at all.

They were being held at Camp Ford near Tyler, Texas, hundreds of miles in any direction from friendly Union territory. Stout stockade walls eight feet high, buttressed by an outer embankment of earth, penned them in. Watching over them were prison guards whose vigilance against escape was reinforced by eager bloodhounds taken on an outside circuit of the prison walls every morning.

Camp survivor Burke later wrote that the bloodhounds "rarely failed to discover the trail of any poor devil who had succeeded in eluding the guard during the preceding night, and once scented, the pack would go bellowing through the woods, only to return with the recaptured prisoner, jaded, weary and sick at heart."

Inside the camp, conditions were so bad, the morale among the Union prisoners so low, discipline among them so lax, that fights were "a daily occurrence," with dozens, sometimes many more, involved, according to Burke. "At times hundreds of men would engage in them ["fisticuffs"] at the same time and more than once the ministers of the Gospel were driven from their improvised pulpits in the open air, by a fighting, surging mass of maddened men."

Only "sometimes" did their Confederate wardens enter the interior grounds to stop the fighting "at the point of a bayonet."

Typically, too, in 1864 the average prisoner's daily rations at Camp Ford consisted of a pint of cornmeal and half a pound of unsavory beef.

Then, too, there were the lice. "It was necessary to scald our clothing daily to prevent this pest from devouring us," wrote Burke many years later. "The writer saw some of the men who neglected this precaution eaten to the bone, and their deaths hastened by this small but indefatigable foe."

Could the outlook have been any worse? Well, for three of the seven, yes, it could. Brothers George and Martin Tucker and fellow Union soldier Patrick somehow escaped one night. But the blood-hounds soon tracked them down, and that was that. Back to Camp Ford they and their exultant captors came. A *really* low point!

Meanwhile, and far more happily, fate had smiled upon Michael Tucker. Wounded in the foot at the time of the brothers' capture near Marks Mills, Arkansas, on April 25, 1864, Michael had been allowed to leave the pestiferous prison camp as part of a prisoner exchange. Upon his departure, the seven became six.

With the enforced return of the three who attempted to escape, discouragement and resignation very well could have set in among the six, all of them from Indiana outfits . . . but no, instead, only fresh resolve to escape gripped the remaining Tuckers, Cousin Michael, Burke, Behen, and Patrick. They—and a large number of prisoners—now laid plans for a massive breakout by means of a tunnel snaking under the high stockade.

First, of course, they must dig the tunnel without detection by the guards.

Allowed to build a wooden hut as shelter, the Tuckers and their cousin became the key figures in the escape plan . . . since the tunnel would reach out from their own hut. And indeed, the tunnel did begin as a hole dug in the center of their hut, an excavation three feet square and six feet deep, reported George Tucker's descendant James Tucker and fellow writer Norma Tucker (actually, no relation) in *America's Civil War* magazine (March 1995).

Soon abandoning a stolen spade that proved too long for the tight confines of their tunnel, the diggers pried and dug at its face with a purloined butcher's knife. They could only crawl into the tunnel and back out. Discarding the dirt they loosened of course was a problem, too . . . but they dealt with it. "A small sled was made with a pen knife," Burke later explained. Imagine, though. A penknife!

"To this sled, with a capacity of about one cubic foot of earth," he continued, "a rope was attached. Then the person whose turn it was to work would enter the tunnel, pulling the sled after him, his companion[s] in the hut holding the other end of the rope." Once the sled had been filled with dirt—"by means of the butcher knife and a wooden paddle"—the digger signaled with a tug on the rope, and his companions simply pulled the sled out and then spread the dirt elsewhere.

In retrospect, it may sound simple, if a bit laborious, but the fact is that out of fifty-one known escape attempts at Camp Ford, "only four met with modest degrees of success." Clearly, if flight by tunnel had been a simple matter, wouldn't there have been more escapes of the successful variety?

On the other hand, the overland trek of some three hundred miles to the closest friendly territory had to be a major failure factor for anyone managing to breach the camp perimeter by whatever means . . . as witness the role of the bloodhound brigade.

Even so, the Tuckers and their co-conspirators (forty or so, it seems) were not altogether discouraged by fears of failure, whether tunneling inside the stockade or making their way cross-country outside that same stout wooden fence.

For that, outside, is where many of the tunnel workers at last, after two months of hard work, did find themselves—the remaining two Tuckers, cousin Michael Real, and friends Burke, Patrick, and Behen all included. The escaping prisoners were organized into small squads taking different routes, and Real soon vanished into the night with his companions of a three-man squad. The original seven were now five, five who would be sticking together for the difficult journey ahead.

"Our squad was third on the program exit," Burke later wrote, "and on the night of September 27th, 1864, as the Rebel patrol was crying the hour: 'Half past ten o'clock, post number nine, and all's well,' I, the last of our squad, passed out [of the tunnel]. On emerging from the ground outside, the first object that caught my eyes was the dark figure of the guard sharply outlined against the sky. Looking cautiously down the slope, I saw the track made by my predecessors through the grass, and I crawled silently away into the darkness to join my companions in the woods. Then we set out at a rapid pace in the direction of Natchez [Mississippi]."

There was no smooth road to travel—nor would they have chanced a road in any case. They simply bumbled and barreled on in the dark, crashing through deep woods, brush, briar patches, or over fallen trees, sometimes, to be sure, "falling headlong," but always pressing on as fast as they could go, "resolved to strain every nerve to achieve liberty," wrote Burke.

The early sunshine of dawn found them on top of a gentle hill. "The forest was bathed in beauty. The golden sunlight penetrated the pine foliage, illuminating the pendant needles that glittered like burnished lances, swayed gently by the balmy breeze."

With the world around them silent but for the "sighing of the pines and the chastened melody of the brook hard by," the escaped prisoners paused to drink in "the exhilarating air of freedom that morning." But they had not yet gone far, and they still faced a trek of hundreds of miles before they could count on keeping their freedom. They must move on. And on.

Guided by a hand-traced map and sustaining themselves on strips of dried beef gathered back in the prison camp, they advanced in single file, Indian fashion, and spoke only in whispers. There was no harm in the fact that just about all the escapees were used to hunting in the woods, that the Tucker brothers were experienced Union army scouts.

Behind the Indiana Five, fortunately, a heavy rain had kept the bloodhounds from following their trail by scent. Even so, fully half of the escapees from the tunnel had been rounded up in short order. Cousin Michael and his two companions, however, went eighteen days before their recapture . . . but four days later, they escaped again! This time for good, too.

None of these developments was known to the Tucker party forging eastward toward Mississippi from Confederate-held territory in Texas. Steadily progressing over hill and through forest, that is, but with occasional reason for alarm. One time, they detoured to avoid the "white tents of a Rebel camp." George Tucker slipped ahead to scout their path, then, in a field of small scrub pine, had to flatten himself when a horse and rider suddenly appeared on a nearby road.

The rider, apparently a local doctor absorbed in his own thoughts, never noticed Tucker but the horse did . . . and shied. Even then the horseman never looked around.

No harm done, the escapees moved on. They forded the Sabine River with their tattered and skimpy clothes piled on their heads. They shared their deep woods from time to time with parties of woodchoppers or hunters, but those they managed to avoid. They plucked berries in the wild and stole corn and sweet potatoes from an occasional farm to sustain themselves, and always, always, they kept on moving.

They struck a fast-running stream, an outlet from a lake. Patrick, terrified of the water, needed strong urging to attempt the crossing even with a piece of wood to keep him afloat. Partway across he panicked and let it go—Behen had to rescue him. The Tucker brothers, meanwhile, neither of them a swimmer, simply jumped in and were washed downstream, ending up on the opposite side of the stream anyway.

That same night the five hit upon the Red River, a major goal but also a major stream and a challenge to cross. Robbing a sweet potato patch at a nearby plantation, they were interrupted by the guard, a sympathetic black man, it turned out, who then guided them to a ferry close by. "Hauling themselves across the river on the ferry, they went forward with rising spirits," noted authors James Tucker and Norma Tucker.

The next night, though, by now a full day's march beyond the Red River, they were startled to hear the distant baying of hounds behind. "But they outdistanced the trackers and came to the edge of a small lake. There, they caught and roasted a pig—the first real food they had had in several days."

As their trek continued, they hit another lake and a swath of sword grass so high and thick they were forced to detour again and go around. They soon crossed the Little River and then the Ouachita (once more on a ferry pointed out by a sympathetic black).

Another night's exhausting travel brought them to the banks of the Tensas River, within striking distance of their ultimate goal, the mighty Mississippi. Again with the help of friendly blacks, they hid until late at night to avoid a passing Confederate patrol, then sought out a nearby ferry, a mere dugout this time.

Unfortunately, it had been moored for the night on the opposite bank. But . . . no problem. Burke shucked his clothing (what there was of it), took to the water, and brought back the dugout.

As events turned out, that was their last real obstacle. The quotable memoirist Burke recorded the last stage of their incredible journey: "In a short time we found ourselves upon the great road leading to Natchez. We pulled off our shoes that we might make as little noise as possible, and for the first time since leaving Camp Ford Prison marched upon a highway. We traveled single file as usual, and about seventy-five yards apart. The moon was shining and about two o'clock in the morning we saw a picket far down the road."

Union or Confederate? "After holding a consultation we resolved that one man should advance, and if it was not a Federal Guard he was to give the alarm signal and we were to leave the road and try to make our way to Natchez separately the best we could."

Martin Tucker was the man chosen to advance and make contact, and happily he found no need for alarm. It seems they had stumbled across a group of Union scouts. By morning the five escapees were in Union-held Natchez on the eastern banks of the Mississippi, safe, fairly sound . . . and far, far from their starting point of Camp Ford at Tyler, Texas. Amazingly, they had crossed the entire state of Louisiana on their escape trek.

A New Orleans newspaper reporter was among those astounded by their sudden emergence from Confederate territory. Pointedly saying he believed their unbelievable-sounding tale, he wrote: "They crawled, walked, ran, waded and swam across three hundred miles of the most inhospitable land in the Confederate states." As he noted also, "They suffered from insect bites, dysentery and general exposure." For good measure, the newspaperman threw in pursuit by "guards with blood-hounds and hunters with coon dogs." Further, they had to subsist on "stolen corn, yams and berries in limited quantity."

The Indiana Five created such a stir when they appeared in Natchez that happy morning that a throng gathered to stare and one onlooker pressed forward to give the escapees a stake of $10. No doubt they did look like charity cases of the most pitiful kind, too. As the New Orleans writer noted, their clothing was in shreds. "The five men arrived in Natchez wearing among them three pairs of worn shoes, three pairs of trousers, two shirts, no stockings and one hat. One poor fellow had only the remnants of small clothes around his loins."

Brothers with Separate Fates

BROTHERS AND LAW PARTNERS Elliott and Samuel Rice of Oskaloosa, Iowa, both joined the Union army as military neophytes and rose to general's rank before the shooting ended.

Taking part in one battle after another—Shiloh, Corinth, and the Atlanta campaign among them—younger brother Elliott began service in 1861 as a private and served all the way through the battle of Bentonville, North Carolina, in April 1865. He survived an amazing seven wounds in all. At his death in 1887, twelve years after the Civil War ended, he still had a bullet in his body, acquired in the November 1861 battle of Belmont, Missouri.

Older brother Samuel, on the other hand, entered army service as a colonel after organizing the Thirty-third Iowa, served only in Missouri and Arkansas, and suffered one wound, a blow that struck the spur on his right foot. Due to the primitive medical procedures of the day, however, that one minor-sounding injury was enough. The bullet striking his lower right leg drove fragments of the metal spur into his ankle and shattered the bone. He died three months later.

Masons at War

PICTURE THIS: A MOUNTED UNION officer dashing, completely alone, into the midst of the Fourth Virginia's Black Horse Troop outside of Waynesboro, Virginia, one day in late September 1864, the Yankee's sword flailing away at Rebels to either side.

He burst upon the Confederates, "sabering the men right and left, wounding several," wrote the Fourth Virginia's Capt. A. D. Payne later. "This bold assailant succeeded in forcing his way through the Confederate column and might possibly have escaped, but a shot fired by a Confederate brought his horse down, and he fell with it."

As Payne also said, the intruder "in all probability" would have been killed on the spot but for one factor, the same factor that saved many a Yank or Johnny Reb throughout the Civil War. He was a Freemason, and he was "recognized" as such by a fellow Mason among his enraged enemies.

Payne continued: "In all probability he would have been slain on the spot, but [for] the timely interference of Captain Henry C. Lee . . . who, seeing the struggle, rode up and put an end to it. It is said that Captain Lee recognized in the prostrate man a brother Mason, through some sign or cry used by the Masonic order in time of distress or danger."

The spared man then taken prisoner was Capt. George N. Bliss of the First Rhode Island Cavalry, later to become a useful citizen and judge back in Rhode Island. During that peaceful postwar period, too, he received a letter from former Confederate Brig. Gen. Thomas T. Munford saying that he saw Bliss that night, "sitting behind a Confederate cavalryman, with blood streaming down your face, going to the rear, a prisoner."

The onetime general and war veteran was well aware of the good works done by and among the Freemasons on the opposing sides of the war . . . even unto their sworn enemy. Munford seemed not at all to mind. "I am not a Mason," he wrote to Bliss, "but most of my staff were Masons and I know they frequently did many things that seemed to give them extra pleasure for the unfortunate on the other side. I was sure the institution was full of good works, and although I was only a poor soldier who tried to do his duty, without being a Mason, I believed the organization was based upon Christian principles, and [I] was always in sympathy with the work of the fraternity."

With an estimated five hundred thousand Masonic lodge members spread, thick as butter, across the land on the eve of the Civil War, Mason repeatedly met Mason, Mason served with Mason, Mason fought Mason—from the moment that Confederate Mason P. G. T. Beauregard opened fire on Mason Robert Anderson's Federals at Fort Sumter to the very end of the Civil War. And many were the stories of succor and rescue among the Masonic fraternity that emerged, regardless of who was enemy and who was not.

The irony is that many a Masonic act of brotherly succor not only crossed the frontlines but also, from a military purist's standpoint, could have been considered a boon to the enemy, albeit usually on a small scale. In one case, for instance, a Confederate officer allowed a Union prisoner of war to escape. The incident took place at Guntown, Mississippi, on June 10, 1864, according to the book *House Undivided* by Allen E. Roberts, himself a Mason.

By this account, John Grim of the Seventh Ohio Independent Battery had been taken prisoner. And then . . . Grim espied the "Masonic square and compasses" visible on a watch chain worn by the Confederate lieutenant in charge of the prisoner. "Grim immediately let him know he was a Mason."

In response, allowing his men to ride ahead a few paces, the Rebel officer urged Grim to make a run for the nearby Federal lines. That almost wasn't very good advice. Grim did make his dash for freedom. "But the Confederates opened fire and he fell wounded. He started to get up when he heard a whisper, 'Lie still; pretend you are dead.' Grim's advisor then shouted: 'You fixed him that time boys. Go ahead; we will leave him here. We have no time to bury Yanks.'"

Still able to move about despite his wound, Grim soon rejoined his Union compatriots. "He never did learn the name of his benefactor." No matter—the bottom line here was that Union soldier Grim arbitrarily had been granted the freedom to fight another day . . . to fight against his benefactor's own compatriots.

In another wartime incident, an apparently doomed Union prisoner, again a Mason, was spared execution by John Singleton Mosby's men. The ugly result was that another man had to take the spared man's place.

The incident at Front Royal, Virginia, came during the harsh conflict between Union Gen. Phil Sheridan's forces in the northern end of the Shenandoah Valley and Mosby's hit-and-run raiders of the same area. When the Federals executed six rebels presumed to be Mosby's men, Mosby responded by ordering the execution of six Union prisoners, their names to be drawn by lot from a pool of twenty-seven prisoners.

One of those chosen in the first drawing was a drummer boy only sixteen years old. Mosby, not on the scene, excused the youth from condemnation and ordered a second drawing among the other nineteen men with a Capt. Richard P. Montjoy in charge.

"On the next round," wrote Roberts in his book, "a Mason was among those selected. He was released by his fellow Mason, Montjoy." That naturally meant another of the POWs would have to take his place. Eventually, all six candidates for execution were chosen, but Roberts noted that two of the condemned men managed to escape. The remaining four, however, were hanged.

If any one of *them* had been Masons, perhaps he, too, would have been spared . . . and still another unfortunate chosen to take *his* place. Would that have been fair? Yet, in war, is anything really fair?

Masons of course helped Masons in many other incidents of the Civil War without such unfortunate and highly visible repercussions, but still . . . would their commanders always have approved? As Roberts also related, a Union officer named Murray stopped his men from looting a Masonic lodge at Lawrenceburgh, Tennessee, shortly before the battle of Shiloh at Pittsburg Landing on the Tennessee River.

The officer, himself a Mason, ordered them to return every stolen item to its rightful place, then placed a guard at the door.

A Confederate soldier dressed in civilian mufti happened to witness the incident.

Later, Murray posted his pickets outside of Lawrenceburgh, then rode his horse back into the center of town by himself. Only days later would he discover how lucky he was to complete that short trip in safety. A freshly captured Confederate doctor, also a Mason, told Murray he almost was ambushed as he rode alone. He would have been bushwhacked for sure, but he wasn't, thanks to the very same Confederate soldier who had been privy to Murray's orders protecting the Masonic lodge in town. Naturally, the onlooking Rebel had been a Mason. Naturally, he was in command of the ambush squad. And naturally, he told his men to hold their fire.

The newly spared Murray was commander of the Third Ohio Cavalry. He lived to command the Third Ohio in the battle of Shiloh shortly after the planned ambush was aborted. The Third Ohio fought and did harm to the compatriots of the would-be bushwhackers . . . it might have done so without its long-time commander, true, but would the Ohio horsemen have been as effective if Murray had been captured, wounded, or killed in the planned ambush?

More simple to contemplate are the many times a fellow Mason rescued a fallen soldier of the opposing side . . . or rushed to the aid of a wounded Mason on the same side. Or played the chivalrous role of white knight in other circumstances.

A Southerner once recalled the time as a child during the Civil War that he was awakened at home in Mississippi "by cursing and screams, and found the room in which my mother and I were sleeping full of Federal soldiers." Worse, "mattresses had been piled in the hallway and set on fire."

As the terrifying rampage by fifteen to twenty soldiers continued, however, one of the Union men came across a carefully wrapped package in a nearby bureau drawer. After he saw its contents, his attitude changed completely. He went to the mother's bed, spoke to her in a low tone for a moment, then rushed out of the room.

"A few moments after the soldier left the room, a tall handsome man suddenly walked in," Frank Brame recalled years later, "and all the soldiers suddenly ceased their depredations and brought their hands up and stood at rigid attention. The tall man immediately ordered the fire in the hall extinguished and also ordered the premises vacated and guards placed at the several gates of the yard."

Then turning to the boy's mother, he bowed and apologized for "the rudeness of my soldiers." He promised payment for damages done to her home and pledged that he and his men, while commandeering her plantation's meat supplies, would leave enough for her "reasonable needs."

The episode ended. As the Yankee troops were settling in on the Mississippi woman's property and their cooking "was fairly started," Nathan Bedford Forrest's cavalrymen appeared on the scene, "charging down through the woods, yelling and shouting." In seconds, the Union troops were in retreat.

And what was the item in the package from the bureau drawer that had spared the boy's home from arson and pillage? Roberts explained: "What the soldier had discovered was a Masonic apron of curious workmanship and material that had been in the Brame family since 1676."

Once again, whether the military purist or the ultimate commander of either side in the Civil War would have approved, the Masonic ideal of brotherly love had been exercised, had crossed a significant boundary to help others. (Neither R. E. Lee nor U. S. Grant, incidentally, was a Freemason.)

One more exercise of fraternal kinship cited by Roberts in his exhaustive history of Freemasonry during the Civil War involved a writer for the *Masonic Monthly* of that era. Present for the battles of South Mountain and Antietam, John Edwin Mason came across a badly wounded Confederate on the mountainside after sundown. The writer, himself an unabashed Union man, was alerted "when someone sitting against a tree uttered in a clear, distinct voice the never-to-be-forgotten words accompanying the sign of distress among Masons."

Pushing through the slope-side underbrush, he found a colonel from a South Carolina unit leaning against a tree. "He was shot through the right leg and also through the shoulder, the latter wound being very painful."

The narrator bathed his fellow Mason's wounds with water from a canteen, stopped the bleeding, then proposed to call a stretcher-bearer—Union of course—to carry the wounded man to a field hospital. When the Rebel officer protested that he wasn't "entitled" to such kind treatment, Mason replied, "You are entitled to *all* I can do for you and to the kindest care and treatment our field hospitals afford because you have proved to me you are a *Freemason*."

The next day, Mason visited the Confederate officer in the hospital and again explained he had been so helpful because the South Carolinian was a fellow Mason in need. "But," said the wounded man, "I have been fighting against you, and all such as you for a year, and aiding in all ways in my power to kill you."

In response, the Union man delivered a short, chiding speech. "Then go and sin no more," he said, "for this you should feel ashamed as a Mason. It is your country and not your State you have sworn to support and be a good citizen in, and you have been trying to subvert the best government ever framed by man, and blessed by Almighty God. It has done you no injury, but has watched over and protected you, as faithfully as a brother Mason. It has protected your life and property, and you owe it a debt of gratitude. Return, then, to your allegiance, and be as true to your country as you have been false. It is your duty *as a Mason*."

Rather than resent the chiding, the South Carolina officer was obviously much moved. If he survived his wounds, he pledged, "I will never be found in our army again."

His doctor just then appeared. He turned to him, according to the narrator of the story, and said, "I will never cease to love the flag I honored in boyhood, until we three . . . meet together in heaven."

And what was the outcome for the wounded man and his pledge? According to a postscript by John Mason, a nameless angel of mercy became well known two years later to Union soldiers held prisoner in Charleston, South Carolina, under "atrocious" conditions. The mysterious benefactor took food to the "starved" POWs, sat up all night with them when they were sick or even dying, and provided them a doctor's care at his own expense. "His countenance became familiar to all imprisoned in Charleston, and he was often asked why he dared perform such duties, being a native South Carolinian."

He never really said why and his identity remained unknown. Oddly enough, though—or perhaps not so oddly at that—he was "a nameless hero *who was wounded in the right leg and severely wounded in the shoulder*." Just like the officer John Edwin Mason once rescued on the slopes of South Mountain.

Presidential Woes

ROGER A. PRYOR, THE OVERLOOKED Confederate general who later opted to seek action as a private, had the social standing to pay a courtesy call at the home of President Jefferson Davis in Richmond the summer of 1863—not as a supplicant seeking a command, but to extend his condolences for the defeat at Gettysburg in the first three days of July.

In Richmond, where he had been "serving on a court-martial," recalled Pryor's wife, Sara, "every house was in mourning, every heart was broken."

Arriving at the presidential home, the White House of the Confederacy, her husband was told that President Davis couldn't see him, but his wife, Varina Howell Davis, the first lady of the Confederacy, indeed would receive him. "The weather was immensely hot," reminisced Sara Pryor later, "and he felt he must not inflict a long visit; but when he rose to leave, Mrs. Davis, who seemed unwilling to be left alone, begged him to remain."

Minutes later, Davis himself appeared—"weary, silent, and depressed." Soon after, so did the presidential couple's child Joe—"a dear little boy . . . [dressed for bedtime] in his night-robe." Kneeling at his father's knee, the four-year-old "repeated his evening prayer of thankfulness and of supplication for God's mercy on the country."

The president "laid his hand on the boy's head and fervently responded, 'Amen.'"

Minutes later, the visiting Roger Pryor departed with appropriate expressions of gratitude and farewell. Only the next day did he learn of the Confederate surrender at Vicksburg—"news of which Mr. Davis had been forewarned the evening before," added Sara Pryor's account in her memoir *My Day*.

Taken together with the setback at Gettysburg, the loss of Vicksburg was the second half of a double blow to the South dashing all hopes of ultimate victory—or strong position in any future peace negotiations.

Then, too, as presage for a further burden of woe for Varina and Jefferson Davis, noted Mrs. Pryor, "the Angel of Death was hovering near to enfold the beautiful boy and bear him away from a world of trouble."

She referred to the fact that in less than a year little Joe Davis fell to his death from an upper porch at the White House of the Confederacy to a brick walk below.

Star-Crossed Recruit

JOHN SUMMERFIELD STAPLES SURE SEEMED to be a lucky man. Not a hero, not a slouch, either . . . but a man lucky enough to emerge from the Civil War without a scratch, despite a unique status that set him apart from every other soldier in the Union army.

It wasn't so much that he was a volunteer paid to take another man's place in the ranks. After all, there were many Union army volunteers who were paid to take the place of others. And yet, even in that crowd, John Staples stood out from all others. The reason of course being the man who had paid him $500, the man he represented in the ranks . . . that man at 1600 Pennsylvania Avenue, one Abraham Lincoln.

For Staples, then just twenty, the unlikely story began when a stranger approached him and his father, the Reverend John Long Staples, a Methodist minister, in Washington, D.C.—on Pennsylvania Avenue itself—one day in the fall of 1864. Although their home was in Stroudsburg, Pennsylvania, the father-son team had been working as carpenters at the Washington Navy Yard.

The younger of the pair was only about five feet, six inches in height, but in appearance he was "well formed, stout and healthy," the *Washington Star* soon informed its readers. Not only that, "There is every indication that he will be proved an excellent soldier."

In fact, young Staples already had been a soldier for the Union—as a paid substitute serving in the 176th Pennsylvania Volunteers. That had been back in 1862 and 1863, a seven-month stint interrupted by hospitalization for typhoid, followed by a medical discharge.

By the time he and his father encountered the stranger on Pennsylvania Avenue, young Staples apparently was more than ready to take the plunge into army life again.

That stranger was Noble D. Larner, president of a local "draft club," and he had been asked to find a man who could be Lincoln's "representative recruit." Under the Union's conscription laws, Abe Lincoln, as president and as a man then fifty-five, wouldn't have been drafted, but he and his cabinet members were seeking volunteer recruits to represent them as a good example. The fact is, relatively few volunteers had stepped forward in response to the draft call of July 18, 1864.

Lincoln asked his provost marshal general, Brig. Gen. James Barnet Fry, to find a suitable Lincoln recruit. Fry had then turned to Larner, president of the city's Third Ward Draft Club. On the very next day, Larner came across the Staples father-and-son pair on Pennsylvania Avenue.

He came right to the point. "I am looking for a young man to represent the president in the army as a recruit," Larner announced. "Will you accept?"

When the young man and his father agreed, arrangements swiftly fell into place. On the first Saturday in October, they were ushered into the White House and into the presence of the president himself. Young Staples was already outfitted in an army uniform as he twice shook hands with his eminent sponsor, while the older Staples, Fry, and Larner looked on.

The *New York Herald* reported on the scenario that unfolded: "Mr. Lincoln shook hands with Staples, remarked that he was a good-looking, stout and healthy-appearing man, and believed he would do his duty. He asked Staples if he had been mustered in, and he replied that he had. Mr. Larner then presented the President with a framed official notice of the fact he had put in a representative recruit, and the President again shook hands with Staples, expressed the hope that he would be one of the fortunate ones, and the visiting party then retired."

Since the draft laws allowed payment for a recruit representing someone ineligible for the draft, Lincoln paid Staples the going rate of $500. The young Pennsylvanian then more or less melted into the Union army ranks—specifically into those of the Second District of Columbia Volunteers, with no further ado . . . or distinction.

With his father also joining up as chaplain for the same regiment, young Staples was posted across the Potomac at Alexandria, Virginia, sometimes serving as a clerk under the provost marshal and sometimes as a guard at the Prince Street Prison, also under the provost marshal. He once again fell ill in the spring of 1865 and was allowed to go home to recuperate. He thus missed the end of the war and the assassination of his mentor the president. He was discharged from service in September 1865 with no further incident. "No special valor or spectacular wartime service was recorded by Staples," reported Allen D. Spiegel in *America's Civil War* magazine (November 1991).

Even so, Staples did survive the devastating conflict without even being wounded—he was "one of the fortunate ones," as Lincoln had put it back on October 1, 1864. But now the young man's luck, fate, whatever you wish to call it, would take a turn for the worse.

Briefly returning to the family wheelwright, carriage, and carpentry business in Stroudsburg, Staples married in 1869. His wife died just five years later at the age of twenty-six. By then they had a son, and Staples had gone to work in Waterloo, New York, repairing railroad cars for the Delaware and Lackawanna Railroad. He married a second time in 1876, but three weeks after presenting him with a baby girl in 1878, his second wife also died.

Placing his children with his parents back in Stroudsburg, Staples moved from job to job, town to town—from a supervisor's job at the Waterloo Wheel Manufactury to Scranton, Pennsylvania, to a job again repairing railcars, this time in Dover, New Jersey. The latter move, in 1884, placed him closer to his children.

But now the young widower fell ill. He applied for a government disability pension.

The request, however, was denied. The illness was ruled not service-related.

Still, that or another illness was real enough to force him to go home again for another recuperative period. That was in January 1888.

He returned to his job on January 11. At his boarding house in Dover three days later, Spiegel recounted, Staples sat down in a rocking chair to rest and . . . consistently unlucky after all, died. Heart attack. Age forty-three.

Now, with "Lincoln's recruit" dead, crowds turned out for the funeral and Stroudsburg's newspaper, the *Jeffersonian,* editorially issued a call for a monument in his memory. Indeed, a monument then was erected . . . one commissioned by his minister-father and created by a local tombstone maker.

On the one hundredth anniversary of Lincoln's birthdate, however, a newspaper article on special "recruit" John Staples recalled his story . . . and triggered a congressional bill calling for erection of a truly significant, $20,000 monument in his memory in Court House Square at Stroudsburg. But . . . the bill disappeared in committee.

In 1933 a highway plaque marked a J. Summerfield Staples Bridge over Pocono Creek in Pennsylvania. Two decades later, both bridge and plaque were washed away in a flood.

The only permanent recognition John Staples ever would receive consisted of a commemorative plaque placed at the entrance of the Stroudsburg Union Cemetery in 1941 and a 1987 replacement for his old grave marker . . . so weathered by that time as to be illegible. And so passed Lincoln's recruit, fortunate in war, but unlucky in love, life, . . . and even death.

Contradictions, Contradictions

IF CONFEDERATE PRESIDENT JEFFERSON DAVIS was expectantly depressed by the double losses at Gettysburg and Vicksburg in the first four days of July 1863, he appeared surprisingly ebullient, even optimistic, just days later.

Was he simply putting on a brave face?

In the first instance, he struck Confederate Brig. Gen. Roger A. Pryor as "weary, silent, and depressed," as Pryor's wife, Sara, later noted. Pryor, the Confederate general who turned private to get back into action, had paid a courtesy call on Davis and his wife, Varina, the very evening they learned of the surrender at Vicksburg. News of Robert E. Lee's great defeat at Gettysburg on July 3 had already reached the Confederate capital of Richmond, Virginia.

"Every house was in mourning, every heart was broken," recalled Sara Rice Pryor years later in her memoirs.

Less than ten days later, Confederate Maj. Gen. Daniel H. Hill, in charge of Richmond's defenses during the fighting at Gettysburg, was sitting "in a yard of a house in the suburbs of Richmond" when Davis came galloping up with an escort. As Hill later described the scene, the president was "dressed in a plain suit of gray and attended by a small escort in brilliant uniform."

Surprised as he was to see Davis at that spot and moment, D. H. Hill was even more surprised by the orders he now received.

"Rosecrans is about to advance upon Bragg," said Davis. "I have found it necessary to detail Hardee to defend Mississippi and Alabama. His corps is without a commander. I wish you to command it."

Translated, that meant that Union Maj. Gen. William Starke Rosecrans ("Old Rosey" to his troops) was advancing against Confederate Lt. Gen. Braxton Bragg, a Davis pet in charge of the Army of Tennessee, and that Confederate Lt. Gen. William Joseph Hardee (known as "Old Reliable") would take over the defenses of Mississippi and Alabama, whereas D. H. Hill himself would assume command of Hardee's corps in the Army of Tennessee. And all this, although none of the principals yet knew the details, would be the prelude to the battles of Chattanooga and Chickamauga.

As Hill digested the implications of his abrupt transfer, he saw one immediate problem. "I cannot do that, as General Stewart [out]ranks me," he told his commander in chief. Hill meant Maj. Gen. Alexander Peter "Old Straight" Stewart, a fellow West Point graduate but a civilian and a mathematics professor before the Civil War broke out.

Stewart's rank was no problem so far as Davis was concerned. "I can cure that," he said, "by making you a lieutenant-general. Your papers will be ready to-morrow."

Hill indicated that he could be ready to leave within twenty-four hours.

The president then "gave his views on the subject, some directions in regards to matters at Chattanooga, and then left in seemingly good spirits."

Hill couldn't quite understand the last. *Good spirits!* And yet, oddly, it seems that he could!

As Hill later wrote in *Century* magazine's "Battles and Leaders" series: "His cheerfulness was a mystery to me. Within a fortnight the Pennsylvania [i.e., Gettysburg] campaign had proven abortive. Vicksburg and Port Hudson had fallen, and Federal gun-boats now were plying up and down the Mississippi, cutting our communications between the east and west. The Confederacy was cut in two, and the

South could readily be beaten in detail by the concentration of Federal forces, first on one side of the Mississippi and then on the other. The end of our glorious dream could not be far off."

But Hill acknowledged that he himself had been cheerful at their meeting, "as cheerful at that interview as was Mr. Davis himself."

How to explain that?

Perhaps it was rationalization, perhaps it was something that only those long-ago actors in the great drama could feel and understand, but Hill went on to say, first, "The bitterness of death had passed with me before our great reverses on the Fourth of July."

Just weeks before, in May, he then noted, "the Federals had been stunned by the defeat at Chancellorsville," adding that the shaken Union "probably would not have made a forward movement for months." In that time, "a corps could have been sent to General Joe Johnston [in the Department of the West, nominally overseeing the Vicksburg campaign], Grant could have been crushed, and Vicksburg, 'the heart of the Confederacy,' could have been saved."

In short, Hill seemed to be saying the South had had the strength to take such winning steps even if it had failed to do so . . . an odd yet seemingly soothing thought.

He went on to add, none too clearly either, "The drums that beat for the advance into Pennsylvania seemed to many of us to be beating the funeral march of the dead Confederacy. Our thirty days of mourning were over before the defeat of Lee [at Gettysburg] and [Lt. Gen. John C.] Pemberton [at Vicksburg]."

On the other hand, surmised Hill as well, perhaps Davis that day had been buoyed by talk that England and France might yet recognize the Confederacy as an independent nation. Thus, perhaps, "the calmness of our Confederate President may not have been the calmness of despair."

Meanwhile, Hill traveled to Tennessee and, on July 19, reported to Bragg at Chattanooga . . . a reunion with ironic overtones. "I had not seen him since I had been the junior lieutenant in his battery of artillery at Corpus Christi, Texas, in 1845," Hill noted. His fellow lieutenants in Bragg's battery, Hill added, had been George H. Thomas and John F. Reynolds.

"We four had been in the same mess there," Hill wrote in his article for the *Century* series. "Reynolds [a Union general] had been killed at Gettysburg twelve days before my new assignment. Thomas, the strongest and most pronounced Southerner of the four, was now Rosecrans's lieutenant."

Thus, at the pending battle of Chickamauga, Confederates Bragg and D. H. Hill soon would be opposing Union generals Rosecrans and Thomas, the Virginian destined to be known as the "Rock of Chickamauga" for his steadfast performance in what was otherwise a Federal debacle. As Hill noted, too, "It was a strange casting of lots that three messmates of Corpus Christi should meet under such changed circumstances at Chickamauga."

Among other ironies affecting the overall situation in Tennessee and Mississippi, incidentally, Joseph Johnston, as noted in Ezra J. Warner's *Generals in Gray,* had been "in the anomalous position of attempting to retrieve the situation at Vicksburg, while the city's commander, General Pemberton, was receiving contrary orders from Richmond."

Then, too, after Hill commanded a Confederate corps in the same battle of Chickamauga, he was so outspoken in criticizing Bragg's performance as a field commander that Jefferson Davis refused to ask the Confederate Senate for approval of his own promotion of Hill to lieutenant general. Relieved and brought back east, Hill was largely inactive until joining Johnston in North Carolina for the final weeks of the war—as still a major general only.

Hill later served as president of the University of Arkansas and the Middle Georgia Military and Agricultural College. He edited a magazine, *The Land We Love,* and he authored the book *North Carolina in the War Between the States.*

Additional note: Upon joining Bragg's Army of Tennessee, D. H. Hill immediately noticed a major difference from Robert E. Lee's command back east, the Army of Northern Virginia. "The want of information at General Bragg's headquarters was in striking contrast with the minute knowledge General Lee always had of every operation in his front," Hill wrote. As the Federals approached Chattanooga with no advance warning from Rebel sources, Hill added, "I was most painfully impressed with the feeling it was to be a hap-hazard campaign."

While Hill allegedly felt "sympathies" for Bragg as a commander whose forces had suffered "reverses," Bragg himself had not inspired

Hill to feel great confidence in his leadership. "My interview with General Bragg at Chattanooga was not satisfactory," wrote Hill. "He was silent and reserved and seemed gloomy and despondent. He had grown prematurely old since I saw him last [in 1845], and showed much nervousness."

As Hill already knew, Bragg didn't get along with many of his subordinates, and "his many retreats had alienated the rank and file from him."

Little-known facts: D. H. Hill was a brother-in-law to Stonewall Jackson, who died shortly after the battle of Chancellorsville in May 1863. Like General Stewart, whom he feared would outrank him, Hill was a West Point graduate but a civilian and a professor of mathematics before the Civil War broke out.

The Variegated Lincoln

HE OCCASIONALLY WROTE POEMS, THIS quicksilver man . . . who once described himself as nearly six feet, four inches in height . . . who also considered himself "lean in flesh, weighing, on an average, one hundred and eighty pounds, dark complexion, with coarse black hair, and grey eyes—no other marks or brands recollected."

He posed for many paintings, but somehow he came out looking different in every one. Said his secretary John Hay: "There are many pictures . . . there is no portrait of him."

Through his life he sat for photographers at least sixty times, with more than a hundred alleged likenesses resulting . . . but, again, he looked so different in so many of them!

He himself seemed to favor an 1857 photograph taken by Alexander Hesler and showing a rather homely, beardless, big-nosed man in profile, unconcerned that his hair is completely tousled and windblown. Abraham Lincoln called that likeness "a very true one; though my wife, and many others, do not." He opined that their objection "arises from the disordered condition of the hair."

But then, he also said, "My judgment is worth nothing in these matters."

A later photo, a three-quarter view shot in 1864 by Anthony Berger, shows him with beard, his sizable nose no longer etched so prominently in profile . . . and still a man serene within himself, unconcerned by appearances. This, the favorite of his oldest, longest-surviving son, Robert Todd Lincoln, would become the model for the image on the five-dollar bill.

Oddly, it is a photo at fault in one significant, everyday detail. Lincoln's hair on the five-dollar bill is parted the wrong way! Both the bill and the photo show Lincoln's hair parted on the right instead of his customary left.

Oh, well, what did he care about such trifles? He had other considerations to dwell upon. His poetry, for instance. The night he received news of the great Union victory at Gettysburg, he danced in glee—in his nightshirt—with his secretary of war, Edwin Stanton. Two weeks later, still on a Gettysburg high, he wrote his last bit of poetry—doggerel, really.

> In eighteen sixty-three, with pomp and mighty swell,
> Me and Jeff's Confederacy, went forth to sack Phil-del,
> The Yankees they got arter us, and giv us particular hell,
> And we skedaddled back again, and didn't sack Phil-del.

Interesting, is it not, that he, like the Confederacy's own Jefferson Davis, was born in Kentucky; that they were born but sixty miles apart; that both left their respective homes (Illinois for Lincoln, Mississippi for Davis) to assume their respective presidencies on the same day, February 11, 1861? That Lincoln, exulting in the Union victory at Gettysburg, should narrate from a Confederate perspective?

Some might say that Lincoln wrote better rhymes in earlier years. Here's one—recalled by Mark E. Neely Jr. in his 1982 tome, *The Abraham Lincoln Encyclopedia*—from Lincoln as a teenager:

> Abraham Lincoln
> his hand and pen
> he will be good but
> god knows When

Many years later, Lincoln was more exacting, more serious as he looked back upon his childhood, noted Neely. Hence these lines from 1846:

> The friends I left that parting day,
>> How changed, as time has sped!
> Young childhood grown, strong manhood gray,
>> And half of all are dead.
>
> I hear the loved survivors tell
>> How nought from death could save,
> Til every sound appears a knell,
>> And every spot a grave.
>
> I range the fields with pensive tread
>> And pace the hollow rooms.
> And feel (companion of the dead)
>> I'm living in the tombs.

Was Lincoln preoccupied with thoughts of death? Despite his famous homespun humor, he certainly was prone to melancholy—or "the hypo," as he himself called it (for hypochondria). After his engagement to Mary Todd foundered on New Year's Day of 1841, Lincoln, by now an Illinois state legislator, described himself as "the most miserable man living." Fortunately, the young couple resumed their courting and married late the next year.

Still, Lincoln did struggle with depression, did think often of death. As President-Elect Lincoln prepared to leave Springfield, Illinois, for the White House in early 1861, a sense of foreboding marked the leave-taking.

According to Lincoln's law partner William Henry Herndon (his details sometimes questioned by some historians), Lincoln's stepmother, Sarah Bush Johnston, said good-bye "with tears streaming down her cheeks" and "expressing the fear that his life might be taken by his enemies." Then, too, the mother of a client Lincoln had successfully defended in a well-known murder trial was "filled with a presentiment that she would never see him alive again." Lincoln himself told Herndon he would like to come back to Springfield and resume their law practice together . . . "if I live."

Furthermore, "He said the sorrow of parting from his old associates was deeper than most persons would imagine, but it was more marked in his case because of the feeling which had become irrepressible that he would never return alive."

Keep in mind, though, that in Lincoln's frontier environment, in his era, death—early death—was commonplace. Noted historian Neely:

"Death was an ever-present frontier companion. When [Lincoln] was 9 years old, his mother died in an epidemic that took others close to the family. His older sister died while he was a teenager, and Lincoln himself had a brush with death, in 1819, when a horse kicked him in the head and rendered him unconscious and, to all appearances momentarily, dead."

Add to all that the dangers obviously inherent for the man guiding, leading, the Union through a harrowing civil war often raging within stone's throw, relatively speaking, of the Federal capital on the Potomac. The dangers that did, in fact, result in his death at the hands of a fanatical Southern sympathizer, John Wilkes Booth, less than a week after Robert E. Lee's surrender at Appomattox on April 9, 1865. Oddly—or perhaps predictably?—Lincoln, according to his close friend and sometime bodyguard Ward Hill Lamon, just days before his assassination dreamed that his body was lying on view in the White House.

By historian Neely's analysis, meanwhile, "The philosophical expression of Lincoln's tendencies toward depression and of his occasional preoccupation with death was fatalism, a doctrine to which Lincoln was attracted on and off throughout his life." Even as president, for instance, Lincoln once, in 1864, said, "I claim not to have controlled events, but confess plainly that events have controlled me."

That would seem to square with his statement of two decades earlier, in 1846, that "in early life I was inclined to believe in what I understand is called the 'Doctrine of Necessity'—that is, that the human mind is impelled to action, or held in rest by some power over which the mind itself has no control."

All of which leads to Lincoln's reflections, probably in 1862, on the most sublime of all mysteries concerning the Civil War—on whose side was God?

"The will of God prevails," Lincoln wrote on an undated piece of paper, then went on to ruminate further. "In great contests each party claims to act in accordance with the will of God. Both *may* be, and one *must* be wrong. God can not be *for*, and *against* the same thing at the same time."

But such a conclusion was one of mere human logic, he may also have considered, for here Lincoln noted, "In the present civil war it is quite possible that God's purpose is something different from the purpose of either party—and yet the human instrumentalities, working just as they do, are of the best adaptation to effect His purpose."

And now on to the most sublime consideration of all. "I am almost ready," added Lincoln, "to say this is probably true—that God wills this contest, and wills that it shall not end yet. By his mere quiet power on the minds of the now contestants, He could have either saved or destroyed the Union without a human contest. Yet the contest began. And having begun, He could give final victory to either side any day. Yet the contest proceeds."

Truly, a mystery to us mere mortals. Imagine, as Lincoln obviously did, the fact that good men, women, and children on both sides, along with their leaders, looked to the same God for salvation, prayed to Him, sought His succor in battle . . . and in the ultimate outcome. As Lincoln soon would note publicly, in his second inaugural address, that of March 1865: "Both [sides] read the same Bible, and pray to the same God, and each invokes His aid against the other. . . . The prayers of both could not be answered; that of neither has been answered fully. The almighty has His own purposes."

His own purposes. As with Lincoln's death just a few weeks after he uttered those very words.

☆ ☆ ☆

Additional notes: Do not forget Lincoln's seemingly inexhaustible fund of "down-home" humor. He spun his parablelike tales so frequently that clever publishing entrepreneurs were quick to seize upon the presidential wit as the basis for books. One such was the popular (in the North) ten-cent paperback titled *Old Abe's Joker; or Wit at the White House,* reported historian Neely. Another book based upon Lincoln's quips and stories was called *Lincolnana; or the Humors of Uncle Abe.*

Like a twentieth-century successor named Ronald Reagan, all his adult life Lincoln was a quick study and master of the one-liner. When the burly Lamon accidentally tore the seat of his trousers in front of a country courthouse back in Illinois one time, Neely reported, Lamon's fellow lawyers on the Eighth Judicial Circuit got up a fund drive to finance repairs. To which tongue-in-cheek effort Lincoln responded: "I can contribute nothing to the end in view."

Another time, told that his debating rival Stephen A. Douglas's brother-in-law was caught peering over a transom to watch a woman undressing, Lincoln wryly commented that the offender, an army officer, "should be elevated to the peerage."

Not everybody, however, appreciated Lincoln's seeming devotion to homespun humor. Perhaps, though, they didn't see how all those "country-fried" stories served Lincoln himself, if not always his audience, as a form of relief.

Once, upbraided by a visiting congressman for storytelling at the time of a particularly stinging defeat for the Union, Lincoln immediately turned serious and told his visitor: "I respect you as an earnest, sincere man. You cannot be more anxious than I am constantly, and I say to you now that, were it not for this occasional vent, I should die."

At another time of Union disaster, Lincoln revealed his true emotions before Union Maj. Gen. Robert Schenck. "You have little idea of the terrible weight of care and sense of responsibility of this office of mine," Lincoln said. "Schenck, if to be at the head of hell is as hard as what I have to undergo here, I could find it in my heart to pity Satan himself."

★ Part 6 ★
1864–65

Winding Down

By now, it could only end one way, the way it did end. And if it were a terrible, terrible shame the war itself had to happen, worse still was the fact that it still went on . . . and on.

The Dahlgren Papers

HE CAME WITH SECRET ORDERS to destroy this devoted city, hang the president and his cabinet, and burn the town."

Ugly times, ugly deeds to come.

"He came with secret orders . . ." Those were the words of a Civil War diarist writing in the capital of her country at a bleak stage of the Civil War. Writing about an enemy raiding party that approached her city's very gates and then fell short of its goal. Writing about an attempted raid in early 1864 that may have set the stage for assassination attempts against civilian leaders—such as Abraham Lincoln or Jefferson Davis and their respective cabinet members.

It was an ill-conceived attempt leaving bitter, bitter fruit as its legacy, along with controversy and even mystery. Men died in the resulting combat, naturally, but one—a black man acting as a guide—was hanged when he led a cavalry column astray. Whether he simply bumbled his way along, thoroughly lost, or was a spy was one mystery that resulted.

Another lay in the documents a teenage boy found on the body of one cavalry column's commander, a young officer who carried a crutch tied to his saddle and wore a wooden leg. Documents saying the raid would free all prisoners, burn the city, and slay the enemy's leaders.

But were there really such documents? Did they really call for such vengeful acts?

At home base two days later, the young officer's admiral father would go to the president and ask for news of his raider-party son.

In Richmond, Virginia, the other capital city, diarist Mary Boykin Chesnut's pen flew with the usual combination of gossip, social tid-bits, and real news.

Union Brig. Gen. H. Judson Kilpatrick, leader of the abortive raid on Richmond in which Ulric Dahlgren was killed.

Her husband, Brig. Gen. James Chesnut, an aide to President Davis, had come home close to dinnertime and ordered up his horse. "It is so near dinner," she said wonderingly.

"But I am going with the president," he replied. "I am on duty. He goes to inspect the fortifications. The enemy, once more, are within a few miles of Richmond." Truly *within?* After he left, Mary added to her diary entry of March 3, 1864: "The enemy's cannon or our own are thundering in my ears."

As she also would note, the threat to Richmond, capital of the Confederacy, had been real. "Once more," Chesnut wrote, "we have repulsed the enemy. But it is humiliating indeed that he can come and threaten us at our very gates whenever he so pleases. If a forlorn negro had not led him astray (and they hung him for it) on Tuesday night, unmolested they would have walked into Richmond."

"They," Union cavalrymen, had set out for Richmond on February 28 to free Union prisoners held there; *they* consisted of a thirty-five-hundred-man cavalry column commanded by Brig. Gen. Hugh Judson Kilpatrick, a "boy general" graduated from West Point in 1861 and sometimes called "Kil-Cavalry" because of his hard use of horsemen.

The next day, February 29 (1864 was a leap year), Kilpatrick kept moving south despite a brush with Confederates at Beaver Dam Station, but he ordered Col. Ulric Dahlgren, twenty-two, the admiral's one-legged son, to split off toward Goochland Court House with a separate five-hundred-man force.

The plan called upon that small detachment to ford the James River, turn downstream, then recross the river to attack Richmond from the south while Kilpatrick's main force engaged the northwest defenses, all this on Tuesday, March 1. Dahlgren, deprived of his lower right leg by a wound suffered the previous summer, counted upon a black man named Martin Robinson as his guide to the anticipated ford across the river. When no ford was found, as noted by Chesnut, Dahlgren ordered the unfortunate guide hanged.

Kilpatrick's main force, in the meantime, found the city's home guard and other defenders fully alerted and bristling at the Union cavalry's approach. By nightfall the normally aggressive Kilpatrick felt he was making little progress and broke off his attack.

He now decided to go east and south, toward Federal lines near the Chickahominy River.

Dahlgren and his men by nightfall of that same Tuesday were themselves hardly more than two miles outside the Richmond city limits. But Dahlgren also had split his force, and now he, too, ran into stiff resistance from hastily gathered defenders, these led by Robert E. Lee's usually deskbound eldest son, Brig. Gen. Custis Lee, another aide to President Davis.

Discouraged, confused, and by now realizing Kilpatrick must have turned away from Richmond, Dahlgren also pulled back and gathered his remaining men for a fast retreat in the dark. The raid was off, but grim repercussions still lay ahead.

Heading north and then east at the head of ninety or so troopers, Dahlgren pointed toward King and Queen County east of Richmond and rode the semicircular pathway of an outer "beltway" eventually leading him there.

The next day, March 2, Kilpatrick rode for a link-up with elements of Maj. Gen. Benjamin Butler's command in New Kent County east of Richmond, and Dahlgren followed a similar path but encountered Rebel opposition in Hanover County. As he moved eastward, elements of Fitzhugh Lee's (R. E. Lee's nephew) cavalry raced ahead to set up an ambush at Manapike Hill, between King and Queen Court House and King William Court House.

That night Dahlgren rode into the trap awaiting him and was killed, and all but four of his men were captured.

William Littlepage, a teenager serving in the home guard, searched the Union colonel's body and found a notebook and three sheets of official stationery from a Union cavalry division. The youth dutifully gave the papers to his captain, Edward W. Halbach.

The captain in turn, with the coming of daylight, read the papers then, later that day, handed them over to Lt. James Pollard of the

Ninth Virginia Cavalry, the man who had set up the ambush. No doubt both officers were stunned at what they read . . . and Pollard the next morning set out for Richmond to present the papers to his superiors there.

It wasn't long, about midday apparently, before Pollard had presented the shocking documents to Fitzhugh Lee, who then rushed off to present them to Jefferson Davis. After a hurried conference with Secretary of State Judah Benjamin, the papers, a hot potato indeed, went next to Maj. Gen. Samuel Cooper at the War Department, the Confederacy's adjutant general.

One of the documents, two pages in length, apparently was the substance of a short speech to the troops, while the other seemed to be added plans for conduct of the raid.

Both documents urged the destruction of Richmond, and one called for the slaying of Davis and his Rebel cabinet.

In Washington on Friday, March 4, Rear Adm. John Dahlgren, inventor of the Dahlgren gun, visited President Lincoln to ask for news of his son, Ulric, a favorite of the president. In Richmond that same day, diarist Mary Chesnut made note of new Union moves against Richmond: "Enemy reinforced and on us again," she wrote. That was Kilpatrick attempting retaliation for the death of Dahlgren.

The next day, on March 5, Richmond's newspapers published news of the instructions contained in the Dahlgren documents. The South, predictably, reacted with shock, while from the North came denials and claims the documents were forged as a propaganda ploy.

The truth of the matter has been a mystery debated by historians ever since. Could it be that Southern authorities, with or without the connivance of Richmond's newspaper editors, made up the apparent assassination plan in its entirety? That the Confederate government forged the Dahlgren Papers?

Or, another view . . . expressed by James O. Hall in the *Civil War Times* of February 1999? To wit: "The authorities at the [Confederate] War Department did not even know that such papers existed until [Fitzhugh] Lee delivered them to [General] Cooper. Out of the resulting confusion and cumulative outrage, a decision was made to call in Richmond newspaper editors and furnish copies of the documents for publication the next morning, March 5. There was not enough intervening time for a sophisticated forgery to be concocted, for new stationery to be printed with the necessary letterhead, and get everyone in agreement on a cover story. The conclusion has to be that there was no forgery."

Whatever the case there, the repercussions lingered on. On March 5, Mary Chesnut wrote that she walked with a friend, probably South Carolina cavalry Maj. Thomas Ferguson, and, "He told me of Colonel Dahlgren's death and the horrid tablets found in his pocket.

"He came with secret orders to destroy this devoted city, hang the president and his cabinet, and burn the town."

Then, too, three days later (March 8), she noted still more of the talk, true or untrue, making the rounds in the capital of the Confederacy, as related this time by local resident Lucy Webb: "At her hospital there was a man who had been taken prisoner by Dahlgren's party. He saw the negro hung [*sic*] who had misled them—unintentionally, in all probability. He saw Dahlgren give a part of his bridle to hang him."

As Mary Chesnut also reflected, the episode had been a melancholy affair all 'round. "This Dahlgren had also lost a leg," she noted in a final diary comment.

Additional notes: Robert E. Lee, when he heard of the raid and the Dahlgren documents, called it "a barbaric & inhuman plot."

The fact is, though, attitudes on both sides of the Civil War had hardened by the time of the Kilpatrick-Dahlgren raid in early 1864. "Whether Lee liked it or not," wrote Emory M. Thomas in his 1995 biography of the general, "the war was turning obviously ugly. And the looting, burning, and random killing on both sides would only accelerate during 1864."

In the North, meanwhile, "a streak of ruthless determination, not hitherto noticeable, began to appear in Lincoln's character," wrote David Herbert Donald in his 1995 biography of the president—a streak not of any innate cruelty, but rather due to "his sense that the war had gone on too long, with too much loss of blood and treasure, and that it was time to force it to a close."

Shortly beforehand, Lincoln had been outraged by Confederate threats to shoot captured black soldiers of the Union. He retaliated with an executive order: "For every soldier of the United States killed in violation of the laws of war, a rebel soldier shall be executed; and for every one enslaved by the enemy . . . a rebel soldier shall be placed at hard labor on the public works."

But Lincoln's order was only "an empty threat," says Donald's Pulitzer Prize–winning biography. To be sure, Lincoln continued "to fume over mistreatment of Union prisoners," but he also told Secretary of War Edwin Stanton, "blood can not restore blood, and government should not act for revenge."

Still, added Donald, "out of this frustration and out of his growing sense that something had to be done to break the military stalemate, arose the plan for . . . [the] daring raid against Richmond."

The original idea, as presented to Lincoln by young General Kilpatrick himself, was to assault Richmond's defenses from two sides at once and free Union prisoners held at Libby and Belle Isle prisons.

The raid's abortive outcome—accompanied by the hanging of Dahlgren's black guide, the young officer's own death, and the discovery of the shocking documents—suggests another, more subtle mystery than that of the authenticity of those documents. Did the raid, in some quarters, inspire Southern retribution against Lincoln himself?

During the failed raid, Kilpatrick's column attacked and destroyed this mill on the James River and the Kanawha Canal.

Or was the raid merely a manifestation of hardened attitudes already in place on both sides of the war?

Postscript: In any case, young Colonel Dahlgren's remains were destined to rest temporarily in the Virginia countryside. Not where he fell in combat and initially was buried, but on a farm closer to his goal of Richmond, thanks, as stated before, to the secret reburial conducted by colleagues of Union spy Elizabeth Van Lew in Richmond.

He Lifted His Hat

THE BAD NEWS FOR ROBERT E. LEE, for every man of his Army of Northern Virginia, came in the notoriously rough, wild, and tangled country just west of Fredericksburg, Virginia—not once but twice—in a pair of battles fought almost exactly a year apart, in May 1863 and May 1864.

The names still resonate hauntingly today. They still evoke a sense of foreboding, even as mere echoes from the past. And they do deserve a respectful pause, perhaps a whisper as we say the names. Quietly now, even reverently, in view of all their dead, their burned, and their maimed, we dare to say their names.

Chancellorsville.

The Wilderness.

Today, people whiz by in their cars with scarcely a thought. On a modern road map, prosaically enough, the two locations would almost merge as a single dot.

In each instance of the bad news back then, when all was so different, "Marse Robert's" men, after many hours of exhausting battle, were attempting an end run around the Union's mighty Army of the Potomac—a flank attack. Out of sight, they filled the back roads, pathways, woods.

In each instance, too, there came a scattering of unexpected shots from unexpected quarters, followed by startled shouts. In each instance, a year apart, there came more than the usual grief at the sight of a fallen comrade—for these two were no ordinary soldiers but Lee's two valued corps commanders, Thomas J. "Stonewall" Jackson and James Longstreet.

Worse, each had been shot by his own men. In the first such mishap, at Chancellorsville on May 2, 1863, it was Jackson who fell victim to his own, to the troops of the Eighteenth North Carolina Infantry, as he was returning from a reconnaissance of the lines in gathering darkness. He was not mortally wounded, it seemed, but the surgeons did have to take his left arm. Then, just as recovery seemed entirely possible, he came down with pneumonia and died late on Sunday, May 10.

The dreaded news spread quickly among his compatriots. "An irreparable loss," said a shaken Lee, who just days before, with deliberate irony, had called Jackson "my right arm." For the Confederacy, despite its victory at Chancellorsville, that was a bitter day, but there remained many more sad encounters as Americans fought Americans at many other sites strewn with additional casualties, Gettysburg and Vicksburg among them.

In May 1864, a year after Jackson's fatal wounding, the rival forces once again were drawn up opposite one another in that wild and tangled terrain just west of Fredericksburg. This time they prepared for the appropriately named battle of the Wilderness—notorious not only for its storm of shot and shell, not only for the staggering numbers of more men killed, but also for the fire that sprang up and cremated both the dead and the untended wounded.

Longstreet's First Corps had arrived on May 6—late, but still in time to strike at the left flank of Union Maj. Gen. Winfield Scott Hancock's Second Corps at 11 A.M. and threaten to roll it up, as Hancock himself later admitted, "like a wet blanket."

In the midst of the tumult that followed came the moment when one of the officers in the group, Maj. Gen. Joseph Kershaw, saw errant rifles being leveled and pointed toward them, noted Jeffrey D. Wert in his biography of Longstreet.

"Friends!" Kershaw shouted, but too late. In the volley of rifle fire that already had been loosed, two officers and an orderly went down, never to rise again.

Another officer, Brig. Gen. Moxley Sorrel, saw Longstreet hit. "He was actually lifted straight up and came down hard," Sorrel said later.

"Longstreet reeled in his saddle, his right arm hanging limp at his side," wrote Wert. The general had been struck in the throat by a bullet

Confederate Lt. Gen. James Longstreet, who, like Stonewall Jackson a year before, was wounded by his own men . . . but in Longstreet's case not fatally.

that passed through his shoulder and severed nerves.

Now Longstreet, too! Every onlooker had to wonder and fear for the South. Just a year earlier, with the loss of the great Stonewall, many had felt the cause of the South was irretrievably lost. And now, could Longstreet be gone as well?

It did appear that way as he struggled to speak, face ashen, bloody foam on his lips.

He did force out a few words. He whispered them to Sorrel. "Tell General Lee to have General Field [Maj. Gen. Charles Field] to assume command of the First Corps," he managed to say.

Somehow, with Field then by his side, Longstreet summoned the strength to explain the flank maneuver already under way. Then it was time to leave the fight to others. A shuffle forward as Longstreet was carried off on a stretcher, a solicitous officer placing a hat over his face.

"When the troops saw Longstreet, they shouted he was dead," wrote Wert.

But not this tough soldier. With his good left hand, Longstreet lifted the hat. They saw he was alive. "The burst of voices and flurry of hats exultantly thrown into the air," he himself said later, "eased my pains somewhat."

Yes, he himself . . . since this would *not* be a full repeat of May 1863. Not only would Longstreet recover well—and quickly enough to go through the remaining months of the Civil War—he would outlive most of his fellow stars of the Confederate firmament. Both Gens. A. P. Hill and Jeb Stuart, for instance, were mortally wounded before war's end, and Lee himself died just a few years later.

Ironically, too, Longstreet also lived to turn Republican and serve as a minor federal official appointed by President U. S. Grant—the very man, of course, who had commanded the Union at the Wilderness affair that almost cost Longstreet his life.

Letter to Mrs. Bixby

IT WAS ONE OF THE most moving and also most famous of all letters composed by President Abraham Lincoln—the Bixby letter.

"Dear Madam," he wrote to the widowed Lydia Bixby of Boston on November 21, 1864, after his second election to the presidency,

> I have been shown in the files of the War Department a statement of the Adjutant General of Massachusetts that you are the mother of five sons who have died gloriously on the field of battle. I feel how weak and fruitless must be any words of mine which should attempt to beguile you from the grief of a loss so overwhelming. But I cannot refrain from tendering to you the consolation that may be found in the thanks of the Republic they have died to save. I pray that our Heavenly Father may assuage the anguish of your bereavement and leave you only the cherished memory of the loved and lost, and the solemn pride that must be yours to have laid so costly a sacrifice on the altar of freedom.
>
> Yours very sincerely and respectfully,
(signed) A. Lincoln

Wonderful words, and who is to diminish Lincoln's fine sentiments if—as happened—it turned out he had been misinformed as to the extent of the Widow Bixby's loss?

She did not lose five sons to the war, although she had seen that many sons go off to war . . . and two of them did die in combat. More than enough for any mother, any war.

As for the rest, noted historian Mark E. Neely Jr. in his *Abraham Lincoln Encyclopedia,* "one was honorably discharged, one deserted and one either deserted or died a prisoner of war."

More than enough, all right . . . and surely Mrs. Bixby was still grieving when personally presented Lincoln's letter by the adjutant general of Massachusetts, William Schouler.

The Boston papers picked it up the afternoon of the very same day; the letter then was reproduced and reprinted over and over again. As late as 1891, said Neely, "a New York print dealer named Michael F. Tobin copyrighted a facsimile . . . and sold copies for $2." Further, "The proprietor of Huber's Museum, also in New York City, sold similar facsimiles for $1."

The Bixby Letter even appeared in a Liberty Bond handbill disseminated by the federal government during World War I.

Oddly, the original text of Lincoln's famous letter quickly vanished. "The text of the letter is known only by the newspaper accounts," added Neely. "The original handwritten copy has never been found."

Unsung Heroes III

THEY LIVED IN A HOUSE named Boxmere for its magnificent boxwood, and when the war came to town, the two young men of the house—boys, really—at first just wanted to see all the excitement.

Their widowed mother, Mrs. Thomas Hardeman Figuers, and their two little sisters had retreated to a friend's safer-appearing home nearby. At Boxmere, though, young Harden Perkins Figuers had climbed a yellow poplar tree behind the house at the first sound of cannon at Fort Granger. All the better to see the pending action, of course.

But the rifle fire accompanying one of the Civil War's greatest battles soon drove him out of his tree and into the house, where he joined brother Tom and their dog Fannie for a vigil in the cellar.

Years later, wrote Reid Smith in his 1975 book *Majestic Middle Tennessee,* Harden Perkins Figuers "would recall how the cranky crackle of Rebel rifle fire had finally driven him from his lofty perch." Since the family home at Franklin, Tennessee, was just inside the Federal lines, that "Rebel rifle fire" was aimed young Harden's way!

In short time, the rifle fire now thudding into the rear walls of the stately Figuers home, the backyard began to fill up with the forms of fallen Federals.

Then "a cannonball suddenly slammed into an overhead sill and sent both boys scurrying up to the first floor."

Upstairs, they found "the house . . . crawling with captured Confederate wounded and no doctor anywhere to be found."

Swallowing their shock, the boys set to starting fires, heating and hauling water, tearing up the family linens to make bandages, anything to help, but most important . . . they needed a doctor. How to bring one there?

Young Harden accepted the inherent risk. Setting out for "downtown" Franklin at a run, the battle still raging around the town, he raced to a local doctor's office, found the physician in, and begged him to come quickly and tend the wounded back at Boxmere. But . . . the doctor shook his head no. Harden returned to Boxmere dejected and disillusioned. "The doctor had refused to leave the safety of his office and venture into the streets."

Back at Boxmere, the boys continued to do their best for the wounded until, "later in the evening" they were heartened by the arrival of their mother to help out . . . to see how her young heroes were faring.

When all was said and done at Franklin, thousands on both sides had been killed and wounded, but both the Rebel and Yankee armies moved on. Stunned Franklin residents gradually settled back into their normally quiet rural routines, the Civil War itself destined to grind down to an end only months after the battle of late November 1864. For many years later, though, the owners of Boxmere continued to find unexploded cannonballs "beneath the lone boxwood that lent Boxmere its unusual name," wrote Smith. "Such were the grim mementoes of a day of sound and fury this grand old place will never be able to quite forget."

"Lee to the Rear!"

NOT ONCE BUT TWICE IN two days' time the venerated Robert E. Lee came close to becoming a statistic . . . a more immediate casualty of the Civil War than his suffering and sorrow made him later as the leading figure of defeat.

It happened at the Wilderness, May 1864, just before the frightening wounding of James Longstreet. And who knows what course the Civil War might have taken had Lee himself become a casualty of the worst kind . . . here or elsewhere? In any case, he definitely was in danger of death, wounding or capture, and not for the only time in his career as commander of the Army of Northern Virginia.

One moment of danger came as Lee rode with Gens. A. P. Hill and Jeb Stuart on the Orange Plank Road early in the battle in an effort to locate Dick Ewell's corps and/or the Union forces. The three Confederate generals came to a clearing on the Widow Tapp's property and dismounted. Quite suddenly, recalled Emory M. Thomas in his biography of Lee, "a line of blue-coated soldiers emerged from the woods to the left of the Confederates."

But the Union soldiers apparently didn't realize what opportunity lay before them, for they withdrew. Added Thomas, "Had these men seized the moment, they could have easily captured or killed Lee, Hill, and Stuart."

Imagine the possibilities! Not only Lee, but three major personalities of the Confederate leadership in mortal danger at the same moment. What an impact their deaths or capture would have had on the Confederacy's will to continue . . . although, sad to say, neither Hill nor Stuart was destined to survive the war. Stuart, in fact, was only days away from his mortal wounding at Yellow Tavern.

Then, too, with Hill's men in ragged retreat the next morning, Lee was planted in the Orange Plank Road trying to stem the flow to the rear. Spotting Brig. Gen. Samuel McGowan, he shouted, "My God, General McGowan, is this splendid brigade of yours running like a flock of geese?"

Suddenly, though, the advance elements of Longstreet's anxiously awaited corps were pouring into the potential gap, stemming the tide of retreat.

"Who are you, my boys?" asked Lee.

And when they replied they were from Texas, he shouted, "Hurrah for Texas!"

Then the clearly excited Lee guided the newcomers "into line," wrote Thomas, and "rode at their heels as they swept forward to the attack."

The Texans soon noticed that Lee was still with them, "about to charge with them."

A flurry of shouts erupted. "Go back! Lee to the rear!"

But at first he wouldn't . . . would not go back. "For long moments Lee was oblivious to these cries; he seemed possessed."

Finally, his own staff officer Charles Venable had the good sense to catch Lee's mount Traveller by the bridle and lead horse and rider to the rear, out of immediate danger.

But there also came a similar situation a week later at the Mule Shoe salient (also known as the Bloody Angle) during the battle of Spotsylvania. With Union troops pouring into the Mule Shoe on May 12, Lee rushed to the scene and tried to rally his troops in a counterattack. When he appeared ready to lead it himself, his Rebels wouldn't move. Again they shouted: "Lee to the rear! Go back!"

He did, and it was on this day that a cannonball whizzed beneath his rearing horse Traveller, another near miss for Lee.

Late in the day, too, he once again was ready to ride into battle, this time with a fresh brigade of infantry, but these soldiers also yelled, "Go back, General!" And no wonder—the firing in the salient was so intense that day, a twenty-two-inch oak tree was chopped down by the minié balls that struck it in a never-ending torrent.

Lee's closest call of all during the Civil War may have come almost two years earlier—during the battle of Second Manassas. Lee had ridden forward on August 29 for a better view of the terrain when a Union sharpshooter's bullet grazed his cheek and left a scratch mark.

No Place to Fall

IF ANTIETAM AND ITS COMBINED casualty list of more than twenty-three thousand qualified as the bloodiest single day in American military history, perhaps the battle of Franklin, Tennessee, with nearly eighty-six hundred combined casualties, would qualify as the bloodiest two to five hours (estimates vary) in American history.

How, though, to translate such cold, large-scale numbers into their more individual human terms?

Perhaps it would be a bit more personal to recall that five Confederate generals were all laid out together late that evening of November 30, 1864, on the rear veranda of the nearby Carnton plantation, all five awaiting burial.

Or to recall that one of them, Irish-born Patrick Cleburne, had stopped by St. John's Episcopal Church not long before, not far away. Cleburne knew that fellow Rebel Gen. Leonidas Polk, an Episcopal bishop in civilian life, and four Polk brothers had built this church on the Columbia–Mount Pleasant Pike in 1842.

Cleburne may *not* have known that two years before his own stop, Yankee troops serving under Don Carlos Buell had passed through this part of Middle Tennessee on their way to the battle of Shiloh and stolen organ pipes from the church as souvenirs.

But Cleburne did know he was approaching a major battle. Struck by the quiet serenity of St. John's, he reportedly said, "If I am killed in the impending battle, I request that my body be laid to rest in this, the most beautiful and peaceful spot I ever beheld."

Days later, his wish was granted . . . Cleburne, a casualty at Franklin, was temporarily laid to rest at St. John's. So, in fact, were two more of the six Confederate generals felled in the battle of Franklin, H. B. Granbury and O. F. Strahl.

Also killed outright during the conflagration at Franklin, then laid out on the back veranda of the Carnton mansion had been States Rights Gist and John Adams. Succumbing to his wounds later, the sixth general lost to the Confederacy was John C. Carter.

Before Carter died, he was carried back to the nearby Harrison house, built by High Sheriff William Harrison of Williamson County in 1848 or so. Here, after lingering in pain for nearly two weeks, the youngest of the "Franklin Six" finally died on December 10. ("Just two months earlier," noted Reid Smith in his book *Majestic Middle Tennessee*, Confederate Brig. Gen. John H. Kelly, wounded leading a cavalry charge at nearby Parry Station, also had died in the Harrison House, and he had been the youngest general in the Confederate army.)

All six general officers killed at Franklin, it may be recalled, had served in Gen. John Bell Hood's ill-fated Army of Tennessee. Coincidentally, the same white-columned Harrison house apparently was the scene on November 30 of Hood's own planning for his army's hopeless assaults against well-entrenched Union troops at Franklin, a simple farm community near Nashville.

That morning Hood and his subordinates had discovered Union Gen. John Schofield's surprise nighttime move past the worn and tattered Army of Tennessee at Spring Hill. And now Cleburne counseled against Hood's proposal to mount a frontal attack in response. Far better, additionally argued Nathan Bedford Forrest that afternoon at the Harrison house—correctly but in typical hot temper—far better to go against the Union flank. But no, Hood argued, heatedly also, *he* was in command, not Forrest, and frontal the assault would be.

And so it came about, wave upon wave of Rebel troops futilely dashed against the solid rock of Schofield's entrenchments. "At four o'clock," wrote Reid Smith, "the attack order was given. The next two hours saw the Confederates hurl themselves at Schofield's men with the frenzied fury of thirteen separate charges that killed the attacking Southerners so fast the dead often could find no place to fall."

Standing just behind the Union lines that late afternoon, just south of town, it's also worth noting, was the landmark Carter house

At the center of the man-made storm that shook Franklin, Tennessee, in late November 1864 was the Carter House . . . where a family awaited word of a son's fate just outside.

Both O. F. Strahl (left) and States Rights Gist were among the six Confederate generals fatally wounded in the battle of Franklin.

. . . where seventeen family members and five neighbors anxiously hid in the stone cellar and awaited the end of the storm sweeping over and around the sturdy brick house.

It had been built in 1830 by local merchant Fountain "Fount" Branch Carter, whose three sons all volunteered for the Twentieth Tennessee Infantry in 1861. One son, Moscow, had been captured and turned loose on parole; Francis, youngest of the three, still in his teens, had been "shot down at Shiloh," and the third, Tod, about twenty-four years in age, was that very moment out there, just beyond the house he was born in, somewhere in the mob of Rebels assaulting the Union line.

As Moscow Carter and his father watched through a small cellar window, recounted Smith, "the spearhead of Hood's first attack hit the Federals between 'Fount' Carter's cotton gin and his barn just west of the [Columbia] Pike." As a result: "In a frenzy of tooth-and-claw hand to hand fighting, his ragged Rebels temporarily split the Union line and surged past the front door of the Carter House, only to be met and thrown back by Col. Emerson Opdyke's determined Yankee reserves."

Again and again, though, the Confederate waves spent themselves all around the Carter house, with young Tod Carter's family inside worrying over his whereabouts, his safety. Between the Carter cotton gin and the Carter barn, a stretch equivalent to two city blocks, added

Smith, "four of the five Confederate generals to die on the field at Franklin would be killed. . . . Of the six to be [mortally] wounded, five were shot down along this sector of the Yankee lines."

By nine o'clock that night only an occasional rifle report punctuated the groans of the wounded—more than six thousand of them Confederate.

At the Carter house, by now, a quick, hushed meeting with a visitor come on a vital errand. Out there, in the "wreckage of Hood's army," young Master Tod lay wounded, too. "Guided by his young son's commanding officer, Gen. Thomas Smith, 'Fount' Carter, along with three daughters and a daughter-in-law, would find Tod lying on the battlefield within a stone's throw of the house where he had been born."

Worse still, "in a matter of hours, beneath the roof of his childhood home, Capt. Tod Carter, CSA, would breathe his last."

Just one more of the eighty-six hundred individuals who made up the single afternoon's total casualty count.

"May We Meet in Heaven"

NO PARENT WOULD EVER WANT to receive a letter like this . . . like Confederate soldier J. R. Montgomery's final words for his father back in Mississippi, written in May 1864 from somewhere in Virginia near the battleground known as Spotsylvania.

"This is my last letter to you," the young man began. "I went into battle this morning as courier for General [Henry] Heth. I have been struck by a piece of shell and my right shoulder is horribly mangled and I know death is inevitable."

He went on to say, according to Emory Thomas in his biography of R. E. Lee, he knew his father would want to hear from him, and he tried to offer reassurances. "I know that death is near, that I will die far from home and friends of my early youth but I have friends here too who are kind to me."

One of those, a fellow soldier named Fairfax, would write later with the "particulars" of young Montgomery's pending death.

Some posthumous plans for Montgomery had already been made. "My grave will be marked 58 that you may visit it if you desire to do so, but is optionary with you whether you let my remains rest here or in Miss. I would like to rest in the grave yard with my dear mother and brothers but it's a matter of minor importance."

Were there any reassurances for the wounded soldier himself? In his faith, apparently yes. "Let us all try to reunite in heaven," he had continued. "I pray my God to forgive my sins and I feel that his promises are true that he will forgive me and save me."

And now, farewell, his words trailing off.

"Give my love to all my friends my strength fails me. My horse and equipment will be left for you. Again a long farewell and you. May we meet in heaven. Your dying son, J. R. Montgomery."

Custer Does a Favor

NOT MANY SOUTHERN TOWNS HAD reason to thank George Armstrong Custer for a gratuitous act of kindness during the "recent unpleasantness." After all, this young and colorful general, graduated from West Point the very year the Civil War erupted, was, if brave (insanely so, some would argue), also headstrong, cruel, and even ruthless.

Oh, no, the faint of heart might rear back and say, not *our* Custer! Not the brave hero of the Last Stand at the Little Bighorn. Surely not!

Ah, but yes. *Brave?* Absolutely. Case in point: Outside Richmond, Virginia, May 1862, Union forces on the one side of the Chickahominy River, Johnny Reb sequestered somewhere on the opposite bank and beyond, the question for Union commanders concerned the river's depth. Was it fordable?

Riding forward and into the water, no hesitation over the obvious fact that he would make a prime target, was the young West Pointer Custer. As the Union commander George McClellan said years later, Custer's action was reported on up the chain of command as "an act of desperate gallantry."

Another time, also in Virginia, one of his men had been shot in the heart and was, in Custer's own words, "even then in the death struggle." No matter that he was already doomed. The young Custer, unable to "bear the thought of his being struck again," dashed beyond the front line, scooped up the man, and carried him to the rear.

But what about cruel? Well, Custer's first "kill" in battle apparently was a Confederate officer in flight upon a fine thoroughbred horse. "I selected him as my game," Custer later wrote his sister Lydia. Yes, *game.*

Custer rode after the Rebel officer. They jumped a rail fence, relates Evan S. Connell's biographical *Son of the Morning Star.* He shouted at the Southerner to surrender, but the man rode on. Custer shot him . . . of necessity, it would appear, in the back. The fleeing officer reeled in the saddle, then tumbled to the ground.

A fellow Union officer saw Custer's victim rise to his feet, turn with his hands over his head, then fall over dead.

In the aftermath, the dust of combat settled, Custer appropriated the unknown officer's handsome horse, his red morocco saddle studded with nails of silver and his double-edged, extra-long sword. "It was his own fault," Custer wrote to Lydia. "I told him twice to surrender."

In battle, of course, these are the things that happen. War is not fair—by the time of the Civil War, chivalry was on the way out; mass slaughter was in.

In that context, was Custer cruel and even ruthless? According to Connell's study, Custer "lost more men during his berserk charges than most cavalry officers." Peel away Custer's boyish pranks and colorful, self-designed uniform, and there "rode a killer."

If unwilling to take Connell's word alone, consider, please, these thoughts penned years later, out in the West, by a fellow serving officer, Maj. Gen. David Stanley: "I have seen enough of him [Custer] to convince me that he is a cold-blooded, untruthful and unprincipled man. He is universally despised by all the officers of his regiment excepting his relatives and one or two sycophants."

If General Stanley was an avowed Custer-hater, never mind; just slide back a few years, to the months immediately after the end of the Civil War. Here was Custer leading four thousand troops to Houston, Texas . . . and administering the lash to men committing minor acts of disobedience.

Okay, insubordination, if you wish. Still, forty lashes each to two men who butchered a calf en route or twenty-five strokes of the whip for

NATIONAL ARCHIVES

Brave but sometimes ruthless, the Union's "boy general" George Armstrong Custer showed a kind side to a Confederate officer and his family in Charlottesville, Virginia.

a soldier who stole fruit? Considering that the men were, by Connell's account, "half-starved" on their "interminable" march to Texas, was that appropriate punishment? Considering that Congress four years earlier outlawed flogging, was it even Custer's legal right?

During the Civil War itself, it may also be recalled, Custer was widely blamed—perhaps erroneously—for the outright execution of six of John Singleton Mosby's rangers, again in Virginia. The facts are not entirely clear, but orders had come down from U. S. Grant himself for the summary execution of captured Rebel partisans, Mosby included. In response to that outrage, and another that soon followed, even the supposedly genteel warrior Robert E. Lee went along with Mosby's proposal to hang the same number of men captured from Custer's command.

Seven such unfortunates were selected, a handful were hanged, and two to four of Custer's men managed to escape.

Whatever the exact numbers in that bloody affair, and whatever may be said for or against the controversial Custer, one Civil War incident has eluded most of the history books . . . and it did involve an act of kindness that left a Southern town and family most grateful, indeed.

In March 1865, the war almost at end, Custer briefly occupied Charlottesville, Virginia, the home of the University of Virginia.

He had already agreed to spare the school any harm by his troops, but then came the issue posed by Charlottesville resident Thomas Farish, a captain in the Confederate army caught skulking, it did appear, near town in civilian clothes.

Union troops hustled him before Custer, who was staying at a Charlottesville home called the Farm, a fine brick edifice on East

Jefferson Street. Oddly, as the prisoner in tattered laborer's garb was brought in, a child who lived there exclaimed, "Oh, Mama, they've got Papa!"

True enough—it was Capt. Tom Farish's own home. He, in fact, had rushed back from southwest Virginia, on furlough, to make sure his family was safely enduring the Federal occupation of his hometown.

With the situation explained to Custer in Farish's parlor, the unpredictable Union officer graciously saluted and said, "I don't know if it is my duty to ask you to take a seat or yours to ask me, under these peculiar circumstances of war."

A good start to such a meeting, you might say . . . except that Custer's superior, Gen. Phil Sheridan, ordered the Southerner hanged as a spy. That very evening, Union men began building a gallows on the front lawn of Farish's home.

About midnight, however, came a countermanding order. After hours of argument on the prisoner's behalf, Custer had persuaded Sheridan to spare the Charlottesville resident and release him on parole.

So it was, years later, that a certain Southern town and its surrounding county—Charlottesville and Albemarle County—responded to Custer's death at the Little Bighorn with a donation for an out-of-town monument to be erected in his memory. According to Edward C. Mead in a January 1905 issue of the *Baltimore Sun,* a Custer memorial ball held in Charlottesville produced the proceeds for a "large contribution" to the monument's cost.

Unexpected Benefactor

In the aftermath of the battle of Franklin, Tennessee, Nicholas Edwin Perkins found himself standing defiantly before an upstairs door in Meeting of the Waters, his fine Georgian brick home near the battle site. Below a small mob of Yankee looters swirled through the stately first-floor rooms. Their shouts indicated they planned to set the house afire once they had finished with their looting.

Despite a crippled right arm, Perkins was ready to defend the family members he had hastened into the upstairs room behind the door he now so zealously guarded.

To fight off the Yankee rabble, he could count only on the sword he held in his left hand—his right arm had been crippled in a pistol duel with a classmate at Centre College many years before.

From below there suddenly came more shouts and even "frenzied" commotion, according to Reid Smith in *Majestic Middle Tennessee.* "From out of nowhere a saber-swinging Union officer had ridden up to the house and waded into the looters with a torrent of oaths that cleared the downstairs chaos within a few head-splitting moments."

Going downstairs minutes later to thank his unexpected—and most welcome—benefactor, Perkins discovered he knew the man. The Yankee officer was the old college classmate who had crippled Perkins's right arm in their gun duel at Centre College years before.

Crook's Embarrassment

IN THE CIVIL WAR, BROTHER fought brother, it is well known. In the case of Union Maj. Gen. George Crook, however, that sort of pairing went a bit further—when his future brother-in-law joined in Crook's capture by a Confederate raiding party.

Worse, it was an embarrassing, even ignominious capture in a quiet hotel, far from any battlefield . . . with friendly troops encamped close by. For Crook also, it resulted in brief confinement at Libby Prison in Richmond as a prisoner of war.

Hardly mitigating for Crook was the fact that a fellow Union general, Benjamin Franklin Kelley, also was captured in the same raid on Cumberland, Maryland, by Capt. Jesse McNeil's partisan rangers in February 1865. Cumberland was Kelley's headquarters, but Crook was the superior officer in rank.

Both Union generals were lodging at the time in the Revere House, a hostelry owned by a man named Daily or Dailey, whose apparently beguiling daughter Mary soon enough would become Mrs. George Crook, the still-to-be-famous Indian fighter's wife. As fate would have it, Kelley also had met a young lady around town and soon would be marrying her as well.

For the moment, though, neither general had given enough thought to Mary's absent brother, Daily's son, who was a member of McNeil's spirited troop of rangers. Nor had the Union pair given enough thought to the remaining sixty or so partisans who quite suddenly the night of February 21 were romping through the Cumberland hostelry just about at will.

In no time at all, the Rebels scooped up their high-ranking prey and sent them southward, in the direction of Richmond and its Libby Prison hostelry.

They say that Edwin Stanton, Lincoln's secretary of war, was livid with rage when he heard of the raiding party's easy escapade. For one thing, Kelley was supposed to be guarding the Baltimore and Ohio rail line against disruption by Confederate raiders such as McNeil himself. At the time, too, Kelley's superior, Crook, commanded the entire Department of Western Virginia.

When captured, Crook and Kelley could have called upon the helpful services of ten thousand Federal troops on duty nearby.

While an official investigation and relief of General Crook were options under consideration in Washington for a time, no sanctions were ever imposed—perhaps because the war soon ended, perhaps in view of his yeoman service, or perhaps both. West Pointer Crook, after all, had served at Antietam and South Mountain, at Chickamauga, at Cloyd's Mountain—a signal victory for the Ohio-born officer—and at Winchester, Fisher's Hill, and Cedar Creek. Upon his exchange from embarrassing POW status, meanwhile, he would command a cavalry division for the Union Army of the Potomac and take part in the pursuit of Robert E. Lee's disintegrating forces all the way to Appomattox.

Crook had begun army life (after graduation from West Point in 1852) as an Indian fighter who survived an early wounding by a poisoned arrow. Now, with the end of the Civil War, he returned to the far West and Indian fighting—except that toward the end of his life he argued for peaceful pacification of the Native Americans and greater recognition of their rights.

Kelley, meanwhile, also was exchanged the month after sharing in Crook's embarrassment. Leaving the army in June 1865, he later entered into other forms of federal service—first, by President U. S. Grant's appointment, as a tax collector, then as superintendent of a military reservation, and finally—by President Chester Arthur's appointment—as an examiner of pensions.

His Civil War experience had been limited geographically to the Virginia-Maryland region, but was intense, nonetheless. Born in New Hampshire, and later a resident of Wheeling, West Virginia, Kelley was a freight agent for the B&O when the Civil War broke out. He organized the First (West) Virginia, a regiment he then led in the early battle of Philippi. Severely wounded there, he eventually recovered and soon was commanding forces protecting the vital rail line supplying Union forces to the west.

Kelley and his men took part in the pursuit and harassment of Lee's retreating army after Gettysburg. He also fought at Cumberland, Moorefield, and New Creek.

All very commendable . . . and too bad the most spectacular moment in Kelley's military career came the night he and Crook were routed from their hotel lodgings and hustled into captivity. For Crook, though, such rude intrusion by an enemy that included his future brother-in-law had to be especially embarrassing.

One of Fourteen Honored

JUST NORTH OF THE JAMES RIVER and east of Richmond the order came down the line. Put aside your percussion caps. For the morning's assault against Johnny Reb, bayonets only.

The first wave of men from Union Brig. Gen. Charles Paine's Third Division, Twenty-seventh Corps, moved out at 5:30 A.M. that September 29, 1864. On that Thursday morn, they would cross three hundred yards of rising ground, then negotiate a tangle of stakes and defensive brush piles before confronting Gen. John Gregg's Texas Brigade and the twenty-fourth Virginia Cavalry.

Out of 683 Union men sent forward in the 5:30 wave, 365 soon would lie dead on the battlefield.

First Sgt. Powhatan Beaty waited with others of his Company G for the signal sending forth the second Union wave minutes after 6 A.M.

A native of Richmond itself, that slowly disintegrating Confederate capital lying just beyond the Rebel line, Beaty was a bit of an oddity . . . but his place of birth was but a minor detail in the sweep of events that day. For this would be a significant battle, a clash of arms major enough to call for U. S. Grant's personal direction of Union moves and Robert E. Lee's personal command of Confederate forces. Sometimes called the battle of Chaffin's Farm, the two days of fighting now are better known as the battle of Fort Harrison, are better known for the fact that possession of the fort permanently changed from Confederate hands to Union.

Often forgotten in the retelling of the Fort Harrison story is the role of Powhatan Beaty . . . and that of another baker's dozen men who all took part in that small segment of the overall battle called New Market Heights, a clash along New Market Road in Henrico County, today a suburb of Richmond.

All fourteen men won the Medal of Honor, "the largest single number of soldiers ever so honored in a single day's battle in American history," according to Gary Robertson in the *Richmond Times-Dispatch* of February 4, 2000. Beaty, one of four Virginia natives among the fourteen but the only one born in Richmond, was cited for both his leadership and gallantry. He "took command of his company, all the officers having been killed or wounded, and gallantly led it," says Beaty's Medal of Honor citation (which spells the overall battle's alternate name as *Chapins* Farm).

As was the general rule among the Union's 180,000 African-American troops, those officers were white. Beaty and his thirteen fellow Medal recipients all were enlisted men, all were black, all were members of Paine's Third Division, Twenty-seventh Corps, U.S. Colored Troops.

Beaty, it seems, had left the Richmond area before the Civil War to become a farmer in Ohio. He had joined the Union army at Camp Delaware, Ohio, on June 5, 1863, at the age of twenty-four. He was chosen first sergeant of Company G, Fifth U.S. Colored Troops, just two days later. Not much else is known about him today. "Details about his personal life are lost to history, as was the case with many soldiers of the time," said the *Times-Dispatch* account of his heroism outside of Richmond in the fall of 1864. "Little is known about his life after the war. The date of his death is not known."

Fluttering Through the Air

MOVING INTO PETERSBURG, VIRGINIA, EARLY in January 1864, into a brother-in-law's substantial house, Sara Pryor and her small children were out of harm's way . . . but only for the moment, it turned out. It was June when the two armies of Lee and Grant took positions inside and outside the city gates, hardened their lines, and settled down for a siege that would last until the following April.

Excepting already-existing food shortages, the static confrontation of armies didn't seem all that terrible to Sara Pryor at first. For one thing, she might now see more of her husband, Roger, the former general voluntarily turned private but acting as an independent agent in his scouting forays for Robert E. Lee. Roger Pryor was joyful when he told her he would be based nearby, right in Petersburg—his hometown, it so happened.

But he wouldn't be with his family at all times . . . and even if he were, there wouldn't be much he could do about the terrifying new development that suddenly intruded with a bang. "The next Sunday," Sara Pryor wrote in her memoir, "a shell fell in the Presbyterian Church opposite our house."

No mere vagrant shot, that explosion was only a beginning. "From that moment we were shelled at intervals and very severely. There were no soldiers in the city. Women were killed on the lower streets and an exodus from the shelled districts commenced at once."

No advance notice of the shelling was given, no opportunity offered "for the removal of the non-combatants, the sick, the wounded, or the women and children."

The artillery at first was aimed at the city's Old Market section, its rail depot presumably a gathering spot for soldiers. "But the guns soon enlarged their operations, sweeping all the streets in the business part of the city, and then invading the residential region."

Church steeples seemed a favorite target, "all of them coming in finally for a share of the compliment."

Now the citizenry learned what its soldiers on the frontlines of the war already knew about artillery. Certainly Sara Pryor did. "To persons unfamiliar with the infernal noise made by the screaming, ricocheting, and bursting of shells," she wrote, "it is impossible to convey an adequate idea of the terror and demoralization which ensued. Some families who could not leave the besieged city dug holes in the ground five or six feet deep, covered with heavy timber banked over with earth, the entrance facing opposite the batteries from which the shells were fired. They made these bomb proofs safe, at least, and thither the family repaired when heavy shelling commenced."

She and her little boys were quick to distinguish "the peculiar deep boom of the one great gun which bore directly upon on us." Her boys called it "Long Tom." Mysteriously, the big gun would remain silent for weeks at a time—"rested or slept," she wrote—but then would make up for lost time."

A neighbor, Charles Campbell, a historian, cleared out a dry coal cellar, scattered rugs on the floor, and moved in chairs. "There we took refuge when the firing was unbearable."

But there still were dangers and close calls. One day a shell struck a chimney on Sara Pryor's borrowed house and "buried itself, hissing, at the front door." Another time, the house shaking from the fury of a heavy nighttime bombardment, she and the children were in the street rushing to their bomb cellar at Mr. Campbell's, "when a shell burst not more than twenty-five feet before us."

As the siege of Petersburg, Virginia, wore on, pigeons, rats, and mice disappeared. Cats began to starve, but still the Union shells came "fluttering" in.

NATIONAL ARCHIVES

Fortunately no harm done, but what a pyrotechnic display! "Fire and fragments rose like a fountain in the air and fell in a shower around us." Strangely, not only were they all unhurt, the children were unafraid.

On yet another occasion, a shell fell in their yard and dug into the ground. "My baby was not far away in her nurse's arms." The baby, in fact, was fascinated by the sound of the flying shells, so much so that "the first word she ever uttered was an attempt to imitate them." The shells "made a fluttering sound as they traversed the air, descending with a frightful hiss." The servants said they sounded like birds with broken wings.

Sometimes a shell would explode in midair—"a puff of smoke, white as an angel's wing, would drift away, and the particles would patter down like hail."

Near the temporary Pryor abode was a sunken street with embankments rising on each side. "Into this hill the negroes burrowed, hollowing out a small space, where they sat all day on mats, knitting, singing, and selling small cakes made of sorghum and flour, and little round meat pies."

Neither whites nor blacks could find much food during the siege, but Sara Pryor was proud to say: "With all our starvation we never ate rats, mice, or mule meat. We managed to exist on peas, bread, and sorghum. We could buy a little milk, and we mixed it with a drink made from roasted and ground corn." The corn, though, was scarce.

As time passed, the shortage of food only worsened. "The famine moved on apace, but its twin sister, fever, rarely visited us. Never had Petersburg been so healthy. Every particle of animal or vegetable food was consumed, and the streets were clean. Flocks of pigeons would follow the children who were eating bread or

U.S. ARMY MILITARY HISTORY INSTITUTE

The Dunlop house shows the kind of shell-fire damage suffered by Petersburg homes and other buildings. There was nothing left inside this once fine brick edifice but debris.

crackers. Finally the pigeons vanished, having themselves been eaten. Rats and mice disappeared. The poor cats staggered about the streets and began to die of hunger. . . . To keep food of any kind was impossible—cows, pigs, bacon, flour, everything was stolen, and even sitting hens were taken from the nest."

The constant shelling, though, was such a strain that Sara Pryor jumped at the chance to move into yet another suddenly vacated family home three miles outside the city, but still within the Confederate lines. She had been there only a few days, though, when R. E. Lee moved his headquarters close by. "The whole face of the earth seemed to change immediately. Army wagons crawled unceasingly in a fog of dust along the highroad just in front of our gate. All was stir and life in the rear, where there was another country road, and a short road connecting the two passed immediately by the well near our house. This, too, was constantly traveled; the whir of the well-wheel never seemed to pause, day or night."

Then a general who was an old friend asked to establish his headquarters in the backyard. Sara found herself "in the center of a camp" with his staff's tents stretching to her doors. But Roger Pryor couldn't have been happier—"my husband rejoiced at his [the general's] presence and protection for our little family."

From her garden now, Sara Pryor could see the Confederate trench lines. She did not yet know that behind her farm site, Grant's men were building a line of strong Union fortifications opposite the Rebel lines. Still, "the most painful circumstance" for her "little family" in their latest quarters was "the picket firing at night, incessant, like the dropping of hail, and harrowing from the apprehension that many a man fell from the fire of a picket."

Then, too, she always worried about her soldier husband. "He was now employed day and night, often in peril, gleaning from every possible source information for General Lee." This meant "perilous scouting expeditions, sometimes being absent a week at a time." It meant going across the lines and into enemy territory to scout out his movements and troop dispositions.

As Lee had explained to former general Pryor, "Grant knows all about me, and I know too little about Grant. You were a schoolboy here, General, and have hunted in all the bypaths around Petersburg. Knowing the country better than any of us, you are the best man for this important duty."

Thus, Sara Pryor could be proud of her husband and fearful for him . . . while herself living on the very edge of the siege lines dividing Union and Confederate forces at Petersburg.

Middlings All Gone

AS THE SIEGE OF PETERSBURG wore on in late 1864 and early 1865, Robert E. Lee did his selfless best with what little he had. He was very much in public view. "General Lee passed my door every Sunday morning on his way to a little wooden chapel nearer his quarters than St. Paul's Church," wrote Sara R. Pryor." I have a picture of him in my memory, in his faded gray overcoat and slouch hat, bending his head before the sleet on stormy mornings."

When a cousin had the remarkably good fortune to receive a whole turkey from a country friend, he "consented to share it with her."

At their dinner, she gave him only a moderate portion, for there was only one turkey and there were many friends, noted Sara Pryor.

But the cousin then noticed General Lee "laying on one side of his plate part of his share of the turkey."

What could be the matter? Was he not hungry . . . not well?

"Madame," he informed her, "Colonel [Walter] Taylor is not well, and I should be glad to be permitted to take this to him."

That autumn in starving Petersburg a mere chicken would cost $50, bacon was $20 a pound, and flour $1,500 a barrel.

At another dinner during the difficult siege, Lee himself was the host to a number of gentlemen, reported the *Mobile Advertiser.* "General Lee, in a fit of extravagance," said the newspaper, "ordered a sumptuous repast of bacon and cabbage. The dinner was served, and behold, a great sea of cabbage and a small island of bacon, or 'middling,' about four inches long and two inches across. The guests, with commendable politeness, unanimously declined the bacon, and it remained in the dish untouched."

The next day, though, "remembering the delicate tidbit which had been so providentially preserved," Lee ordered his servant to bring him the scrumptious leftover.

But the servant painfully related that the "middling" had only been borrowed in the first place, and he had had to return it to its original source. "General Lee heaved a sigh of disappointment, and pitched into the cabbage."

Meanwhile, when Sara Pryor's husband was captured in late November 1864, a general came to her borrowed home and "gently" told her the bad news.

Then came a staff officer, his clanking spurs announcing his presence at the door.

"Madame," he said, "General Lee sends you his affectionate sympathies."

Sara Pryor somehow felt another presence. "Through the window I saw General Lee on his horse, Traveller, standing at the well. He waited until his messenger returned—I was too overcome to speak—and then rode slowly towards the lines."

"Andy Ain't a Drunkard"

OF ALL TIMES FOR A vice president–elect to turn up drunk! Of all times for this one in particular, too!

And what a speech he gave! So bad, so rambling, Attorney General James Speed leaned into a companion's ear and said, "This man is certainly deranged."

Seated nearby, awaiting his own turn, a humiliated Abraham Lincoln seemed to be studying the floor in minute detail.

Unfortunately, too, speaking without benefit of notes, the vice president began by saying he didn't know enough parliamentary procedure to preside over the Senate—one of its members sitting close by, incidentally, chose to bury his face in his hands. As also recalled by Michael Dorman in his book *The Second Man,* the incoming veep "downgraded not only his own qualifications but those of members of the Lincoln Cabinet."

The ill-conceived speech finally over, he took his oath of office and made way for Lincoln, whose own finely tuned second inaugural speech was momentarily overshadowed in all the furor that greeted the startling performance of newly installed Vice President Andrew Johnson.

The sad irony was that Johnson in reality was a self-made man, a U.S. senator and military governor (Union of course) from Tennessee who had risen from a humble start as a tailor. He previously was known to be a sober, industrious man . . . but now he was a laughingstock.

Going around Washington, Dorman's book recalled, was this ditty:

> Oh, was it not a glorious sight,
> To see the crowds of black and white,
> As well as Andy Johnson tight
> At the inauguration.

Lincoln may have been embarrassed by Johnson's conduct at their inaugural ceremony on March 4, 1865, but he quickly, a few days later, came to the defense of his vice president. "I have known Andy Johnson for many years," Lincoln said. "He made a bad slip the other day, but you need not be scared. Andy ain't a drunkard."

Since, by most accounts, he really wasn't, what had happened?

Well, both the night before and even the morning of the inauguration he had imbibed, true. But Johnson had suffered a bout of typhoid after the Lincoln-Johnson ticket won the 1864 national election. Still recuperating, he would have begged off on attending the joint inauguration the following March, but Lincoln wanted him there. The mistake the still-shaky Johnson now made was to have one or two too many drinks at a celebratory party the night before, then try to sooth his hangover the next morning with a bit more to drink . . . a bit too much for a man in his weakened condition.

The episode that resulted was an unfortunate embarrassment for the loyal legislator from East Tennessee who had remained in the U.S. Senate after his fellow Southerners left town as the Secession fever of 1860–61 took hold. "It was an act of political courage that earned the respect of Lincoln and numerous others," wrote Dorman. "On the Senate floor Johnson railed against his fellow Southerners for seceding—arguing that they were committing treason."

When his fellow Democrats in Tennessee aligned themselves with the Confederacy, Johnson left his old party to join the Unionist (i.e., Republican) Party of Lincoln. "In 1862, Lincoln asked Johnson to take on the job of returning federal authority to war-torn Tennessee. With a presidential appointment as military governor of the state, Johnson embarked on the seemingly thankless assignment. For his efforts he won the undying enmity of many Southerners. But he also earned the plaudits of countless Northerners."

By the time the Republicans gathered in Baltimore in 1864 to choose their national standard-bearers for that year, Johnson was clearly favored to succeed Lincoln's first vice president, former Maine senator Hannibal Hamlin, as the number-two man on the Union-Republican ticket.

As events turned out, of course, the hardworking Johnson, a humble tailor turned politician, succeeded to the presidency itself after Lincoln was assassinated just weeks following their inauguration. Thus the very public drunkenness episode of their joint installation in office was not the end of the Johnson story. Thrust suddenly into the national spotlight, it was he who had to deal with a defeated, economically shattered South on the one hand and with radical Republicans in Congress pressing for revenge on the other . . . pressing also, as time went on, for his impeachment, a move ultimately turned aside in the Senate by just one vote in Johnson's favor.

Johnson turned over the White House in 1869 to the Union's Civil War hero, Ulysses S. Grant. Johnson then returned to the Senate in 1875, but only briefly, since he died the same year.

☆ ☆ ☆

On the other hand . . . there is that story told by Nevada's U.S. Sen. William M. Stewart, a Johnson-hater, to the effect that Vice President Johnson was clearly befuddled with drink the morning that Lincoln died of his gunshot wound to the head.

According to Stewart's account, fellow senator Solomon Foot of Vermont, leader of the chamber's Republican caucus, rounded up Chief Justice Salmon P. Chase to visit Johnson at his lodging in the Kirkwood House and swear him in as president. "It will not do to be without a President in the White House in times like these," Foot supposedly said.

It took "repeated poundings" on the door of Johnson's bedroom, wrote Lloyd Lewis in his book *Myths After Lincoln,* to bring the vice president to the door, "blinking, matted mud in his hair, liquor on his breath, his feet bare."

As his visitors entered the room, Senator Stewart included, Johnson sat down. Announcing the grim news that Lincoln had been shot and had died that very morning, the chief justice said, "I have come to administer the oath of office to you."

The vice president naturally was stunned. "Slowly the fact worked through Johnson's mind," wrote Lewis, "and all at once he popped up to his full height, reaching upwards extravagantly with his right arm, and thickly announced, 'I'm ready.'"

The story only gets worse. Stewart hurried off to find War Secretary Edwin Stanton, and when they returned together, the other two officials were gone. Johnson allegedly was "down again, flat on his bed," according to Lewis's recapitulation.

Wrote the historian also: "The two men [Stewart and Stanton] fell to work, dressing the drunken President as respectably as they could, helped him down into Stanton's carriage, and drove him to the White House, where they hid him while attendants ran for a doctor, a tailor, and a barber."

Those specialists, each in his own way, did what they could to spruce up the newly sworn president. "Late in the afternoon a few chosen individuals were allowed to see him, as Stewart said, 'just to satisfy themselves that there was a President in the White House.'"

Johnson's defenders of course were quick to point out that he didn't actually move into the White House until a few weeks later, in deference to the grieving Mary Todd Lincoln. "Still," wrote Lewis, "Stewart might have been wrong about this detail and right about the others. He was, he said, an eyewitness." Or Johnson might have been at the White House for a short period that "lunatic Saturday" in Washington simply to show the presidential flag, as it were. In the judgment of Lewis, even though Stewart was known to despise Johnson, "he [Stewart] was never a careless liar."

Human Moments for Lee

IF ROBERT E. LEE COULD be saintly at times during the final months, during the siege of Petersburg, he could also be sour. He could be very human.

Robert E. Lee was photographed by Mathew Brady in Richmond just days after the surrender at Appomattox. At left is his son Custis Lee and at right his faithful (and newly married) aide Walter Taylor.

LIBRARY OF CONGRESS

After all, the world was tumbling down all around him. He and his disintegrating Army of Northern Virginia, losing more than a hundred deserters a day in early 1865, were trapped now in the Petersburg-Richmond corridor with no hope of victory ahead. Only fifty-eight, he nonetheless was suffering occasional chest pain from cardiovascular disease. During the war years, he had lost a daughter, Annie Carter Lee, twenty-three, to typhoid. His son Rooney had been badly wounded at Brandy Station and then captured and held hostage by the enemy. He had lost Rooney's wife, Charlotte, and two of his grandchildren to disease and poor health. His own wife, Mary, was afflicted with crippling arthritis. Also a blow, the couple had lost control of their grand Arlington estate overlooking Washington, D.C., from the Virginia side of the Potomac . . . probably forever.

All that—plus the suffering of soldiers and citizens on every side, every day—was enough to leave anyone (but a real saint) in bad temper from time to time. Not even Lee could be an exception.

And a few people did notice. His long-time aide, Col. Walter Taylor, for instance, in a letter to his future wife, described Lee "as a queer old genius" and said the great commander "is so unreasonable and provoking at times."

Reporting that he and the general "lost temper with each other yesterday," Taylor also said, "I might serve under him for ten years to come and couldn't love him at the end of that period."

Another witness to Lee's sometimes short fuse was Brig. Gen. E. Porter Alexander, who wrote about the time he had been instructed to be ready at two o'clock one morning to ride with Lee, only to be surprised by staff officer Charles Venable at 1:30 A.M. instead. "Come on!" urged the visitor. "The Old Man is out here waiting for you & mad enough to bite nails."

Artillery officer Alexander protested that he had been told two o'clock, to which Venable readily agreed. "Yes," he said, "two o'clock was the hour he told us all last night, but now he swears he said one. And he scolded everybody & started off all alone, & with scarcely any breakfast because nothing was ready. I overtook him & the rest of the staff are coming along as fast as they can get their horses."

Outside, Porter found an impatient Lee waiting. "Good morning, General Alexander," he said frostily. "I had hoped to find you waiting in the road for me on my arrival."

Alexander tried to point out that Lee had stated their meeting time as two o'clock.

But not according to Lee. "One o'clock was the hour, Sir, at which I said I would start!"

When Alexander said he must have misunderstood, Lee reiterated: "One o'clock, Sir, was the hour!"

Lee then asked where their guide was. Alexander again was taken by surprise. Since Lee had never mentioned a guide, Alexander said, "I supposed no guide would be needed & I would only have to follow you."

That only made Lee bristle anew.

"Well, Sir, when I was a young man & had a march to make in the morning, I never went to bed until I had procured some citizen of the neighborhood who could conduct me."

Lee then turned in Venable's direction and instructed him to guide the party.

But here was fresh, if petty, frustration for the icon of the Confederacy, reported Emory M. Thomas in his biography of the general. Venable was busy talking to someone else and didn't hear Lee's order.

Fuming all the more, Lee turned to a nearby courier and told him to act as a staff officer that day, "for all my officers are disappointing me."

Lee of course had long since seen the proverbial handwriting on the wall, and all it offered was disappointment on a grand scale. In early March 1865, he made a remarkable statement to his son Custis, who had spent a good part of the war as an aide to Jefferson Davis.

"Mr. Custis," he said, "when this war began, I was opposed to it, bitterly opposed to it, and I told these people that, unless every man should do his whole duty, they would repent it; and now they will repent it."

By "these people," he meant the Confederate Congress, which he had visited that same day on a brief trip to Richmond that included consultation with President Davis and dinner with Custis and other Lee family members. "I have been up to see the Congress," the bitter-sounding Lee told his son, "and they do not seem to be able to do anything except to eat peanuts and chew tobacco, while my army is starving. I told them the condition my men were in and that something must be done at once, but I can't get them to do anything, or they are unable to do anything."

From what Lee told Custis, it would seem (a) he never had held much hope of ultimate victory and (b) there now was no hope whatsoever.

Then, too, memoirist Sara Pryor, trapped in Petersburg during the long siege along with Lee and his army, recalled a conversation Lee apparently had with Maj. Gen. John Brown Gordon of Georgia just before that short journey to Richmond. "Before daylight on March 2," she wrote years later, "General Lee sent for General Gordon, who was with his command at a distant part of the line." Gordon found Lee "standing at the mantel in his room, his head bowed on his folded arms." A single lamp dimly lighted the room and the embers of a fire smoldered away in the fireplace. "The night was cold, and Lee's room chill and cheerless."

Lee told Gordon he had sent for him "to make known to you the condition of our affairs and consult with you as to what we had best do." In "dejected" voice, Lee then listed the grim facts. They had barely 45,000 men at their disposal. Overall, the Confederate forces in the East numbered only 60,000, compared to U. S. Grant's 250,000.

His men in Petersburg, Lee said, were starving. "They are already so weakened as to be hardly efficient. Many of them have become desperate, reckless, and disorderly as they have never been before."

Discipline was obviously breaking down. "It is difficult to control men who are suffering for food," Lee apparently said. "They are breaking open mills, barns, and stores in search of it. Almost crazed from hunger, they are deserting in large numbers and going home."

As for horses, vital for mobility in Lee's day, the situation was equally bad. "The supply of horses in the country is exhausted. It has come to be just as bad for me to have a horse killed as a man. I cannot remount a cavalryman whose horse dies. General Grant can mount ten thousand men in ten days and move around your flank. If he were to send me word to-morrow that I might move out unmolested, I have not enough horses to move my artillery."

Here, though, Lee was able to add a wry comment. "He is not likely to send me any such message, although he sent me word yesterday that he knew what I had for breakfast every morning." To this Lee added: "I sent him word I did not think that this could be so, for if he did he would surely send me something better."

It was right after his despairing consultation with General Gordon, Sara Pryor noted, that Lee traveled to Richmond "to make one more effort to induce our government to treat for peace."

He returned to the besieged ramparts of Petersburg saying, "I am a soldier! It is my duty to obey orders." And now she added, "the final disastrous battles were fought."

In one of them, Lee's March 25 attack against Federal Fort Steadman just east of Petersburg, Gordon's men did briefly capture the Union fortification and almost a mile of Federal trench lines, but counterattacks then drove the Rebels back. "The battle was over by 8:00 A.M.," wrote Thomas in his Lee biography, "and Lee had lost another 4,000 soldiers in the process of inflicting 1,500 casualties upon Grant."

Just days later, Lee had to abandon Petersburg and set out on the road to Appomattox, Virginia. Richmond quickly fell to the Union. But more battles still were fought, hundreds more men died . . . and all for naught, really. Lee surrendered his army at Appomattox on April 9, roughly a month after his futile visit to the corridors of political power in Richmond.

☆ ☆ ☆

Additional note: Crazy as it may seem to us today, Lee's adjutant Walter Taylor approached his boss late in the afternoon of April 2, just hours before the Confederates were to evacuate Petersburg, and sought permission to be gone for a while that evening. What on earth could be so important that he would leave headquarters at such a critical juncture?

Well, Taylor explained to Lee, he planned to marry that night in Richmond . . . but he would be back, he promised; he would be back by next morning.

According to Taylor's later writings, Lee "promptly gave his consent." As a result, wrote Thomas in his Lee biography, Walter Taylor and Betty Saunders became man and wife before sunup April 3. With Lee's permission for brief leave, Taylor had left Petersburg behind by commandeering the locomotive of an ambulance train that "overhauled another train bound for Richmond." The adjutant's courier set out for Richmond separately with their horses.

"When Taylor arrived in Richmond, the government, the army, and anyone else able to do so either had fled or were fleeing the Confederate capital." But . . . no matter. He and his prospective bride had made their plans and would go through with them. Just minutes after midnight, "the Reverend Dr. Charles Minnigerode, Rector of St. Paul's Church, blessed the marriage in the presence of some family and friends at the home of Lewis D. Crenshaw on West Main Street."

Shortly after that, Taylor was on his way back to Lee.

"By the time Taylor set out to fulfill his promise to rejoin Lee, it was four o'clock in the morning. Most of the official Confederates (government and military) had left; a mob of residents were looting warehouses containing military rations of food, and lapping and scooping up from gutters the whiskey that flowed from barrels dutifully broken to keep people from drinking it. Fires raged out of control in much of the city as Taylor and his courier rode over Mayo's Bridge to the south bank of the James."

Epilogue: Taylor indeed would catch up to Lee west of Petersburg and be with him through the surrender at Appomattox. He, in fact, rode back into Richmond with Lee and his small entourage of crestfallen staff officers after Appomattox. Soon parting company and going their separate ways, they saw each other one more time—during Lee's visit to Norfolk, Virginia, the spring of 1870, the year of Lee's death.

Meanwhile, Lee's eldest son, Custis, himself a major general in rank, finally saw action in the futile last battles of the war . . . and suffered capture in the bloody battle of Sayler's Creek on April 6. Almost immediately paroled in deference to his ill mother, he was destined to succeed his father as president of Washington College (now Washington and Lee University).

John Brown Gordon returned home to Georgia to serve his state as governor and as a three-term U.S. senator. Living until 1904, he also became a founder and the first commander in chief of the United Confederate Veterans.

Custer Arrested by Custer

HIS NAME WAS CUSTER. He was the only Civil War soldier (Union, of course) to win the Medal of Honor twice. He later was killed by rampaging Sioux Indians at the Little Bighorn.

But he was *not* George Armstrong Custer.

This Custer, Thomas Ward by name, did *not* attend West Point. Instead, he joined Company H of the Twenty-first Ohio in September 1861, as a private, age seventeen.

Tom Custer served for three years and was mustered out of service in October 1864. In the interim, he had seen some of the Civil War's major actions—Murfreesboro, Chickamauga, Chattanooga, and the Atlanta campaign.

His fervor for the Union cause unabated, however, he now, in November 1864, joined the Sixth Michigan Cavalry with the rank of second lieutenant. With less than a year of warfare remaining, he had not yet been cited for even his first Medal of Honor.

He was sent to join the staff of a general-grade officer operating in the Shenandoah Valley of Virginia—his flamboyant, already-famous older brother, George Armstrong Custer. The older Custer, graduated from West Point in 1861, the year the war began, had been in command of the Michigan cavalry brigade since before Gettysburg (July 1863); now, by the time of the battle of Cedar Creek in the fall of 1864, he led a full division for the latest of the Shenandoah Valley campaigns.

Soon after, though, the two Custers were assigned to the Army of the Potomac and posted with the Union forces besieging Petersburg, Virginia, just below the Confederate capital of Richmond. Weeks and then months passed, marked by sporadic outbreaks of fighting. Worn down on all fronts, the Confederacy obviously was in its final days as weary soldiers on both sides of the siege lines checked off the passing days of early 1865.

The end, marked by the fall of both Richmond and Petersburg, followed by Robert E. Lee's surrender at Appomattox, wouldn't come until April of that year. And still, even as April arrived, Tom Custer was yet to be cited for his first act of gallantry in battle.

Then came April 3, a Monday. The Petersburg siege lines broken, Lee's army was in retreat, to fetch up a few days later at Appomattox. Ulysses S. Grant was proceeding westward on a parallel course, but Phil Sheridan, George Armstrong Custer's immediate commander, was sniping right at the heels of the retiring Confederates on the Namozine Church Road. Here, in a skirmish at Namozine Church, west of Petersburg, Lt. Tom Custer seized a Rebel flag, the act of bravery that earned him his first Medal of Honor.

This also was the day the Federals took Richmond. Jefferson Davis and remnants of his Confederate government had fled the night before. More obviously than ever, time was running out for the Confederacy.

But there still would be action, more action, on the roads to Appomattox. While not great in total numbers involved, one of the bloodiest fights of the entire war lay ahead at Sayler's Creek—a bitter battle marked by ugly, individual hand-to-hand combat. And here, too, just three days after his first notable action, young Lt. Tom Custer was a conspicuous participant. "He leaped his horse over the enemy's works, being one of the first to enter them," reported no less a personage than General Sheridan himself, "and captured two stand of colors, having his horse shot under him and received a severe wound."

One result would be Tom Custer's second Medal of Honor for actions coming just three days apart in the very last days of the Civil War. Not that he cared at the moment. Although wounded in the face, the excited Tom Custer turned over the captured colors to his older brother George, then tried to return to battle. Told to desist and be treated for his wound, Tom still wanted to re-enter the fighting. George Custer finally had to place his own brother under arrest to force him to undergo medical treatment.

Three days later, on April 9, came Lee's surrender at Appomattox. Only a few more flare-ups of fighting remained before the Civil War ground to its final halt.

Both Custer brothers had served the Union well, and now they were destined to go west, together, with George Custer's Seventh Cavalry, to a shared destiny on the Little Bighorn in Montana.

Tom, sometimes as colorful as his brother, liked to catch snakes with the fork of a stick and carry them off the trail, a practice that often spooked his horse. He still carried a scar on his left cheek from his wounding at Sayler's Creek.

Now, by another body of water, in 1876, he would fight one final fight—the massacre on the Little Bighorn, 265 men and officers killed. And among those killed by the aroused Sioux Indians, not only George Armstrong Custer, but younger brother Tom . . . not only George and Tom, in fact, but an even younger brother, Boston Custer, present as a so-called guide. All three were victims of the Indian onslaught at the Little Bighorn. Of the three, though, it was Tom's body that suffered the worst mutilations inflicted by their Indian enemy.

More on Brothers

OTHER BROTHERS OF COURSE FOUGHT on the *same* side in the Civil War, whether as enlisted men or officers, and a second conspicuous pair were the Birneys, David and William—Alabama-born, the sons of an Alabama slave owner who saw the light and became an abolitionist.

Considering their father James Gillespie Birney's antislavery views, it shouldn't be any surprise that his two sons fought, both as generals, for the Union . . . although only one would survive the war.

But that one, William Birney, the older of the two, went a bit farther than most Union generals to advance the cause of emancipation. A lawyer, writer, and newspaper publisher in the North before the hostilities, he first served with two New Jersey infantry regiments, the First and the Fourth, in the Army of the Potomac and took part in all its campaigns through Chancellorsville (May 1863).

At that point, he became colonel of the Twenty-second U.S. Colored Infantry, but he didn't stop there. Also made a brigadier general of volunteers, he soon recruited enough blacks to fill out seven more "colored" regiments. Freeing the inmates of slave prisons in Baltimore, reported Ezra J. Warner in his *Generals in Blue,* William Birney "expedited emancipation in Maryland."

After fighting in the battle of Olustee in Florida, he took over a division of black troops in the Union's Tenth Corps and then, for the Union drive ending with Robert E. Lee's surrender at Appomattox, he commanded a division of Godfrey Weitzel's Twenty-fifth Corps.

After the war, he continued writing and practiced law. After residing in Florida for a time, he moved to Washington to ply his attorney's trade there—even to serve as the federal city's U.S. attorney, or federal prosecutor.

Younger brother David Bell Birney, reaching major general's rank during the war, won both praise and criticism for his performance in some of its major battles in the East. Also an attorney, he began the war with the Twenty-third Pennsylvania and soon was its commander. Moving up the ladder, he took over a brigade in Philip Kearny's division for the Peninsula campaign of 1862, then took over the division upon Kearny's death. In the meantime, Birney had been charged with disobeying a superior's order in the battle of Fair Oaks outside of Richmond but was acquitted.

According to Warner again, the younger Birney "served with distinction with the Army of the Potomac until July 1864." Then came another blow. "He was again charged with dereliction of duty at Fredericksburg, but the charge was not substantiated and Birney was, in fact, highly praised by General George Stoneman."

Like brother William, David Birney served at Chancellorsville (displaying "able leadership," said Warner). He then moved on to Gettysburg, where he took over the Third Corps after its commander, the controversial Gen. Daniel Sickles, was badly wounded.

As the Union moved into its final campaign against Lee's Army of Northern Virginia at Petersburg and Richmond in 1864, U. S. Grant gave Birney permanent command of the Tenth Corps—the same corps that encompassed the all-black division his brother commanded before moving on to the Twenty-fifth Corps. David Birney, veteran of many battles by now, most recently had also survived Grant's Overland campaign taking the Union army to the gates of Petersburg . . . but that was as far as he was destined to go.

Contracting a raging case of malaria, he managed to reach his home in Philadelphia before he succumbed . . . on October 18, 1864. Older brother William, on the other hand, would live well beyond the war years . . . to August 1907.

Additional notes: Their father, Kentucky-born James Gillespie Birney, once a slave owner and planter in Madison County, Alabama, was well known both in the North and the South for his antislavery views and abolitionist work until he died four years before the Civil War. A controversial figure, and an attorney like his sons, he had freed his slaves and moved to Ohio years before his death. Once arrested for violation of the Fugitive Slave Act, he made his views known through his antislavery publication *The Philanthropist* and was active with the American Colonization Society and with the American Anti-Slavery Society as its executive secretary.

He formed the abolitionist Liberty Party in 1840, then ran as its nominee in the presidential elections of 1840 and 1844.

He didn't come anywhere near victory, but in the view of political historians he siphoned off enough votes from the Whigs and their candidate, Henry Clay of Kentucky, to throw the 1844 election into the corner of Democrat James Polk of Tennessee.

One effect, ironically, would be the demise of the fractured Whig Party and the birth of the Republican Party, former Whig Abraham Lincoln's vehicle to the White House. The Liberty Party in the meantime merged with the Free Soil Movement in 1848.

Odd coincidence: If you back then had mentioned the words "U.S. attorney of Washington, D.C." to Union Gen. Dan Sickles, watch out! As mentioned here, that was the post to be filled by William Birney some years after the Civil War. Then, too, it was his brother David Birney who took over the Third Corps at Gettysburg when its commander, Dan Sickles, was incapacitated by a wound that would cost him a leg.

Before the war, in February 1859, the same Sickles, at that time a U.S. House member from New York, shot and killed the son of Francis Scott Key in broad daylight in the square (today's Lafayette Park) in front of the James Buchanan White House.

The murder victim, Philip Barton Key, just happened to be the U.S. attorney for Washington at the time. He also had been exposed as the lover of Sickles's young wife.

In the trial that followed, Sickles "got off" scot-free even though he had ignored his victim's pleas for mercy and repeatedly shot him before a dozen witnesses. The verdict was temporary insanity. One of his eight attorneys was Edwin Stanton, future secretary of war under Abraham Lincoln.

Artilleryman's Ironic Demise

CONFEDERATE COL. STAPLETON CRUTCHFIELD, a graduate of Virginia Military Institute, was considered a leading artillery commander until he lost a leg at Chancellorsville. He had already served with Stonewall Jackson in the Shenandoah Valley campaign, in the Seven Days' battles outside Richmond, at Cedar Mountain, at Second Manassas, at Antietam, and at Fredericksburg. Recovering from his leg trauma, Crutchfield took on a less active role as an artillery inspector and then as commander of the artillery defenses of Richmond.

Following along when Robert E. Lee withdrew from Petersburg on the road to Appomattox, just three days before Lee's surrender there, artillerist Crutchfield had his head taken off by a cannonball.

"You Sockdologizing Mantrap"

ON STAGE, ACTOR HARRY HAWK spoke a line that told John Wilkes Booth exactly how far the play had progressed. In *Our American*

Cousin, Hawk played the role of unsophisticated American Asa Trenchard, a seemingly simple but surprisingly shrewd country rube visiting England to claim an inheritance from a haughty English nobleman also named Trenchard.

April 14, 1865. The Lincolns—Abraham and wife, Mary Todd—had arrived a bit late. With them, instead of U. S. Grant and wife Julia, were a young engaged couple, Army Maj. Henry Rathbone and his future bride, Clara Harris, stepson and daughter, respectively, of a U.S. senator from New York.

The play had been interrupted as the audience in Ford's Theatre stood to applaud the newly arrived occupants of the flag-draped presidential box, but then the drama unfolded . . . real-life drama on the level of ancient Greek tragedy. At the very moment of triumph, his armies victorious in the field, the great Union about to be reunited, the divisive issue of slavery settled by force of arms, the leader of the nation would himself fall victim to an enemy of all he had stood for.

No lightning bolt flung from a Greek god on high, the deathblow was administered to a simple, humble man sitting in an upholstered rocking chair and watching a play.

True, it was the "statebox" at Ford's Theatre and, true, Abraham Lincoln was the president of the United States. And yet it still was so simple a cruel act, so steeped in small, petty, mundane detail—a police guard who had wandered away . . . a stagehand named "Peanuts John" holding a horse in the back alley outside for the famous actor who came and went all the time . . . a bone broken in the foot of the actor-assassin as he leaped down to the stage ten feet below . . . and then hobbled off into the night.

Well, yes, ever the thespian, he did shout, *"sic semper tyrannis!"*—Latin for "Thus ever to tyrants." Or, "The South is avenged!"

John Wilkes Booth earlier in the day had thought to pick up his mail. That evening he had a few drinks in a nearby tavern, it seems, then went on to the theater—armed, of course, with his small derringer.

He knew exactly where the presidential box was. He knew the lines of the play unfolding onstage. He had told his fellow conspirators to do their part—attack the vice president and the secretary of state in concert with his own action, all at 10:15 P.M. And it was just about then, at 10:13, according to reliable accounts, that actor Harry Hawk, still playing the role of Asa Trenchard, would say, "Well, I guess I know enough to turn you inside out, old gal—you sockdologizing old mantrap."

Believed to be the rocker in which Lincoln was sitting when shot, this upholstered chair years later was acquired by the Henry Ford Museum in Dearborn, Michigan, where it may be seen today.

Booth just moments before had found it convenient that metropolitan police officer John Parker left the door to the Lincolns' double box unguarded— to see part of the play himself, it is said. Only White House footman Charles Forbes was on hand in the passage to bar the way. But Booth, one of Lincoln's favorite actors, disarmed any suspicions Forbes might have held by showing him a calling card. The actor then entered the box from the passageway outside.

The actor found Lincoln right in front of him, facing away, naturally, looking down at the stage, chin in hand and so intently watching the play that he was angled forward with one arm leaning on the rail at the front of the box. Just seconds later, with Harry Hawk's Asa line still a lingering echo in the quiet theater, Booth fired his derringer into the back of Lincoln's head.

At the pop of the small pistol, Rathbone whirled about. But Booth was also armed with a hunting knife. Before Rathbone could intervene, the actor-turned-assassin slashed the army major's left arm, elbow to shoulder, then vaulted to the stage below . . . but a spur snagged momentarily on a blue U.S. Treasury Guard banner adorning the box. Thrown off balance, Booth stumbled on landing and broke a bone just above his left ankle.

With his shout of "*sic semper tyrannis*" he was off and running anyway. Hopping, actually, but in any event gone before anyone could stop him or, in most cases, even move. In a flash, Booth was in the back alley and leaping upon the horse held by a bewildered "Peanuts John" Burroughs. Horse and rider then plunged into the web of Washington streets leading to the Navy Yard Bridge over the Anacostia River.

Pictured here is the so-called Statebox at Ford's Theatre in which the Lincolns and their two guests were sitting when John Wilkes Booth slipped in behind them, unnoticed until too late.

For the moment, Booth was intent upon reaching southern Maryland, a hotbed of Southern sympathizers.

Inside Ford's Theatre, meanwhile, pandemonium finally had struck. Shouts, yells, and sobs suddenly swelled up in a discordant chorus after Mary Lincoln's unnerving shriek, "They have shot the President! They have shot the President!"

First among those hastily moving toward the presidential box was a young army surgeon, Dr. Charles Leale—and he found what appeared to be a dead man. "With his eyes closed and his head fallen forward on his breast, he was being held upright in his chair by Mrs. Lincoln, who was weeping bitterly," wrote David Herbert Donald in his 1995 biography of the president.

But no, the gunshot victim wasn't quite dead. Leale felt a faint pulse.

He thought perhaps Lincoln had been stabbed, but when he pulled back Lincoln's eyelids, he saw evidence of brain damage—massive damage left by Booth's single bullet as it coursed diagonally from an entry point behind Lincoln's left ear to lodge behind his right eye.

Ordering Lincoln lowered to the floor, the doctor explored further—and found the deadly wound at the back of the president's head.

"He removed the clot of blood that had accumulated there and relieved the pressure on the brain," wrote Donald also. "Then, by giving artificial respiration, he was able to induce a feeble action of the heart, and irregular breathing followed."

In moments, reportedly, the famous actress Laura Keene also was in the box to offer the supine victim water. That night's production was to have been her last appearance in the Washington run of *Our American Cousin* . . . and now she was in the presidential box, holding Lincoln's head in her lap as she tried to comfort him.

He was unconscious but still living at this point.

Leale was soon joined by two more physicians, and all three agreed the president must be moved immediately but doubted he could survive a transfer over the bumpy streets to the White House, although it was only seven blocks away.

The best choice appeared to be a house just across the street from the theater, Swedish tailor William Petersen's house. A hastily formed party of strong men, soldiers among them, placed Lincoln's long frame on a shutter or removable partition pressed into service as a stretcher and struggled across the street with him.

There they found a small room, first floor rear, rented out to a member of the District of Columbia Infantry who served in the headquarters of the Union army's Department of Washington as a clerk.

The tall president didn't quite fit the bed inside William Clark's room—his helpers had to lay him diagonally on the bed, feet to the wall at the far end, head near the door.

And so he stayed for hours, until 7:21 the next morning, with an estimated sixty-five persons squeezing in and out of the small room to attend Lincoln, to see him, to weep and to pray over him. The visitors of course included his two surviving sons, Robert and Tad, and his wife, Mary Todd . . . but after a while, she was banned from the room (by War Secretary Edwin Stanton) because of her racking emotional storms.

Appointed to keep track of the visitors, their observations and other statements important for posterity, was a wounded Union soldier who knew shorthand from business school and who happened to be living next door, Cpl. James Tanner.

At 7:21 A.M., April 15, 1865, with an estimated fourteen persons jammed into the room next to the small bed—among them the president's pastor, the Reverend Phineas Gurley of the New York Avenue Presbyterian Church—Abraham Lincoln died.

This is both when and where Stanton, himself racked with grief, uttered the famous epitaph, "Now he belongs to the ages." Some hold that Stanton really said "to the angels."

Either way, it was a fitting tribute to the humble man from Illinois who had served—and now died for—a noble cause. But in his death, there was the small, mundane, ironic detail to emerge later. For Abraham Lincoln, president of the United States, in front of all those witnesses, had died in a boarding house room recently occupied for the better part of a year by a young actor who was a great friend of John Wilkes Booth. Thus, Booth doubtless visited his friend in the same room, historians say. Quite likely, the future assassin even sat on the bed . . . the very bed upon which his future victim died of the gunshot wound to the head inflicted by the same John Wilkes Booth.

Killer at Heart

HE FOLLOWED HIS FATHER AND an older brother on the stage and soon was such a star himself that women besieged him with love letters, his fans once shredded his clothing, and a president of the United States sent a message asking if he could come backstage and meet the famous actor.

John Wilkes Booth said no to the message . . . and later, in the most infamous assassination of American history, he shot and fatally wounded the same president.

Where did this fanatic come from? Who was "J. B. Wilkes"?

Why wasn't he in uniform as a soldier for his beloved Southern cause? Where did the real Booth begin and the actor leave off?

He came from a farm in rural Maryland, a slave state north of the District of Columbia that was known for its distinctly Southern leanings. He attended a military school whose cadets also were Southern sympathizers.

The farm, though, had little to do with his or his family's real calling—the theater. His late, British-born father, Junius Brutus Booth, was a famous actor, and so was an older brother, Edwin Booth. Their shared name was so well known that Edwin's younger brother John, as an aspiring thespian himself, at first used the stage name J. B. Wilkes to establish a theatrical identity all his own.

John, only in his late teens, at first "bombed," as the saying goes, in his early attempts at stock theater in Philadelphia. After a solid apprenticeship for two years or so in Richmond (1858–60), however, he graduated into the theatrical "big time" of his era.

His confidence and reputation as an actor both well advanced by the end of his stay in the future capital of the Confederacy, he embarked upon a stage tour of the South just before the Civil War broke out—now willing to go by the family name, as J. Wilkes Booth.

He then took to the theater circuit in the North and soon, during the war, reached matinee idol status.

At the same time, rumor and confirmed actions indicated or demonstrated long before the assassination of Abraham Lincoln that Booth was a fanatic who was also a hypocrite, a liar, a womanizer, and a drunk.

On the fanatic side, he joined the Richmond Grays late in 1859— "with the sole intention," says a National Park Service history, "of witnessing the December hanging of the fiery abolitionist John Brown in Charles Town, Virginia."

Having accomplished that goal, he returned to Richmond and was discharged. Thus ended this hotheaded Southern advocate's only military experience.

When later asked why he stayed in the North during the Civil War if he was so committed to the Southern cause—why, in fact, he did not care to don a uniform and fight for the Confederacy, like many another Maryland native—he said he had promised his mother to stay out of the war.

But he also told his sister Asia that he was smuggling expensive, hard-to-get quinine into the South, recalled M. Christopher New in the March 1993 issue of *America's Civil War* magazine. Thus, Booth argued, as a blockade-runner he was more valuable to the Southern cause than he could be as a mere soldier. Since he was often earning up to $900 a week, he could afford to purchase the expensive medicine.

Meanwhile, a *proven* Booth lie concerned a tumor Dr. John Frederick May removed from his neck during the Civil War. As recalled by Lloyd Lewis in his 1929 book *Myths After Lincoln,* Booth not only asked the doctor to say he had removed a bullet but told his fellow actors that a pistol ball inflicted in a shootout down South had just now worked its way out.

What about the womanizing? Booth apparently did enjoy the excitement his presence seemed to cause in the distaff ranks . . . whether onstage or in the audience. In an oft-cited incident, the actress Henrietta Irving cut Booth in the face one night in 1861 after learning he had no plans to marry her, then returned to her hotel room and slashed herself. Neither wound was serious. Then, too, when trapped and killed in 1865, Booth carried pictures of five women on his person—one of them his betrothed, who of all things was the daughter of a U.S. senator who was both a Republican and a well-known abolitionist.

Ironically, too, for all his fame, dashing good looks, and frequent stage bookings, J. Wilkes Booth was not that great a success as an actor, argued Lewis in his book. Greeted by sneering reviews in New York, Booth was consigned to the theater circuit outside the big cities of the East, it seems. "New York and Philadelphia were always too critical of him. Even in Boston, which alone of Eastern capitals gave him prosperous engagements, his audiences were mainly women, a situation that an actor of the '60s felt belittling to his reputation."

What he lacked in acting ability he made up for in action and agility. "Pathetically believing that it was more wonderful to stun audiences with a brilliant personality than to capture them with art, he was forever rearranging Shakespeare and Schiller so that his entrances might be made in staggering leaps off precipices and battlements," wrote Lewis. This proclivity was so pronounced that the *Baltimore Sun,* close to being Booth's hometown newspaper, called him "the gymnastic actor."

He was also a frequently drunk actor, Lewis noted. "Often, said the actors who played in his companies, he was so drunk that his negro servant had to lift him from dressing-room to stage." Also "notorious for forgetting his lines," he would try to mask the gaps with "violent bellows and sword-wavings."

And yet his fellow actors apparently liked him, "rating him as good-hearted and merely 'frothy' in his talk of violence." His friends simply didn't place much credence "in his claims to a reckless love of the South."

That he actually could be bold about his feelings for the Confederate cause was shown in an incident that took place in Union-held New Orleans in March 1864. Ignoring an official fiat against the popular

Rebel song "The Bonnie Blue Flag," Booth began to sing it in full voice one evening while walking down the street with several companions.

Quickly surrounded by unfriendly looking Union soldiers, "Booth gave a performance worthy of any he had played on the stage," wrote Christopher New in his magazine article. "Feigning innocence, Booth quietly explained that he did not know there was a law against singing the song." He said he had heard someone else singing it, liked the song, and sang it too. "Incredibly, the soldiers let him go. His companions were certain that had the perpetrator been anyone other than the famous John Wilkes Booth, he would have spent the rest of the war in a prison cell. As one noted, 'He had a way about him which could not be resisted, the way which permits a man to overstep the boundaries of the law, and do things for which other people would be punished."

It was not long after this that Booth quit the stage to speculate in a Pennsylvania oil field—and began planning the abduction of Abraham Lincoln. When that idea didn't come to fruition before Lee's surrender at Appomattox the next year, Booth turned to his most radical idea yet—the assassination of Lincoln, coordinated with assassination attempts by his fellow conspirators against Vice President Andrew Johnson and Secretary of State William Henry Seward.

Booth, as is all too well known, succeeded in his self-imposed role as Lincoln's murderer, a heinous act complete with a dramatic leap from presidential box to stage, while a conspirator did attack and badly injure Seward. Johnson was not attacked.

Ironies, ironies . . . It was on November 9, 1863, that Lincoln attended the play *The Marble Heart* in Ford's Theatre and was so impressed with Booth's performance in the drama that he sent a message backstage asking to have a word with the actor . . . only to be turned down. Then, too, it was Booth's own brother Edwin, by some accounts, who some years earlier pulled back a young man from the path of an oncoming train at a New Jersey railroad station. The young man rescued by Edwin Booth was Abraham Lincoln's oldest son, Robert Todd Lincoln.

★ Part 7 ★
Endings

A schism in the American experience, the war begun in general violence affecting so many now would end coincident with a single act of individual violence . . . but with repercussions again affecting many. Still, the war's survivors, a nation struggling toward new unity, would move on.

No Recriminations Forthcoming

MARYLAND FARMER THOMAS A. JONES, a courier running Confederate mail between Richmond and Baltimore during the Civil War, lived within three miles of the Potomac River. Two days after the Lincoln assassination, at the request of his foster brother, Samuel Cox, he agreed to help hide John Wilkes Booth and his fellow conspirator, David E. Herold.

Jones gave them food and shelter for six days. He did so with full knowledge of Booth's deed. Jones later said that Booth eagerly snapped up the newspapers brought to him—Booth "seemed very desirous to know what the world thought of his deed." The Maryland farmer added, "Murderer though I knew him to be, his condition so enlisted my sympathy in his behalf that my horror of his deed was almost forgotten in my compassion for the man."

After helping the fugitives hide out for the better part of a week, Jones—his misguided sympathy still intact—took them to the nearby river and sent them on their way across to Virginia. He gave them food, and it was he who provided the small boat that carried them across.

Jones also directed them to a woman on the Virginia side who would aid in their continuing flight from justice.

Thomas Jones thus passed up a $100,000 federal government reward for information leading to Booth's capture.

His own deed soon known to the authorities, Jones was arrested. He was never tried, however; nor was he called as a witness in the trial of the Lincoln conspirators.

Booth's after-the-fact accomplice, Jones, in fact, wound up with a federal job in the Washington Navy Yard.

Fired in 1869, he later produced a book, *J. Wilkes Booth: An Account of his Sojourn in Southern Maryland* (1893), now considered a major source of information on Booth's flight from Washington.

A Body's Long Saga

THE MAN HAD DIED OF a gunshot wound in the back of the head, almost in the same spot as Abraham Lincoln's fatal wound. This shooting victim expired on the porch of a farmhouse a few miles south of Fredericksburg, Virginia, a little while after the fatal wound was inflicted. But now . . . now what to do with the body?

Few bodies, as events turned out, ever went through such a saga of travel and secrecy as this one would.

From the front porch the body, now sewn or wrapped into a blanket, first traveled by a black neighbor's farm cart toward the Potomac River, the first stage of a convoluted path leading back to Washington, D.C. But Secret Service Lt. Luther B. Baker was pushing the black driver, Ned Freeman, too hard. Bouncing along a dirt road, the horse-drawn cart lost a key axle bolt—snapped in two. The front end dropped to the ground with a thud, and the body almost flew out of the cart.

It didn't quite, but the mishap required a pause to fix the problem. As Freeman bent to the task, blood from the still form above began to drip on his hands.

With a shriek, the driver bolted upright. It was the blood of a murderer, he cried. It would never wash off.

Giving up on Freeman and his conveyance, detective lieutenant Baker paid him off with $2 and found another farm wagon in the neighborhood, together with a driver able to complete the trip to the Virginia banks of the Potomac.

There he was joined by the band of Union cavalrymen who also had been at the scene of the shooting that morning. They waited a short while for the steamer *John S. Ide*, sent by Secretary of War Edwin Stanton for the body.

When it arrived, the entire party boarded and rode upstream as far as Alexandria, Virginia, across from Washington. There the body and a live prisoner, captured that morning at the same Virginia farm, were quietly transferred to a tugboat.

That was at 10:40 P.M. Roughly three hours later, at 1:45 A.M., the tug drew alongside the Union ironclad *Montauk* lying off the Federal city in the middle of the river. Here yet another transfer took place. The prisoner, David E. Herold, was moved into the hold. The body, though, was left on the *Montauk's* deck, and there it stayed all that day—until the next evening, actually.

During the afternoon, unbelievably, civilians making their way to the navy warship in skiffs somehow got aboard and even opened the shroud covering the body. Col. Lafayette C. Baker, head of the Secret Service, told War Secretary Stanton he himself had caught a woman just cutting off a lock of hair from the body but managed to wrest it away from her. The civilians then were sent packing.

Also during the afternoon, an autopsy committee went aboard to examine and identify the body. Both a hotel clerk, Charles Dawson, and a physician who once had operated on the deceased, Dr. John Frederick May, identified the body . . . confirmation of the deceased's identity was announced, although no autopsy report was made public.

Oddly, although May recognized the scar where he once removed a small tumor from the back of the deceased's neck, he did not at first glance recognize his onetime patient. "The cover was removed from the body," he later said, "and to my great astonishment revealed a body in whose lineaments there was to me no resemblance to the man I had known in life."

If the scar on the back of the neck and a closer look at the dead man's face finally did convince the doctor, he still remained astonished. "But never in a human being had a greater change taken place, from the man in whom I had seen the vigor of health and life to that of the haggard corpse before me."

Meanwhile, the body's macabre odyssey was far from over. Going by the reconstruction of its travels by Lloyd Lewis in his book *Myths After Lincoln,* the next move came just before dark that same day, April 27, 1865.

Cousins Colonel Baker and Lieutenant Baker of the Secret Service rowed out to the *Montauk* at twilight, seemingly paying little attention to the crowds lining the shoreline and staring out at the ironclad. Still in view of the onlookers in the gathering dusk, a makeshift coffin (a gun box in reality) was lowered into their skiff, along with a ball and chain.

The skiff then eased on downstream, the more anxious onlookers following on the shoreline, sometimes running to keep up. As the sun went down, it became difficult to keep the skiff in sight. "For two miles," wrote Lewis, "the watchers kept even with the drifting detectives, then lost them." The floating skiff, it seems, had reached a huge and notoriously foul swamp alongside the river.

Like a scene from a horror movie, this was a forbidding sea of muck where the Union army customarily disposed of dead mules and horses. Few persons would venture here even in the daylight hours . . . which is exactly what Stanton, the Bakers, and company were counting on. "Alone in the silence of this dread morass, the two detectives lay on their oars and waited for midnight," added Lewis.

But it was *not* their plan to dispose of the body here. Just ahead was the point in southeast Washington where the Potomac and the Anacostia Rivers met—Greenleaf Point then and today the site of Fort Leslie McNair. And on that peninsula that night loomed the dark outlines of the Washington Penitentiary, the oldest Federal penitentiary in the country. Built in the 1820s, it was closed, empty, according to Stephen M. Forman, official historian for the Congressional Cemetery, in his book *A Guide to Civil War Washington*.

Moving on in silence now, their oars carefully muffled, the conspirators rowed to the side of the prison structure—where they would find a helpful entryway already chopped through the wall in anticipa-

The grim Washington Penitentiary was destined to be Booth's first burial place . . . and the scene of the hanging of four persons convicted of taking part in the Lincoln assassination, among them boarding house keeper Mary Surratt.

LIBRARY OF CONGRESS

tion of their secret arrival. Another few minutes, and the box of white pine was hoisted by four soldiers, carried to a warehouse room inside, and buried under the floor. "The door was locked, the four soldiers swore by sacred oaths never to disclose what they had seen or done, and the key to the room was given to Stanton," added Lewis.

The next day, it was shown that the ruse had worked. "Scores" of ghoulish searchers were reported wading, rowing, pawing through the awful swampland near Greenleaf Point in frantic hunt for the body in the gun box.

But had the ruse not "worked" all too well? For the secret disposal of Lincoln assassin John Wilkes Booth's body, with never a public glimpse of the remains, only fed wild rumors that he had not been killed, that he was still alive and well, still at large in parts unknown and eluding the harsh justice that should be his.

In the meantime, Booth's fellow conspirators were held in the isolation cells at the same old penitentiary—they were tried by a military court there, and four of them were hanged there, including David Herold, captured early the morning of April 21 at that Virginia farm where Booth was shot and fatally wounded in a tobacco barn.

Like Booth himself, the hanged Lincoln conspirators were buried for a time under the floor of the penitentiary structure. All five corpses then were disinterred in 1869 and turned over to their families for private reinterments.

The Booth body saga was now almost at an end. It was outgoing President Andrew Johnson (Lincoln's successor, of course) who, just days before leaving office on March 4, 1869, gave the order to have Booth's remains removed to Christ Church in Baltimore, Maryland. On February 16 and 17, wrote Mark E. Neely Jr. in *The Abraham Lincoln Encyclopedia,* several persons, including a dentist, "identified the decaying body, and on the 18th it was put in a vault in Green Mount Cemetery."

Weeks later, on June 26, "the Booth family had John's body interred [at Green Mount] with an Episcopal service performed by the Reverend Fleming James."

Epilogue: The Reverend James, assistant minister at St. Luke's Hospital in New York City, was dismissed for officiating at Booth's final interment.

The Truth About Booth?

LIKE ELVIS PRESLEY, DID JOHN WILKES BOOTH survive his own death? Did Lincoln's assassin somehow emulate Napoleon's marshal Michel Ney, "Bravest of the Brave," who "survived" his execution by firing squad (which fired blanks of course) and turned up later as a schoolteacher in North Carolina?

Of such stories are legends, historical myths, and even conspiracy theories made.

And no exception was the mythology that greeted the demise of John Wilkes Booth, last seen shot and killed on April 26, 1865, when Federal troops trapped him in a burning Virginia tobacco barn after his flight of some days through southern Maryland from Washington . . . from Ford's Theatre.

But not so, *not killed,* argued various researchers and a variety of people claiming to have seen or known Booth after his reported death. One of the most enduring of those "have seen him" accounts was still making the rounds as late as the 1990s, when Nate Orlowek of Silver Spring, Maryland, told radio talk-show host Woody Woodland of Nashua, New Hampshire, about a Booth "mummy."

According to Woodland's subsequent "Spotlight" column— appearing in *Network Publications,* February 1994—"He [Orlowek] believes that someone else was killed at Garrett's Farm on that April day and that John Wilkes Booth lived until 1903. And he believes that a storekeeper named John St. Helen is the key to changing history."

A storekeeper in this case, rather than a Carolina schoolteacher? Could it possibly be? Let's hear the man out.

As a first step in the story told by history buff Orlowek, it seems that St. Helen turned up in Granbury, Texas, in 1877 and was sick, so sick he thought he was dying. He "confessed" to his best friend—an attorney it so happened—that "he was really Booth."

But he then recovered and, having already revealed himself, went on to tell his attorney friend a long, more detailed story. Among the details was information generally not known, "because all of the government papers on the case were [still] secret," Orlowek told Woodland.

LIBRARY OF CONGRESS

This mild-looking young man was a killer at heart—John Wilkes Booth, an assassin supposedly seen again and again for years after a manhunt allegedly ended with his death in Virginia.

Meanwhile, wrote Woodland, "St. Helen was remembered by town residents as handsome, poised, and well educated. After a few drinks he was likely to recite Shakespeare or launch into a dissertation on Roman history." Such, of course, would have been the lingering attributes of the accomplished actor Booth.

But then why would he be in Granbury, Texas? Could it be because the town was named for Confederate Brig. Gen. Hiram Bronson Granbury, one of the six Southern generals killed at the battle of Franklin, Tennessee?

We'll probably never know . . . and let's in any case move on with the story. Both St. Helen and the attorney, a gentleman named Finis Bates, themselves moved on from little Granbury—Bates to Memphis, Tennessee, which became his springboard to achieving the office of attorney general of Tennessee, and St. Helen to . . . well, "parts unknown," Woodland wrote.

In those years of separation from one another, Bates remained fascinated by St. Helen's story and "spent much of his spare time trying to verify it." And really, one does have to wonder why any man would risk claiming, much less admitting, that he was the notorious John Wilkes Booth.

But now comes step two in the story. In Enid, Oklahoma, on January 13, 1903, a housepainter named David E. George lay dying "in a small room in the Grand Avenue Hotel."

Surrounding him were the owner of the hotel, a desk clerk, and a local doctor. "This man," Orlowek told Woodland, "as he was about to die, gasped out that the only man who knew his real identity was this man Bates." Not only that, he went ahead and told his three onlookers he really was John Wilkes Booth!

Now the story takes its really bizarre turn. By Woodland's summary account: "Though the men were skeptical they did send for Bates. In the meantime, the local funeral director mummified the body. When Finis Bates arrived and saw the body, he immediately recognized his old friend John St. Helen. He brought the body back to Memphis, where he stored it in his garage."

Unwilling to rest there, Bates continued with his research and in 1907 published a book entitled *The Escape and Suicide of John Wilkes Booth.* "In the book," added the Woodland account, "Booth alias St. Helen alias George identifies Vice President Andrew Johnson as the prime mover of the plot to kill Abraham Lincoln."

Of course, "the book was generally dismissed as nonsense," even if Harry Houdini, for one, gobbled up all the copies he could find. The sordid sequel to the story is that when Finis Bates died in 1923, "his widow sold the mummy and it became a sideshow exhibit throughout the Midwest and South," added Woody Woodland. And . . . should anyone be surprised? The mummy eventually disappeared.

How to prove or disprove the bizarre story of Booth's long-term "survival"? Orlowek, the youth director at a synagogue, argued that a first step would be to see who really is buried beneath the John Wilkes Booth headstone at Green Mount Cemetery in Baltimore. He and others intrigued by the Finis Bates story, he told Woodland, "feel it's necessary to exhume the body and do forensic tests on it and by doing that, determine the truth once and for all."

Now, however, for another side to the same story, let's look at a savage denunciation presented by debunker Lloyd Lewis in his 1929 book *Myths After Lincoln.* For openers, he painted John St. Helen as a "ruffian" and no storekeeper, but a "drunken saloon-keeper." Finis Bates was "a gaping boy from Memphis" and "greenhorn traveler."

St. Helen had boasted of a telltale scar on the back of his neck, similar to a scar on the real Booth, but "the townspeople of Granbury remembered that he had acquired the scar by a knife in a brawl at his groggery."

Continued Lewis: "The youth, Finis L. Bates by name, grew up to be a lawyer in Memphis, and dallied with the tale. In 1903, while touring the Southwest on business, he read that a man claiming to be Booth had committed suicide in Enid, Oklahoma. Arriving at the frontier town, he found it in a state of delighted fervor over the romance, and exhibiting the body with pride."

Through its local newspaper, asserted Lewis, Enid "was crying to the world that here was the escaped hero-villain, although its people had known the fellow as David E. George, a drunken morphine-fiend."

Apparently housepainter George at least twice had claimed to be Booth. "Both confessions had been made while he was bed-fast from drugs, a fact that did not hamper the credulity of Finis L. Bates in the least. The lawyer, looking upon George's remains, jumped to the conclusion that here was his great informant of Granbury, Texas, a quarter of a century before, John St. Helen. The two men, he declared, were one, and that one—Booth."

And so, yes, Bates carried the late housepainter's body back to Memphis—"where it rests today [in the 1920s], owned by Bates' heirs, often exhibited across the South and Southwest in its mummified state at ten cents or twenty-five cents a look."

The Tennessee lawyer's "curious" book was a popular item for quite some time. "This book, read by thousands and thousands of eager-eyed believers in the folk-story, fanned the smoldering mystery flame briskly in the years following its publication in 1907." It also let loose "a flood of pamphlets that supported its claims, interviews from self-styled relatives of Booth who 'verified' it, statements of persons who insisted that this or that portion of it was known by them to be true."

Naturally, one of the reasons such myths could take hold was the public's recollection that the body of the man killed at Garrett's farm in Virginia had been spirited back to Washington and buried in secret. Nor was the Bates book the only Booth-seen-alive report to crop up in the years after the Lincoln assassination. Among many wild reports, an Ohio man swore that Booth stayed at his house one night on a flight to Canada. A Southwest-based story asserted that "Booth owed his escape from Union troopers to his membership in a powerful fraternal order, which spirited him away rather than see him hanged."

Any evidence of a *dead* Booth also caught the public fancy. "Soon Booth's skull was on simultaneous view in different side-shows and carnivals across the country." Then, too, a Chicago theatrical manager related to Confederate cavalry leader Nathan Bedford Forrest claimed his and just two or three other Southern "clans" shared the "secret" of where the real Booth was buried.

Well, does it have to be a myth? Could someone other than Booth have been shot at that tobacco barn, with the real Lincoln assassin somehow escaping capture and deserved punishment?

Doubtful, really doubtful, since proof of that theory would require equal proof that someone else was shot and killed in Booth's place. Moreover, Lewis himself located and interviewed an eyewitness who asserted he personally saw the body in question . . . and it really was Booth.

His witness was William B. Lightfoot, a twentieth-century resident of Richmond, Virginia (1717 Hanover Avenue), but in his youth a bedraggled Confederate soldier who had returned home to Port Royal, Caroline County, Virginia, after the surrender at Appomattox. Some days later, hearing about a shooting at a neighbor's farm four miles away, he hurried on over.

He saw a man lying dead on the porch at the Garrett farmhouse. He hung around, as the saying goes, until a doctor pronounced the man dead, until the Union cavalrymen on the scene wrapped the body in a blanket and placed it in a black laborer's wagon. "I followed the wagon," he told Lewis, "back to Port Royal and saw it cross the Rappahannock over to Port Conway on the other side and go off toward the Potomac."

How did he know the dead man was Booth? First, Lightfoot said, he heard the Union troopers at the scene "all saying that it was Booth dead there on the porch."

But couldn't they have been mistaken? Not too likely, according to William B. Lightfoot, a notary public at the time. "You want to know if that body was Booth's," he said. "Well, I'll tell you. I never saw Booth in real life, but I knew his picture; had seen it many, many times, for he was a great stage favorite in Richmond before the war and his photographs, like those of other actors, were to be seen everywhere. I would have recognized him from his photographs and, sir, I did. I knew him right away, and never thought of it being possible that it could be anybody else. The dead man on Garrett's porch was John Wilkes Booth."

Moreover, said Lightfoot, his neighbor Richard Garrett recognized the dead Booth as "the same man who had come to his house begging shelter two days before."

In addition, Lewis pointed out in his book, the real-life Booth's accomplice Davy Herold told his Union captors that it had been Booth trapped in the tobacco barn with him. The doctor who once operated on Booth's neck and later assisted in the autopsy said the body still bore the scar from his previous work on the assassin's neck. Still another witness, hotel clerk Charles Dawson, said the "J.W.B."

initials tattooed on the real Booth's hand were still there when he also was asked to help identify the body for the official record.

Case closed?

Additional note: Richard Garrett apparently was hoping the Federal government would pay for the tobacco barn he lost when the Union cavalrymen set it afire to smoke out Booth, William Lightfoot also told author Lewis. "As a notary public, I took down Garrett's story when he put in a bill to the government for the barn the soldiers had burned," Lightfoot said. "He lost the case."

No Hiding the Hour

SOMETIME BEFORE 2 P.M. on July 7, 1865, young David Herold, twenty-three years in age, was scheduled to die by hanging for his role in the conspiracy that brought about the assassination of President Lincoln. He was a simple, immature lad, easily led by older, more forceful friends, according to testimony in his defense.

Unfortunately, those friends included John Wilkes Booth. And young Davy had accompanied Booth on his flight through southern Maryland into Virginia after the assassination. There was no doubt. Herold was captured right at the barn where Booth was trapped then fatally shot. And in July, Herold, a navy clerk's son, would be executed sometime before two o'clock in the afternoon—a terrible, anxious, heart-rending hour awaiting his recently widowed mother, Mary Porter Herold. So distraught was she that family members stopped every clock in the house so she wouldn't know the exact time and realize when the two o'clock deadline came.

Unfortunately, she knew that her Davy was no more when nearby church bells rang out precisely at the dreaded hour.

Of Little News Value

HEADING FOR HOME AFTER WEEKS, months, even years of captivity in Southern prisons and camps, the Union soldiers piling aboard the steam-powered side-wheeler *Sultana* at New Orleans and Vicksburg were jubilant . . . ecstatic. And why not? It was late April 1865, and the war was over. They at last were going home! And so they piled aboard.

On a Mississippi crawler licensed to carry 376 passengers and 80 crew, probably 2,200 to 2,400 Federal soldiers, plus 100 civilians, 90 crew, 100 horses and mules, and 150 tons of sugar, all somehow were squeezed aboard.

At Vicksburg, Capt. J. Cass Mason, part owner of the vessel, resorted to heavy timbers to hold up the decks. But it wasn't the over-crowding or the excess weight that doomed the steamboat; it was the

Despite being overload, the sidewheeler Sultana *did not sink or capsize of her own accord. It apparently was a boiler explosion that did her in, with grievous loss of life resulting.*

gigantic explosion—probably the boilers—followed by a devastating fire that sank her just above Memphis the night of April 27, 1865, in a few minutes' time.

Greater even than the *Titanic's*, the *Sultana's* death toll of 1,800 or more souls would be the greatest single-vessel loss in modern maritime history until World War II. And yet the disaster received little publicity—in the *New York Times,* for instance, a single paragraph on an inside page. With the war just ending, Lincoln assassinated, and 623,000 dead to mourn, North and South, the *Sultana* just wasn't the big news it would be today.

PERSONAL GLIMPSE
Bridge a Family Affair

ONLY A FEW OF THE men emerging from the soldiery of the Civil War still whole and full of life's ambitions could be considered absolutely unique in terms of their later accomplishments. Two such men were Henry Stanley, who found Livingston in the wilds of Africa, and Lew Wallace, author of *Ben Hur.* Fellow writer Ambrose Bierce perhaps could be considered another . . . but then, still to be counted in this rare lot was Union Col. Washington Roebling, the remarkable civil engineer who built the Brooklyn Bridge (with a little help from his late father as its designer and from his wife, Emily, as acting foreman!).

When the Civil War broke out, Roebling, only twenty-three, was already a professional engineer working with his pioneering father, John, in the construction of suspension bridges.

A major feat emanating from their joint efforts would be the Niagara International Bridge at Niagara Falls, New York, the world's first modern suspension bridge . . . but now, just days after the shelling of Fort Sumter in the spring of 1861, the younger Roebling joined the New Jersey State Militia as a private.

By spring of the following year, an officer no longer attached to the militia unit, he was building bridges in the hotly contested Shenandoah Valley of Virginia . . . with occasional interruptions, such as the day Stonewall Jackson found him and his Union men building a bridge at Front Royal and drove them off.

By the spring of 1863, now assigned to the staff of Union Gen. Gouverneur K. Warren, Roebling went aloft many mornings in an observation balloon overlooking the Virginia countryside around Chancellorsville, just recently the battleground that had seen the last of Jackson. From his perch so far above the ground, Roebling was able to see that Robert E. Lee was moving his Army of Northern Virginia north and west, as prelude to the Confederate "invasion" of Pennsylvania . . . and the battle of Gettysburg.

On the second day of that momentous collision between North and South, Roebling and Warren, just then chief engineer of the Army of the Potomac, rode over to the "rugged little knob" later to be known as Little Round Top and discerned that the lightly manned promontory loomed as an invitation to Union disaster. Roebling later wrote that Warren stopped momentarily to confer with Gen. Stephen Weed while Roebling himself "ran up to the top."

And there, "one glance sufficed to note the head of [John Bell] Hood's Texans coming up the rocky ravine which separates little and big Round Tops."

Alerted by Roebling, Warren, after one look from the crest, also saw the need for immediate action to stop the Rebel advance. He immediately sought the help of Weed's brigade and that of Col. Strong Vincent to stuff the gap. This is when Col. Joshua Chamberlain and his Twentieth Maine Infantry, from Vincent's Third Brigade, so famously did halt and drive off the Confederates in an outburst of furious action that may have saved the day for the Union . . . and, many historians assert, the battle, perhaps even the war.

"Largely because of his rank," wrote Edward C. Smith of American University in the *Washington Times* of May 4, 1996, "Warren received the lion's share of the credit for rescuing this strategic position from being overrun and would deservedly be honored as one of the heroes of Gettysburg."

But Warren generously passed along a good part of the praise to his staff officer, saying, "Roebling was on my staff and I think performed more able and braver service than anyone I knew."

Warren must have approved of Roebling in other ways as well— once the younger man married the general's sister Emily, the two Union officers would wind up as brothers-in-law. Roebling met the

Union Maj. Gen. Gouverneur K. Warren, whose sister and brother-in-law were destined to complete the Brooklyn Bridge.

general's sister at a ball in early 1864, and they married, Smith reported, within a year. "He said privately that he thought she was the 'medal' he had earned for valiantly serving in the Army."

As another aspect of that valiant service, Warren and Roebling had been very much involved, together again, in still another highlight of the war—the battle of the Crater at Petersburg, Virginia. There, Roebling's engineering expertise had been most useful to the Union men tunneling under the Confederate lines in hopes of blasting open a huge hole in Lee's fortifications. At one point just before the pending explosion and assault, Roebling and Warren together "had risked their lives by crawling through the tunnel to the edge of Lee's position," reported Smith.

The outcome of the ambitious plan was a Union rather than a Confederate disaster, with hundreds of Federals trapped and killed in the huge crater created by the explosion, because they had charged into the gaping hole rather than around it to attack the Southern line. Roebling "lamented that the tunneling had not accomplished its goal, which had been 'to end this miserable war as soon as possible.'"

The war indeed would continue, futilely, for almost another year. But Roebling, confident of imminent Union victory, resigned from the army in January 1865 with the rank of colonel . . . and now came the Civil War hero's *real* life's work.

Returning to his father's bridge-building enterprises, the younger Roebling first was assigned to supervise construction of the giant masonry towers supporting the suspension cables for the Cincinnati-Covington (Kentucky) Bridge on the Ohio River. Just ahead, though, was the crowning achievement for both Roeblings—the challenging Brooklyn Bridge project.

Envisioned years earlier by the elder Roebling, the 1,595-foot span high above the East River would connect Manhattan and Brooklyn. It would be another bridge suspended by cable from two giant towers, but the first to use steel wire as the all-important cables (each one sixteen inches in diameter).

The older Roebling, it should be explained, had become a "cable pioneer" years before by suggesting the replacement of hempen hawsers used to tow canal boats with wire cables. He then had perfected his own method of weaving and stranding wire cable and founded a family wire-manufacturing firm destined to sustain three generations of Roeblings. After building four major suspension bridges, he had won approval from the state of New York for his design of the Brooklyn Bridge and had been appointed chief engineer for the mammoth project.

He now sent his son Washington to Europe to study the latest methods for sinking tower foundations in an underwater-underground environment such as the muddy bottom of the East River, no small engineering feat.

But then, in 1869, with construction on the massive new span barely begun, family tragedy struck—John Roebling was injured in a construction accident and died three weeks later.

The mishap that took his life wouldn't strike us today as all that serious . . . not by modern, twenty-first-century standards anyway. The story is that John Roebling was standing on pilings at a ferry slip taking compass readings when a docking boat he hadn't noticed bumped its way into the slip. One of his feet was crushed between the pilings, and his injured toes had to be amputated. What proved fatal for the German-born engineer was the tetanus that then set in.

As a remarkable next chapter in the construction of Roebling's Brooklyn Bridge, however, his son Washington now would step in and take over the thirteen-year project as chief engineer in place of his father. As Professor Smith noted in his article, that would be no easy task. The bridge's intricate design and demanding specifications left no margin for error. The project was such an all-consuming activity that it required Roebling to develop and demonstrate his expertise in many other areas beyond engineering. He proved to be a master manager in his difficult dealings with politicians, investors, contractors, laborers, journalists, and others.

Wearing work, twelve to fourteen hours a day, six days a week, it was, too. And often dangerous—in addition to Roebling's own father, the bridge cost another twenty-six lives before it was completed and opened with colorful fanfare in May 1883. By then, the younger Roebling himself had fallen victim to the great project's demands—apparently as a result of "the bends" that once posed a major risk for deep-sea divers.

Like those very same divers, Roebling's construction crews worked and breathed in compressed air while preparing foundations for the span's twin towers of granite. To excavate huge holes in the muddy bottom of the river and then lay the tower footings, they worked in watertight pneumatic caissons containing compressed air, with more than a hundred cases of decompression sickness ("the bends") resulting.

It wasn't fully understood in those days that it took time—slow decompression—to ease dangerous nitrogen bubbles out of the bloodstream, or a man could be paralyzed for life.

After spending twelve hours in such a compressed-air caisson one day, Roebling himself was carried out unconscious—and he now joined the ranks of those permanently affected by "the bends."

Ingeniously, though, as still another remarkable chapter in the development of the Brooklyn Bridge, he and his wife, Emily, found a way to keep the project going under his supervision—incredibly, he "supervised" from the window of their home in Brooklyn Heights at the Brooklyn end of the bridge. To a degree, he could see what was going on, what needed to be done. Then, to observe more closely, to convey his orders to his work crews, Emily went to the bridge itself and acted as his "foreman" on the job.

As Professor Smith noted, Emily proved the ideal wife for Roebling in unexpected ways. "She was Roebling's nurse, private secretary and 'ambassador' to the engineers and various other constituencies. Most important, however, she was his most faithful friend and confidant."

Fortunately also, she was accepted in her unofficial foreman's role by Roebling's men on the job, even though the women of that time "had limited connection with construction work." Her contribution to the final stages of the bridge made it a Roebling project three times over—credit John, Washington, and Emily Warren Roebling for its creation, start to finish.

Although Washington Roebling remained in poor health at the time the bridge was opened in 1883, he was only in his midforties. He in fact would live another four decades before dying in 1926 at the age of eighty-seven.

The Brooklyn Bridge was his last major construction project, but thanks largely to the family wire-cable business, he died a rich man worth an estimated $30 million.

The bridge of course remains in heavy use today as an enduring monument to the efforts of all three Roeblings from the Civil War era who contributed so much to its creation.

Unhappy Fates Ahead

AS IF THE CIVIL WAR itself were not dangerous enough for its leading combatants, consider the violence that a startling number of them encountered *after* the fighting had died down. More precisely, consider first the cruel fate awaiting several of the Confederacy's surviving general-grade officers:

• Brig. Gen. James Holt Clanton, Georgia native, Alabama state legislator, and presidential elector before the war, survived Shiloh and other battles. He recovered from a serious wound suffered at Bluff Spring, Florida. Returning to his law practice after the war, he soon resumed a leadership role in the Democratic Party of Alabama.

But not for long. At Knoxville, Tennessee, in September 1871, he encountered an ugly drunk, a former Union officer who was the son of T. A. R. Nelson, Tennessee Supreme Court justice and former Union congressman from eastern Tennessee. Nelson's son provoked a quarrel, and Clanton ended up dead.

• Brig. Gen. William Felix Brantley, Alabama native and Mississippi resident, began the war as captain of the company-sized Wigfall Rifles but ultimately became a brigade commander. He fought at Murfreesboro, Chickamauga, Chattanooga, in the Atlanta campaign, and, at the end, in North Carolina, never suffering a serious wound the entire time.

In November 1870, however, riding in his buggy near Winona, Mississippi, he was murdered by an unknown party or parties, apparently as the product of an old feud.

• A major general and near legend for his aggressive tactics and narrow wartime scrapes was Bryan Grimes, North Carolina native and the last major general to be appointed in Robert E. Lee's Army of Northern Virginia. After leading one final attack on the very morning of Lee's surrender at Appomattox, Grimes retired to plantation life in North Carolina. Fifteen years later, however, as the product of still another long-standing personal dispute, Grimes was ambushed and killed one summer evening by hired assassin William Parker.

• And then there was the mysterious fate of former Confederate Brig. Gen. Robert Vinkler Richardson, an associate of Nathan Bedford Forrest before, during, and after the Civil War. In business with Forrest and Gideon D. Pillow in Memphis, Tennessee, before the war, Richardson, a lawyer and now colonel, formed the First Tennessee Partisan Rangers early in the conflict. At different times during the war, he fought with Pillow, Forrest, and James R. Chalmers.

Briefly going abroad after the war, Richardson returned to Memphis and went into the railroad business with his former associate and wartime superior, Forrest.

Traveling in pursuit of that business, he stopped the night of January 5, 1870, at a tavern in Dunklin County, Missouri. There, for reasons unknown, a gunman hidden behind a wagon in the yard fired upon the former brigadier general with a shotgun. Mortally wounded, Richardson died the next morning.

• Still another notable Confederate officer to die a violent death after the Civil War was Catesby ap Roger Jones, Confederate naval officer who commanded the ironclad CSS *Virginia* in its historic battle (a draw) against the Union ironclad *Monitor* in Hampton Roads, Virginia, on March 9, 1862.

Later in the war, former U.S. naval officer Catesby Jones was in charge of the Confederate naval foundry at Selma, Alabama. Leaving Confederate service with the rank of commander, Jones entered the business world after the Civil War. But a quarrel with one J. S. Harral in 1877 resulted in Jones being shot and mortally wounded.

• More conventional, in a sense, was the postbellum violent fate awaiting former Confederate Brig. Gen. Mosby Monroe Parsons, a native of Charlottesville, Virginia. With former Confederate Congressman A. H. Conrow and four companions (six in all), he plunged into the Mexican civil conflict over Emperor Maximilian's claim to the Mexican throne. While the facts are uncertain, it is thought that Parsons and his party were killed in August 1865 in Mexico's state of Nuevo Leon by Republican insurgents after aligning themselves with the Imperialists.

It of course wasn't only the surviving Confederate officers who suffered from the violence of their times—terrible things could and did happen to Union men, too. In only one generation's time, barely forty years from the end of the Civil War, the newly unified nation lost three sitting presidents to assassins. That is, not only Abraham Lincoln in April 1865, but also onetime Union army officers James A. Garfield (shot July 2, 1881, and died of his wounds on September 19) and William McKinley (shot September 6, 1901, and died September 14).

Well known, too, is the violent fate that awaited Union Gen. George Armstrong Custer (plus his brothers Tom and Boston) on the Little Bighorn in Montana in 1876.

Additional notes: Disease of course struck down many a Civil War leader in the early postwar years—Robert E. Lee in 1870 (stroke); former president Ulysses S. Grant in 1885 (throat cancer); Spanish-born Union Gen. George G. Meade, of Gettysburg fame, in 1872 (pneumonia); Confederate Gen. Braxton Bragg in 1876 (dropped dead walking down a street in Galveston, Texas), former U.S. vice president John C. Breckinridge, onetime general and secretary of war for the Confederacy, in 1875 (complications from major surgery).

Pure irony attended the death of former Confederate general Joseph Eggleston Johnston, who died in 1891, reportedly after catching cold while attending old Union foe William Tecumseh Sherman's funeral—Johnston marched in the funeral procession bareheaded. Just weeks later, he died of pneumonia. Sherman, meanwhile, had died of asthma after himself catching cold.

Accident occasionally took a toll, as well. Jubal Early, left without gainful employment and bitter over the Confederacy's defeat, found momentary financial relief in helping P. G. T. Beauregard supervise the Louisiana Lottery for a handsome $10,000 a year in earnings . . . but no boost to either man's reputation. Early, far from wealthy, gave away much of his income—$1,000 to Stonewall Jackson's widow, $1,000 to a former servant, $1,000 to help raise a statue of Lee in Richmond.

He lived until 1894 and in the interim served as president of the Southern Historical Society while also engaged in a running, years-long feud with former Confederate comrade James Longstreet. Early's death was prosaic in the extreme—he fell down the U.S. Post Office stairs at Lynchburg, Virginia, went into shock, and died two weeks later.

Like Early, meanwhile, like Beauregard, like Longstreet, and like many other Confederate comrades of note, John Bell Hood retreated to New Orleans after the Civil War . . . but his was to rank as one of the saddest postwar stories of all. He had already lost his last major battles (Franklin and Nashville, Tennessee), an army (the Army of Tennessee), an arm and a leg and a fiancée (Sally "Buck" Preston of Columbia, South Carolina). Now, in New Orleans, he did find short-term happiness. He married well, he achieved financial success in the insurance business—and in a mere decade's time he sired an amazing eleven children. The secret there was three sets of twins!

But then, in the winter of 1878–79, came a yellow fever epidemic that took more than three thousand lives.

Hood and his family at first escaped harm, but the epidemic had undermined his and many other business ventures in New Orleans. Had his business affairs fared better, Hood would have taken his family out of town the following summer—away from the mosquitoes carrying the deadly disease. But he didn't.

That year, the epidemic claimed six more lives . . . only six, but three of them, it so happened, were John Bell Hood, his wife, and one of their children, a daughter.

Career Changes of Note

SOME MADE THEIR NAME, THEIR history, in the Civil War, but others—such as a future president or Maj. Gen. Lew Wallace, future author of the novel *Ben Hur*—made their real mark, as we have seen, in "second careers" far removed from the fields of battle.

Along those lines, Union Brig. Gen. William Sooy Smith in fact was noted during the Civil War—for an ambitious but essentially disastrous raid across Mississippi. In the postwar years, on the other hand, he was destined to emerge as a true pioneer in civil engineering. For here was the man who built the world's first all-steel bridge—across the Missouri River at Glasgow, Missouri. Here, too, was the man who subsequently became such an expert in the support structure for skyscrapers that he could claim a role in the construction of just about all the really tall buildings erected in Chicago until shortly after the turn of the century.

Not quite so important but a unique man nonetheless, Robert Cumming Schenck—Union general, diplomat before and after the Civil War, eight-term member of the House of Representatives—built himself a postwar reputation in some (admittedly narrow) circles as an authority on draw poker. He even wrote a treatise on the subject.

Not too many Civil War histories will devote major space to the wartime exploits of Union Gen. Clinton Bowen Fisk, abolitionist, teetotaler, future New York banker, future presidential candidate on the Prohibitionist ticket . . . but still known in educational circles today as founder of Fisk University in Nashville, Tennessee.

Then, too, remember Charles Pomeroy Stone, West Point graduate, wartime brigadier general, Union officer held prisoner, basically, for more than half a year by his own Union army? Well, who does, except perhaps a few descendants . . . and military historians in Egypt, where he served as chief of staff of the Army of the Khedive for thirteen years after the Civil War in America.

Confederate Maj. Gen. John B. Gordon (left), future U.S. Senator from Georgia, and Union Brig. Gen. Charles P. Stone (right), blamed for the disaster at Ball's Bluff, Virginia.

As for his months of confinement at Union military posts, the problem was the blame attached to Stone for the Federal debacle at Ball's Bluff, Virginia, an unfortunate assault engineered, actually, by Stone's subordinate, Col. Edward D. Baker, the U.S. senator from Oregon who was an old friend of Mary Todd and Abraham Lincoln. As recounted by Ezra J. Warner in his compendium *Generals in Blue,* "Stone was made to bear the burden of the disaster at Ball's Bluff [Baker having been killed in the action]."

Further, "The Radicals in Congress . . . demanded his [Stone's] removal. On February 8, 1862, at midnight, without charges then or ever preferred, Stone was arrested and subsequently confined for 189 days in Forts Lafayette and Hamilton. He was grudgingly released on August 6 without reparation or even acknowledgement of error."

Stone went another nine months with no command whatsoever, briefly found service and performed "with gallantry" in the Port Hudson and Red River campaigns before finally being forced out of the Union army altogether, even though the Civil War still raged. "On April 4, 1864," reported Warner's book, "Secretary of War [Edwin] Stanton caused him to be mustered out of his volunteer commission (as brigadier general), and, as a colonel of the Regular Army, he was again without employment. He finally resigned on September 13, 1864."

Stone's postwar, post-Egypt career also included serving as the engineer in charge of the foundation laid for the Statue of Liberty.

Another Civil War general who later served in the Egyptian army, incidentally, was Confederate Brig. Gen. Henry Hopkins Sibley, who spent four postbellum years in Egypt as an artillery specialist. He also goes down in history as inventor of the Sibley tent. Still another Civil War figure to accept the opportunity of service in Egypt was Confederate Maj. Gen. William Wing "Old Blizzards" Loring.

Among the die-hard Confederates, meanwhile, neighboring Mexico briefly was a magnet for those seeking new vistas . . . and/or time to lick the wounds of defeat. Most, like Kentucky-born cavalryman Joe Shelby, eventually came back to the newly reunited United States to settle down in quiet civilian roles. As Ezra J. Warner reported in his book *Generals in Gray,* "General Shelby with a few of his command buried their battleflag in the Rio Grande and then crossed into Mexico to ally themselves with either the party of the Emperor Maximilian or his opponent, General Juarez." It was after Maximilian's downfall that Shelby and others returned to their war-scarred homeland to build new lives as best they could.

Many a veteran of both sides became a political figure of considerable note in the postwar years. First and foremost in that crowd, of course, were the five Union combat veterans who were elected president of the United States—U. S. Grant, Rutherford B. Hayes, James A. Garfield, Benjamin Harrison, and William D. McKinley. Ironically, after surviving the rigors of combat, two of the Union's veteran-presidents, Garfield and McKinley, were destined to die in office as victims of vicious, gun-armed assassins.

The Confederacy produced its own share of postbellum political stars, albeit none on the order of a future president. One was the widely esteemed Maj. Gen. John Brown Gordon of Georgia, survivor of a near-fatal head wound at Sharpsburg (Antietam) and later governor of Georgia and three-term U.S. senator from his home state. Contrarily, Kentucky's John C. Breckinridge, vice president of the United States before the Civil War, both a general and secretary of war for the Confederacy during the conflict, did not seek any further political office after the war.

As another twist of sorts, the Confederacy's well-known Lt. Gen. James Longstreet entered the service of the Federal government after the hostilities came to a close—as U. S. Grant's appointed minister to Turkey and, later, as commissioner of Pacific railroads under Presidents McKinley and Theodore Roosevelt. Another Confederate icon who accepted postwar Federal service was John Singleton Mosby—the famous Gray Ghost, Confederate raider par excellence . . . and, many years later, U.S. consul in Hong Kong, followed by a stint as assistant attorney, U.S. Department of Justice. The once hard-riding cavalry raider Joe Shelby, for that matter, years after returning from Mexico, accepted President Grover Cleveland's appointment as a U.S. marshal in Missouri.

Meanwhile, few figures of the Civil War era would ever match the fame, totally unrelated to the war, that came to Lew Wallace for writing the novel *Ben Hur: A Tale of the Christ* fifteen years after the conflict that seared the nation's very soul. Wallace himself went through difficult, soul-testing experiences—not only in combat, but in other situations calling for a resolute frame of mind. His combat experience ranged from a division command at Fort Donelson, to participation in the Shiloh-Corinth campaign, to his crucial delaying stand against a much larger Confederate force at the Monocacy River outside of Washington, D.C.

Battle in the field was one thing, but Wallace, a major general of volunteers from Indiana, also had to lead a commission investigating the conduct of fellow Union Gen. Don Carlos Buell, then make life-and-death decisions as a member of the military court hearing the government's case against the conspirators in the assassination of Abraham Lincoln. In addition, Wallace presided over the postwar military court convicting Henry Wirz, the cruel commandant of the notorious Andersonville Prison.

Wallace next (in 1878) was asked (by fellow Union veteran and now president Hayes) to serve as governor of the New Mexico Territory . . . with the special charge of resolving the bloody "Lincoln County War" that had been disturbing the territorial peace for some time. Wallace did succeed in cooling tempers on both sides of the cattlemen's war, with a welcome and commensurate decline of the violence seen earlier, but he never did succeed in pacifying one William H. Bonney—otherwise known as Billy the Kid.

Wallace didn't have long to brood over that aspect of his New Mexico "career" since he suddenly (1881) was off to distant climes as Garfield's U.S. minister to Turkey, a diplomatic post he held for four years before returning to his earlier life as an attorney in Crawfordsville, Indiana.

Remarkably, Wallace had begun writing and publishing a series of historically based novels as early as 1873. His first, based on Hernando Cortés's conquest of Mexico, was *The Fair God.* Then, in 1880, came the famous *Ben Hur,* based upon the Roman Empire's early Christians . . . the model for two blockbuster movies of the twentieth century and never out of print since 1880. Soon thereafter came *The Boyhood of Christ* (1888) and *The Prince of India* (1893). Finally, Wallace was working on his own autobiography when he died in 1905 at the age of eighty-seven. It was published the next year, in 1906.

Also quite different from most of the military men who served either side in the Civil War was the French-born Prince de Polignac (Camille Armand Jules Marie), a volunteer Confederate general who returned to his native France after the rending American conflict just in time to serve in the Franco-Prussia War of 1870 as commander of the French First Division. He thus wound up serving two ill-fated causes in a row. Nonetheless, he then became a noted expert in mathematics . . . and when he died in Paris in 1913, oddly enough, Prince de Polignac, a

Frenchman through and through, was the Confederacy's last surviving major general.

Additional note: Aside from the generals of the Civil War period, there were others who would become world-famous for postwar exploits in unrelated fields. Leaping to mind are the poet Walt Whitman, a hospital volunteer during the war; Scottish-born Allan Pinkerton, detective before and after; the low-ranking soldier-turned-writer Ambrose Bierce, later to disappear on a trip to Mexico; the artist (during and after) Winslow Homer; and the German observer of Thaddeus Lowe's balloon experiments, Count Ferdinand von Zeppelin, inventor of . . . what else but the zeppelin!

PERSONAL GLIMPSE
Stanley, We Presume

NOT MANY CIVIL WAR VETERANS would turn up late in life as members of the British Parliament . . . as a knight of the realm, at that! But then, few participants in the war served on both sides, Union and Confederate. Even fewer, probably a minority of one, managed to switch sides . . . and then become both a soldier and a sailor for his new allies.

Three military "careers" in all—the first ended by capture, the second by discharge, and the third, frankly, by outright desertion.

Born a housemaid's illegitimate son, he was John Rowlands for the first eighteen years of his life, but then he acquired a new name. And it is as Henry Morton Stanley that the Welsh-born newspaperman remains world-famous today . . . but for none of the activities cited above.

Rather, he is known for his short utterance on the shores of Africa's Lake Tanganyika six years *after* the Civil War, for those four little words—"Dr. Livingston, I presume?"

A bit impulsive from early age but always colorful, he ran away from an English workhouse at fifteen, boarded and worked here and there for nearly three years, then, in January 1859, became a cabin boy aboard an American packet boat, the *Windermere,* setting sail for New Orleans.

He jumped ship upon arrival and almost immediately found the older mentor whose name he would assume for life, American cotton broker Henry Morton Stanley. The older man took a liking to the young Welshman, found work for him, and encouraged his interest in reading (and discussing) fine literature.

After the Civil War erupted in 1861, Rowlands-Stanley joined the Dixie Greys (Company E, Sixth Arkansas). He attended the battle of Belmont, Missouri (November 1861), but with his regiment held in reserve, his first real taste of combat would come at Shiloh just a few months later.

There, as the Dixie Greys and fellow Confederates swept aside their Union foe early in the battle, young Stanley was struck in the belt buckle by a musket ball and knocked silly. Recovering after a time, then catching up to his greatly slowed—and woefully thinned—company, he didn't like what he had found in battle. "For it was the first field of glory that I had seen and the first time that glory had sickened me with its repulsive aspects," he wrote later.

But he survived the day, and he was with his company when the battle began again the next morning. This time, however, he became a reportable statistic—captured by the enemy.

Sent north as a POW, to the Union's Camp Douglas near Chicago, the future explorer and hunter for Dr. David Livingston saw things a bit differently after a few weeks of incarceration. He now joined the Union army!

As events turned out, his military career no. 2 didn't last very long, either. Assigned to an Illinois artillery unit that was posted at Harpers Ferry, Virginia, he was discharged in the summer of 1862 as physically unfit to continue soldiering. Like many of his fellow Civil War participants, blue or gray, he had been hospitalized for dysentery.

Weak as a kitten, lacking in money, he took to the road and wandered as far as Hagerstown, Maryland, then on to the outskirts of Sharpsburg, where a helpful farmer allowed him to sleep in a farm shed for the rest of the summer—and fully recover his strength. Fit again, Stanley accepted the farmer's offer to pay his train fare to Baltimore, and from there he set sail as a merchant seaman, a trade he would ply for about two years.

During that period, he made an attempt to reconcile with his mother back in Britain, but she wanted none of it, so he returned to the sea. Once again drawn to America and its still-raging Civil War, he now—in August 1864—joined the Union navy! Stationed aboard the USS *Minnesota,* he was witness to the Union's amphibious assault upon Confederate Fort Fisher near Wilmington, North Carolina, late in 1864.

By March of the next year, before the war ended, however, he had jumped ship at Portsmouth, New Hampshire—deserted.

Now began his newspaper career . . . for the *Missouri Democrat* in St. Louis.

In Africa, meanwhile, the veteran missionary and explorer David Livingston had already discovered Lake Ngami and the Zuga River, the Zambezi River and its spectacular Victoria Falls . . . now, in 1866, he was in search of the source of the legendary Nile. By the end of 1867, in fact, he reached the southern end of Lake Tanganyika. By now, though, the Western world had lost sight of him and was worrying over his safety.

The *New York Herald* would gamble upon creating a spectacular story for itself and send a reporter in search of Livingston. That reporter was Henry Morton Stanley.

Stanley, after studying the situation, jumped off from Zanzibar, on the east coast of Africa above Madagascar, in March 1871. Trekking through hard, virgin territory for eight months, he finally, on October 28, 1871, met a fellow—albeit somewhat older—white man in the native village called Ujiji on Lake Tanganyika. And then those famous four words: "Dr. Livingston, I presume?"

Indeed it was . . . and Stanley stayed with him until March of the next year. Livingston died in 1873, and Stanley, upon hearing the news, vowed to continue Livingston's explorations of the "Dark Continent." The Welshman in 1874 plunged back into Central Africa with three fellow white men and more than three hundred African bearers. The expedition took them to Lake Victoria and then down the Congo River from its sources to its mouth all the way across the continent on Africa's west coast. Only Stanley and about 150 of the Africans survived the arduous trip, which lasted until 1877.

After failing to interest his own British countrymen in the colonial spoils to be found in the Congo, Stanley returned at the head of another expedition, this time on behalf of Belgium, which colonized the Congo. He made one last trip to Africa in 1888 to rescue German-born Emin Pasha, governor of the Sudan, when he was trapped by a native uprising while exploring the Upper Nile. (Emin later was murdered by natives of the Upper Congo region . . . at Stanley Falls on the Congo.)

Returning to the land of his birth, Stanley became a naturalized British citizen, was knighted, and served for a time in Parliament. He died in 1904 at the age of sixty-three.

Command of English

THE DOCTOR HIMSELF COULDN'T TAKE it. The dead, the maimed . . . the stranded wounded crying out when the fires reached them. The amputations, one after the other. All at the Wilderness, his first real combat exposure. And then, afterward, being ordered to brand a deserter on the face with a big *D*. Branding the Irishman, literally, with a fiery-red branding iron. Then, too, the autopsies—many autopsies at his military hospital.

Perhaps it was what we today call post-traumatic stress disorder—certainly it was *something* like that. In any case, Union Capt. William C. Minor began acting strangely. He claimed that Irishmen were slipping into his bedroom at night to bother him. Temporarily confined at a government insane asylum in Washington (today's St. Elizabeth) for treatment, he was retired from the army on disability.

Hoping for rest, time to read and to resume an old hobby of painting, he set sail for Europe. But in England he wandered into a London street one night and shot a complete stranger.

Doctor Minor, found to be insane, was subsequently confined to the Broadmoor asylum for the criminally insane for the better part of four decades. Even so, long a student of literature, he used his Union army pension to buy books and to create a formidable library at Broadmoor.

For years also, this troubled veteran of the American Civil War would become a major contributor to a unique work-in-progress destined to become a literary monument of the English-speaking world, the *Oxford English Dictionary.*

Love Found in Yankeeland

HE WAS TWENTY-EIGHT AND SHE twenty-three when they met two decades after the war, the American Civil War. He was—let's face it—a Yankee, born and raised in upstate New York. And even the grandson of a famous abolitionist who helped runaway slaves find their freedom before the Civil War.

She, born a year before her family had to flee from Richmond, was known far and wide in her native South by her special nickname.

Her real first names were Varina Anne and her last name, Davis. At her birth, her mother, also Varina by name, exclaimed that the baby girl looked "like a little rosebud." The family didn't call her Rosebud, however; the family didn't even call her Varina or Anne. She quickly and endearingly became "Winnie," the very same affectionate name her father always called her mother.

The South, the Confederate States of America, to be precise, knew her by another nickname altogether. It was a title, really, a title given and meant to be borne with pride . . . but in her later life one that proved a sad and intervening burden.

Talk about star-crossed lovers! The question here was: Could a young Yankee, even two decades after the last shots had been fired, marry and live happily ever after with the winsome Winnie, still known far and wide as "Daughter of the Confederacy"?

Actually, his answer was yes. And hers was yes . . . but then maybe no. And let's put this off. And . . . well, to go back to that proud burden she carried is to go back to June 1864, to the White House of the Confederacy in Richmond, Virginia. For that was when she was born, the last child of Confederate President Jefferson Davis and his wife, Varina.

It was a poignant moment for the Confederacy's first couple—they had lost their five-year-old son Joe to a fatal fall from an open porch at the Confederate White House just two months before Winnie's arrival. Her birth came at a low ebb of Confederate fortunes, too, a matter of more than ordinary concern in the Davis household. The losses at Vicksburg and Gettysburg were "old" history; the battles of the Wilderness and Cold Harbor were fresh and horrifying memories, and now came the siege of Petersburg, leading irrevocably to Appomattox the next April.

Winnie would be too young to remember, but that was when her mother had to gather up her young ones and flee the Confederate capital. That was a time also when, quite separately, her father had to gather up his chief governmental ministers and flee the enemy at the gates as well.

The two entourages met up in Georgia for only a brief reunion before the Federals caught up and nabbed them all. Jefferson Davis then languished for months as a Federal prisoner held at Fort Monroe, Virginia. And then, upon his release, began the family's wanderings— to Canada, to Europe, to Memphis, Tennessee, back to Europe, and finally to Beauvoir, a Gulf Shore estate at Biloxi, Mississippi, where Davis composed his personal history of the Confederacy with wife Varina's help.

He didn't finish his mammoth, two-volume work (*The Rise and Fall of the Confederate Government*) until 1881—by then, of course, Winnie, the Daughter of the Confederacy, was growing up. In just a few years she was a most attractive young lady, and that's when she fell in love—with a Yankee!

It came about in 1886 when Winnie and her mother attended a party in their honor at the home of an old family friend in Syracuse, New York—Dr. Thomas Emory, a Confederate army veteran.

A local attendee, quickly smitten with the visiting Winnie Davis, was Alfred "Fred" C. Wilkinson, a young patent attorney whose forebears included his banker father, his jurist grandfather on one side— and on the maternal side his abolitionist grandfather, Samuel J. May, a minister widely known for his role in antebellum slave escapes from the South through the Underground Railway.

At first, the young couple, separated by geography, didn't reveal their feelings to Winnie's mother and father, but the letters flying thick and fast between Syracuse and Biloxi for the next two years were evidence enough. Clearly, a day of reckoning was soon to come . . . and it did, when Fred turned up in Biloxi one day in 1888 with marriage on his mind. Mrs. Davis, previously aware of the heavy correspondence but opposed "to union with a Yankee," soon relented and even conceded that Winnie's young man was a "refined well-born Yankee, full of energy, spirit and love (for Winnie)."

Jefferson Davis was a tougher nut to crack. His reaction to the newly arrived suitor's intentions: "Death would be preferable."

But wait. According to Anita Monsees in the New York Historical Society's publication *Heritage* (January–February 1991), Winnie's father eventually "was swayed by Fred's evident love for his daughter, and the two became companionably close, with the Confederate leader issuing a warm invitation to Fred to return."

Before this, it might be noted, Winnie had suffered "both physical illness and bouts of profound depression." Now, said her mother, a suddenly blooming Winnie was "like one out of prison." Even better, it at first seemed, her father the next year agreed to the couple's marriage plans.

Winnie at last had her parents in her corner, but not, it turned out, her friends and others in the South. With her family receiving threatening letters after word of the romance seeped out, "Winnie slumped." Her health took a nosedive. "That fall, the Davises packed a wan and depressed Winnie off to Europe with their friends, the Pulitzers." (Who, incidentally, urged her to go ahead and marry Fred "in spite of Confederate sentiments.")

But now, in 1889, harsh fate intervened—Jefferson Davis died while Winnie was still in Europe. "Winnie's response was to undergo a severe nervous breakdown." At the Widow Davis's urging, Fred rushed to her (and the Pulitzers') side in Naples, where he stayed for months.

When he returned in April 1890, Mrs. Davis "insisted on announcing the engagement," news that "hit the nation's press like a bombshell." In the South, "the earlier adverse reaction . . . increased exponentially."

Winnie returned in midsummer, apparently still shaken by all these events. Soon, in August, a postponement of the proposed marriage was announced—"Miss Davis not desiring to be married until after a year of the date of her father's death," was the only explanation given.

The final sad step came in October of that same year: The engagement was off. No personal details revealed, certainly not by the chastened Fred, a gentleman to the end. Reported the *New York Tribune:* "If Miss Davis had broken off the engagement, he [Fred] had no doubt that she had good reasons for doing so."

Winnie's mother publicly blamed her daughter's fragile health, but it also seems Mrs. Davis and Fred had argued over his discovery that summer that she was secretly investigating his financial status.

However all the factors should be weighed today, the fact is the marriage never took place. In the years to come, Winnie published a pair of syrupy Victorian novels and frequently took part in ceremonial events . . . as the Daughter of the Confederacy, naturally. She died young, at age thirty-four. Her onetime fiancé Fred died at age fifty-seven . . . while recuperating from a nervous breakdown of his own.

The fact is, too, neither one ever married. And who today can deny they died as latent casualties of a war concluded decades before they passed from this earth?

Odd Day to Die

IT WOULD HAVE GALLED THE distinguished Virginia educator Lyon Gardiner Tyler in the extreme to foresee the day of his death. The son of President John Tyler, Lyon was only a child when the tide of war swept across the Virginia Peninsula and forced his Northern-born mother, Julia Gardiner Tyler, to abandon the magnificent Tyler mansion, Sherwood Forest, to Union forces and flee the Old Dominion.

Young Lyon's presidential father had led a peace convention in Washington that sought, in the spring of 1861, to avert the pending hostilities, but to no avail. Then elected to the Confederate Congress of 1862, meeting in Richmond, John Tyler died before he could take his seat.

All of which were traumatic events in the life of the preteen who had to flee Virginia with his mother.

Nor would he forget . . . or forgive. Becoming president of William and Mary College in later years, "he spent the rest of his life defending the Lost Cause by attacking Lincoln," according to the characterization offered by historian Mark E. Neely Jr. in his *Abraham Lincoln Encyclopedia.*

Thus, in his privately published work of 1930, *A Confederate Cate-chism,* Lyon Tyler argued that Lincoln wanted war "to fix the tariff for protection forever on the South," that Lincoln's Union armies used barbarous means to achieve victory, and that the Emancipation Proclamation was no more than a military ploy intended to incite slave revolts. Slavery in any case soon would have gone to "a peaceful and natural death with the development of machinery consequent upon Cyrus H. McCormick's great invention of the reaper."

By freeing the slaves, Tyler also asserted, Lincoln "was the true parent of reconstruction, legislative robbery, negro supremacy, cheating at the polls, rapes of white women, lynching, and the acts of the Klu Klux Klan."

Lincoln, he argued, had taken the U.S. Constitution and treated it "as a doormat and wiped his feet upon it."

Lyon Tyler, the strident Lincoln critic, died in 1935 at the age of eighty-one. He passed away on February 12, Lincoln's birthday.

The War's Last Casualty . . . Almost

NINETEENTH-CENTURY WAR, twentieth-century postscript . . . Outside of Richmond one day in 1995 a tree shuddered internally. A big branch cracked off at its base and fell. And out tumbled a long-spent cannonball, six pounds of solid metal that narrowly missed Karen Storer, who was washing her car beneath the old gum tree.

Both the tree and her caretaker's cottage were on farm property belonging to country singer and sausage impresario Jimmy Dean just southeast of Richmond in a still-rural Varina (no relation to Mrs. Jefferson Davis) section of largely suburban Henrico County.

At first, Storer, a gardener and caretaker for Dean, was startled by the near miss of the ancient cannonball, which most likely was fired by soldiers fighting the last months of the Civil War in the area of Fort Harrison and nearby Chaffin's Bluff . . . the very area in which Powhatan Beaty and his fellow black troops won their Medals of

Honor. And all that 130-odd years before Karen Storer was washing her car one day beneath the old gum tree.

"After I realized I wasn't hit and the car wasn't hit, it was sort of funny," she told *Richmond Times-Dispatch* staff writer Gary Robertson in 1999. "But I didn't think anybody would ever believe that cannonball was up there that long. They were going to think I made it up."

With such doubts in mind, she left the cannonball in her yard.

And now another four years passed . . . but one day in 1999 Jimmy Dean and his wife, Donna, dropped by for a visit. At one point, Donna noticed the ball at her feet and asked about it.

Storer explained, "Well, I was washing my car three or four years ago and the wind was blowing and a big limb came out of that big gumball tree.

"And when the limb fell, the cannonball fell, too."

Dean was obviously taken by the story. By Robertson's account he let loose a "rolling guffaw" as he exclaimed, "Isn't that the dangdest thing you ever heard of!"

As Robertson added in the *Times-Dispatch* of November 15, 1999, "Having a Civil War cannonball fall out of a tree is clearly not something that occurs every day."

On the other hand, noted Robert Krick, National Park Service historian based at the Richmond National Battlefield Park, discovery of the cannonball in an area known for its Civil War artifacts should have been no major surprise—aside from the spent ball's twentieth-century manner of delivery, that is.

"That whole [Chaffin's Bluff] area was heavily fortified by the Confederates as part of the defense of Richmond during the war," Krick told Robertson. After the Federals captured Fort Harrison in September 1864, Krick added, the Union troops settled into the former Rebel bastion for the remainder of the war, while the Confederates clung grimly to nearby Fort Gilmer. "The armies were within sight of each other down there, firing mortars and sharpshooting and living the trench lifestyle," Krick said.

The cannonball that tumbled out of the gum tree "probably was an overshot from the Fort Harrison–Fort Gilmer area," added Krick. "Geographically that makes the most sense."

Now that he knew about it, singer–sausage maker Dean decided to keep the cannonball on his mantelpiece—but only after having police experts determine that the ball was solid and contained no explosives.

Park historian Krick noted that Dean has long shown a lively interest in the history attached to his farm property and its old Civil War fortifications.

Nineteenth-century war, twentieth-century postscript? As Dean pointed out to his gardener-caretaker Storer the day he learned about the cannonball, *she* could have become a postscript of sorts. If the falling cannonball had struck her in the head, Dean suggested, she might have wound up "a fatality of the Civil War"!

Perhaps even its *last* casualty.

Glimpses of the Great Men

And here came **Stonewall Jackson** . . .

Berry Benson, a sergeant with the First South Carolina Volunteers, heard the faint yell far down the line, and then the yell grew louder and louder. Jackson, did it say?

> But the yell continuing and growing louder and nearer, everybody says, "It's Jackson—it is Jackson!" And directly came the sound of horses' feet galloping as all then rose, waving hats in the air and cheering the rider. Then came Jackson at a furious gallop, looking neither to the right nor the left—not even paying the least heed to a stand of arms belonging to my company that stood in the road, but riding over them[,] scattering them right and left as though they had been broom sticks only. And after him, some fifty yards behind, his aide, trying to keep him in sight.

And there, astride his mount Traveller, sat **Robert E. Lee** . . .

Col. L. L. Polk, later founder of *The Progressive Farmer* and first commissioner of agriculture for the state of North Carolina, was there as Lee reviewed some troops.

> I took a good look at the illustrious hero. He was certainly born to command. He is about six feet tall, weighs about 190, finely pro-

portioned, perfectly erect, and sits a saddle with the ease and grace which is seldom commanded by our younger and prouder commanders. His manly and military bearing, his face covered with grey whiskers, his dark keen eyes make one feel that he is a man of no ordinary character or intellect.

Abraham Lincoln, seen at his first inaugural ball by young Henry Adams—grandson of President John Quincy Adams, great-grandson of President John Adams. This the Lincoln newly come to Washington, as later described in the onlooker's autobiographical *The Education of Henry Adams* (1906) . . .

> Had young Adams been told that his life was to hang on the correctness of his estimate of the new president, he would have lost. He saw Mr. Lincoln but once; at the melancholy function called an Inaugural Ball. Of course he looked anxiously for a sign of character. He saw a long, awkward figure; a plain, ploughed face; a mind, absent in part, and in part evidently worried by kid gloves; features that expressed neither self-satisfaction nor any other familiar Americanism, but rather the same painful sense of becoming educated and of needing education that tormented a private secretary, above all a lack of force.

Ulysses S. Grant, as recalled by Confederate Gen. James Longstreet upon hearing of Grant's death in 1885, was "the truest as well as the bravest man that ever lived."

Newly captured **Jefferson Davis,** seen by Confederate Lt. Gen. Joseph "Fighting Joe" Wheeler, also newly captured, aboard the Federal steamboat carrying them both northward to a highly uncertain future as prisoners of the victorious Union . . .

> As for President Davis himself, he showed not the slightest trepidation, but reviewed the situation as calmly as if he had no personal interest in it. He discussed the war, the men and its incidents, in the same dispassionate way that a traveler might speak of scenes and incidents in some foreign land.
>
> He was affable and dignified, as usual, and if he felt any fear, he certainly showed none.

Why was **Lincoln** so often called Honest Abe? Well, according to his wife, Mary Todd, "Mr. Lincoln . . . is almost monomaniac on the subject

Lincoln had been invited to the ceremony of April 14, 1865, restoring Old Glory to Fort Sumter for the first time since April 1861, but on that Good Friday Lincoln instead remained in Washington and that evening went to his fate at Ford's Theatre.

of honesty." According to good friend Leonard Swett, "He believed in the great laws of truth, the rigid discharge of duty, his accountability to God, the ultimate triumph of the right and the overthrow of the wrong." According to a minister who knew him well, the Reverend Albert Hale, First Presbyterian Church, Springfield, Illinois: "Abraham Lincoln has been here all the time, consulting and consulted by all classes, all parties, and on subjects of political interest, with men of every degree of corruption, and yet I have never heard even an enemy accuse him of intentional dishonesty or corruption."

And **Abraham Lincoln,** speaking here himself . . .

"I have no doubt that favorable news will soon come, for I had, last night, my usual dream that has preceded nearly every important event of the war. I seemed to be in a singular and indescribable vessel, but always the same, and to be moving with great rapidity toward a dark and indefinite shore." On Good Friday, April 14, 1865, a relaxed and happy Abraham Lincoln was meeting with his cabinet in Washington. To the south, at Fort Sumter, Brig. Gen. Robert Anderson would be raising the American flag once more over the man-made island in Charleston Harbor that he had been forced to abandon exactly four years earlier after taking down the same, the very same, American flag. Joining Lincoln and his cabinet secretaries for their regular Friday meeting was the triumphant Ulysses S. Grant, freshly returned from Robert E. Lee's surrender at Appomattox five days before, on April 9. Grant, though, was not quite ready to kick up his heels in pure joy—William Tecumseh Sherman still faced a Confederate army in North Carolina under Joe Johnston, he reminded. But that's when Lincoln, envisioning still another, perhaps final victory, mentioned his recurring dream. "It must relate to Sherman," he said. "My thoughts are in that direction, and I know of no other very important event which is likely just now to occur." And that afternoon, riding in a carriage with his wife, Mary, after telling his cabinet there should be no mistreatment of the defeated South, Lincoln was so excited and joyful, she, suddenly fearful, blurted out, "I have seen you thus only once before; it was just before our dear Willie died." (Another version of this quote reported by historians is: "I have not seen you so happy since before Willie's death.") That very night the Lincolns went to Ford's Theatre to see the play *Our American Cousin* . . . their last outing together.

Sightseeing at Old Libby

CIVIL WAR BUFFS SEARCHING THESE days through historic Richmond, Virginia, for a glimpse of that notorious warehouse-turned-prison known as Libby Prison should have gone first to Chicago, Illinois . . . a century or so ago.

There they would have seen Libby Prison itself, its timbers, sills, capstones, and almost all 600,000 of its bricks. They would have seen an unappealing, three-story building 150 feet long, 100 feet wide.

No replica, it really was the same Libby warehouse from Richmond that became a detention facility holding Union prisoners in pestiferous conditions during the Civil War.

Originally a warehouse for Libby and Son, ship chandlers and grocers, it was moved, brick by brick, to Chicago in the spring of 1889 to be rebuilt as a sightseeing attraction expected to benefit from the crowds drawn to the pending World's Columbian Exposition of 1893. It took 132 railroad cars to haul all its carefully marked pieces from Richmond to Chicago.

If the entrepreneurs behind that gigantic effort had any doubts as to their project's future public appeal, a slight accident on the rail line west should have been encouraging. After one of the freight trains hauling pieces of the onetime prison derailed in Kentucky, the *New York Times* reported, "people flocked to the scene all day to secure old bricks and lumber as mementoes."

Even so, most of Richmond's Libby warehouse safely reached Chicago, reported Bruce Klee in the *Civil War Times* of February 1999, "and the building was reconstructed on half a city block on South Wabash avenue, below the Loop, as the city's central business district was known." In addition, "a monumental Gothic wall of artesian stone quarried in Chicago was built around the property."

By September 20, 1889, the Libby Prison War Museum Corporation was ready to open for business, with brass bands and hundreds of Union Civil War veterans on hand. If the crowds that day included only four former inmates from Libby, wrote Klee, "some 3,500 others visited over the next decade."

And when they did: "Each man was asked to identify the place where he had slept so a marker could be displayed on a nearby wall. Each of these brass plates was inscribed with a soldier's name, rank, place and time of capture, and present residence."

All kinds of authentic Civil War artifacts were displayed in rebuilt Libby Prison, among them a love letter from Jefferson Davis to his future bride, Varina Howell; an iron shoe lost by John Wilkes Booth's horse as he fled from Ford's Theatre; even a chisel used by Union prisoners during the war to dig a tunnel that allowed 109 men to escape the prison one night early in 1864, 59 of them permanently.

This is the infamous Libby Prison as it appeared in the Confederate capital of Richmond, Virginia, before the brick-by-brick removal of the old warehouse to Chicago.

Indeed, another display was a re-creation of the escape tunnel's opening. But there were also some odd embellishments totally unrelated to the Civil War—"shrunken heads of Incas" and the "skin of the serpent that tempted Eve in the Garden of Eden," the promoters claimed.

Naturally, the Libby re-creation project's commercial overtones (including an in-house gift shop selling bullets from Gettysburg and other souvenirs) did not evoke universal favor. There were many detractors, North and South. The city's own *Chicago Tribune* deplored the apparent fact that "good citizens of Chicago would attempt to make money out of horrid memories."

A Union veteran was publicly unhappy with "unprincipled speculators who conceived the selfish and despicable idea of violating the sanctity of soldiers' sufferings and to many the very spot of their deaths."

Even so, the Libby museum attracted one hundred thousand visitors during its first three months of operation, "and attendance swelled during the Columbian Exposition in 1893 [honoring Christopher Columbus]," wrote Klee. But then the size of the crowds steadily dwindled until, in 1899, the Libby museum entrepreneurs formed the Chicago Coliseum Company. The old warehouse was dismantled once again, and "in its place rose the gigantic coliseum that hosted Chicago's political conventions, sports events and entertainment for more than 80 years."

The coliseum had swallowed up small sections of the old Libby—a piece of the outer Libby wall was a part of the arena's front wall, and a part of its rear wall was built of Libby bricks. Thus, when the time came in 1981 to replace the coliseum structure itself, "preservationists made a futile attempt to save it by having it placed on the National Register of Historic Places."

Today, the only vestiges of the old warehouse-turned-prison-turned-museum, said Klee, are "a small wall of Libby bricks, an original door, and a handful of prisoners' artifacts [that] remain inside the Chicago Historical Society to document the prison's reincarnation as America's most unusual Civil War memorial." And back in Richmond . . . a plaque marks the spot where Luther Libby's warehouse once stood on East Cary Street.

Additional note: While Libby Prison was chiefly known for its *Union* prisoners of war and their sufferings in severely overcrowded conditions, there came a day when the old warehouse served as a temporary detention center for ranking Confederates. For here, in the days immediately after Appomattox, were held Alexander H. Stephens, vice president of the Confederacy, along with Confederate cabinet members James Seddon and Robert Hunter, who had served the same Confederacy as secretary of war and secretary of state, respectively.

"And into a cell in the rat-infested basement went warden [Confederate Maj. Thomas P.] Turner, who faced charges of cruelty and robbery," wrote Bruce Klee. "He remained there until June [1865], when he was discharged for lack of evidence." Turner subsequently became a dentist in Memphis, Tennessee.

And what of Luther Libby, whose name would forever be attached to the infamous prison? He had been forced out of his own warehouse on forty-eight hours' notice early in the Civil War by Confederate officials. The ship chandler departed as ordered but left his business sign behind, thus consigning his name to an unhappy fate . . . especially for a native Yankee from Maine.

Mary Todd Lincoln

Troubled First Lady

By Ingrid Smyer

By THE TIME SHE WAS five, she had lost her lilting double name to a newborn sister, Ann. From now on, "Mary Ann" would simply be Mary . . . Mary Todd.

So began a lifetime of losses for perhaps the most troubled and certainly one of the most maligned first ladies ever to step across the White House threshold. Even as first lady, she would encounter truly crushing losses . . . along with bizarre reminders of the childhood difficulties that began with the loss of her name to a sibling. Unbelievably, in the midst of the Civil War, married to the president of the United States, commander in chief of the Union armies, she would find herself playing hostess—in the White House—to a much younger half sister who was the recent widow of a Confederate general!

Not only "politically incorrect," the weeks-long visit of Emilie Todd Helm to the Lincoln White House, coming after her pleas for safe passage through Union lines, was a sharp reminder for Mary Todd Lincoln of her days as a little girl in the Todd home in Lexington, Kentucky—as a child who hardly had time to enjoy being the baby of the family. Baby brother Levi arrived barely a year after Mary. Then, a year after Levi, came Robert Parker Todd, but in fourteen months he died of natural causes. His death from a common childhood illness left "Mary Ann" with a deep sense of loss, aggravated only a short time later by the bestowal of half her name to a newborn sister.

Years later Mary, in her unforgiving way, described this unfavorite sister (named for a childless and favorite aunt) as "poor unfortunate Ann, inasmuch as she possesses such a miserable disposition and so false a tongue."

Ironically, Mary herself would be the one to go down in the history books as having a sharp and even shrewish tongue, not always a fair judgment.

Meanwhile, after losing a baby brother at the tender age of four, and shorn of half her name at the age of five, Mary at age six encountered the worst loss yet—her mother died from childbirth complications after delivering another son, who was named George Rogers Clark Todd.

Compounding this loss, Mary was only seven when a stranger would claim the affections of her father—young Mary had to endure yet another upheaval as her father brought a new wife into the Todd family.

Like the wicked stepmother of fairy tales, Betsey Humphreys Todd was detested by all six of Mr. Todd's children, but in age and temperament, Mary apparently was the most vulnerable to the effects of all this family trauma. Mary's two older sisters, Elizabeth and Frances, had long ago bonded and would remain close friends throughout their lives, while Ann, the youngest sister, would be a favorite of Aunt Ann, who came to run the household for a while before Mary's father, Robert Smith Todd, remarried. Mary's two brothers, in an age that tended to honor boys more than girls, could expect to be treated as the future standard-bearers of the proud and prominent Todd name.

Betsey Humphreys came from the wealthy and prominent Humphreys family of Frankford, Kentucky. Her mother, Mary Brown Humphreys, absolutely ruled Frankford society. But Betsey, at age twenty-five, was well on her way to spinsterhood until she met the widower Robert Todd in 1826. Since she could be adept at hiding her age, some say she may have been as old as twenty-eight! Years later her five daughters would omit her birthdate from both her obituary and her tombstone.

Whatever her true age, Mr. Todd's new wife demanded her own standards of order and elegance in the Todd home and would not be daunted by a household full of stepchildren. Though she would never endear herself to the first Todd children, it was not totally her fault. The children's formidable grandmother, who lived in the big house on the hill above the Todd house, had prepared her grandchildren to reject any substitute for her daughter and their mother, Eliza Parker Todd, who was connected to the Todd clan by not only marriage but also through their other grandmother . . . who herself was a cousin of the Todds.

The Widow Parker, as the maternal grandmother was known, to distinguish her from the many Parker relatives of Lexington, often reminded her grandchildren of the patriotic exploits of their ancestors on both sides of the family. At the time of the Revolution, Robert Parker and Levi Todd, along with brothers Robert and John Todd, had come to the Kentucky wilderness and established the beginnings of a town that was little more than a fortification against the Indians. The year was

1775, and they named it after a distant battle just past in Massachusetts, the double battle of Concord and Lexington. As family legend would have it, these men served with valor in the Revolutionary War that followed. John in particular was a hero at the battle of Blue Licks, Kentucky, in 1782 as he joined Daniel Boone and fellow frontiersmen in a desperate fight against a marauding force of British soldiers and Chickasaw and Miami Indians. Riding on a white horse—family stories were always a bit bigger than life—he paid the ultimate price by laying down his life for country, for family, and for fellow Kentucky settlers.

After serving in the Revolution, Robert Parker and Levi Todd proceeded to promote their town with glorious and exaggerated accounts of the prospects in their frontierland. Both men accumulated vast land estates spread over three counties of Kentucky, but unlike the plantation owners of the Deep South, planting crops and managing farms was not how they created their wealth and prominence. Todd once emphasized his bent for other enterprises in a letter to a friend: "I believe you have as little taste for farming as myself."

Much of Levi Todd's wealth came about after Kentucky's first governor, Isaac Shelby, appointed the younger brother of the hero of the battle of Blue Licks to the important position of clerk of the Fayette County Court. In this position from 1780 until his death in 1807, Levi Todd was keeper of all important records from road surveys to deed registrations—in essence, he was a one-man government.

Robert Parker, meanwhile, was busy making his own mark as surveyor, miller, merchant, and clerk of the city's governing body. According to Jean H. Baker's biography *Mary Todd Lincoln,* in this capacity Robert Parker "collected four shillings every time a property exchanged hands in Lexington, just as Levi, in a similar annuity, collected a fee on all legal documents processed in Fayette County."

Then, too, if ambition and hard work rewarded these two pioneers, so did their extensive family connections—sisters marrying into prominent families, sons, brothers, and nephews also finding their way into important positions, all made the saying "first families" a truism. Thus, young Mary Todd's grandfathers and grandmothers represented two thriving branches of a leading Kentucky family.

In keeping with the family's storied success, Robert Parker built the first brick house in Lexington, and Levi Todd built the first one in Fayette County. According to family legend also, Levi named his estate Ellerlie for the Scottish village of his sixteenth-century Todd ancestors.

Into this promising and secure world Robert and Elizabeth Parker's daughter Eliza—later to become Mary's mother—was born in 1794. When she was only six years old, her father died and her mother built a large two-story house near the center of town. Here, from the second-floor window, most of Lexington could be seen, wrote biographer Baker, adding that the view included "the expectant eighty-foot-wide Main Street, the brick-pillared courthouse, and Cheapside Market." Even Lexington's slave markets could be seen and heard from this vantage point. Here too, in this prominent house, the formidable Widow Parker would spend the rest of her long life.

Life was circumscribed for "little misses" in this town of Southern graciousness. Young girls had only one vehicle to success and that was to marry well. Known as a "rising beauty," Eliza attended tea parties, cotillions, theater, and the inevitable round of gossip sessions with her girlfriends. Schooling for girls was not stressed even though the family had endowed the local university for men, Transylvania.

In the meantime Robert Smith Todd, the third of Levi's six sons, lost his mother but soon acquired a young stepmother. He graduated from Transylvania and went on to study law under the famed jurist George Bibb. Then, with his law studies under his belt, he was ready to start out—some say "like a house afire"—to capture the lovely "Liza" Parker. But as new winds of war stirred the men of this frontier state to action against the British and their ally, Tecumseh, even before the official opening of the the War of 1812, Robert was ready to serve. In the tradition of oft-told stories of father Levi's role in the same fight at Blue Licks that cost the life of Uncle John Todd, young Robert now asked one of the Parkers to recommend him to U.S. Sen. Henry Clay for a commission.

Many frontier families boasted oral histories that endowed each generation with a need to further serve the cause of patriotic glory. But the Todds and Parkers raised such historical imperative to rare heights. Even the women had their family stories of bravery in wartime roles. Eliza Parker's own grandmother had brought food and clothing to her husband, Capt. Andrew Porter, during the terrible winter that George Washington and his men spent at Valley Forge, Pennsylvania. She often rode out with provisions to the log-hut encampment, "where one day she met an unfamiliar officer who led her to her husband, complimenting her, as they rode through the snow on a bitter cold day, on her devotion to her husband and, through him, the republican cause." The officer was none other than George Washington.

Meanwhile, Eliza Parker accepted her cousin Robert Todd's proposal, and they were married in 1812. Despite the latest war and the fact that he would be away with Kentucky's volunteer forces part of the time, they went to live with the Widow Parker, who gave them the lower half of her lot. There, in 1814, the newlyweds established their own home in the family compound.

Into their world a third daughter was born in 1818—Eliza and Robert named her Mary Ann, soon to be just Mary . . . Mary Todd.

With babies arriving every two to three years, Eliza often needed help running her household, and the Widow Parker sent her slaves down the hill to assist with the chores. One such slave, the house servant called Mammy Sally, became a parental-like presence for the little third daughter, a role that was even more pronounced after the death of Mary's mother a few years later.

Mammy Sally was the archetypal Southern mammy whose terrifying stories of ghosts, spirits, devils, and phantoms, often invoked while also calling upon the good name of the Christian God, were certain to keep her wards on their good behavior. One of Mammy Sally's especially terrifying stories was the West African myth about the jaybird who kept records of all the bad children and reported to the devil every night. For a sensitive and impressionable child like Mary, these stories loomed as entirely true. Mammy's mix of Christian theology and transplanted African tales reinforced her little ward's cherished hope that the dead, perhaps even her mother who had abandoned her, would return in spirit.

But it was to the affairs of the world, specifically political affairs, that Mistress Mary turned her thoughts as time passed. And here she hoped to gain her busy father's ear. At the tender age of nine she joined his political party and as a Whig refused to attend a public rally in Lexington for the visiting Democrat Andrew Jackson on the eve of his election in 1828.

For this young miss to follow a political bent was most unusual. Proper ladies of her generation and her social standing, young or old, were expected to remain in the domestic sphere, and Mary, constantly surrounded by sisters, half sisters, stepmother, mammy, and other female servants, was expected to prepare herself accordingly. The women of Lexington, it should also be noted, were known for their high fashion. As the wife of the president of Transylvania, Mary Holley, a proper New Englander, once noted, after the ladies of town had paid their obligatory morning social calls, "I was astonished to see callers arrive in satin and silk as if they were going to an evening function." Drawing a fetching word-picture of the same visiting ladies, she added that they would "adjust their flounces, scarcely touching their backs to the parlor chair lest they form a wrinkle or disturb a hair."

The small demands on women, especially unmarried ones in Mary's society, left plenty of time on their hands to indulge in idle gossip, parties, and pretty dresses, until such time as a husband would rescue them from the dread of spinsterhood. Politics and education were of the man's realm.

For all of Mary's desire to fill her wardrobe with pretty clothes, she was eager to fill her head with more than idle gossip. Fortunately, her father was of like mind that women should not be boring. Robert Todd, who probably had been exposed to many books in his father's library, was aware of early feminist Mary Wollstonecraft's revolutionary ideas that education was a natural right for girls. He saw to it that his daughters as well as his sons had a formal education. Accordingly, Mary at age nine entered Shelby Female Academy, or Ward's as it came to be called after the Reverend Ward and his wife. Here and later at Madame Mentelle's boarding school Mary excelled. While most of her contemporaries finished their schooling at about age fourteen, Mary stayed in school.

The eccentric Madame Mentelle and her husband had escaped with their heads from the excesses of the French Revolution and made their way to Lexington, where Madame opened her "select family school." In this environment Madame made a lasting impression on her pupils. In addition to introducing Mary to a lifetime fluency in French, plus a love of reading and writing, Madame opened young Mary's eyes to theater. Here, in school plays, Mary Todd became a "star actress," as one cousin put it, and began to develop an uncanny ability later used to mimic friends and, most hilariously, her hated enemies. It was also Madame Mentelle, according to biographer Baker, who left Mary with "an unshakable fascination with royalty, indelible images of female independence, aristocratic snobbishness, and individ…… ntricity."

…… 1832, meanwhile, would bring three major changes in …… e entered Madame Mentelle's boarding school, which …… afterward, her father and stepmother and entourage …… ouse in Lexington. This was painful for Mary, since she was not simply losing the home that held memories of her earliest childhood, she was also losing the place where she had lived with her mother. And the third upheaval was the marriage of her favorite sister, Elizabeth, to the young lawyer Ninian Wirt Edwards, son of an Illinois governor. As a result, Elizabeth would be moving away, to his home in Illinois.

In the fall of 1839, seven years later, Mary herself left Lexington and moved to Springfield, the new capital of Illinois, to live with sister Elizabeth and her husband Ninian—a sensible arrangement if only because it meant escape from a home presided over by the stepmother Mary had not yet learned to like. Further, Mary's sister Frances in an earlier visit had had the good fortune to meet her own future husband, local physician and druggist William S. Wallace. As described in Ruth Painter Randall's book *Mary Lincoln,* the convivial Edwards home was the "center of the aristocratic 'Edwards clique.'" All the most distinguished visitors in town, "especially when the legislature was in session, found their way up the gentle slope to the house on the hill where hospitality was on a lavish, old-fashioned scale."

Just in case Mary expected to match the matrimonial experience of sister Frances, the Edwards mansion was the right and proper place to be.

Mary quickly made friends with another visitor to this bustling capital city, Mercy Levering of Baltimore, also destined to be swept up in the "lively coterie," as the younger set called themselves. Soon after Mercy's arrival at a brother's local home, she was being courted by a young lawyer, James Conkling, an arrangement that then blossomed into an engagement. "Dear Merce," as Mary called her, had to return home temporarily in the spring of 1840, but the young women kept in touch by mail, with Mary filling in Mercy on the latest gossip and changes taking place since her departure.

Revealing a serious side, Mary responded to one of her friend's letters by saying, "Would it were in my power to follow your kind advice, my ever dear Merce, and turn my thought from earthly vanities, to one higher than us all."

Apparently feeling a bit guilty over the frivolity of the coterie, Mary continued, "Every day proves the fallacy of our enjoyments & that we are living for pleasures that do not recompense us for the pursuit."

All well and good, but the fact was that Springfield, a little town so young, so vigorous, so fast growing as a new state capital, could itse at times ring with the sounds of excitement and frivolity. As historian Randall wrote, it was a burgeoning community "full of young people and their enthusiasms and love affairs."

Into this town in 1837 a young lawyer not much given to frivolity had ridden with all his worldly possessions packed in two saddlebags.

It was not long before the unlikely Abraham Lincoln, tall, thin, awkward, uncouth and even ugly, was included in the smart set around town. Seemingly a contradiction in terms, yes, but then, as noted by one observer who had heard him in the legislature, this Lincoln "spoke with such force and vigor that he held the attention of all." More important, he was well known as the man most responsible for the removal of the state capital from Vandalia to Springfield.

The day of course came when Mary Todd, one of the belles squired about town by several eligible bachelors, first saw the up-and-coming legislator across a dance floor in 1839. It was not love at first sight, but, wrote Ishbel Ross in her book *The President's Wife,* "by some magic a fire was lit that burned through a quarter of a century of love and sorrow."

And here was another seeming contradiction—that popular Mary Todd, described by sister Elizabeth as having "clear blue eyes, long lashes, light brown hair with a glint of bronze, and a lovely complexion," should be smitten by the poor country lawyer with few of Mary's own social graces. And it certainly did make for an odd match—the tall, gawky Lincoln alongside such a sophisticated young lady associated with the "lively coterie."

That Lincoln should find Mary alluring was far less a surprise. Consider the fetching picture that Mary made that year, as somewhat lavishly described by an obviously loving niece: "Mary, although not strictly beautiful, was more than pretty. She had a broad white forehead, eyebrows sharply but delicately marked, a straight nose, short upper lip and expressive mouth curling into an adorable slow-coming smile that brought dimples to her cheeks and glinted in her long-lashed blue eyes."

The same niece went on to say: "Those eyes, shaded by their long silky lashes, gave an impression of dewy violet shyness contradicted by the spirited carriage of her head."

As soon would discover, there was an intellectual side to this young woman, who had been better educated than her contemporaries, was well read, and was even given to a real understanding of politics. In a letter to Mercy in late 1840, for instance, Mary confessed to her strong interest in the recent election of William Henry Harrison as president: "This fall I became quite a politician, rather an unladylike profession, yet at such a crisis, whose heart could remain untouched while the energies of all were called in question?"

Sometimes what is not written tells more than the actual script, for Mary did not mention that her heart by then belonged to Lincoln. She said only that they had reached an "understanding." And, in her chatty way, that his "lincoln green" suit had gone to dust, apparently a reference to an unbecoming suit the two women had laughed over in the past.

But then, just as the unlikely lovers were making marriage plans, the informal engagement was off! And to this day no one really knows why. Most probably the socially attuned Edwards couple did not consider the raw Lincoln a suitable husband for their Mary. Then, too, Lincoln himself felt he was a dreary prospect as a future husband.

While Mary Todd held her head high during the eighteen months the star-crossed lovers were apart, Lincoln became depressed, even physically ill. In a letter to his law partner at the time, Congressman John Todd Stuart, Lincoln lamented: "I am now the most miserable man living. If what I feel were equally distributed to the whole human family, there would not be one cheerful face on the earth." And worse: "Whether I shall ever be better or not I can not tell; I awfully forbode I shall not. To remain as I am is impossible, I must die or be better, it appears to me."

If Mary were able to put up a brave face during their schism, in her heart of hearts she, too, felt the sting of their separation, as confided by letter to "Dear Merce" in mid-1841. "Summer in all its beauty has come again," she wrote, while departing winter had left her with "some lingering regrets over the past, which time alone can overshadow with its healing balm."

The Edwardses aside, there were some in Springfield who were determined to bring Mary and Abraham together again. According to Justin G. Turner and Linda Levitt Turner in their book *Mary Todd Lincoln,* such a person was their mutual friend Simeon Francis, editor of Springfield's Whig newspaper, the *Sangamo Journal.* During the summer of 1842, Francis and his wife would be the healing balm that Mary had invoked. They invited the two unhappy people to their home, unbeknownst to either one, with the result that the onetime lovers "were shyly delighted when Mrs. Francis urged, 'Be friends.'"

After two years of romantic ups and downs, love and breakup, family pressures and political interventions, Mary Todd and Abraham finally made a whirlwind decision to wed. Delighted to flout tradition and do without a big, "showy" wedding, Mary at first thought to be married at an Episcopal rectory—destined later to become the couple's first real home—but then accepted sister Elizabeth's insistent offer to hold the wedding at the Edwards home instead.

If the newly married Mary Todd Lincoln was seeking glamour, a continuation of parties and pretty clothes, a showy home and life of ease, well, she had chosen the wrong man.

There would be no elegant trips to Saint Louis and down the Mississippi River to New Orleans—the preferred vacation mode of her Kentucky kinfolk—no travels abroad for these newlyweds. A drive across town to a boarding house called the Globe Tavern would be their wedding trip. Here they would live until the birth of their first child in August 1843, just three days short of nine months from the night they had wed.

It was assumed that Mary would seek the comforts of her sister Elizabeth's ample home for the birthing, but no, Mary's long-smoldering streak of independence, so much a part of her nature and only further nurtured at the knee of Madame Mentelle, caused Mary to manage on her own, without Big Sister. No harm was done as Mary produced a fine, strong, and healthy baby boy. They named him Robert Todd Lincoln after her father.

Now, of course, with the responsibility of a newborn on her hands, loving as Mary might be, surely she realized the contrast with her happy-go-lucky days as a member in good standing of "the coterie." Rather than the gay parties she helped to organize at her very social sister's home, Mary and Abraham now enjoyed all the amenities of a frugal boarding-house existence, for which they paid $4 a week.

THERE IS no doubt that Mary married for love, yet with her intuitive powers she saw in her man, already standing tall in local politics, a potential for achievement, even the hope of greatness. Her competitive spirit found the political arena exciting—an arena where she, along with husband Abraham, could fill a heretofore somewhat empty life of frivolity and satisfy that nebulous but utterly human longing "to be somebody."

Lincoln, too, was ambitious, if in a quieter way. "Nearly always between these two there was a moving undertow of their mutual ambitions," wrote Carl Sandburg in his sentimental biography, *Mary Lincoln*. Their temperaments were startlingly different, but both had a burning desire to achieve. "And between these mutual ambitions of theirs might be the difference that while he cared much for what History would say of him, her anxiety was occupied with what Society, the approved social leaders of the upper classes, would let her have."

Imagine her thrill as she saw predictions come true when, in 1846, Lincoln was elected to Congress! Her husband was going places and she with him. Unlike other congressmen of that day, Lincoln was taking his family—now two sons, the younger one named for a friend and fellow politician, Edward Dickinson Baker—with him to Washington. Not so incidentally either, Mary decided it at last was time to take her husband to meet her family and friends in Lexington. For one thing, stepmother Betsey Todd had never met the rising young politician who was her stepson-in-law.

So it was that before they set out on the long journey to Washington, the Lincolns first went to Mary's hometown, where they spent three weeks. Here Lincoln experienced southern hospitality, and here he saw with glaring clarity slavery at its worst and at its best.

From the porch of the Widow Parker's down past sweeping lawns he viewed the peaceful scene of the town, but not too far away, beyond a spiked fence he could hear the moans and groans of runaway slaves housed in a grim-looking structure run by William Pullum, Lexington's leading slave dealer. Here, in vermin-infested slave pens, poor black souls strained to see out from the high-barred windows. Slave trading went on almost every day, but on Saturdays and court days special auctions were held. Here half-naked men, women, and children were on view and bids were made for human flesh and blood.

And yet at the Todd home, Lincoln could almost believe the stories of contented slaves as he watched the house servants—mostly female—go about their capable management of the household and their gentle handling of children.

The first visit to the state where he was born was an eye opener for the soon-to-be congressman. But Lincoln enjoyed being with his wife's family—he and his father-in-law were on friendly terms, and he was pleased to see that even his wife and her stepmother seemed cordial to one another. Relatives and friends rallied to the visitors. They were graciously entertained—after all, Mary was a Todd, and that carried weight in Lexington.

Robert Todd saw that Lincoln met important people, one of them Mary's hero of her youth, Henry Clay, then mourning the death of his son in the Mexican War. The war was doubly painful for the elder statesman, for he felt that the war was an action of "unnecessary and offensive aggression." Lincoln heard a speech made by Clay claiming also that to take over Mexico would open new territory to slavery. Lincoln could see why the venerable Clay had been such an influence on his wife, even inspiring much of her early interest in politics.

While Lincoln was taking in the lavish estates and grand lifestyle of Mary's family, he must have felt that had she not married him she would surely be living in luxury such as this, in a style he could never even aspire to match. Mary delighted in the parties and seeing old friends, while also enjoying unaccustomed leisure afforded when old Mammy Sally took charge of the two Lincoln boys. But Mary also was anxious to leave for Washington.

Mr. and Mrs. Lincoln and their two sons arrived in Washington on December 2, 1847, a great day in Mary's eyes. If Mary had visions of grandeur, however, they were quickly thwarted—not only because Lincoln housed his family at Mrs. Ann G. Sprigg's simple boarding house, but because Mary would hardly have time to find her way around before her congressman-husband would send her back to Lexington.

As far as Lincoln himself was concerned, Mrs. Sprigg's was the place to be. It was ideal if one were in a hurry to get to the Capitol building. The lodging place was strategically situated where the Library of Congress now stands, so close to the Capitol that another congressman-boarder once explained, "The iron railing around the Capitol comes to within fifty feet of our door." In those days, most congressmen boarded with fellow delegates from their state, but Lincoln originally choose Mrs. Sprigg's on the recommendation of Mary's cousin and former House member John Todd Stuart because it was a Whig stronghold, and he was the lone Whig sent to Congress from Illinois. (But he was only one of the four Lincolns crowded into a single room!)

Hardly a metropolis, Washington in 1847, with a population of thirty-eight thousand, nonetheless was the biggest city Mary—or her husband, for that matter—had ever seen. Newly built on swampland on the banks of the Potomac between Maryland and Virginia, the capital at the center of the old thirteen colonies was hardly on a par with Paris or London, but it was the seat of government, and for Mary that meant an exciting, stimulating center of power.

The weather on the flats of the Potomac was muggy, rainy, or generally uncomfortable, hardly the place for a young wife with two youngsters. Sharing one room with two boisterous boys in tow was no easy feat for the new congressman—or for his wife. Particularly these two boys, since whenever the family went out, onlookers commented on the undisciplined behavior of the Lincoln boys.

Mary both helped and hindered her congressman in their crowded quarters at Mrs. Sprigg's. She demanded his help with the children and yet was able to help him as she read over the legislative reports and gave him her quick analysis. Still he sent his brood back to Mary's family in Kentucky in the early spring.

If he felt that his family interfered with his work when they were with him, without them he was lonely for them. His letters to her were filled with longing, and Mary's expressed equal pining for him. "How much I wish, instead of writing, we were together this evening," she wrote one May evening, and she assured him that his "codgers," as he teasingly referred to their boys, had not forgotten him. "I feel very sad away from you," she wrote.

Thus, on June 12, Lincoln wrote that he would welcome her on one condition: "Will you be a good girl in all things, if I consent?" A rather demeaning way to put it, but he had often referred to Mary as his child-wife. The letter continued, "Then come along, and that as soon as possible. Having got the idea in my head I shall be impatient till I see you."

Joyfully packing her beautiful new dresses, she (and the boys, too) later joined Lincoln on the campaign trail of 1848 for Zachary Taylor, who subsequently won the presidency while Lincoln's own state went for Taylor's opponent, Lewis Cass. This was a real disappointment for the hopeful Lincoln, who would receive little recognition for the part he had played in Taylor's successful run for the presidency.

Mary had not rejoined him in the capital, and when the Thirtieth Congress adjourned in March 1849, he returned to Springfield. These were dark days for the Lincolns. Feeling that his political career was over, he sank into deep depression. Mary suffered from recurring headaches but refused to give up her dreams of someday returning to Washington. According to legend at least, Mary even then declared she would not have married Mr. Lincoln had she not believed he was destined to be president.

During these seemingly hopeless times for Lincoln, came an offer for the governorship of Oregon. If Lincoln thought seriously about this opportunity, Mary said no right off. She held to her belief that her husband was destined for greatness; Oregon would be a political dead end.

Lincoln continued his law practice, traveled the Eighth Circuit, and kept in touch with the people. Mary, meanwhile, kept up with local politics.

But sad events enshrouded the Lincolns during this time. On July 16, 1849, Mary's father, Robert Todd, died of cholera, and soon after Christmas, in January 1850, Mary's grandmother, the Widow Parker, who had outlived her husband by half a century, also died. It was especially hard for Mary to lose two members of her family in a span of six months—the very two who probably had exercised the most influence on her early life. But still worse was to come—less than a month later, her own son, little Eddie, her pride and joy, died of diphtheria.

Mary mourned her little one with an outpouring of grief that was an ominous prelude to the uncontrollable emotions she would display years later upon another young son's death, this time in the White House. Lincoln, for his part, mourned little Eddie inwardly, as evidenced by his deep gloom.

Over the next few years, meanwhile, there were few developments in Lincoln's life and activities to encourage the deep conviction that Mary still harbored of a great destiny awaiting him . . . and her.

One bright spot in this otherwise uneventful period was a visit in 1854 of Emilie Todd, now a lovely young lady of eighteen. Four married Todd sisters who now lived in Springfield began a gay round of parties, which of course delighted Mary. "Little Sister" Emilie, as Lincoln liked to call Mary's favorite half sister, was a keen observer of people and events who years later would write one of the best accounts of the home life of the Lincolns. According to historian Randall, Little Sister not only spent a good deal of time with the Lincolns but kept a diary noting no unhappiness between them. Emilie went so far as to record the pride she saw in Lincoln's eyes as they rested on his comely little wife, and the pains that same little wife took to dress prettily, the effort she made to sparkle and bring that look to her husband's eyes.

But this observer was also aware that sister Mary was nervous and often let her Todd temper run uncontrolled. "Her little temper was soon over," Emilie once wrote, "and her husband loved her nonetheless, perhaps all the more, for this human frailty which needed his love and patience to pet and coach the sunny smile to replace the sarcasm and tears—and, oh, how she did love this man!"

Emilie married Ben Hardin Helm, a popular choice with both Mary and her husband, especially when they discovered his mutual interest in politics, albeit not always of their persuasion. Some of the correspondence between Emilie and Mary over the years fortunately survived the calamitous events of the 1860s to offer a glimpse into the political talk of their day. In November 1856, for instance, Mary wrote to her sister that Lincoln absolutely was not an abolitionist. "All he desires is that slavery not be extended, let it remain where it is," Mary explained. Both she and Lincoln believed in gradual emancipation, she added, with compensation to slaveholders.

But now, suddenly, came a major change in the lives of the Lincolns. The year 1858 would give the busy wife, mother, and letter-writer much to celebrate and to write about. At the Republican state convention on June 16, Lincoln was selected to be his party's candidate for the U.S. Senate! He made an acceptance speech that same evening that included the now-famous line, "A house divided against itself cannot stand."

His Democratic opponent was none other than Mary's former beau, Stephen A. Douglas. Mary of course was proud and excited when her candidate challenged her old suitor to a series of debates. Now, at last, Mary's confidence in her man was dramatically reinforced . . . and she was ready to realize her dream.

The debates gained Lincoln national recognition and followers, but now would come Mary's own turn in the limelight. On the day of the last debate Lincoln's wife would make a grand appearance. It was agreed that the charming Mrs. Douglas, who had been traveling with her husband, needed the competition of a pretty, beautifully dressed, intelligent, and refined lady on the Republican side. Mary's excitement that day was reflected in her comment while watching the two debaters on the platform: "Mr. Douglas is a very little, little giant by the side of my tall Kentuckian, and intellectually my husband towers above Douglas just as he does physically."

At this final debate, too, she heard Abraham repeat his warning that "a house divided against itself cannot stand," uttered with the amendment, "I believe this Government cannot endure permanently, half Slave half free."

Despite all the hurrahs, though, Lincoln was defeated in his bid for the Senate. That Lincoln was disheartened is to say the least, but what of his wife who had held such confidence in their political destiny? They had fought long and hard, and yet she was not totally disheartened. Writing to Emilie, she said, "One feels better even after losing, if one has had a brave, whole-hearted fight."

Then, too, "fizzle-gigs and fire-works" was the surprising, almost-cheery phrase Lincoln used to describe the campaign to a friend. But his disappointment was obvious in a letter to another friend. "I now sink out of view, and shall be forgotten," he wrote, but more prophetically he continued, "I believe I have made some marks which will tell for the cause of civil liberty long after I'm gone."

Like Mary, though, he was not yet ready to give up the quest for the political grail. Lincoln also told a downhearted follower: "Quit that. You will soon feel better. Another 'blow-up' is coming; and we shall have fun again."

Blowup, yes, fun, no—not in the true sense of the word. Excitement aplenty, yes! In May 1860, at the national Republican convention held in nearby Chicago, Abraham Lincoln was nominated to be the Republican candidate for president. Suddenly—was it really possible?—the impossible dream could be, might be, realized!

The firing of a hundred guns in Springfield that November election night indeed did proclaim Lincoln's victory, and as he turned to leave the State House he remarked, "There's a little woman down at our house [who] would like to hear this. I'll go down and tell her."

That night, the Lincoln home became the center of attention for all Springfield—it seemed the whole town had arrived on the doorstep.

Fireworks and rockets, bands blaring their music in the street, and, as one observer said, "even the Democrats, who all liked Lincoln personally, joined in the jubilee." What a night it was for Springfield, adopted home for both Lincolns!

Now the "little woman" who had not so patiently awaited her turn to continue the Todd-Parker saga of legendary feats of patriotism and bravery was ready to march on to her own glory, along with her own triumphant man.

Somehow, though, it wasn't destined to work out quite that way.

The two-story house at Eighth and Jackson Streets that had been their home for fifteen years was rented out; furniture was stored. If there were pangs of nostalgia, Mary brushed them aside as she made ready for a new life of bigger and better things. But already her elation was clouded by ugly threats directed at her husband and by the ominous rumbles of approaching war. Danger would now be a constant companion, making their leave-taking for Washington less than joyful for all in the family. Mary, if she were present at the rail depot that morning of February 11, 1861, must have felt a chill as she listened to her husband say his farewell to Springfield—"I now leave, not knowing when, or whether ever I may return, with a task before me greater than that which rested upon Washington."

Lincoln's special Great Western railroad train then rolled out of town, leaving Mary and the younger boys—Willie and Tad—to catch up with him and Robert the next day in Indianapolis. That day, February 12, after all, was his birthday, his fifty-second.

This trim but innocuous-looking house at Eighth and Jackson Streets in Springfield, Illinois, was home to Mary Todd and Abraham Lincoln—today, as an extraordinary American president's home, it is a National Historic Site open to the public.

The journey east was to be a campaignlike tour taking days and passing through small-town and big-city America alike. The *New York Herald* noted that men carrying American flags were stationed along the tracks at half-mile intervals. "Every town and village passed was decorated." Thousands awaited a glimpse of the gangling giant—their president-elect. Mary, for her part, happily, even dreamily, wandered about the special train, chatting with one and all. As one onlooker said, "She was tickled to death with all she had seen since leaving home." No doubt, too, all talk of dangers aside, she was thrilled to be going back to Washington once again, this time at the side of the most important man in the country.

Always longing to travel and see other places, other people, Mary now had the opportunity—she thoroughly enjoyed the ride through the countryside. Many of her women relatives were in the Lincoln entourage, but it had been a sore subject that few of her Todd relatives had supported her husband in his quest for the presidency. In all of Lexington only two votes were cast for Lincoln. On the other hand, her sister Elizabeth, who once opposed Mary's marriage to Lincoln, was now very much present to share in Mary's triumph, as were Elizabeth's two daughters and a niece, Elizabeth Todd Grimsley—who later wrote an informative account of her time with the Lincolns in the White House.

Along the whistle-stop tour Lincoln would step out on the back platform and greet the well-wishers. Sometimes, heeding cries from the crowd to see Mrs. Lincoln, Mary made her appearance as well. As she stood by his side at one such stop, the president-elect tenderly held her hand as he quipped to the onlookers, "Now you see before you the long and short of the Presidency." Mary Lincoln of course was only five feet, three inches, not unduly petite, but next to her giant of a man she did appear very short. In fact, she would never allow a photograph made of the two of them together, since she was aware of the absurd contrast they made.

The train rolled merrily on, but trouble lay ahead. Fortunately, Lincoln's advisers had engaged the services of Allan Pinkerton, a former Scottish barrel maker who had founded one of the first private detective agencies in America. He had placed spies along the train route, and he was informed of a plot to sabotage the railroad somewhere near Baltimore, "a hotbed of secessionist agitation and notorious for lawless gangs," as Dawn Langley Simmons described the

Maryland city in her biography *A Rose for Mrs. Lincoln*. It was decided that the president-elect would secretly switch trains and arrive in Washington ahead of schedule. Mary and the children would follow on without Lincoln.

MRS. ABRAHAM LINCOLN, soon to be the first lady of the land, thus arrived in Washington rather unceremoniously and not on the arm of her husband, the president-elect. Once again, any dramatic dreams of glory she may have held were thwarted. Arriving in the nation's capital with no fanfare, she was quietly escorted to the hotel where they were to stay until the inauguration, although she at least was greeted in person by the Willard brothers, owners of the hotel that is still a Washington landmark today as the Willard Inter-Continental. Reunited with her husband, she found him "sprawled out in an armchair in their suite upstairs." In seconds, the children had left her side for their father's lap, ready for a good round of play.

The family's split arrival, and the ugly threats imposing these unusual arrangements, were an unpleasant harbinger of the ill feelings that the Lincolns would encounter in Washington's Southern-dominated society. Feelings of resentment ran high as Southerners took their leave, as these new Republicans came in, and as Washington took on the appearance of an armed camp. "The 'aristocrats' who remained looked upon their Southern-born First Lady as a traitor for being married to the champion of anti-slavery, and the leader of a new social revolution," wrote Simmons.

Unfortunately for Mary, and Mary alone, the town's Yankee residents were just as vicious and vitriolic in their conviction that a Southern spy was taking up residence in the White House.

Despite all the unpleasantness, Mary was excited to be in Washington with her now-famous husband and their three sons. Robert, by this time a student at Harvard, was on hand for the family gathering. He was often the life of the party and was playful with his friends. Two chums from school had met him in Indianapolis to bid him farewell on his journey to Washington. They had both hugged him and playfully suggested that he be a good boy in Washington, and then, before Robert knew what they were doing, they triumphantly left with a lock of his hair. Now old enough to join the men in the smoking room downstairs at the Willard, he was known to smoke a cigar or two. He also enjoyed listening to the music in the hotel, but he complained when some anti-Unionists persuaded the band to strike up "Dixie," even then the well-known air associated with newly formed Confederacy. The music-makers diplomatically followed up with "Hail Columbia," noted Simmons.

In preparation for becoming the president's lady, Mary had gone to New York on a shopping spree the month before leaving for Washington. And quite a spree it was! While a Springfield housewife she had been frugal, some say even parsimonious, but in her new role she insisted on the very best no matter the cost. She was especially fond of fancy hats and had found a milliner in New York who could create headpieces that suited her. For the first time in her life she did not have to pay on the spot, since credit was gladly extended to the now-prominent Mrs. Lincoln.

Ready to claim her place in Washington, she was anxious to demonstrate that she was no backwoods matron from Illinois. She in fact had already received approving notices calling her the fashionable Mrs. Lincoln—the *Home Journal* was calling her the "Illinois Queen."

Safe and secure in one of her prettiest new hoop-skirted dresses, the newly arrived Mrs. Lincoln received guests in the parlor of their hotel suite. Here she held court not only as a fashionable lady but as one knowledgeable about politics, which she could and did discuss candidly and intelligently. An admiring Lincoln at one such reception commented to a guest, "My wife is as handsome as when she was a girl, and I a poor nobody then, fell in love with her, and what is more, I have never fallen out."

Inauguration Day arrived. Mary and her sons took their seats on the special platform built out from the Capitol's east portico. At any moment her husband would officially become the sixteenth president of the United States. Chief Justice Roger Taney, for the seventh time in his long career, would do the swearing-in. Could anyone have foreseen the extreme irony in the fact that Taney's Dred Scott decision basically declared that slaves were nonpersons with no rights, and here he was, swearing in the very man destined to become known as the Great Emancipator of slaves in America?

Irony or no, Taney would be the one to hold the red velvet Bible for this unpopular Republican come to place his hand upon the Good Book and take the oath of office.

Anyone looking on could not help but feel the air of sadness that permeated the city. This new adventure in government was taking place in a capital that was barely sixty years old and raw as a construction site. The soldiers lining the streets were there more in their capacity as guards than as celebrating marchers. The Capitol was topped with scaffolding awaiting a cast-iron dome and the bronze figure of Liberty. The great obelisk designed to become the foremost monument honoring the father of his country was a mere one-third finished, with high grass obscuring unplaced stonework all around the foot of the future Washington Monument.

Despite all this, Mary surely felt a surge of pride as she listened to the new president, her Abraham, begin his inaugural address: "In your hands, my dissatisfied fellow countrymen, and not in mine, is the momentous issue of civil war."

"Mary was still half in a dream, carried away by her husband's words, when she realized that he was kissing her," according to biographer Simmons's vision of the moment—"the most solemn kiss of their entire years together." And before Mary knew it they were on their way to the White House while the cannon were booming.

For her first inaugural ball the president's wife wore a watered blue silk gown and trimmed her throat with her ever-present pearls. During the grand promenade, incidentally, she would not be on the arm of her husband, since protocol dictated that she have another partner. Stepping forward to do the honors was none other than her husband's famous debating rival of old—and her early beau—Sen. Stephen A. Douglas. A scene out of an epic movie could not be more perfect than the real-life sight of the first lady accepting the offered arm of her former suitor and gliding across the floor with him.

All who knew must have wondered if she wasn't congratulating herself on having chosen the right suitor so long ago. Settling into the White House after the big day, the new mistress quickly saw that her new home was—to put it bluntly—shabby. With her usual energetic approach she wasted no time. Not only would she dress herself in elegant silks and lace and ribbons, but she determined to refurbish the White House in like style. She was aware that Abigail Fillmore, shy as she was, had unabashedly asked Congress for appropriations for the start of a library and even had spent funds to install a coal cookstove in the kitchen. And during the administration just departed, President James Buchanan had installed a conservatory!

Thus it was, despite the war, that Congress appropriated $20,000 to refurbish the Executive Mansion. What a delight for this first lady, who in all her life had never had so much money to spend as she pleased! This precipitated, even necessitated, a trip to New York to order the various fabrics, furniture, rugs, dishes, and other accouterments. Elizabeth Grimsley, Mary's niece who was on a prolonged visit to the first family, accompanied Mary on this shopping excursion. Mary made many major decisions with much study and effort to dress the nation's mansion in finery. Not only did she enjoy shopping for her new abode, but it couldn't hurt her standing with the social critics who, she had already discovered, were always watching. Naively, she felt compelled to prove that "westerners" like Lincoln and herself were not uninformed country bumpkins. Nor even boors.

For all her best efforts at providing the White House new elegance, however, Mary was horrified at the eruption of newspaper accounts criticizing her extravagance, with her newly chosen china a special target. That elegant dinnerware of solferino and gold with an eagle featured in the center and rimmed in purple was such a favorite of the first lady that she ordered a set for herself with her initials emblazoned on it. According to Elizabeth, this personal set was not on the official bill, although various critics said that it was.

Throughout her four years in Washington, Mary Lincoln lived in two worlds not always of her own choosing. She had married a man in whom she saw great career potential, by modern terminology, yet a man she loved. And through her marriage she was catapulted into the limelight to her unfettered delight. Yet for all her own drive and intelligence, she was very much a part of the female sphere, too, having been surrounded by sisters, half sisters, nieces, and women friends all her life. As biographer Jean H. Baker pointed out, Mary once thanked *New York Herald* editor James Gordon Bennett for a complimentary reference to her "female amiability and reticence" by telling him, "My character is wholly domestic."

At the same time an article in the *New York Times* commented, "Mrs. Lincoln is making and unmaking the political fortunes of men and is similar to Queen Elizabeth in her statesmanlike tastes." This irritated her.

Irritated or not, the truth of the matter is that Mary Lincoln had always been drawn to the stimulating conversations of men—her interest in politics and willingness to express her opinions set her apart from most of her female contemporaries. She once admitted that most women's talk bored her.

Still, she had always relied upon the women among family and long-time friends as a support system, but now she found that women, especially, were in the enemy camp, socially speaking. Now, Washington's social leaders ridiculed her every attempt at hospitality. And there was also the jealousy invariably directed at the wife of just about every president. Among others sharpening their knives, the beautiful and ambitious Kate Chase, daughter of Treasury Secretary Salmon Chase, himself a would-be candidate for president, was adamant in her dislike . . . and perhaps more than a bit envious as well?

Mary was jealous of other women who flocked around the president. To her dismay, she found that her rough-hewn Springfield man, always popular with the menfolk, now was surrounded by sophisticated and flattering Washington ladies who delighted in access to such an important figure. Perhaps a bit of flirting went on, and though Mary herself was good at coquetry, it must have been unbearable for her to see these women fawning over her husband. "Her intense love was possessive," historian Ruth Painter Randall wrote. And indeed quite smothering on occasion, too.

After a time in Washington, Lincoln came to rely less and less upon his wife's astute political insights. Perhaps losing the ear of her president, plus her jealousy over the attention he received from flattering females, plus all the criticism aimed her way, publicly and privately, were now all factors fueling new self-doubts in Mary. She suffered chronic, debilitating headaches more and more frequently. Often, too, she lost control and impulsively said things she later regretted, apologizing with real remorse.

"In the bitter politics of wartime, there was a deliberate launching of a whispering campaign against Mrs. Lincoln as a way of injuring her husband," was Randall's explanation for a good bit of the hostile publicity the first lady faced. William Stoddard, one of the young presidential secretaries living in the White House, befriended the well-meaning Mary and later pointed out she was constantly surrounded by "a jury empaneled to convict on every count of every indictment which any slanderous tongue may bring against her."

But Mary Lincoln had brought a lot of emotional baggage to Washington with her, much of it bound to stir wagging tongues in the restless capital. That she was impulsive, impudent, and emotionally immature there is hardly any doubt. In the words of her friend Stoddard, "Her personal antipathies are quick and strong, and at times they find hasty and resentful forms of expression." But then, hear also the words of a distaff journalist who wrote under the pen name Howard Glyndon, who was sent to Washington as correspondent for the *St. Louis Republican,* and who, after attending a reception in the Blue Room, recorded keen observations of Mrs. Lincoln's dress and very white complexion. Said this writer: "At all events, the charm of her [Mary's] face was not owing to cosmetics. It was a chubby, good-natured face. It was the face of a woman who enjoyed life, a good joke, good eating, fine clothes, and fine horses and carriages, and luxurious surroundings; but it was also the face of a woman whose affectionate nature was predominant."

For all the good and bad said and written about this first lady, she herself did provide grist for the gossip mill. Under the guise of helping her husband, she took an active hand in political affairs. Having spent years advising him in his clothes, social etiquette, and even urging the reluctant eater to finish his vegetables, she felt equally qualified to advise him in such things as cabinet appointments. The president having encouraged her participation in certain areas, she was quick to take an active role. Quite often she wore her official prestige like a uniform, for all to see, even representing her husband in reviewing troops and inspecting ships!

Mary felt so strongly about their Republican cause that she wrote letters to editor Bennett of the *New York Herald,* himself not always to be counted in their corner. On one occasion she was brazen enough to write him concerning cabinet posts.

Fully convinced of the importance of her womanly suggestions, Mary ever so sweetly said, "I have a great terror of strong minded Ladies, yet if a word fitly spoken and in due season, can be urged, in a time, like this, we should not withhold it." The president, though, once told her, "If I listened to you, I should soon be without a Cabinet."

From her schoolgirl days, Mary of course had been intrigued by royalty and the grandeur in which they lived. And now, she was the grand lady living in the Republic's grand Executive Mansion . . . and she would make sure it was turned into an appropriate setting for the leader of a great nation—and, of course, for his wife as well. Approaching the challenge with characteristic energy, she found an ally in the form of William S. Wood, a man of less than impeccable reputation whom she insisted upon having named a commissioner of public buildings. That done, off they went to New York to invade the city's finest shops.

Quite naturally, reporters followed Mary wherever she went, and even though her niece Lizzie Todd Grimsley went with them, tongues now wagged furiously back in Washington. Soon, the president received an anonymous note warning him of the "scandal of your wife and Wood" and asserting, "If he continues as commissioner, he will stab you in your most vital part."

Even though Lincoln reportedly had words with his wife over Wood, she and the commissioner soon had overspent the entire $20,000 allowance Congress had given her for the White House refurbishments. In all, Mary made eleven trips to New York, but Wood eventually became too controversial to remain a companion.

In any case, despite wartime shortages and delays, the White House interiors did sparkle with a new look as Mary held court. She organized various White House receptions and attended them even when miserable with headaches. Enjoying the spotlight that entertaining gave her, she impressed the diplomats with her bright and knowledgeable conversation. The ambassador from Chile and his wife were most grateful to the first lady when she conversed with them in French because they spoke no English. Then, too, a contemporary historian came away from one evening soiree so impressed that he wrote: "She told what orders she had given for renewing the White House and her elegant fitting up of Mr. Lincoln's room, her conservatory and love of flowers . . . and ended with giving me a gracious invitation to repeat my visit and saying she would send me a bouquet. I came home entranced."

But Mary's importance to Lincoln as a political counselor diminished—quite understandably, his preoccupation with the war tended to pull him away from their congenial companionship of old.

Seeking ways to compensate, Mary not only staged formal state dinners and receptions, but she also held her own private salons, attended by stimulating patrons, mostly men. To be sure, a few brilliant women were included in these affairs . . . but only if they could hold their own in the political conversation sure to take place. Though Mary was knowledgeable on women's concerns, she turned a cold shoulder to the idea of woman suffrage—she never lent her name to the feminist causes of the fair sex.

Still, she joined an association to boycott international goods, which put a damper on the elegant and expensive fabrics used in ladies' dresses. Even without European materials, however, the first lady would not be daunted in her quest to be the best-dressed lady in Washington. Her old fascination with royalty, stemming from her school days under Madame Mentelle's tutelage, drew Mary to the fashions favored by the beautiful redheaded Empress Eugenie of France, who had married Napoleon III in 1853. War or not, the American press itself was fascinated with the two "fashion queens."

One member of her salon, Nathaniel Willis, columnist for *Home Journal,* wrote of Mary Lincoln as the "Republican Queen in her White Palace." What he didn't say was that she was an insecure and lonely queen in need of constant companionship. And soon this role was filled by a former slave, a mulatto seamstress who became the first lady's confidante and closest friend.

In fact, on Mary's second day in the historic "White Palace," her first visitor was Elizabeth Keckley, one of Washington's most treasured dressmakers. She came recommended by several well-known customers, and ironically she had made gowns for the first lady of the Confederate States of America, Varina Davis, wife of the former senator from Mississippi who now was president of the Confederacy, Jefferson Davis.

The fact is, the Union's first lady had been raised in the presence of family slaves, had once looked upon her Mammy Sally as a surrogate mother helping to fill the void in her little-girl life after her mother's death. Thus, it was only natural that Mary welcomed Keckley with open arms. In response, the newcomer draped her patron in beautiful clothes and soothed her worried brow through many of the troubles and sadnesses of the first family. And Mary in turn lent a helping hand in 1863 to her trusted seamstress in the latter's campaign to help the "contrabands," newly freed blacks pouring into the city from Union-liberated areas down south.

Keckley convinced Mrs. Lincoln of the desperate situation of these former slaves, many of them dying of want. The president's wife responded so positively, she set herself apart from many other Union women of goodwill, recalled biographer Baker, not for "her attention to good causes but rather her commitment to an unpopular one."

As if such an unpopular cause were not trouble enough for an already much-maligned first lady, she added more fuel to the critical fires by soliciting help from her male friends, most of them counted among what she called "my beau monde friends of the Blue Room." She meant the steady attendees of what is thought to be the first salon in America. Notoriously to some onlookers, she had included interesting men, not all of them boasting an impeccable past. They ranged, wrote biographer Baker, from those who could discuss love, law, literature, and war, to those able to talk of philosophers and kings of the past, of the great writers, of commerce, the church, even of the boudoir.

If Mary stubbornly sought to have her way—and Abraham, too, on a larger, national scale—they could not always shake the always-pursuing shadow of tragedy in their lives. As first lady, Mary was determined to show the political and social forces of Washington that she could bring gracious galas to the White House, grand events reminiscent of Dolley Madison's hospitality. To this end in 1862 she planned with great care her first large party since moving into the White House. Five hundred invitations went out—to a "dancing party," a decided break with tradition. Although the guests arrived in their best ballroom attire, they learned the dancing itself had been canceled.

Despite the ban on dancing, a bow to those critics who viewed such activity in the White House as inappropriate in time of war, the attempt at gaiety, the music, and the serving of fabulous food all went forward as planned. Upstairs earlier that evening the president had come into his wife's dressing room as Keckley was helping her into her new gown. "Whew!" was his reaction to Mary's bold finery. "Our cat has a long tail tonight. Mother, it is my opinion if some of that tail was nearer the head, it would be in better style."

But Mary was determined that her best features—her white shoulders and arms—should be shown, and Keckley agreed. Minutes later, Mr. and Mrs. President walked down the stairs to greet their guests, then together began the traditional promenade around the East Room. Mary of course made a fetching picture in her low-cut gown of white satin. A train of black chantilly lace trimmed in crepe myrtle flowed behind her, while a matching wreath of crepe myrtle crowned her dark hair. Her jewelry—as always—was pearls. But for the war, it should have been a happy occasion for Mary, the hostess, especially. All around her, ladies in jewel-bedecked gowns, hoops, and crinolines swished as they moved about the floor . . . without dancing.

This was to be Mary's triumph, a platform to display her knowledge of fashion and grace. But upstairs in this perfect White Palace a dark cloud hovered ever lower and lower.

In the private family quarters little Willie lay ill, very ill with a fever. The Lincolns had considered calling off the party, but the doctor had assured them that their young son was better. Throughout the evening both parents slipped away to check on their child, who was later diagnosed as suffering from typhoid. Along the hall and stairwells flower-scented air wafted up to the sick room, and music could be dimly heard . . . as Mary came again and again to see her Willie. Keckley, who was at the bedside, reported that his fever had dropped.

But it wouldn't be for long. Both Keckley and Willie's faithful playmate Bud Taft kept the hard vigil in the days ahead with Mary. The end came on February 20. The president, in and out of his son's room for days, said, "It is hard, hard to have him die!" and buried his face in his hands.

"Mrs. Lincoln alternated between bouts of convulsive weeping and total prostration," reported historian Ishbel Ross. Mary couldn't face the funeral that followed, nor would she ever again enter the guest room where her Willie had died.

Mary in fact displayed such paroxysms of grief that her despairing husband finally sent for Mary's sister Elizabeth because she usually had "such a power & control, such an influence over Mary." He knew Elizabeth would have little patience with such incessant grief, especially with the nation at war, its casualty lists growing day by day.

Now emulating Queen Victoria, who had recently lost her dear Prince Albert, Mary draped herself in black taffeta. More than a year later, a visiting Emilie Helm, herself just left a widow by Confederate Gen. Ben Helm's death in battle, was startled by Mary's hallucinations and seemingly serious talk of trying to communicate with Emilie's dead husband. Mary also claimed to have nightly visitations with her departed sons, Willie and Eddie. Emilie felt obliged to discuss Mary's condition with the president, who had already warned her that Mary was highly nervous.

As if the Lincolns didn't have enough to worry about, oldest son Robert's relations with his family were strained. He was anxious to join the ranks with his friends and do his duty for the Union. But his mother was putting every obstacle in the way of his joining the army. She continued to use Willie's death as an excuse, saying, "We have lost one son, and his loss is as much as I can bear, without being called upon to make another sacrifice."

The split nation, North and South, saw the death tolls mounting day by day. Mary herself could count a brother, three half brothers, and three brothers-in-law as casualties, and all on the side of the Confederacy—Rebels in her eyes whom she refused to mourn. She did feel her sister Emilie's loss of her husband, even if he had been a Rebel general. And Mary told Emilie that in his "visitations," Willie had let her know that he was in touch with their brother Alexander, also recently killed in battle.

While Lincoln's religious faith deepened over the profound experience of Willie's death, Mary's nighttime visitations with her dead sons convinced her that a medium could put her in touch with her lost loved ones. It is easy to understand that she would fall into the hands of a charlatan who went by the alias of Colchester. After several séances, the so-called medium was exposed as a fraud, an episode that only added to Mary's many humiliations.

Lincoln desperately needed help in caring for his sick wife and his youngest son Tad, also ill with raging fever. Tad was not only sick, he was prostrate with spasms of crying over his lost brother and playmate. Fortunately, he recovered, but Lincoln in the meantime found a well-recommended nurse, Mrs. Rebecca R. Pomroy, who had lost loved ones of her own . . . and had found consolation in her religious faith. She appeared to be just what the doctor ordered, and a relieved Lincoln greeted her with the words, "I am heartily glad to see you, and feel you can comfort us and the poor sick boy." And indeed she did win over the hearts of everyone in the household.

Mary Lincoln, of course, was more sick at heart . . . an emotional or mental illness, rather than a physical malady. In modern times she or her family would surely have sought help from mental health specialists, but in her day women especially were expected to carry the burden of tragedy stoically. That attitude clearly comes through in letters written by stern older sister Elizabeth, who had hurried to Mary's side right after Willie's death then stayed on in an effort to ease Mary's obvious pain. "Your aunt Mary's manner is very distressed and subdued," Elizabeth wrote to her daughter. "It is a serious crush to her unexampled frivolity, such language sounds harsh, but the excessive indulgence, [it] has been revealed to me, fully justifies it."

Mary might have felt not only the censure of family members, but outside the family circle, the ever-ready hostile tongues also were finding fault with everything she did. As Randall so aptly put it, "Newspapers on all sides were denouncing the invalid who wept in the White House." Mary herself forever felt remorse over the ball that went on despite little Willie's illness. She had wanted to cancel the invitations, she lamented. "I have had evil counselors," she shrieked in front of a friend.

Adding one more cruel blow, Eleanor G. Donelly wrote a widely read poem called "The Lady-President's Ball." The poem was supposedly written by a poor dying soldier who through glazed eyes could see the bright lights of the White House. A typical stanza of it went like this:

> What matter that I, poor private,
> Lie here on my narrow bed,
> With fever gripping my vitals,
> And dazing my hapless head!
> What matter that nurses are callous,
> And rations meagre and small,
> So long as the beau monde revel
> At the Lady-President's ball!

These heartless verses were printed in a newspaper four days before Willie's death. Mary Lincoln had rallied from her little Eddie's death, "with the help of youth," Randall noted. "But now youth was behind her, health was impaired, and she was in the midst of war, suspicion, criticism, slander and hate. The future was dark and uncertain. She would never recover from this blow."

IT WASN'T until ten long months later that Mary would finally emerge from this dark period and stand by her husband's side at their New Year's Day reception of 1863. As the guests passed through the reception line, they no doubt studied with added interest this woman who had been so removed from the public eye, yet not the public's curiosity. Fashionably attired for the occasion but clad in her ever-present mourning clothes, her black hair coiffed in a severe style, Mary was the very picture of a somber Victorian mourner. No lively coterie now, no wonderful White House entertainments in view . . . she had visibly changed.

Perhaps there was a moment's cheer for Mary not long after, when who should come avisiting at the White House but "Gen.

Tom Thumb" (real name, Charles Sherwood Stratton), whose recent marriage to the equally petite Miss Lavinia Warren had momentarily pushed the war news aside (with a little help from that early public relations genius P. T. Barnum of circus fame). Tom Thumb, one of the shortest adult visitors ever to walk into the presidential abode, stood all of three feet, four inches tall. He and his tiny bride had been married in New York's Grace Episcopal Church on February 10, 1863.

But this was also the year of Gettysburg, Vicksburg, and so many other confrontations, with unthinkable slaughter taking place even in the Union victories such as those two benchmark battles. Gen. Ulysses S. Grant was emerging as the man of the hour. War-fattened nouveau riche were flocking into the capital, helping to swell the population from 60,000 to 200,000. Hotels were crowded, gambling flourished, restaurants did a booming business, and the money flowed accordingly. The theater flourished also—Ford's and Grover's were sold out at every performance.

At the very moment that the battle was raging in Gettysburg, Mary Lincoln was out for a ride in her carriage. Suddenly the coachman fell from his seat. The first lady was thrown to the ground and hit her head on a rock. It was later discovered that the seat had been deliberately tampered with. Regardless of the cause, however, the mishap was still another setback for the anguished mourner. Her son Robert believed that his mother never recovered from the accident.

Mary did emerge again to perform her hostess duties and care for Tad, long since recovered from his bout with fever. Now, too, her concern was for her husband's health, since the pressures of the presidency and the war were taking an obvious toll. Even the press began to notice the tired, strained face of the president. So it was a welcome turn of events in 1865 when General Grant invited the Lincolns to view the front at Petersburg and Richmond, where the war was grinding down to its inevitable end. They embarked on the *River Queen* for City Point, Virginia, with a large official party on board, plus the everpresent Keckley. It was an especially happy time for the dressmaker because she would be visiting newly emancipated friends in her birthplace of Petersburg.

While at City Point the Lincolns took a carriage ride by the side of the James River and came upon an old tree-studded graveyard. According to Simmons, the couple walked hand in hand among the peaceful graves. "Suddenly the President, overcome with emotion, said, 'Mary, you are younger than I. You will survive me.'" The next few words he uttered were startlingly prophetic: "When I am gone, lay my remains in some quiet place like this."

The Lincolns' visit to City Point (today's Hopewell, Virginia) unfortunately was marred by embarrassing emotional outbursts on the part of the overly possessive first lady. Mary had always been jealous of the attention showered on the president by other ladies. When she learned that the wife of a young officer had been granted permission to remain at the front, she could not restrain herself. She flew into a rage . . . but that was just her first display of uncontrolled jealousy.

Due to review the troops with the commander in chief and arriving in a carriage with Julia Dent Grant, she was shocked and dismayed to find post commander Edward Ord's beautiful wife riding a handsome mount beside the president. The first lady screamed at Mrs. Grant, "What does this woman mean by riding by the side of the President? Does she suppose that he wants her by the side of him?" According to biographer Simmons, Mrs. Grant tried to quiet the outraged Mrs. Lincoln, but Mary only retorted to the kind general's wife, "I suppose you think you'll get to the White House yourself, don't you?" Mrs. Grant (a slave owner's daughter who later did get to the White House as a first lady herself) was stunned and said nothing.

As if the altercation were not yet enough of a scene, Mary Lincoln then dressed down the patient president in front of his officers and men. He tried to calm her by gently calling her by the pet name he often used, "Mother." The next day the president made excuses for his wife, saying she was not well.

The Lincolns returned to Washington on April 9, the very day that Gen. Robert E. Lee surrendered the Army of Northern Virginia to Grant at Appomattox. On Tuesday evening all government buildings in the Federal capital were ablaze with lights to mark the beginning of peace. From a window of the White House the exultant president addressed a jubilant crowd and magnanimously ordered the musicians to play "Dixie."

Just ahead, obviously, would be heady days for the first family. The war was just about over, the family was safe, and Robert had just arrived from Virginia in his Union army uniform. One night that week, however, Lincoln, awoke from a terrible dream. In it, he had wandered into the East Room and saw a coffin with a corpse inside.

"Who is dead in the White House?" he asked the soldier in attendance, and the chilling answer was: "the president."

Perhaps it was to shirk the gloomy remembrance of the dream (if he told her about it), that the first lady on Friday evening—Good Friday, it was—planned an outing for her tired husband. Knowing how much he enjoyed the theater, she decided on a party at Ford's Theatre, where the renowned Laura Keene was appearing in *Our American Cousin*. Mary invited the Grants to join them, but Julia Grant, still smarting from the recent outburst at City Point, sent her regrets. Maj. Henry Rathbone and his fiancée, Clara Harris, accepted Mary's last-minute invitation.

Earlier that day the president and his lady took their usual afternoon drive in their carriage, just the two of them. "I have never seen you so happy since before Willie's death," she said.

His answer: "Mary, we have had a hard time of it since we came to Washington, but the war is over, and with God's blessing we may hope for four years of peace and happiness, then we will go back to Illinois and pass the rest of our lives in quiet."

It was not to be.

The lights were already dimmed when the Lincolns arrived at the theater. He seated himself in the red upholstered rocking chair that Harry Ford had placed in the presidential box and had once used in his own bedroom. A guard, John F. Parker, was assigned to protect the president. The Lincolns should be snug and secure in their box. Between acts the president and his wife chatted.

In these last few happy moments together, Mary drew closer to her beloved Abraham and took his hand in hers. "What will Miss Harris think of my hanging on to you so?" she whispered.

"She won't think anything about it," her husband the president answered.

His last words.

The assassin's bullet entered the back of Lincoln's head. He would never regain consciousness.

Mary Lincoln began screaming. "Why didn't he kill me? Why wasn't I the one?"

And so it all ended. Many of Mary's hopes and ambitions had been granted and many taken away. As she herself described her plight to a friend after the assassination, "My own life has been so chequered; naturally so gay and hopeful—my prominent desires, all granted to me—my noble husband, who was my 'light and my life,' and my highest ambition gratified—and that was, the great weakness of my life. My husband—became distinguished above all. And yet owing to that fact, I firmly believe he lost his life and I am bowed to the earth with Sorrow."

She indeed became the epitome of mourning. She lived many lonely years and suffered more losses and abandonments. She buried her son Tad in 1871 and felt betrayed by her remaining son Robert when he had her committed for a short time to a mental institution. She exiled herself to Europe then returned to her America. And in the end she returned to Springfield.

Mary Todd Lincoln died on July 16, 1882, in the home of her sister Elizabeth Edwards. Forty years before a gay young woman and her tall gangly husband had left this very house to begin their chequered life together.

─── ⋆ Postscript ⋆ ───

Lincoln's Multiple "Burials"

THIS IS NO HOAX. Abraham Lincoln, "Father Abraham," the Great Emancipator, one of the two or three most towering figures of American history, was destined in the years after the Civil War to be laid to rest in one place after another. Not once or twice, but again and again, and sometimes in secret.

In large part, the shifting around of Lincoln's remains in Springfield, Illinois, came about as reaction to a sordid plot by a band of counterfeiters to "abduct" the Lincoln casket and hold it as hostage for the release of the band's engraver from prison . . . so he could make some more phony plates.

This truly was a gang that couldn't shoot straight. As four members of the gang headed for the cemetery by train the night before the proposed body snatch, one of the four in reality was a federal agent and another a government informant. That left exactly two legitimate conspirators out of the four. Meanwhile, awaiting them in hiding places at Oak Ridge Cemetery, two miles outside of Springfield, was a band of security men.

Yet once the two gang-members-in-earnest had broken into Lincoln's tomb and half lifted out his casket, thus incriminating themselves beyond all doubt . . . they got away, with their would-be captors wildly shooting up the dark cemetery.

How could it all happen, and why was a plumber's assistant named Leon P. Hopkins the last man to see Lincoln's face . . . more than once, as it turned out?

To see it all unravel, revisit the Lincoln assassination itself. He was shot on the night of April 14, 1865, and died the next morning, never recovering consciousness. After lying in state in the East Room of the White House and in the Capitol, Lincoln's body slowly traveled back to Springfield aboard a funeral train largely repeating the route that Lincoln had taken on the way to Washington four years before.

At Springfield, two possible gravesites awaited him. The town fathers hoped to bury their preeminent citizen on a hillside called the Mather Block, future home of the Illinois State Capitol. A suitably grand monument of course would house Lincoln's tomb.

But Mary Todd Lincoln, the grieving and distraught widow, said no, her husband himself had told her he wished, when the day came, to be buried in a quiet, secluded place. Thus she insisted upon the newly established Oak Ridge Cemetery out in the countryside.

Still, there would be a monument. But Lincoln, together with the bodies of his two dead boys, Eddie and Willie, was first placed in the cemetery's receiving vault.

Not yet discouraged, the leading citizens of Springfield still wished for Lincoln's burial in a tomb and monument of their own creation on the Mather Block. They formed a National Lincoln Memorial Association and began planning . . . but Mary Todd Lincoln still said no. If they didn't desist, she ultimately declared, she would carry Lincoln back to Chicago, where she was then living. She could even be "violent" about it, she warned.

Or she might take the body back to Washington to be entombed at the Capitol there.

As a result, Springfield gave in and made plans to build its monument at Oak Ridge. But first there must be built a temporary vault . . . and indeed it was ready to receive him on December 21, 1865. As Lincoln's casket then was moved to that new resting place, six old friends were asked to look through an opening and see that the body inside really was Lincoln. They did and it was.

The plumber's assistant, Leon Hopkins, made the opening . . . and not for a last time, either.

For the next five years, Lincoln rested quietly enough while work on an elaborate monument and tomb progressed on a hill behind the temporary vault. The grand structure included a catacomb, five crypts, and a marble sarcophagus when completed.

On September 19, 1871, the Lincoln casket was moved into the as-yet-incomplete cenotaph. The same six friends again peered in at the Lincoln body through an opening once more created by Leon Hopkins. Sadly, a newcomer just arrived two months before, to be buried at the site also, was Lincoln's grown son Tad, who now joined his brothers Eddie and Willie by their father's side.

Meanwhile, the mahogany casket in which Lincoln had come all the way from Washington was deteriorating. An iron coffin was substituted for it, with Lincoln still encased inside an inner casket of lead.

And now another three years passed uneventfully. Then, on October 9, 1874, it was time to place the body in the marble sarcophagus at the center of the catacomb. But as it turned out, the iron coffin did not fit. Lincoln and his lead casket went into a new coffin of red cedar. And the monument was dedicated on October 15.

In the meantime, a counterfeiting ring headed by Chicago saloon-keeper "Big Jim" Kneally had fallen on hard times after its master engraver, Benjamin Boyd, was sent to prison. Incredibly, Kneally thought he could arrange a pardon for Boyd by robbing Lincoln's resting place and holding the body as his bargaining chip.

As the plot unfolded, he enlisted the services of a self-proclaimed "champion grave robber" who somehow had found his way into Kneally's saloon and struck up a friendship with its personnel and hangers-on, recalled Lloyd Lewis in his book *Myths After Lincoln*. In the nineteenth century, medical schools were so desperate for cadavers that they often bought bodies "from men who came to the back door at midnight with mysterious sacks which they exchanged for so much money down and no questions asked." Lewis added, "Ghouls had become the terror of rural communities, and friends and relatives of bereaved families patrolled cemeteries for nights after burials, shotguns in hand."

As later events showed, however, "grave robber" Lewis C. Swegles was an informant for the Secret Service, the federal agency charged with investigating counterfeiting operations such as Kneally's. Then, as two Kneally confederates and Swegles took the train from Chicago to Springfield to rob the Lincoln grave on election day of 1876, a fourth "conspirator" joining them on the train was a Secret Service agent.

In another car on the same night train were six more federal "operatives." Coordinating with Lincoln's one remaining son, Robert, various security men, official and private, were hidden and waiting at the monument when the attempt was made the next night.

And when those hours of darkness came, the two real grave robbers broke into Lincoln's marble sarcophagus and half lifted out the casket itself as the informant Swegles held a lantern giving them light. At this point, it was his job to bring up a wagon to carry the heavy coffin—instead, he made his way to the hidden detectives and told them it was time to spring their trap.

When they rushed into the catacomb minutes later, however, they found no one there. In the cemetery grounds outside, agents who espied one another among the tombstones and statuary started shooting—at one another. In all the confusion, the two real conspirators had fled

. . . only to be caught ten days later, on November 17. It turned out they had stepped out of the catacomb merely to wait for Swegles and his "wagon," then ran off when they realized the cemetery was alive with strangers.

While the public—an often disbelieving public—might have been reassured to know the plot had been foiled, not so among the guardians of Lincoln's tomb. They realized just the opposite: how vulnerable the Lincoln tomb was. Thus, six days after the bumbled grave-robbing attempt, they secretly removed the Lincoln casket and hid it in a dark corner of the inner passageways, "among the odds and ends of boards left by the [monument] builders."

Meanwhile, with the marble sarcophagus sealed shut again, all appeared to be normal—except that the monument-keepers themselves had stolen Lincoln's body, noted Lewis.

The result was that Lincoln "slept for two years under a heap of boards in a cellar, while pilgrims from all over the world stared, wept, mourned and pondered over his sarcophagus at the other end of the monument."

But then, after a wealthy New York merchant's body was seized for ransom, monument custodian John C. Power panicked and organized two quick reburials of the Lincoln casket in unmarked gravesites within the monument complex, supposedly in secret. His dedicated younger helpers formed a Lincoln Guard of Honor to keep closer watch on the Lincoln shrine, while outside the cemetery confines rumors flew and people were asking out loud if Lincoln's body really were inside the sarcophagus.

But now Mary Todd Lincoln had died, and she, too, would be—should be—placed in the official Lincoln tomb. In a public ceremony she indeed was placed in a crypt next to her three deceased sons. But then her remains also were removed, in secret, in the middle of the night, to be buried next to husband Abraham in his hidden burial place.

"Pilgrims increased as more prairie years slipped along, looking now at two empty tombs," recalled Lewis. The Lincoln memorial monument finally was completed in 1883. Meanwhile, Powers was discomfitted because the questions—legitimate, as it happened—would not stop, and "suspicious visitors badgered him incessantly."

In 1886 "the Monument Association, either to stop the rumors or to ease their anxiety for the corpse, decided to give Lincoln decent burial." The guard of honor was alerted to witness the exhumation and reburial of both Lincolns in a solid and secure tomb "of brick and mortar"—supposedly in secret again. On the twenty-second anniversary of the president's assassination, April 14, 1887, "eighteen persons who had known Lincoln filed past his casket, peeping into the square hole which plumbers had cut in the face of the lead coffin." The last to look in, and to reseal the coffin, again was Leon Hopkins—"thinking to himself that he was the last man ever to see the face of Lincoln."

And so, both Mary and Abraham were entombed in the new vault. And there they would stay, no doubts about it . . . but for only another thirteen years! By then, it had become apparent that the monument was settling unevenly, the foundation "cracking up around that everlasting vault of the Lincolns."

What to do now? No question, the existing monument would not remain intact unless something was done to repair . . . or even to replace it.

The state of Illinois having taken over the matter of Lincoln's tomb by this time, a legislative committee investigated, studied, and came up with majority and minority reports. The minority wished for creation of an entirely new, grander monument in the center of Springfield, that old dream of the town fathers, but the majority prevailed . . . the existing monument complex would be torn apart and rebuilt on a new foundation pad, to "an additional height of twenty feet." The cost of starting all over in town was a persuasive factor in the majority decision.

Either way, of course, the Lincolns would be disturbed in their eternal sleep still again. Or, as Lewis stated the case, "So again Lincoln was moved—wandering, restless corpse."

This time, the guard of honor placed the five Lincolns—Abraham, Mary, and sons Eddie, Willie, and Tad—all together in another temporary vault while the reconstruction work proceeded. Then, in February 1901, they all went into crypts within the new structure, but for the Great Emancipator himself, only temporarily so.

This time, it seems, a grimly determined elder son Robert took steps to make sure there would be no more slipups, no more shoddy hiding places (if, actually, he knew about the latter) in connection with his father's remains. He himself advanced $700 toward the cost of a steel-and-cement vault that would be buried ten feet below ground level at the new Lincoln Monument . . . and so, it would be done.

In September 1901, the three still-surviving guards of honor were there, as were a sprinkle of state officials, some townspeople, all in the monument's Memorial Hall. Once again, the plumber's assistant of old, Leon Hopkins, cut open the casket so witnesses could look in at Lincoln's surprisingly well-preserved features and identify the body. Thirty persons did so before Hopkins closed up Lincoln's coffin . . . once more the last man on earth to gaze upon Lincoln's face. And this time, with the coffin lowered into the new vault and sealed therein, finally, at last, came an end to the dead Lincoln's travels. *Finis.* And please, God, to rest in peace.

Bibliography

Armstrong, Richard L. *West Virginian vs. West Virginian: The Battle of Bulltown, W. Va.* Hot Springs, Va.: R. L. Armstrong, 1994.

Baker, Jean H. *Mary Todd Lincoln: A Biography.* New York: Norton, 1987.

Blockson, Charles L. *The Underground Railroad.* New York: Prentice-Hall Press, 1987.

Brockett, L. P., and Mary C. Vaughan. *Women at War: A Record of Their Patriotic Contributions, Heroism, Toils, and Sacrifice During the Civil War.* 1867. Reprint, Woodbury, N.Y.: Longmeadow, 1993.

Chesnut, Mary Boykin Miller. *Mary Chesnut's Civil War.* Edited by C. Vann Woodward. New Haven: Yale University Press, 1981.

The Congressional Medal of Honor: The Names, the Deeds. Forest Ranch, Calif.: Sharp & Dunnigan Publications, 1984.

Connell, Evan S. *Son of the Morning Star: Custer and the Little Bighorn.* San Francisco: North Point Press, 1984.

Coulling, Mary P. *The Lee Girls.* Winston-Salem: John F. Blair, 1987.

deKay, James Tertius. *Monitor: The Story of the Legendary Civil War Ironclad and the Man Whose Invention Changed the Course of History.* New York: Walker, 1997.

Donald, David Herbert. *Lincoln.* New York: Simon & Schuster, 1995.

Dorman, Michael. *The Second Man: The Changing Role of the Vice Presidency.* New York: Delacorte Press, 1968.

Forman, Stephen M. *A Guide to Civil War Washington.* Washington, D.C.: Elliott & Clark, 1995.

Grant, Julia Dent. *The Personal Memoirs of Julia Dent Grant.* New York: Putnam, 1975.

Grant, Ulysses S. *Memoirs and Selected Letters: Personal Memoirs of U. S. Grant, Selected Letters, 1839–1865.* Library of America. New York: Library of America, 1990.

Harwell, Richard, ed. *Lee: An Abridgement in One Volume of the Four-Volume R. E. Lee by Douglas Southall Freeman.* 1961. Reprint, New York: Collier Books, 1993.

Herndon, William H., and Jesse W. Werk. *Herndon's Life of Lincoln: The History and Personal Recollections of Abraham Lincoln.* 1942. Reprint, New York: Da Capo Press, 1983.

Hudson, Carson O., Jr. *Civil War Williamsburg.* Williamsburg, Va.: Colonial Williamsburg Foundation, in association with Stackpole Books, 1997.

Johnson, Robert Underwood, and Clarence C. Buel, eds. *Battles and Leaders of the Civil War.* 4 vols. New York: The Century Co., 1887–88.

Krick, Robert K. "Armistead and Garnett." In *The Third Day at Gettysburg & Beyond,* edited by Gary W. Gallagher, 93–131. Chapel Hill: University of North Carolina Press, 1994.

Lewis, Lloyd. *Myths After Lincoln.* New York: Harcourt, Brace and Co., 1929.

———. *Sherman: Fighting Prophet.* 1932. Reprint, Lincoln: University of Nebraska Press, 1993.

Long, E. B. *The Civil War Day by Day: An Almanac, 1861–1865.* 1971. Reprint, New York: Da Capo Press, 1985.

MacDonald, Rose Mortimer Ellzey. *Mrs. Robert E. Lee.* 1939. Reprint, Pikesville, Md.: R. B. Poisal, 1973.

McGuire, Judith. *The Diary of a Southern Refugee, During the War.* New York: E. J. Hale & Son, 1867.

McHenry, Robert. *Webster's American Military Biographies.* 1978. Reprint, New York: Dover, 1984.

Morris, Roy, Jr. *Sheridan: The Life and Wars of General Phil Sheridan.* New York: Crown, 1992.

Neely, Mark E., Jr. *The Abraham Lincoln Encyclopedia.* New York: McGraw-Hill, 1982.

O'Connor, Thomas H. *Civil War Boston: Home Front and Battlefield.* Boston: Northeastern University Press, 1997.

Perdue, Charles L., Jr., Thomas E. Barden, and Robert K. Phillips, eds. *Weevils in the Wheat: Interviews with Virginia Ex-Slaves.* Charlottesville: University Press of Virginia, 1976.

Pryor, Sara Rice. *My Day: Reminiscences of a Long Life.* New York: Macmillan, 1909.

Randall, Ruth Painter. *Mary Lincoln: Biography of a Marriage.* Boston: Little, Brown, 1953.

Roberts, Allen E. *House Undivided: The Story of Freemasonry and the Civil War.* N.p.: Missouri Lodge of Research, 1961.

Robertson, James I., Jr. *General A. P. Hill: The Story of a Confederate Warrior.* New York: Random House, 1987.

———. *Stonewall Jackson: The Man, the Soldier, the Legend.* New York: Macmillan, 1997.

Ross, Ishbel. *The President's Wife: Mary Todd Lincoln—A Biography.* New York: Putnam, 1973.

Sandburg, Carl. *Mary Lincoln, Wife and Widow.* New York: Harcourt, Brace and Co., 1932.

Sherman, William T. *Sherman's Civil War: Selected Correspondence of William T. Sherman, 1860–1865.* Edited by Brooks D. Simpson and Jean V. Berlin. Chapel Hill: University of North Carolina Press, 1999.

Sifakis, Stewart. *Who Was Who in the Civil War.* New York: Facts on File, 1988.

Simmons, Dawn Langley. *A Rose for Mrs. Lincoln: A Biography of Mary Todd Lincoln.* Boston: Beacon Press, 1970.

Smith, Reid. *Majestic Middle Tennessee.* Prattville, Ala.: Paddle Wheel Publications, 1975.

Snyder, Louis L., and Richard B. Morris, eds. *A Treasury of Great Reporting: "Literature Under Pressure" from the Sixteenth Century to Our Own Time.* New York: Simon and Schuster, 1962.

Stowe, Harriet Beecher. *Uncle Tom's Cabin.* Oxford World's Classics. Oxford and New York: Oxford University Press, 1998.

Thomas, Emory M. *Bold Dragoon: The Life of J. E. B. Stuart.* New York: Harper & Row, 1986.

———. *Robert E. Lee: A Biography.* New York: W. W. Norton, 1995.

Turner, Justin G., and Linda Levitt Turner. *Mary Todd Lincoln: Her Life and Letters.* New York: Knopf, 1972.

Warner, Ezra J. *Generals in Blue: Lives of the Union Commanders.* Baton Rouge: Louisiana State University Press, 1964.

———. *Generals in Gray: Lives of the Confederate Commanders.* Baton Rouge: Louisiana State University Press, 1959.

Wert, Jeffry D. *General James Longstreet: The Confederacy's Most Controversial Soldier.* New York: Simon & Schuster, 1993.

Wilcox, Arthur M., and Warren Ripley. *The Civil War at Charleston.* Charleston, S.C.: *Charleston News and Courier* and *Evening Post,* 1996.

Index